AF461848

Hidden Treasures of the National Trust

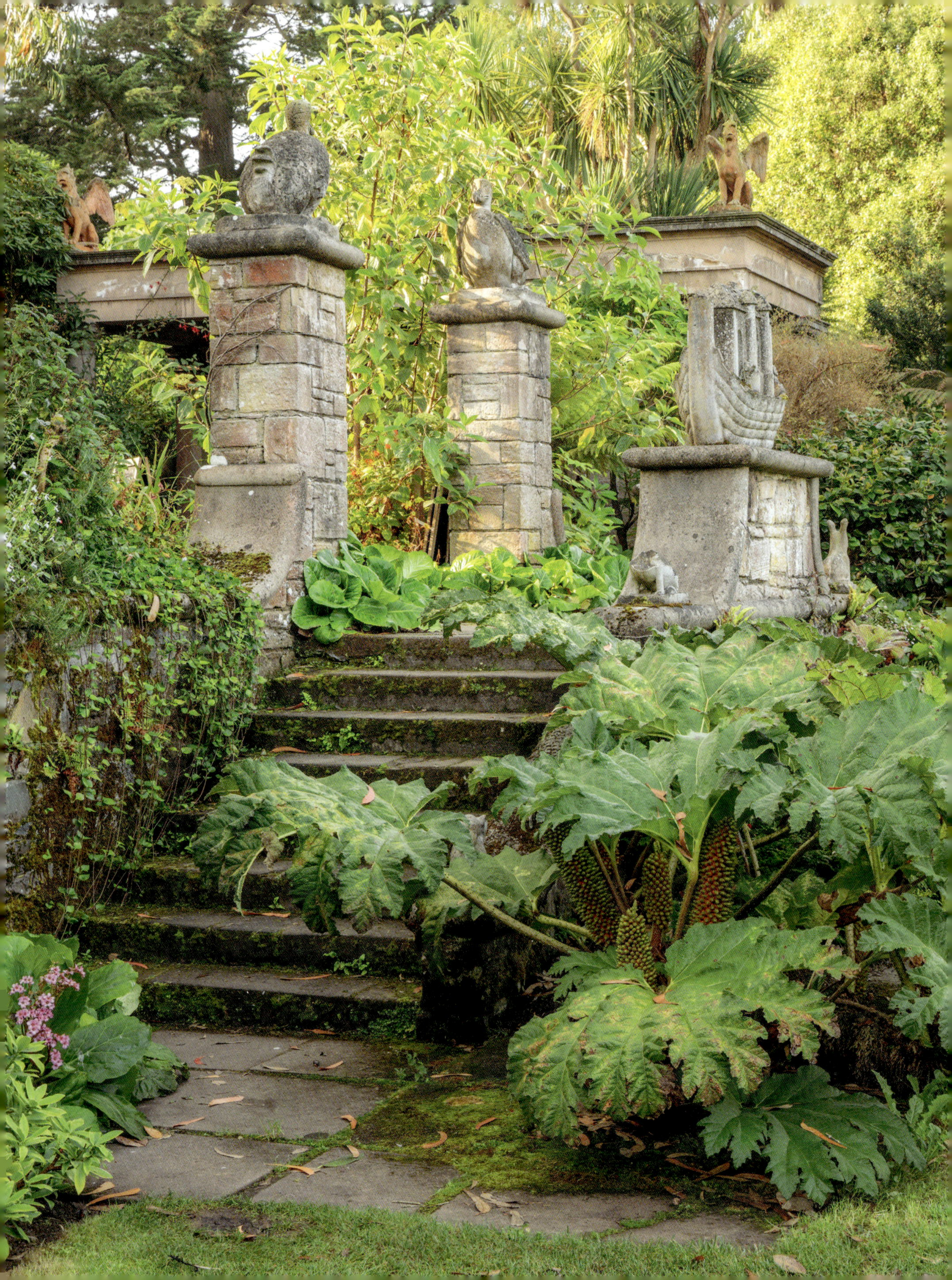

Hidden Treasures of the National Trust

Anna Groves

Foreword by

Mary Beard

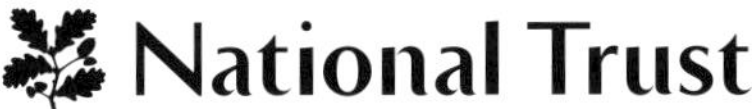

Published by National Trust Books
An imprint of HarperCollins Publishers
1 London Bridge Street, London SE1 9GF
www.harpercollins.co.uk

HarperCollins Publishers, Macken House
39/40 Mayor Street Upper
Dublin 1 D01 C9W8, Ireland

First published 2025

ISBN 978-0-00-871290-7
10 9 8 7 6 5 4 3 2 1

A catalogue record for this book is available from the British Library.
Printed and bound in Bosnia and Herzegovina by GPS.

If you would like to comment on any aspect of this book, please contact us at the above address or national.trust@harpercollins.co.uk

National Trust publications are available at National Trust shops or online at nationaltrustbooks.co.uk

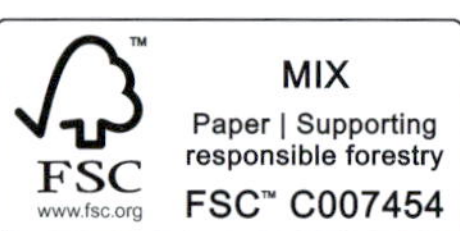

This book contains FSC™ certified paper and other controlled sources to ensure responsible forest management.

For more information visit: www.harpercollins.co.uk/green

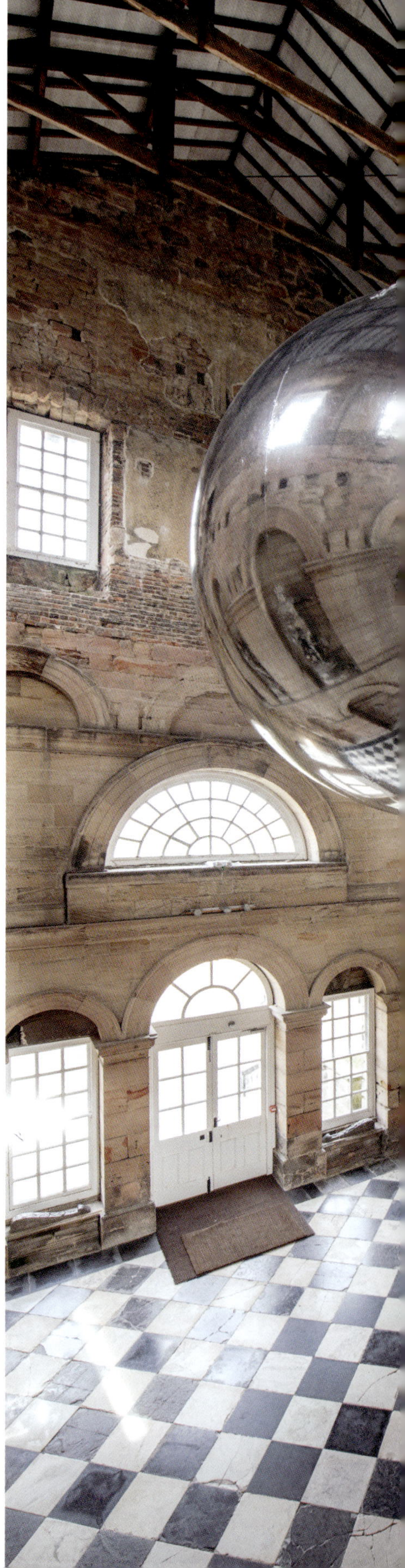

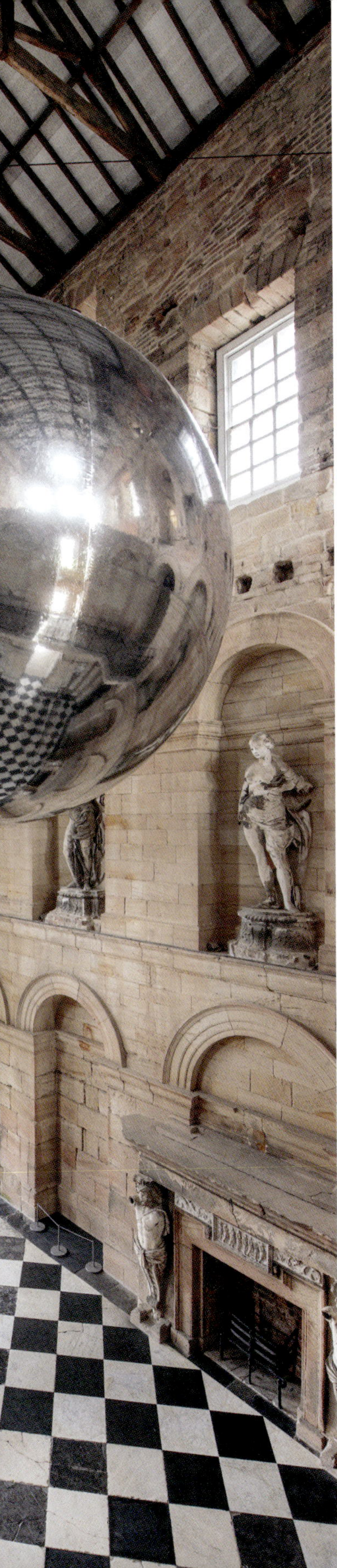

Contents

Foreword by Mary Beard

I grew up a few miles from the National Trust's Attingham Park in Shropshire. I still recall, as a child, being amazed at its huge private picture gallery – built to house the treasures amassed by the second Lord Berwick on his Grand Tour to Italy in the late eighteenth century. It was amazing, but at the same time I found its showy boastfulness slightly off-putting: the huge imitation marble columns, the packed rows of paintings collected by a young aristocrat who didn't know when to stop, and the bravura engineering in cast iron and glass that let daylight in through the roof.

So, I confess that I felt a sneaking satisfaction when I discovered in *Hidden Treasures of the National Trust* that Berwick, and his celebrity architect John Nash, had rather over-reached themselves, with a 'flashy but flawed' design, which had let in rainwater, as well as daylight, from the word go. It was only two centuries later that, in a three-year project, conservation specialists from the National Trust put those flaws right. This saved the whole structure for the future, and in the process opened our eyes to intriguing details of how it had been built and decorated.

There are no better places than National Trust properties for facing up to our history, to its successes and innovations, its errors and even its darker sides. But these properties and their contents don't look after themselves. Simply to survive, they depend on the skills of the Trust's conservators – skills that are the focus of *Hidden Treasures,* which accompanies the fascinating BBC series. Conservators are a wonderfully even-handed bunch. They do not lavish their care and attention only on the great artistic masterpieces that the houses contain (though these certainly make an appearance in the book, from a Tintoretto painting to

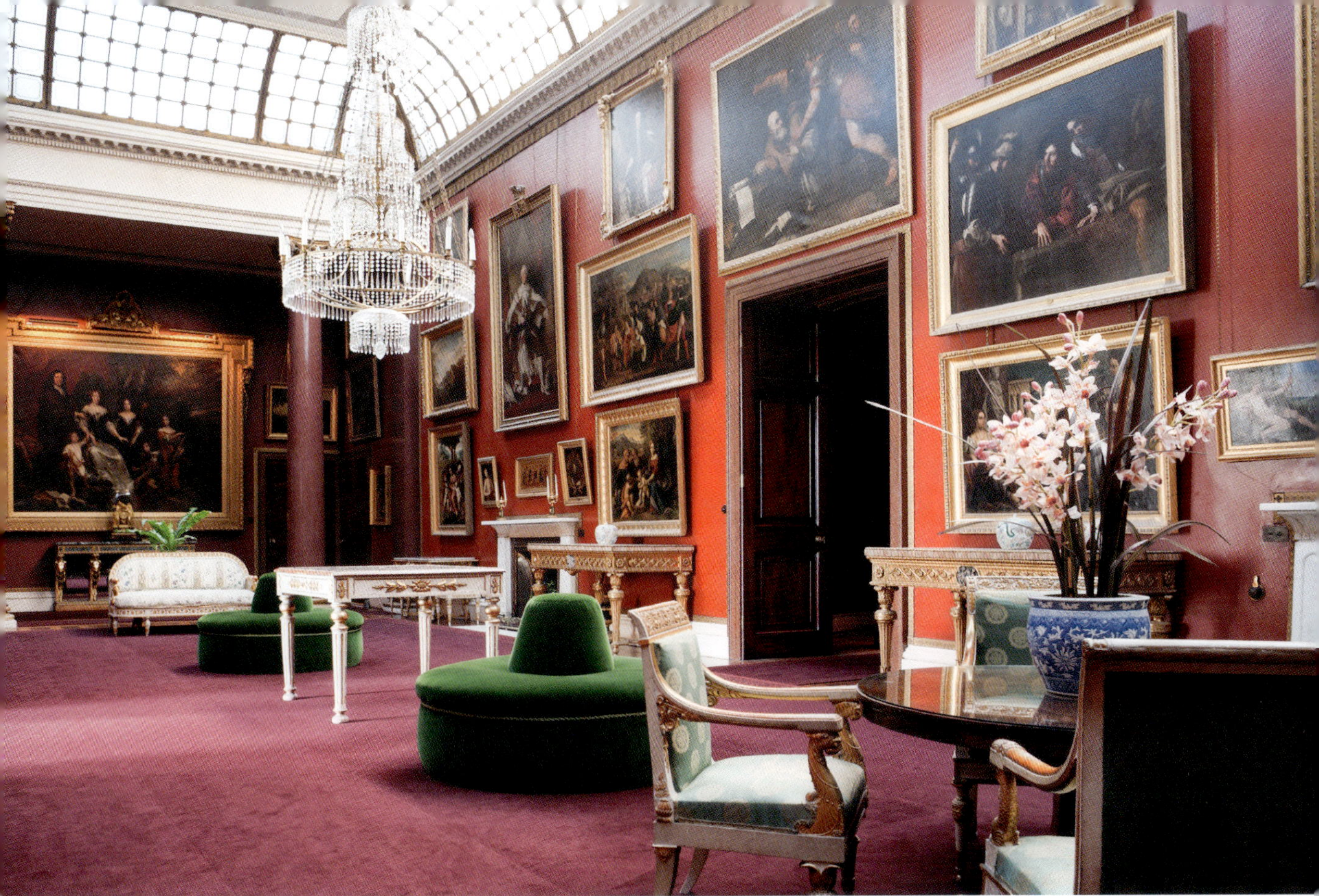

^ Attingham's Picture Gallery roof was a hugely ambitious design for the time.

ancient Etruscan vases). They also keep a watching brief over the clocks, the gates, the squirrels in the grounds, the doll's house furniture, right down to the graffiti in Paul McCartney's old Liverpool house and Lord Berwick's leaky roof (not to mention their running battles against the moths and silverfish, waiting to devour the curtains and the wallpaper).

But conservators and curators do more than conserve. They also reveal the stories and the people behind the objects, from the craftsmen and women who made them and the patrons who bought and sold them, to the housekeepers and handymen who cleaned and mended them over the centuries. As the Trust's houses contain so many riches, it can be easy now to walk past the apparently less 'remarkable' objects, whether the simple writing desk, the old garden flowerpot, or the map collection. In taking us inside the work of the conservation team, *Hidden Treasures* makes every object remarkable, and invites us all to debate and enjoy.

Introduction

The founding principle of the National Trust was that our natural and historic places should be preserved and protected with a view to being shared with as many people as possible. So it might seem surprising that any of the treasures in the care of the National Trust should be 'hidden'. But when you consider that the Trust looks after hundreds of properties that speak to thousands of years of history and contain a million and more objects, each with its own story to tell, it is perhaps less surprising to learn that new discoveries are made every day.

When Octavia Hill and her co-founders established the National Trust in 1895, the focus was on preservation, that is to say, keeping historic places and their contents as close to their original state as possible. Today, 130 years later, the role of the Trust's conservation staff is highly complex. Many of these places and objects had a long history before they came into the care of the Trust. Their stories didn't start and end with when or how they were created. Many will have passed down the centuries through multiple hands, accumulating many more stories, along with some inevitable wear and tear. So one of the challenges of looking after the collections is how to capture and present all these layers of history and reflect the authentic appearance of a place or object while ensuring its continuing survival.

This work is a core activity of the National Trust but often takes place behind closed doors or in a workshop or studio, so as to not disturb visitors or because specialist equipment is required. However, in the BBC series *Hidden Treasures of the National Trust*, millions of viewers are

> The Green Closet at Ham House (see page 63) is a treasure trove of art but is also just one room in one house among the hundreds of properties cared for by the National Trust.

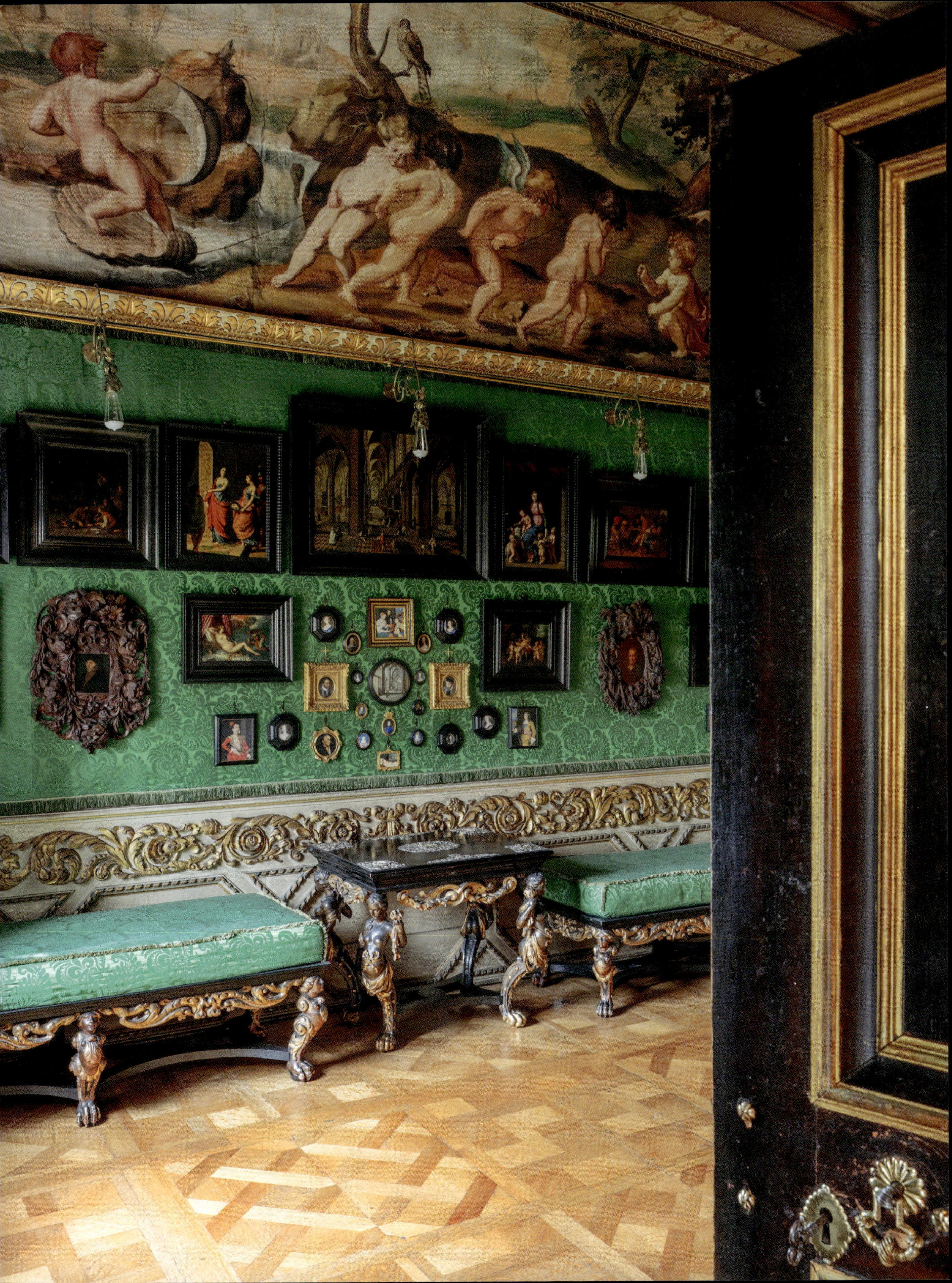

treated to a close-up look at the many and varied conservation projects the Trust has carried out in recent times.

This book is an accompaniment to that series, but it also gives you more. More of the ambitious projects carried out by the Trust, from conserving colossal fireplaces to restoring a Regency roof of iron and glass. More of the unusual objects that draw on all the skills and expertise of conservators. More of the human stories that come to light when an object is so closely scrutinised. It seems that no conservation work simply restores. Some new knowledge or understanding is always gained, which in turn can be shared with everyone.

Long gone is the 'pickling in aspic' approach to curating a heritage scene and its contents – static displays that inform but fail to relate to or connect with their audience. Those of us with an interest in history want to know much more than the physical attributes of a building or object. We want to know about the people who created, collected and valued these things enough to leave them to future generations. It's these stories, as much as the objects themselves, that connect us to our past. But these stories aren't always immediately apparent: they may require the peeling back of layers, further research or detective work, re-examination in the light of new evidence, new approaches, or new findings uncovered by technological advancements. In this book we have the opportunity to look over the shoulders of experts as they meticulously restore, repair and reappraise.

Paintings give up their secrets hidden under layers of aged varnish. Close examination provides the answers to some unsolved mysteries and, in one instance, reveals a rarity that was hidden in plain sight. Some projects delve even deeper, whether it's an archaeological dig in search of a lost castle, or the scraping away of decades of well-intended decoration to reveal marks made by famous musicians.

There's no shortage of eccentricity in the National Trust's collections, often requiring bespoke solutions when it comes to their conservation. Take the 26,000-piece gallery at A la Ronde, made of shells, feathers, rocks, moss and more, or the chronological display of fossils at Biddulph Grange that combines Creationism and geology. These are items that

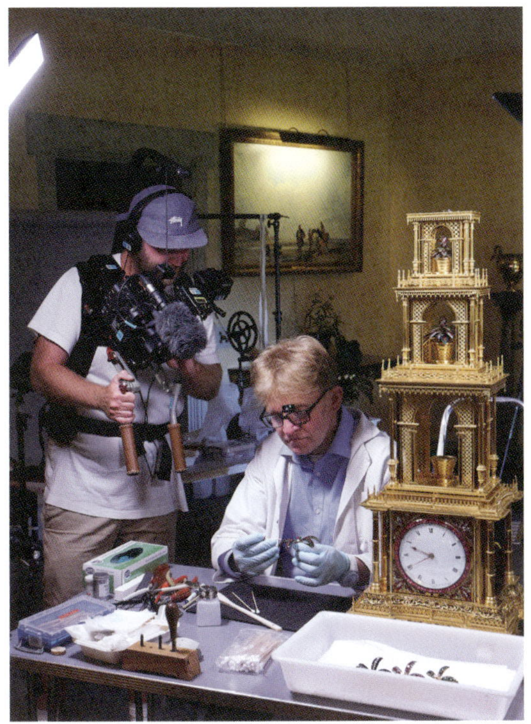

^ A behind-the-scenes shot from the BBC series showing clocks conservator Matthew Read working on the Pagoda Clock at Anglesey Abbey (see page 165).

aroused great curiosity at the time they were made and that continue to puzzle the specialists who care for them.

And then there are objects that had meanings and associations that were regarded one way in the past but which are considered very differently now. These can tell us more about people whose stories have often gone untold – the working classes, women, people of colour, servants – and offer a fuller, more detailed picture of the past than that offered by the homes and belongings of the aristocracy alone.

This book attempts to show just some of the variety and complexity of the conservation work undertaken by the National Trust. That work is exacting but it is also endlessly rewarding. There is the satisfaction of seeing an object returned to a condition that might be appreciated by its original owners. There is also the delight in making new discoveries about an object and uncovering a previously hidden detail or even an entirely new story. Finally, something clearly conveyed in the BBC series is the passion of the conservation teams. This passion comes in part from being at such close quarters with historic objects, some of them created by virtuosic artists and craftspeople; in part from the wonderful novelty of some of those creations and the challenges that come with conserving them; and in part from knowing their work ensures these treasures can be appreciated and studied for generations to come. Conservation today may look very different from the approaches of the past, but the guiding principle of the National Trust, that we should ensure our history survives into our future, remains very much the same.

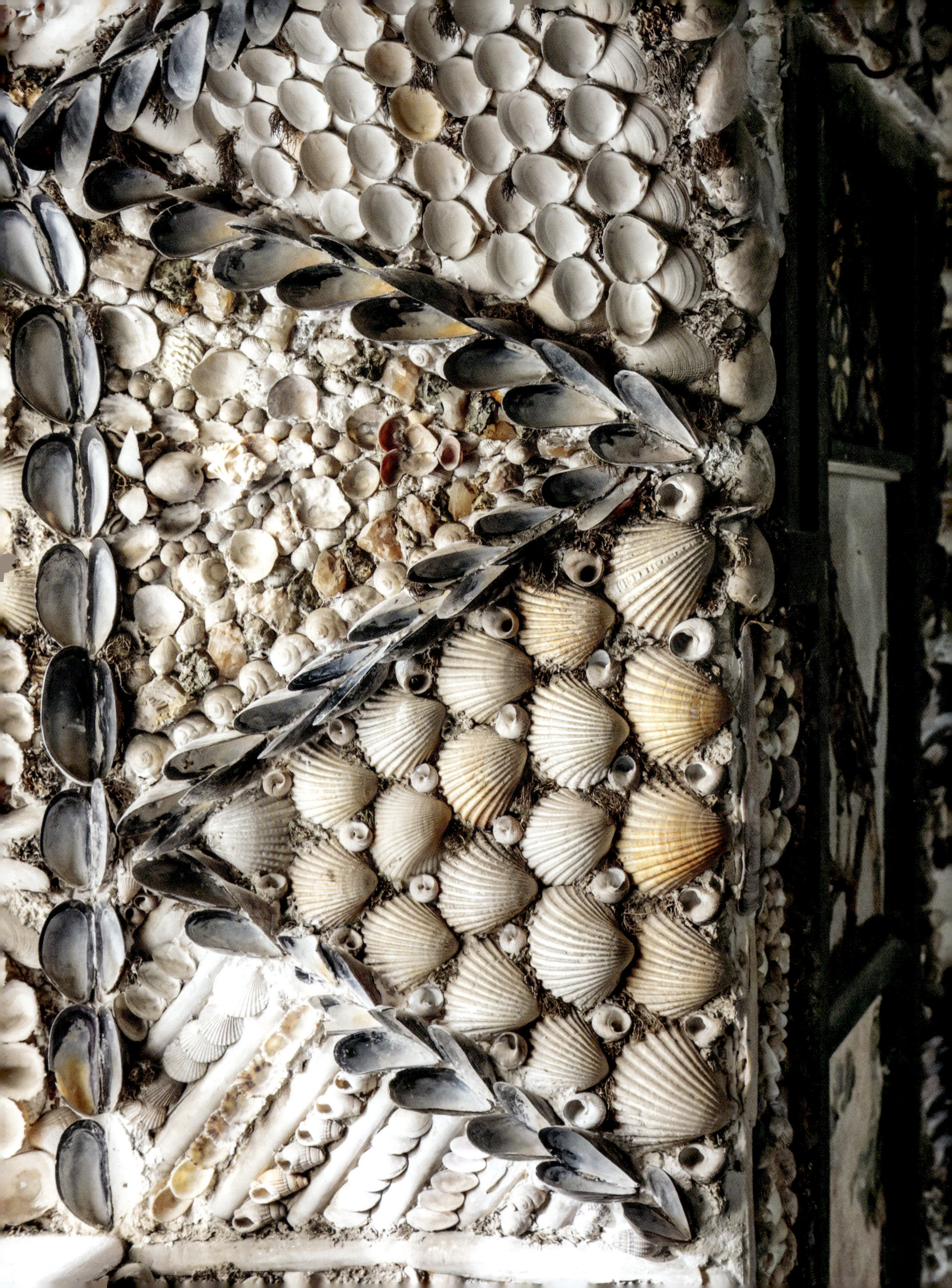

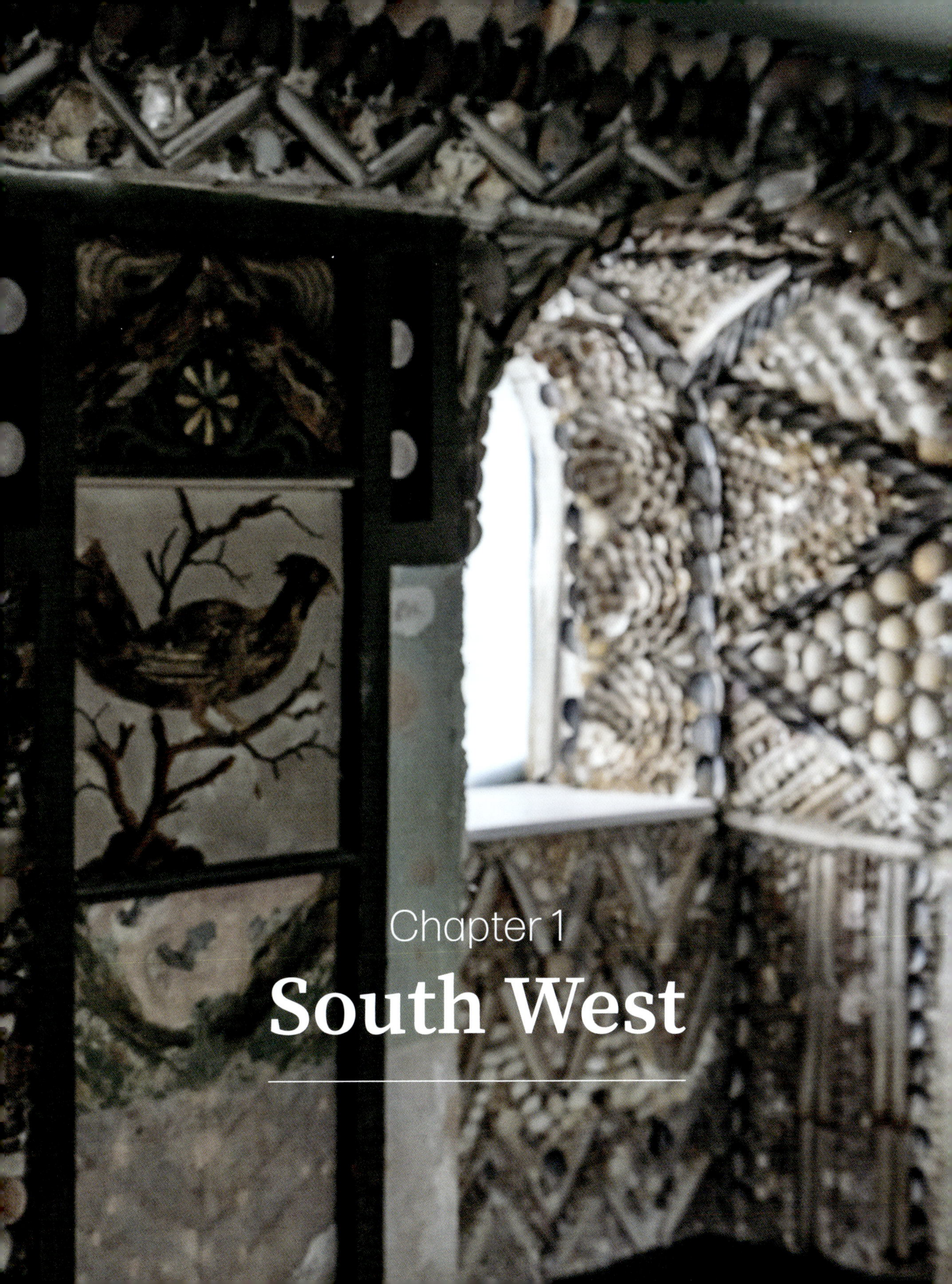

Chapter 1

South West

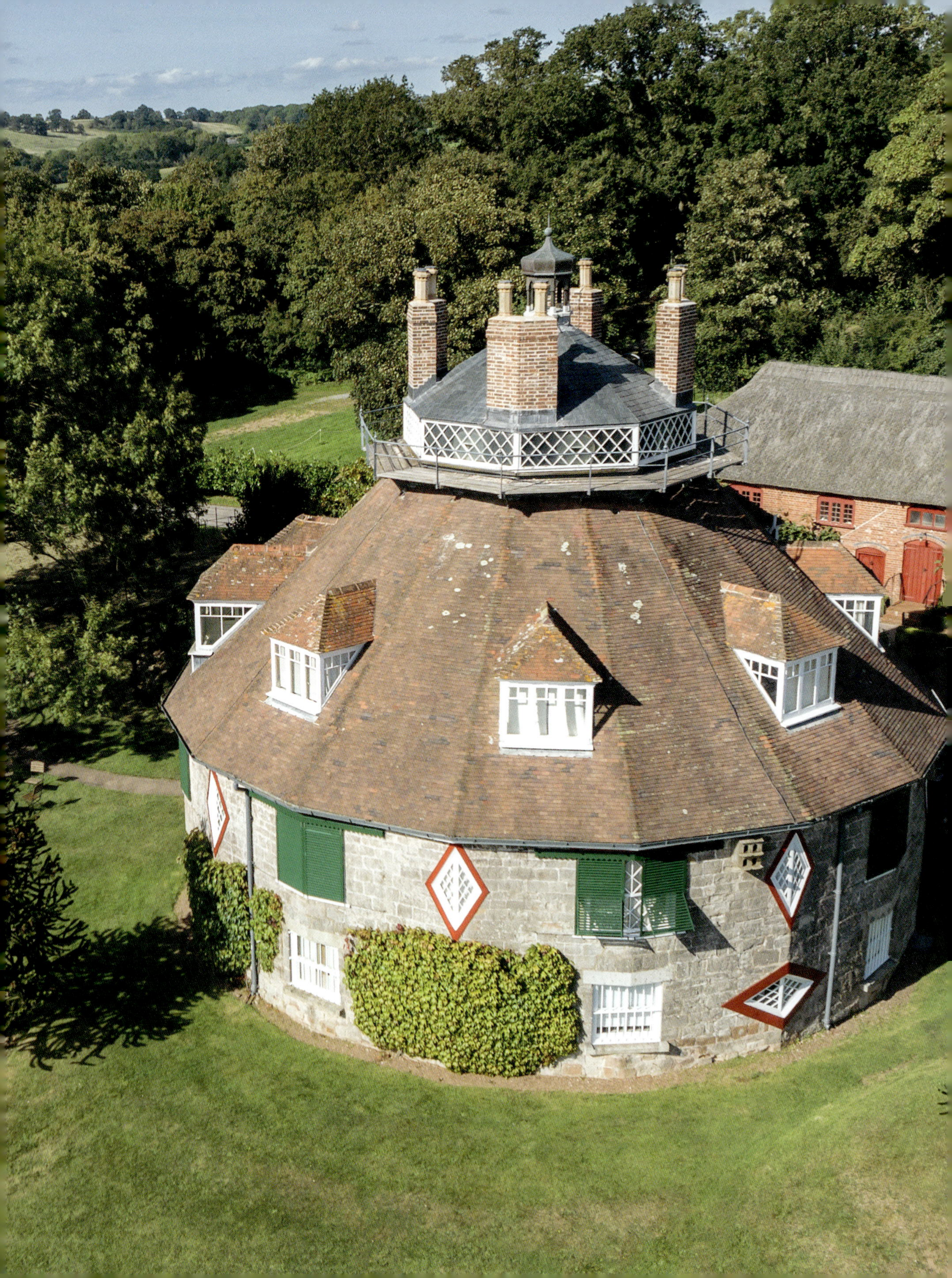

Restoring a Unique Interior

The Shell Gallery

A la Ronde, Devon

If you're familiar with the work of the National Trust, you won't be surprised to hear the properties and collections in its care described as unusual and multifaceted. But we start our journey at a property that in these respects stands some way apart from the rest. The people who conceived of it, who created it, who crafted its contents and who decreed how it should be cared for after their time were truly remarkable. Their legacy takes the shape of the hexadecagonal (16-sided) house known as A la Ronde, with an octagonal gallery at its heart and intricate, shell-encrusted decoration at its peak.

A la Ronde was built at the end of the eighteenth century by two unmarried women, second cousins Mary and Jane Parminter, 17 years apart in age but with a shared outlook on life, one highly unusual for the time in which they lived. The design of A la Ronde's interior is as unique as the circumstances under which it was built, as it was far from typical for women in the Georgian era to retain their independence, and to use their wealth to create an environment following their own vision.

Mary was just five when her mother died and she and her sister came to live with Jane's family. The following year, Jane's own mother died and she became guardian to her cousins while also caring for her younger siblings Elizabeth and John. She was 23 and unmarried and, whether it

< A la Ronde and the estate in which it sits were the creation of two remarkable women and it is invested throughout with their individuality and vision.

was lack of time, opportunity or her own choice, she remained so. Her father, a Barnstaple wine merchant based in Lisbon and Devon, died when Jane was in her thirties and shortly after she set off on a Grand Tour of Europe, then a rite of passage generally reserved for wealthy young men. The party included her sister Elizabeth, a friend, Louisa Combrune (or Comebrune), and Mary, then 17 years old. The women departed in 1784 and travelled extensively and adventurously on and off for about 10 years. They even took up mountaineering and Mary, Jane and Louisa became the first women to ascend Mont Buet, nicknamed 'Mont Blanc des Dames' and also 'Parminter Peak' in their honour. Their travels were undertaken without the customary male chaperone. Elizabeth returned to England part way through their tour due to ill health and died in 1791. But for Mary and Jane, their experiences travelling around Europe shaped the rest of their lives.

On their return to England, Mary and Jane settled back in Devon, purchasing 15 acres (6 hectares) of land just outside Exmouth, where they set about building A la Ronde, said to be inspired by the Basilica of San Vitale in Ravenna, Italy. If it is based on the design of this antique church, it is only loosely so, which is hardly surprising, as the Parminters seem to have been far too driven by their own creative imaginations to imitate very closely. Take the Shell Gallery, in the upper reaches of the hallway they called the Octagon. This 360-degree gallery made largely of shells, but also of rocks, minerals, bones, pine cones, feathers and moss, was an astonishing decorative feat, as much for the 'Why?' as for the 'How?' In the words of project manager Emma Mee: 'It is the creative expression of two very dynamic, well-travelled women.'

But for all the work gone into its

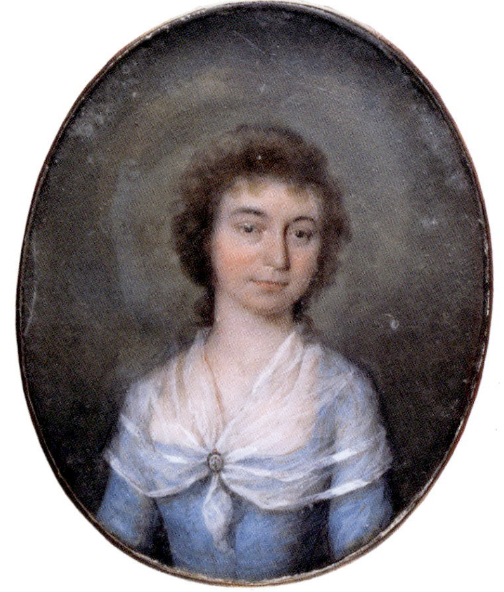

^ A miniature of Mary painted around the time of the Parminters' Grand Tour.

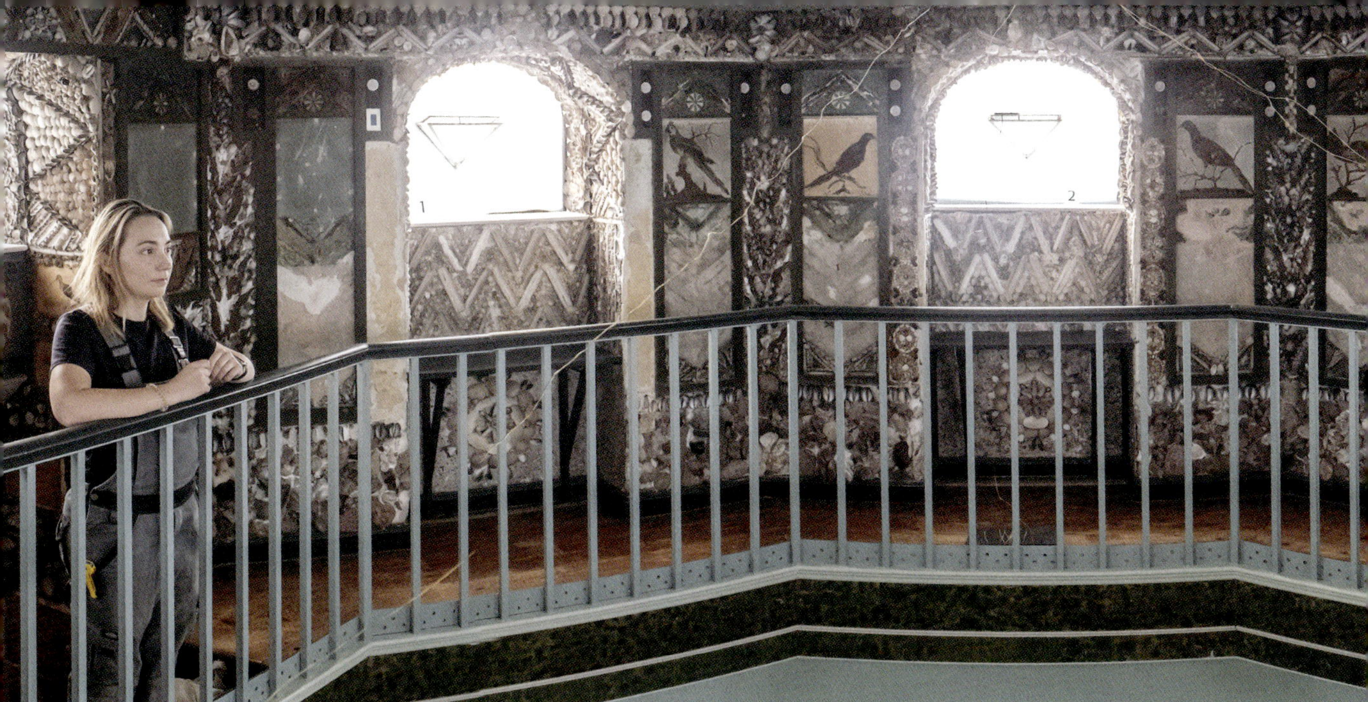

^ Conservator Rachel Lawson surveys the Shell Gallery after months of painstaking restoration.

creation, after more than two centuries Mary and Jane's elaborate labour of love was losing its lustre and more than a few shells. Conservator Rachel Lawson led a team as they repaired and consolidated the walls of the Shell Gallery. It took thousands of hours to conserve this intricate jigsaw. When conservation of the Shell Gallery was completed, the suspended platform that had given the conservators the access they needed was taken down, and the view from the floor of the Octagon restored. It was an emotional and momentous event for the house team, although one person was perhaps more relieved than others that their work was done. Confessing to having something of a shell addiction by the end of the project, Rachel said she could see why the Parminters decorated their gallery in such a fashion, it being 'easy to get carried away'.

Quite what motivated the Parminters to create their Shell Gallery, we'll never know, but we do know very clearly what Mary had in mind for A la Ronde, as she was very specific on the subject. She was determined that the property should remain unchanged and in the care of women; Mary's will sets this out in some detail, stating: 'she may inherit provided she shall not then be or have been married for and during the term of her natural life', marriage resulting in her forfeiting her inheritance. And when it came to bequests to married female servants, she stipulated: 'you must give this money into the hands of this woman and not give it to her husband'. If Mary's insistence on these terms seems excessive or peculiar, set it in the context that it was only when the Married Women's Property Act was passed in 1870, over 20 years after Mary's death, that married women were allowed to be the legal owners of the money they earned and to inherit property.

While Mary's will stated that she wanted A la Ronde to remain as it was, it's hard to imagine that she would have been entirely confident about the survival of some of the more fragile elements of the Shell Gallery – collages of birds made from feathers, sticks and moss on paper. Perhaps Mary believed that she could put her faith in the abilities of women when unburdened by marriage, but she couldn't have foreseen the existence of an organisation such as the National Trust, experts in the conservation of items that, if left to the mercy of time and the elements, would be reduced to dust. Truly, it's amazing to think that these collages should be conserved more than 200 years after they were set into the high walls of the gallery. The gallery itself is so fragile that only specialist staff enter it today; but visitors are still able to gaze up and appreciate it from the floor of the Octagon, just as the Parminters' own guests would have done. The effect is like looking up from the bottom of a rock pool, through the seaweed, to the sunlight above. Its survival, which is amazing to us, was also challenging to book and paper conservator Abigail Bainbridge, as the scale of the project and level of damage required careful thought to determine the treatment. But as we shall see time and time again on our journey, conservators at the National Trust encounter such a dizzying array of rare and unique items that they have to draw on their creativity and problem-solving abilities as much as their knowledge and experience.

What you see at A la Ronde at surface level is striking enough, but once you get to know about the people who made it, digging a little more deeply reveals a treasure trove of information.

> The range of materials used by Mary and Jane Parminter - shells, minerals, bones, pine cones, paper, feathers and moss - challenged the conservation team and drew out creative solutions.

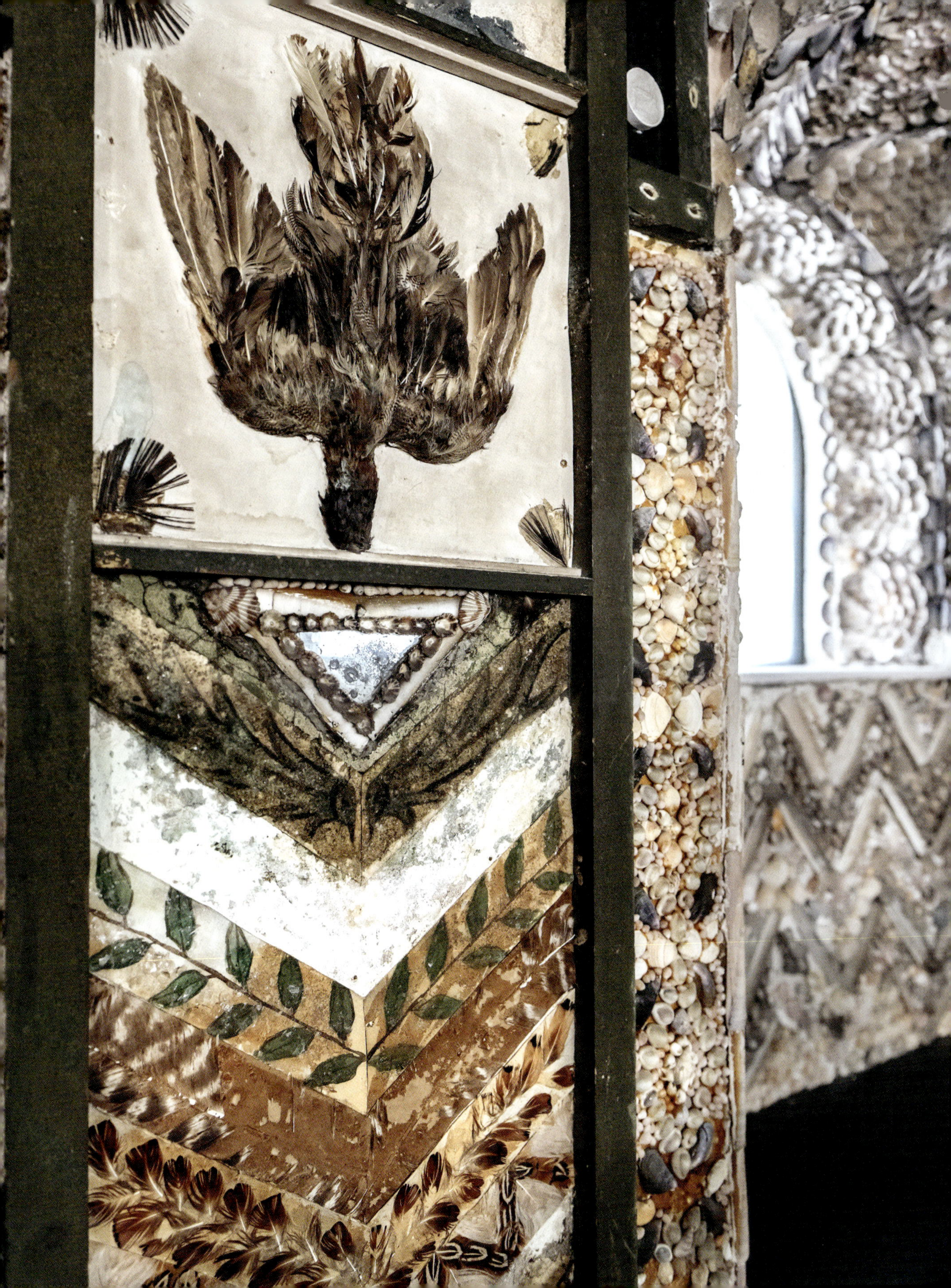

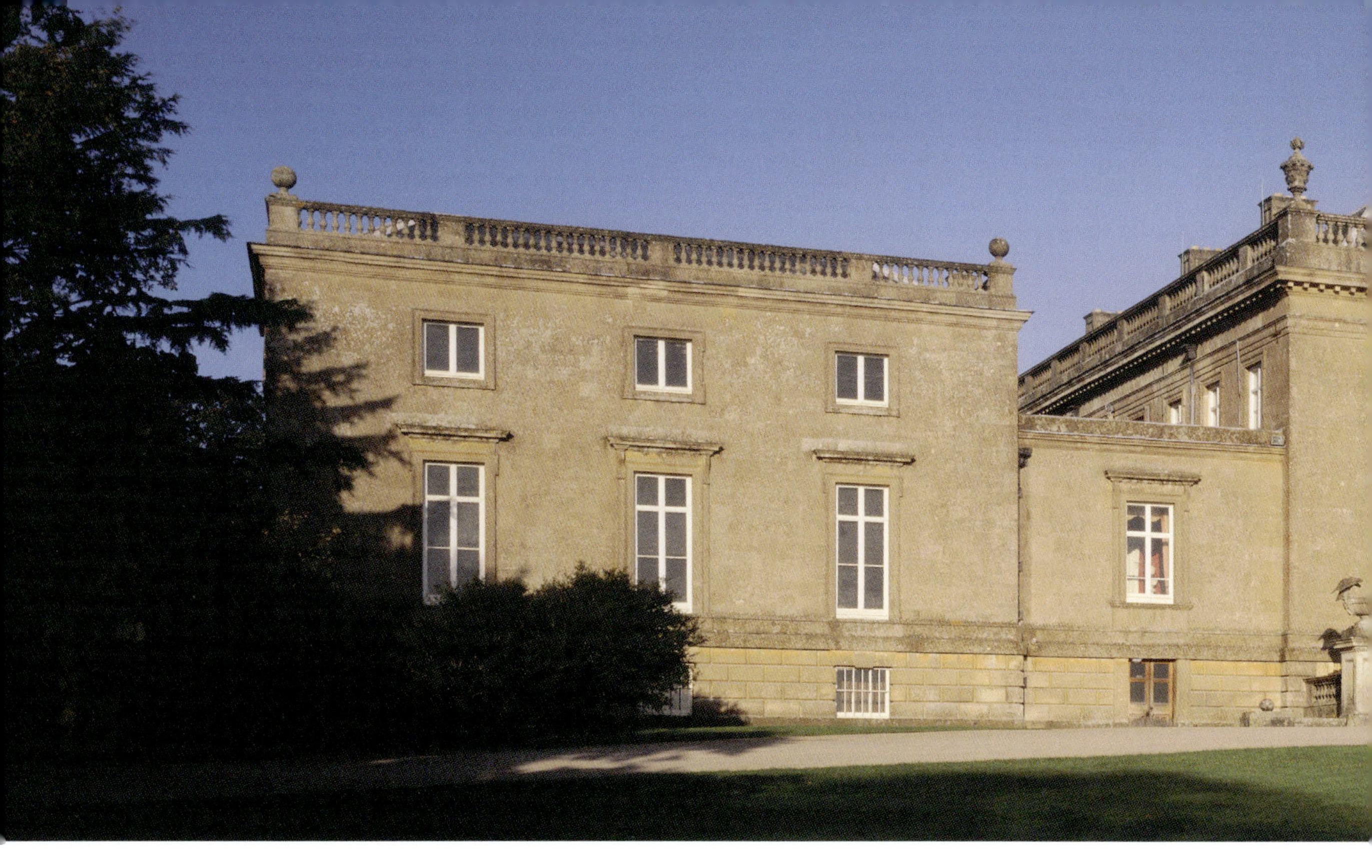

Finding a Lost Castle

Stourton Castle

Stourhead, Wiltshire

The first sight of a place or an object can fill you with a sense of wonder, but it's when you have the opportunity to go beyond and beneath the surface that even more remarkable treasures can be found. This is true of so many of the properties and collections in the care of the National Trust, and can most certainly be seen at Stourhead.

The history of these lands has been set down in layers, left over thousands of years of human occupation. This could be the debris of people's everyday lives or creations they hoped would be a lasting legacy.

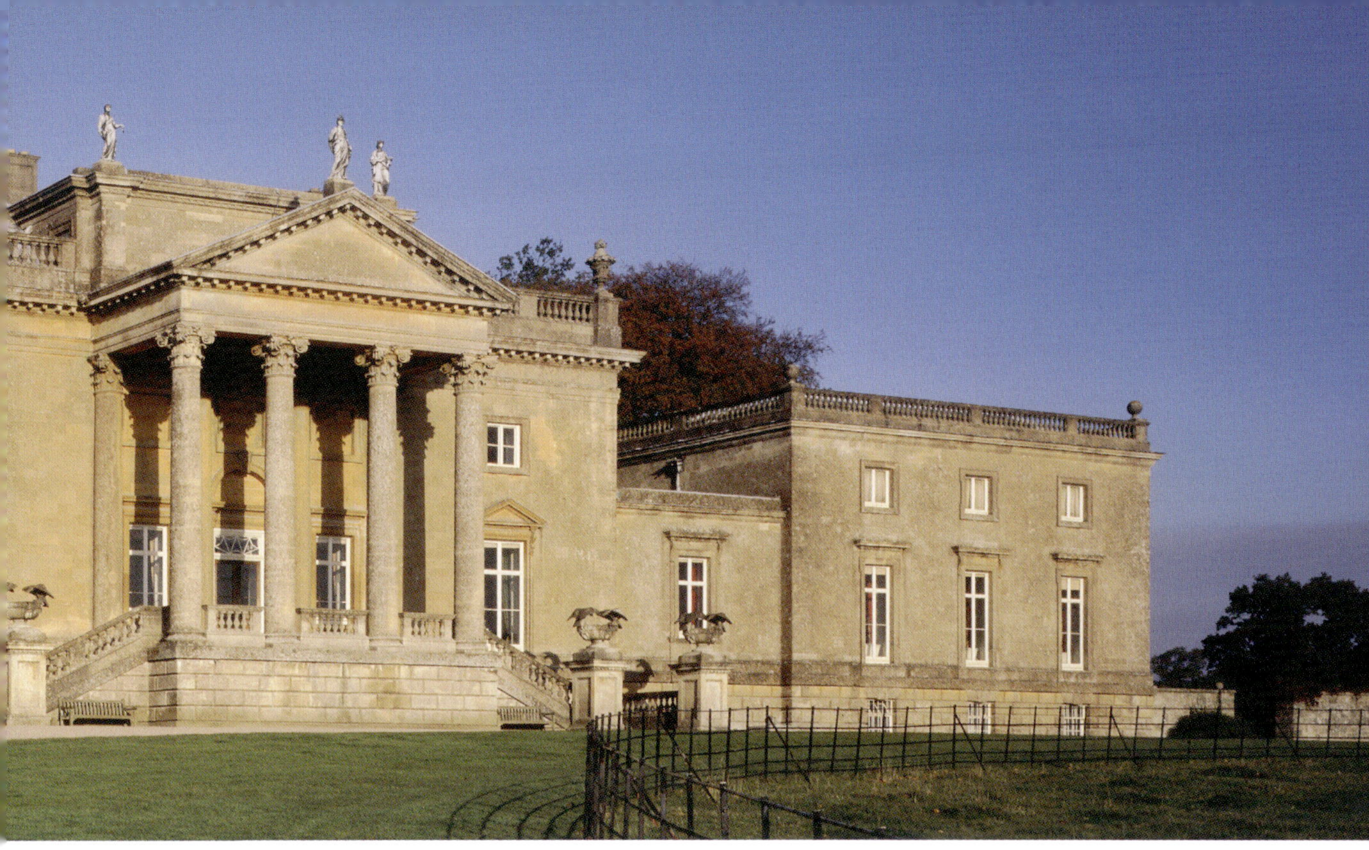

^ The Hoare family demolished the old manor house to make way for a fine Palladian mansion that they filled with art and antiquities.

Layers are something Stourhead has in abundance, as here a family dynasty dwelt for hundreds of years, each generation adding something to the last. This accumulation of treasures collected by generations of the same family is another thing we shall encounter time and time again on our journey.

In addition to leaving behind these material traces, humans have been documenting our history for centuries. And there is a long tradition of people with enquiring minds bent towards our past. A member of Stourhead's own family became a keen antiquarian and archaeologist, publishing many respected titles on local history. But still, for all this enquiry and curiosity, some mysteries remain. So it was with the case of Stourhead's missing castle.

National Trust archaeologist Martin Papworth has known about and searched for Stourhead's lost castle for decades. Antiquarians, historians and mapmakers since the time of its demolition have left useful clues, but establishing its location has long eluded the experts. Until now. In the summer of 2023, Martin set himself and his team the challenge of finally finding the site of the lost castle over the course of a 12-day dig during a festival of archaeology attended by the public, with TV crews scheduled to come back towards the end of the dig to see what the team had found. Pressure layered on pressure.

Before they started digging, they employed twenty-first-century Ground Penetrating Radar technology, using an Ordnance Survey map from 1901 bearing the tantalising legend 'site of Stourton Castle' as the starting point of their treasure hunt. This might make their task sound relatively simple, but the team had to work their way through over a metre (3 feet) of rubble and clay beneath a landscape much altered over generations of human occupancy.

∨ Only a single drawing survives of Stourton Castle.

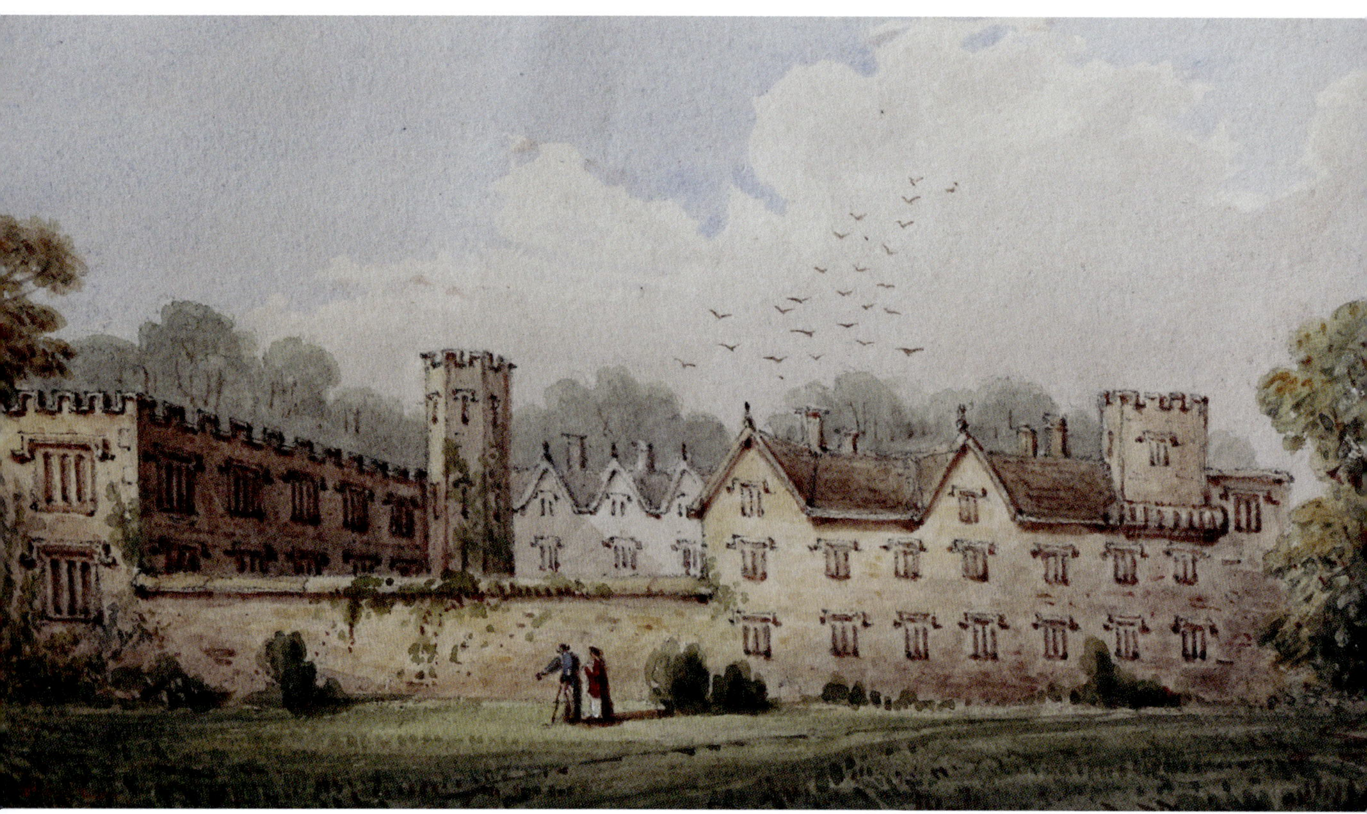

The people who lived here, and about whom most is known, is the Hoare family, who made their fortune with the foundation of C. Hoare & Co., the oldest privately owned bank in the UK. At Stourhead, they created an estate that boasts not only an eighteenth-century neo-Palladian mansion, but also an iconic landscape garden that at every turn creates the feeling of being inside a painting. But in order to achieve their grander visions, in some cases the Hoares swept away what had been there before.

In 1717, Henry Hoare bought the Stourhead estate, formerly and for 500 years the home of the Stourton family, who lived at Stourton Castle. A seventeenth-century sketch of this, by antiquarian John Aubrey, survives. It shows an impressive manor house arranged around two large courtyards with a tall tower and castellated parapets. But for Henry, this did not portray the modern and sophisticated image he wanted, and so he commissioned celebrated architect Colen Campbell to build a new mansion in the style that was the height of fashion at the time. Neo-Palladianism was a resurgence of the style named after Andrea Palladio, an Italian Renaissance architect from Venice, which had been introduced to Britain at the start of the previous century. It is a style seen on buildings in London and other major cities, characterised by their perfect symmetry and temple-like fronts (triangular roof pediments supported by columns). Not confined to city architecture, this style was also much sought after by the wealthy for their country estates.

> Antiquarians, historians and mapmakers since the time of its demolition have left useful clues, but establishing its location has long eluded the experts. Until now.

With the sort of money and ambition possessed by the Hoares, the eradication of the old to make way for the new was something they swiftly achieved, although not in time for Henry to see the finished mansion, as he died shortly before it was completed. The family paid for a survey of their new property in 1722, and the estate map shows the initial construction of the new house completed, but the Hoare family didn't declare it as being habitable until 1724. Stourton Castle was gone, and soon Stourhead's landscape would be radically altered, reworked over the course of 30 years into a scene described by some as more beautiful than any landscape put on canvas.

When Henry's son, Henry II, inherited the estate, he had the means to enhance his father's creation, adding a fine collection of paintings and sculpture, and also turning his painterly eye to the design of the landscape. His patronage of the arts and what he created at Stourhead led to the nickname 'Henry the Magnificent'. Between 1741 and the mid-1770s Henry created a classically inspired landscape set around a large man-made lake, achieved by damming a small stream. The inspiration behind Henry's vision were seventeenth-century painters Nicolas Poussin, Claude Lorrain and Gaspard Dughet, who painted Arcadian (idealised) views of Italian landscapes.

It was Henry's grandson, Sir Richard Colt Hoare, who became a respected antiquarian and archaeologist. It is said he was inspired to take up these studies by the work of antiquarian William Cunningham. Sir Richard may also have used archaeology as a diversion while trying to come to terms with his grief following the death of his wife. We should be thankful for this scholarly diversion, as much of what we know of Stourton Castle is what Sir Richard wrote in his book *The History of Modern Wiltshire*, an invaluable reference work for Martin Papworth and his team. Another fascinating link between the present and the past comes from Audrey Hoare, a descendant living at Stourhead House, who points out a piece of furniture to a BBC camera crew, saying: 'My ancestors obviously suffered from gout. There are quite a lot of gout stools littered around the house.'

So back to the search for Stourton Castle, where days one to eight and trenches A to F yielded nothing conclusive. Then on day nine, the day that the camera crews were due to return, mechanical reinforcements were brought in and trench A was carefully deepened. Martin described the scene: 'The digger began at the east end of Trench A … where we hoped for a wall to be. After a couple of scrapes the machine juddered. "Stop!" cried Nancy [Grace, one of the dig supervisors] and trowelled where the bucket had been. There it was … in the form of three solid, mortared and level blocks of stone … There was no doubt about it. It was actually a wall. The TV cameras turned up, pretty much on cue, and we were soon miked and saying to camera the exciting things we were feeling. The machine then went to F and in an hour had emptied the rubble down to a large area of mortared stone. It had a convenient line of greensand blocks marking a wall edge following the alignment of the Stable Yard wall. The story was the same in trench B. Here too there were stone foundations over 3 metres [10 feet] deep, but this time the corner of a room, and a fireplace still with the ashes of its last fire and a broken wine bottle. Amazing. The hunt for Stourton Castle is over. We have found it!'

∨ The dig and the bid to find a castle took place over just 12 days and was conducted in full view of visitors.

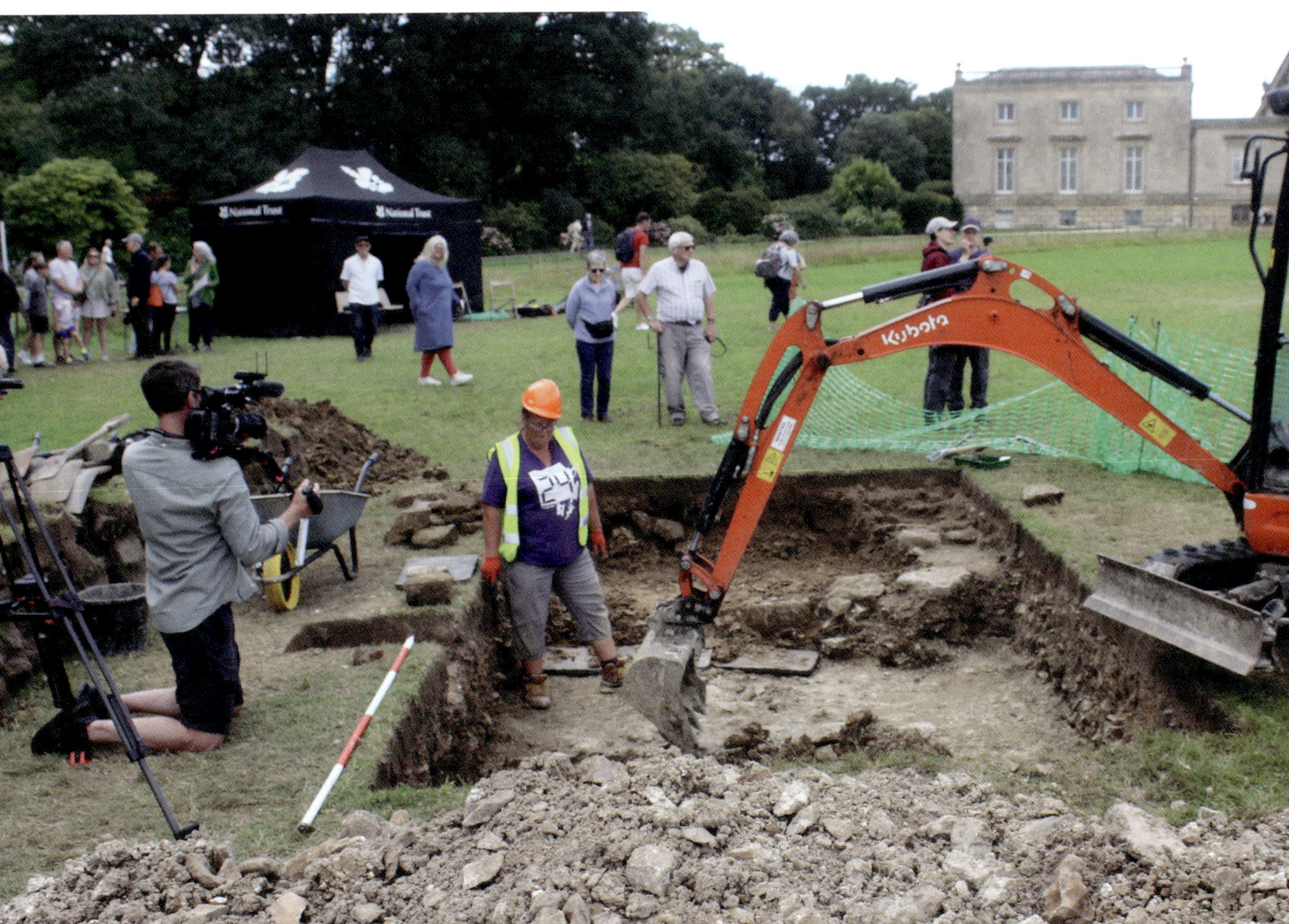

The Drive to Keep Miners' Stories Alive

Levant Mine and Beam Engine

Tin Coast, Cornwall

We've already gone underground on our journey, in search of knowledge rather than material riches. It seems this is just something we're preconditioned to do. Humans have been mining the earth below their feet for as long as they've had tools with which to break the surface, their curiosity and acquisitiveness driving them to go to extraordinary lengths, and depths.

The Tin Coast is located in West Cornwall between Pendeen and St Just in the area of West Penwith. The 7-mile (11-kilometre) route runs from the Pendeen Lighthouse to Cape Cornwall and the valleys to the south. Its importance in mining history has been recognised by UNESCO, which has designated it as part of the Cornwall and West Devon Mining Landscape World Heritage Site. As such, it requires people not only to preserve the remnants of the Cornish tin-mining industry, sometimes precariously perched on cliff-top sites, but also to bring to the surface the stories of those who toiled deep below hillsides now gloriously swathed in heather and gorse.

The landscape is still dotted with the ruined chimney stacks of the engines that once powered a world-leading mining industry, and it is riddled with an underground warren of shafts and levels that was once

> The man engine at Dolcoath Mine, Camborne. This system of reciprocating ladders and stationary platforms conveyed miners between the surface and where they worked hundreds of metres below.

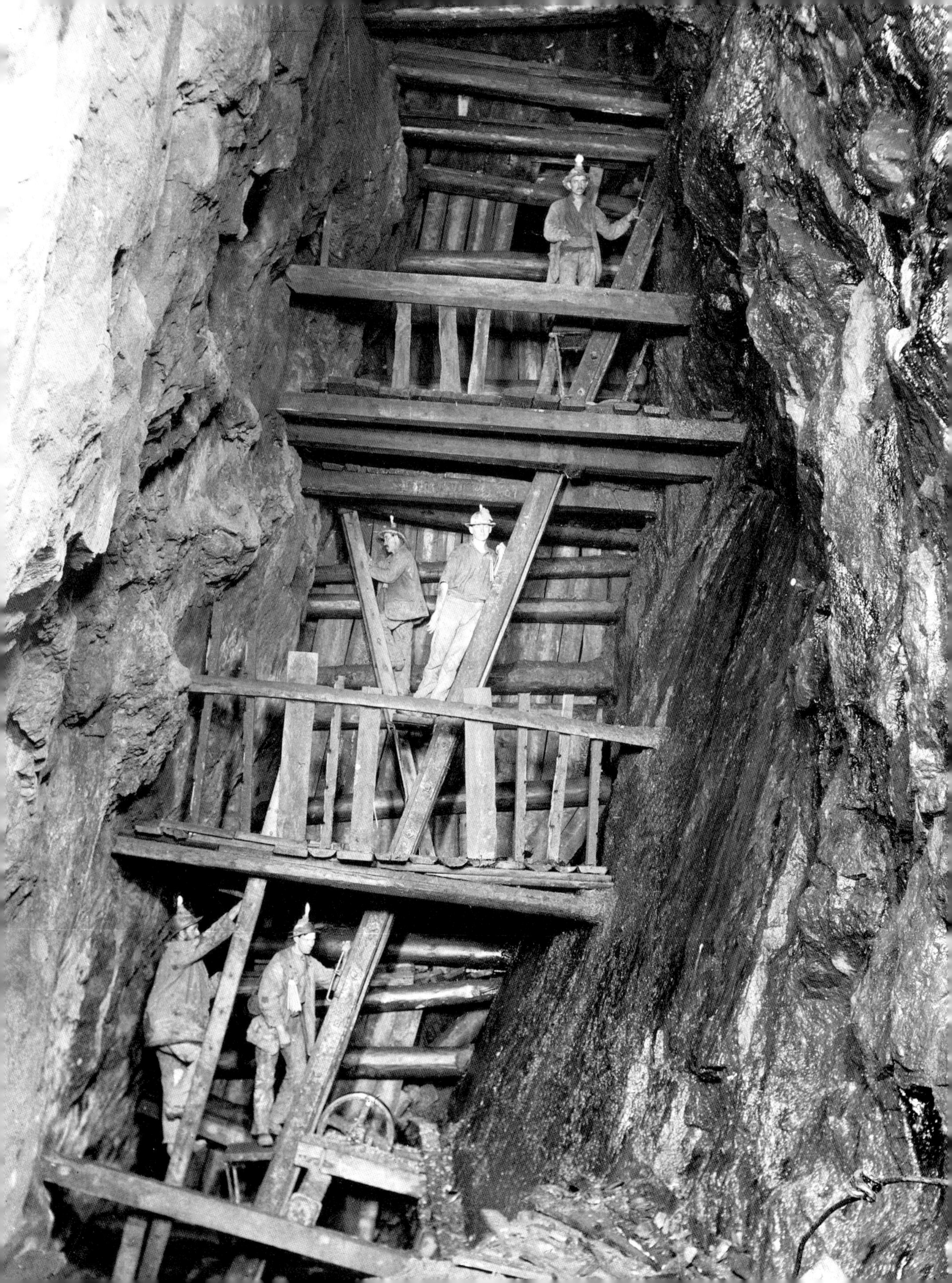

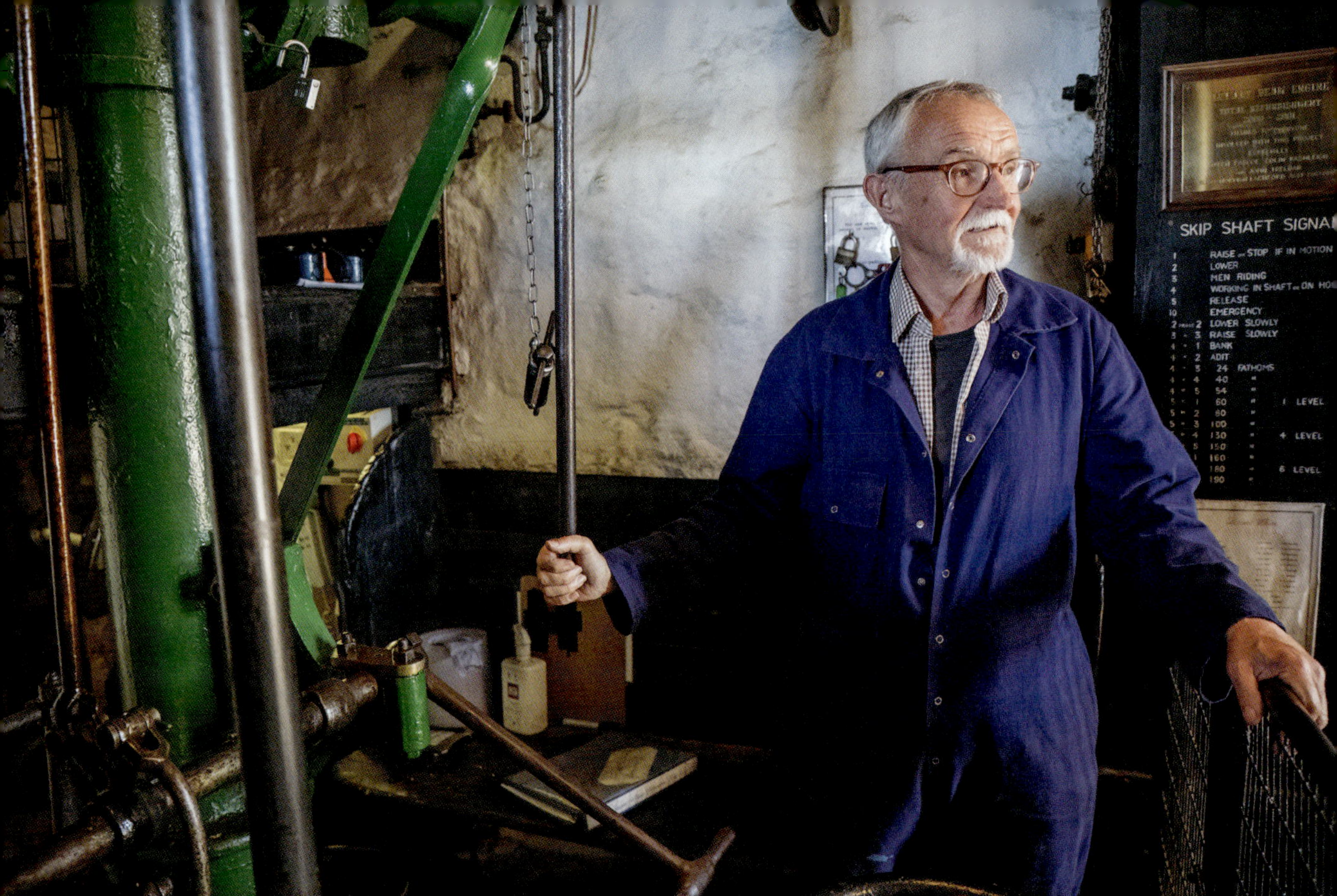

the workplace of thousands of men and boys. Women and girls also worked in the mining industry. Known as bal maidens ('bal' being the Cornish term for mine), they broke up the extracted ore before sorting and pulverising it.

Levant boasts a steam-powered beam engine dating from the 1840s, restored to working order. The engine was used to bring ore up to the surface and sits above a shaft over 1,650 feet (500 metres) deep. It stands as a monument to the engineers who built it, but it is more affecting to think of all the people who laboured in the depths beneath it, in gruelling and dangerous conditions.

Levant powerfully conveys the stories of the men and women who worked here from 1820 until 1930. An estimated 60 miles

^ A volunteer demonstrates Levant's restored beam engine, bringing the site's industrial history to life.

> The surface remains of Levant Mine with its chimney stacks and beam engine houses standing tall in the landscape.

(100 kilometres) of adits (horizontal access passages) and levels perforate the land beneath Levant and even continue out under the sea, in places for over a mile. Into this subterranean labyrinth miners would descend armed with picks, hand drills and gunpowder, a candle mounted on their hats providing the only illumination.

It was incredibly dangerous and yet hugely productive: one source suggests that between 1848 and 1913, Levant's workers extracted and processed 130,000 tonnes of copper ore and 24,000 tonnes of tin ore. The mine employed a great many people and made a few exceedingly wealthy. The number of available workers made them easily replaceable. A by-product of the mining of metals – arsenic – was processed at Levant in a chimney stack that stands close to the Count House, where the mine's shareholders enjoyed lavish dinners. They were aware of the dangers that their workers were encountering daily – arsenic was sold as an insecticide, especially to North America – but these were different times.

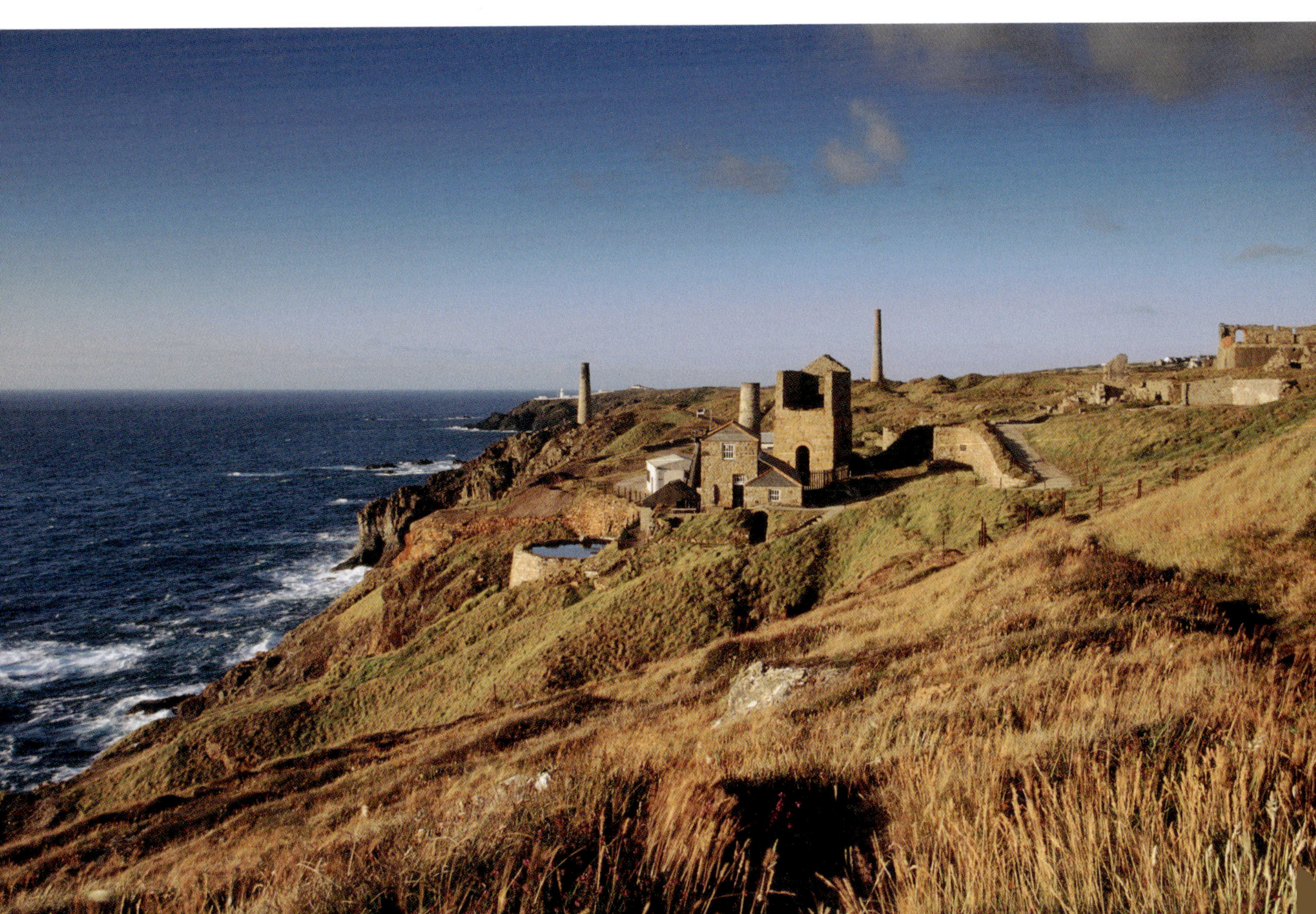

Accidents and horrific injuries were regular occurrences, but the deadliest event at Levant happened on 20 October 1919, when the man engine that was bringing miners back up to the surface at the end of their shift failed. It was around 3 o'clock in the afternoon and the men were close to the top when a vital connection broke. Reports describe 'a living pillar of men' falling down the shaft. Thirty-one died and many more were injured.

The Levant disaster is just one compelling reason to keep *all* the workers' stories alive. At Levant, just as at the other sites along the Tin Coast, volunteers perform that crucial role of storyteller. Without the engine driver, Levant's beam engine would fall into disuse. Instead, it is operated and maintained, and will continue to thunderously evoke the experiences of Levant's workers, all of whom had to labour in the hardest conditions just to survive.

CODE OF SIGNALS	NEW COOK'S KITCHEN SHAFT
1-6	80 FATHOM LEVEL
1-7	148 " "
2-1	175 " "
2-3	195 " "
2-5	205 " "
2-6	225 " "
2-7	245 " "
3-2	290 " "
3-4	315 " "
3-5	340 " "
4-1	360 " "
4-2	380 " "
4-3	380 SLUDGING X CUT
4-4	380 LOADING STATION
1-3	RAISE TO NEXT LEVEL
1-2	LOWER TO NEXT LEVEL
1	STOP (WHEN HOIST IN MOTION)
1	RAISE (WHEN HOIST STOPPED)
2	LOWER
3	MEN ENTERING CAGE
2-2	LOWER SLOWLY
3-3	RAISE SLOWLY
4 & LEVEL SIGNAL	CAGE REQUIRED
15 & LEVEL SIGNAL	ACCIDENT

SIGNED
N.K. KITTO
MANAGER

< Signage demonstrating a code of signals used when lowering men to 380 fathoms (700 metres) below ground.

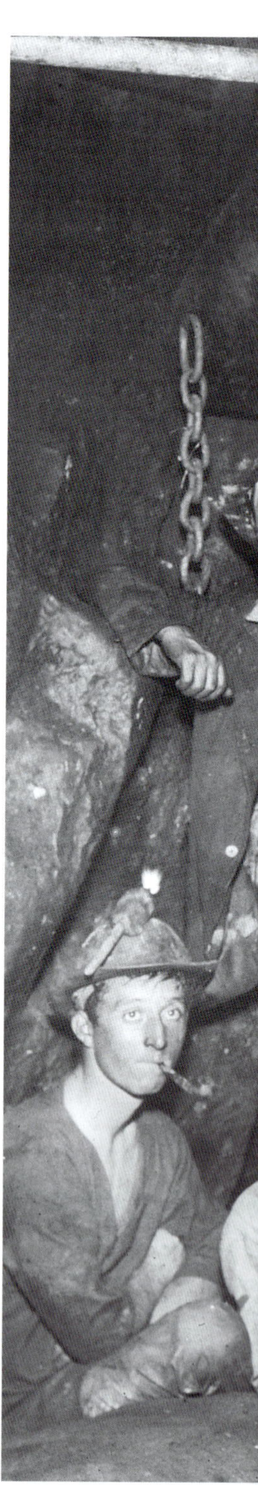

> A group of miners posing for a photograph taken at Levant Mine in July 1894 at 278 fathoms (500 metres).

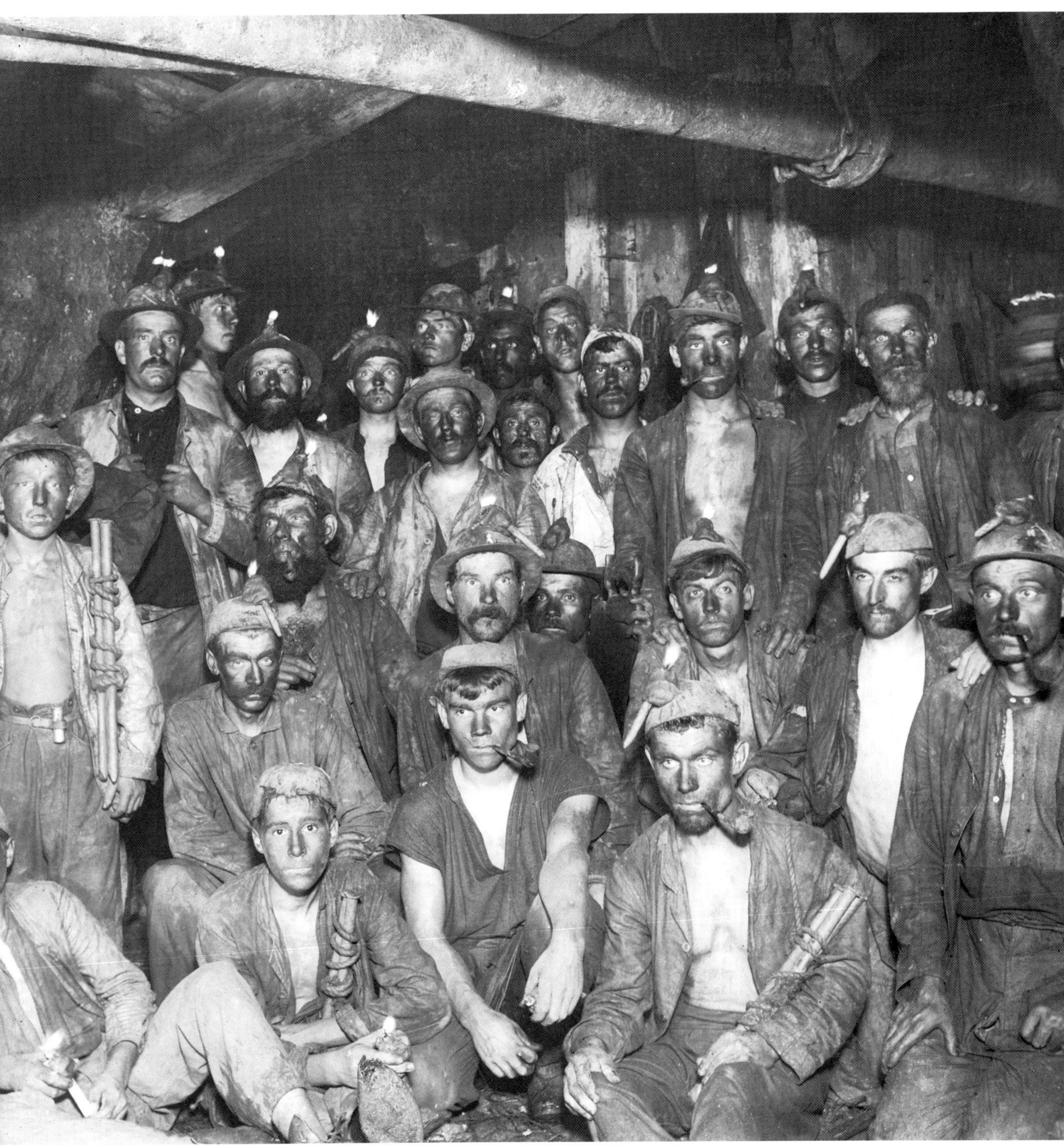

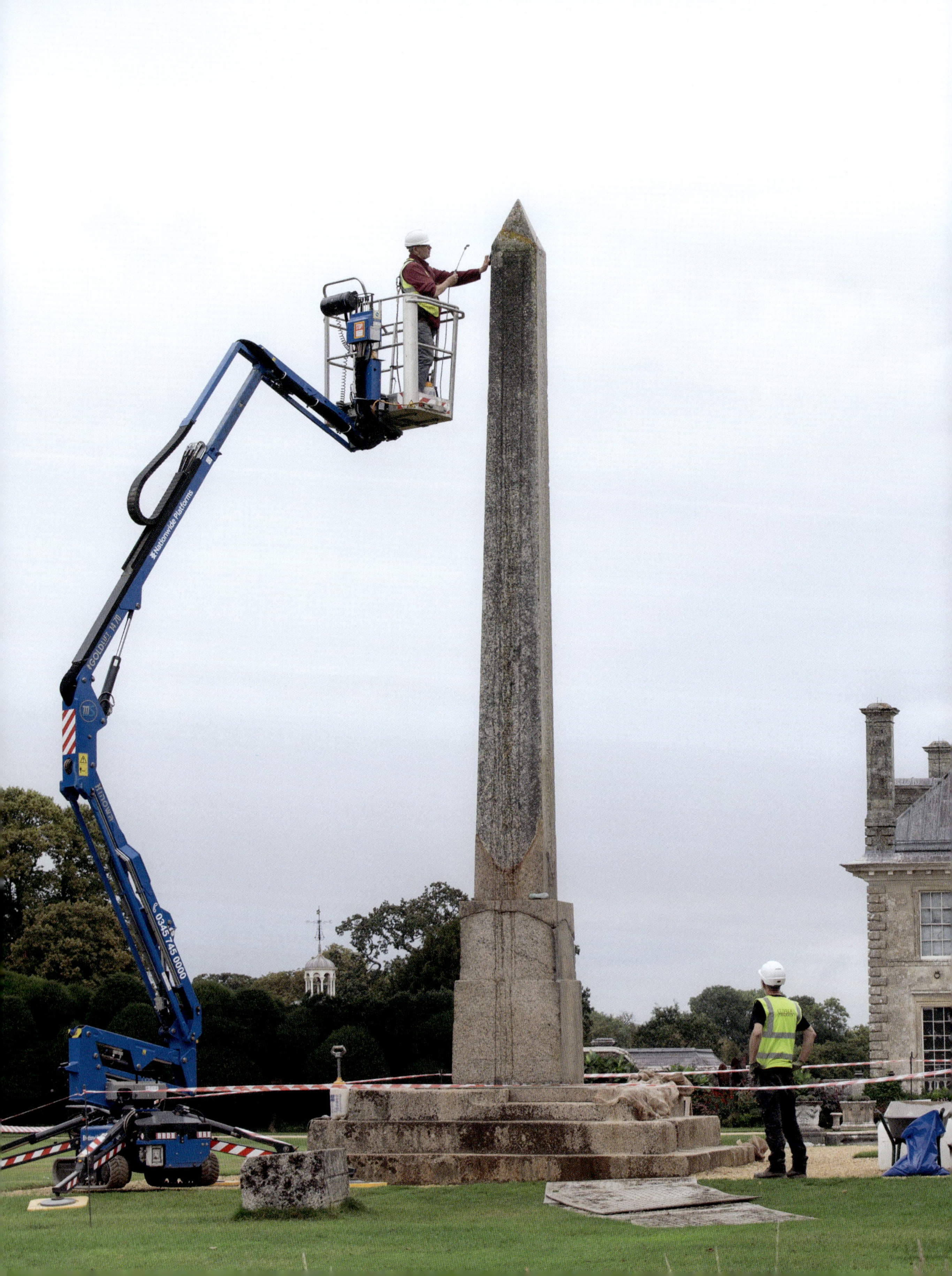
Nationwide Platforms
0345 745 0000

Restoring Dorset's Own Rosetta Stone

The Philae Obelisk

Kingston Lacy, Dorset

Contemporary with Sir Richard Colt Hoare at Stourhead (see page 24), another Georgian gentleman with a passion for collecting antiquities and works of art was politician and explorer William John Bankes. He acquired many ancient artefacts and Old Masters, creating a collection that today is the pride of the National Trust, but one that also induces nervousness when hands-on conservation is required.

A close friend of Romantic poet and professional scoundrel Lord Byron, who called him the 'father of all mischief' during their time at Cambridge University, William John was an avid amateur scholar of Egyptology, and his contribution to the decipherment of hieroglyphs was critical but ultimately undervalued.

On his first trip to Egypt in 1815, William John came across an obelisk dated to the second century BC, outside the Temple of Isis at Philae. Like many men of his class, his classical education meant he was able to read the ancient Greek carved into its bottom section and believed it to be a translation of the Egyptian text carved above, providing a key, like the more famous Rosetta Stone, to unlocking the mystery of hieroglyphs. The discovery of the two texts side by side proved to be more exciting than their translation: both inscriptions were, in essence, the temple's tax-exemption certificate.

< It took six years and the help of the Duke of Wellington to transport the Philae Obelisk from Egypt to Dorset.

It was not unusual for wealthy aristocrats to display antiquities they had collected on their travels on their country estates, and it seems that the Philae Obelisk was relatively easy to acquire. Some accounts say William John actually sought permission from the Ottoman rulers of Egypt. Getting it home, on the other hand, was another story altogether.

It took six years for the obelisk to reach Kingston Lacy. The operation was overseen by Giovanni Battista Belzoni (also known as the Great Belzoni – he had moved to England in 1803 to be a circus strongman), himself a pioneering archaeologist of Egyptian antiquities, and responsible for the transportation of many ancient monuments to European collections.

The obelisk's journey started badly, as the pier constructed to move it onto a waiting boat collapsed under its colossal weight and both pier and obelisk slid into the waters of the Nile. The Great Belzoni persevered and news of this endeavour reached the Duke of Wellington, who had been a friend of William John's father.

When the obelisk reached these shores, the Duke lent his gun carriage for its onward transportation from London to Dorset. The plaque at the obelisk's base confirms that the Duke chose its location at Kingston Lacy and laid the foundation stone on 17 August 1827.

This would not be the last time the Duke would lend his support. In 1833, William John was arrested for engaging in 'indecent behaviour' with a soldier in a urinal outside the Houses of Parliament. He asked the Duke to vouch for his character at his trial, at which the Duke was recorded as saying: 'I should never have believed him guilty of the offence with which he is now charged; his pursuits and habits are honourable and manly – remarkably so; I once gave him a watch – it was in Spain, he had been robbed of his watch at Madrid; he was attacked by two men, and his conduct on that occasion was so firm and manly that it pleased me, and I gave him a watch I had worn for some time.' At this time homosexuality was thought of as a criminal offence punishable by imprisonment, even death, so it was to William John's huge relief that he was found not guilty of the charges against him. However, when he was arrested a second time in 1841, then in his mid-fifties, he had no choice but to leave the country.

William John could not forsake what he had started at Kingston

Lacy. If anything, his enthusiasm for collecting increased. He began to commission and even design works of art to adorn Kingston Lacy, including marble carvings and furniture, and send them back to his siblings in Dorset, in the full knowledge that he would see neither home nor the sum of his life's work. William John died in exile in Venice in 1855.

The Philae Obelisk was already around 2,000 years old when it arrived in Dorset. After nearly two centuries of exposure to English weather, its markings were losing clarity. More worrying still, its base contained conspicuous cracks. Stonework conservators Douglas Carpenter and Richard Ball were brought in to remedy the situation.

They began by carefully removing every piece of lichen from the obelisk's surface. Once cleaned, the needle's pink granite surface showed the inscriptions in greatly sharpened relief. Then they moved on to the task of repairing and consolidating the cracks, which had appeared where the bottom of the needle meets the Libyan granite used to repair the base in the 1820s. Left exposed to many more winters and the damage posed by water ingress as it freezes and thaws, these fissures would only increase in size and destabilise the obelisk. The old mortar was raked out to be replaced with new, but with the addition of sand and other aggregates to help the modern repair blend into its ancient surroundings.

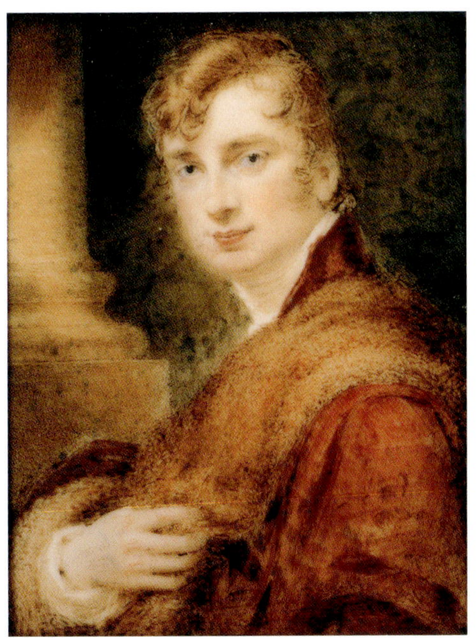

^ William John Bankes travelled widely throughout his life, collecting art and antiquities for his family home.

It's rare to have the opportunity to work on a stone structure of such antiquity, but not as unusual as you may think, in part due to the fashion that saw the very wealthy adorn their country estates with ancient monuments, perhaps turning to the Great Belzoni for help. In any case, Douglas is not easily fazed: 'It's a bit strange seeing an Egyptian obelisk in a garden, but I've seen lots of strange things in gardens now, so it's just another one to add to the list.'

‘Picture of Gray’ Mystery

A Soldier at Newporth Beach, near Falmouth

Clouds Hill, Dorset

Henry Scott Augustus Tuke was a painter who worked in the Impressionist style and who, like the pioneers of that movement half a century before him, loved to paint *en plein air*, or outdoors. He also loved to sail, so it was almost inevitable that, after studying at the Slade School of Art in London, he should move to the coast. Friends from art school suggested Newlyn in Cornwall, a recommendation he must have been grateful for, as he declared the village was ‘simply reeking with subjects’.

Tuke’s themes were generally the sea, sun-worship, health and the male form, often unclothed. In this painting, a Cornwall Royal Garrison Artillery soldier sits on a beach, his jacket and cap beside him on the sand; his braces are down, and he is unwinding the puttees from around his boots as he undresses to join his friend in the water. As was Tuke’s practice, it was likely painted *in situ* on Newporth Beach, close to Pennance Point where he lived. One of Tuke’s favourite models, Frank Jackett, who posed for a painting in the same location years before, recalled in an interview the difficulty Tuke had in getting the canvas down to the beach, because of the high winds.

This scene of two soldiers enjoying their leave, however, is all stillness and peace, in stark contrast to their lives when in uniform. By 1921, the world had seen such horrors that escapist scenes such as this one must have had added appeal. Its first owner was Sydney Lomer, soldier and

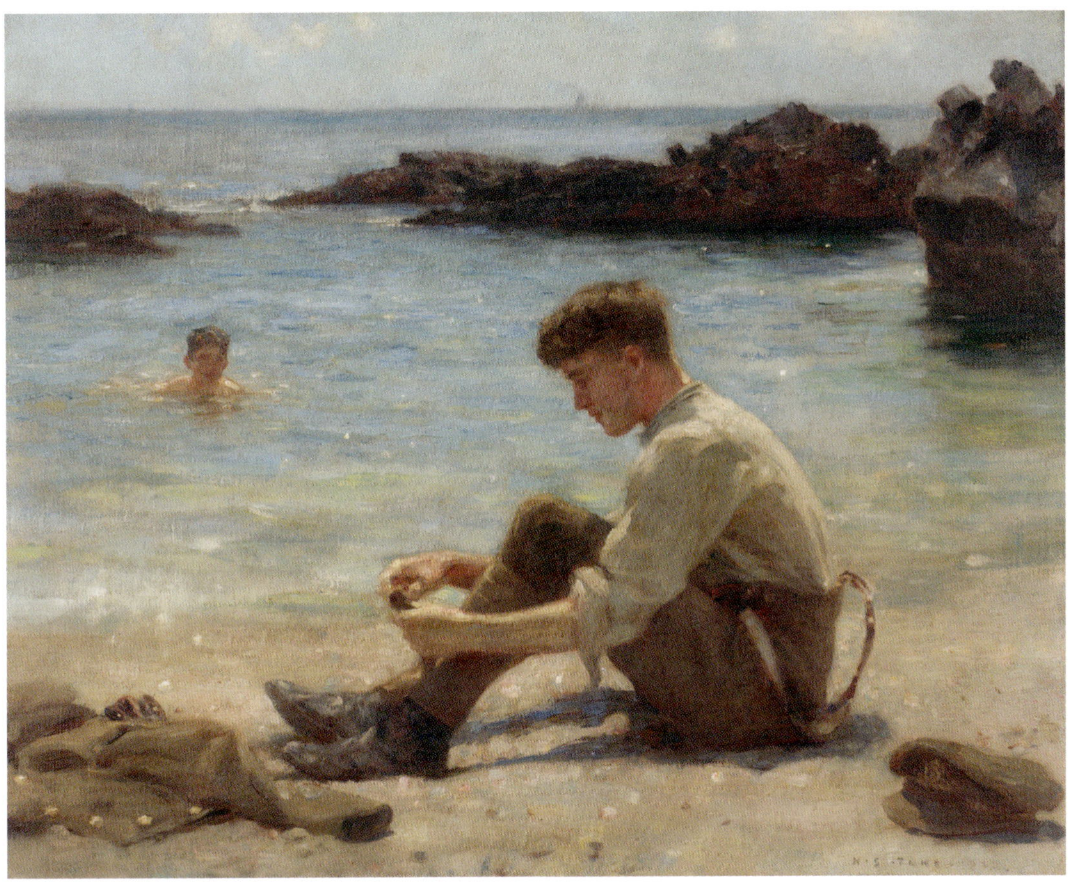

^ Listed both as *A Soldier at Newporth Beach, near Falmouth* and *Picture of Gray*, this painting presented something of a mystery.

war poet. He had received a posting to France in 1915, so would have experienced first-hand some of those horrors in the trenches. Its second owner also served in the First World War, though his military service was spent in North Africa.

That man was T. E. Lawrence, who became famous as 'Lawrence of Arabia'. An American journalist, Lowell Thomas, was gathering material on a visit to the Middle East during the war and met Lawrence while he was there. Thomas went on to create a hugely popular film, featuring images of Lawrence dressed in Arabic clothing, backed by a sensational narrative, which captured the imagination of audiences in America before it had the same effect in London in 1919. The moniker was later reinforced after the publication of *Seven Pillars of Wisdom*. This

1926 autobiography vividly describes Lawrence's involvement in the Arab Revolt of 1916–18, and was hugely successful. The 1935 edition quotes no less than Winston Churchill, who said: 'It ranks with the greatest books ever written in the English language. As a narrative of war and adventure it is unsurpassable.'

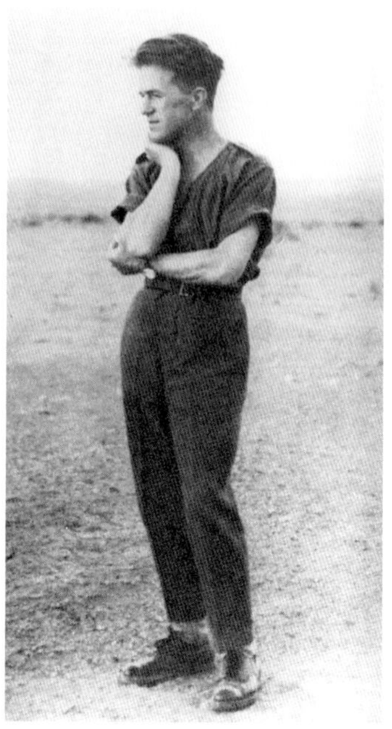

^ T. E. Lawrence, also known as 'Lawrence of Arabia', went by many names.

T. E. Lawrence went by a variety of aliases, one of them being T. E. Shaw, a name that he claimed to have chosen at random, though it is thought that it came as a result of his close friendship with George Bernard Shaw and his wife Charlotte, whom he met in 1922 and whose editorial help he acknowledged in the preface of *Seven Pillars of Wisdom*.

The year after Lawrence met the Shaws, he was stationed at Bovington Camp in Dorset with the Tank Corps, and so initially rented nearby Clouds Hill, before buying it outright in 1929. For the two years Lawrence was at Bovington, he used the cottage as an evening retreat from army life. It had no running water and the accommodation was very basic. He furnished it simply and enjoyed the peace it afforded him.

Clouds Hill was given to the National Trust by Lawrence's brother, Arnold, following his death in a motorcycle accident in 1935. It is now run as a museum dedicated to the life and works of T. E. Lawrence.

Just before the ninetieth anniversary of Lawrence's death, this painting of the Cornish soldiers was sent off for conservation. There had been a long-standing rumour that the face of the soldier on the beach had been overpainted by Tuke to more closely resemble Lawrence. However, due to the painting's complicated provenance, this had been difficult to ascertain.

An inventory of Clouds Hill tells us that Lawrence owned the painting by 1926. It's thought it was painted in around 1922 but, unusually, the date is scratched out. Tuke kept a register of sales – unfortunately not dated but ordered chronologically – in which he records that this painting was one of two originally sold to R. F. C. Scott for 25 guineas. It's believed

R. F. C. Scott was a pseudonym used by Sydney Lomer. The painting is listed as 'Picture of Gray' and its companion as 'Small Bathing Picture', which has the official title of 'Boys Bathing'. Further interest comes from a margin note in the register that reads: 'When R. F. C. Scott died "Gray" bought these two at the sale of his effects for a fiver!' The quotes suggest that this may have also been a pseudonym, further deepening the intrigue. We know that Lawrence at one time owned both paintings, but he gave 'Boys Bathing' to his friend Clare Sydney Smith, who reproduced it in her memoir with the caption 'A Painting of T. E. S. by H. S. Tuke R.A.' (She knew Lawrence by his adopted name of Thomas Edward Shaw.) Research also revealed that Lawrence wrote to his biographers on 2 July 1922 and mentioned that he had just come back from Cornwall, which puts him in the right place at the right time to model for Tuke.

Alongside the conservation treatment, infra-red reflectography was used to study Tuke's paint layering and brush strokes in detail invisible to the naked eye. Stereomicroscopy was also used to magnify areas around the date, signature and model's face. What this technical examination concluded was that the painting contains no extensive retouching or alterations, so the likeness of the soldier was just as Tuke had intended.

It was concluded that for 'Gray' to have been anyone other than Lawrence he would, one, have to have bought the painting on Lomer's death in 1926 and sold it on to Lawrence that same year when it appears in the Clouds Hill inventory, and, two, he would have to have borne a resemblance to Lawrence.

The far likelier scenario is that Lawrence connected with Tuke while he was in Cornwall in the summer of 1922, and either asked or was invited to model for Tuke. That summer's work resulted in these two paintings and when, a few years later, Lawrence heard they were back on the market, he snapped them up, much to Tuke's delight, as noted in his register.

What remains a mystery is why the date was scratched out, something highly unusual as it normally contributes to a painting's authenticity and value. However, Lawrence was such an enigma that it's perhaps apt that an element of mystery should cling.

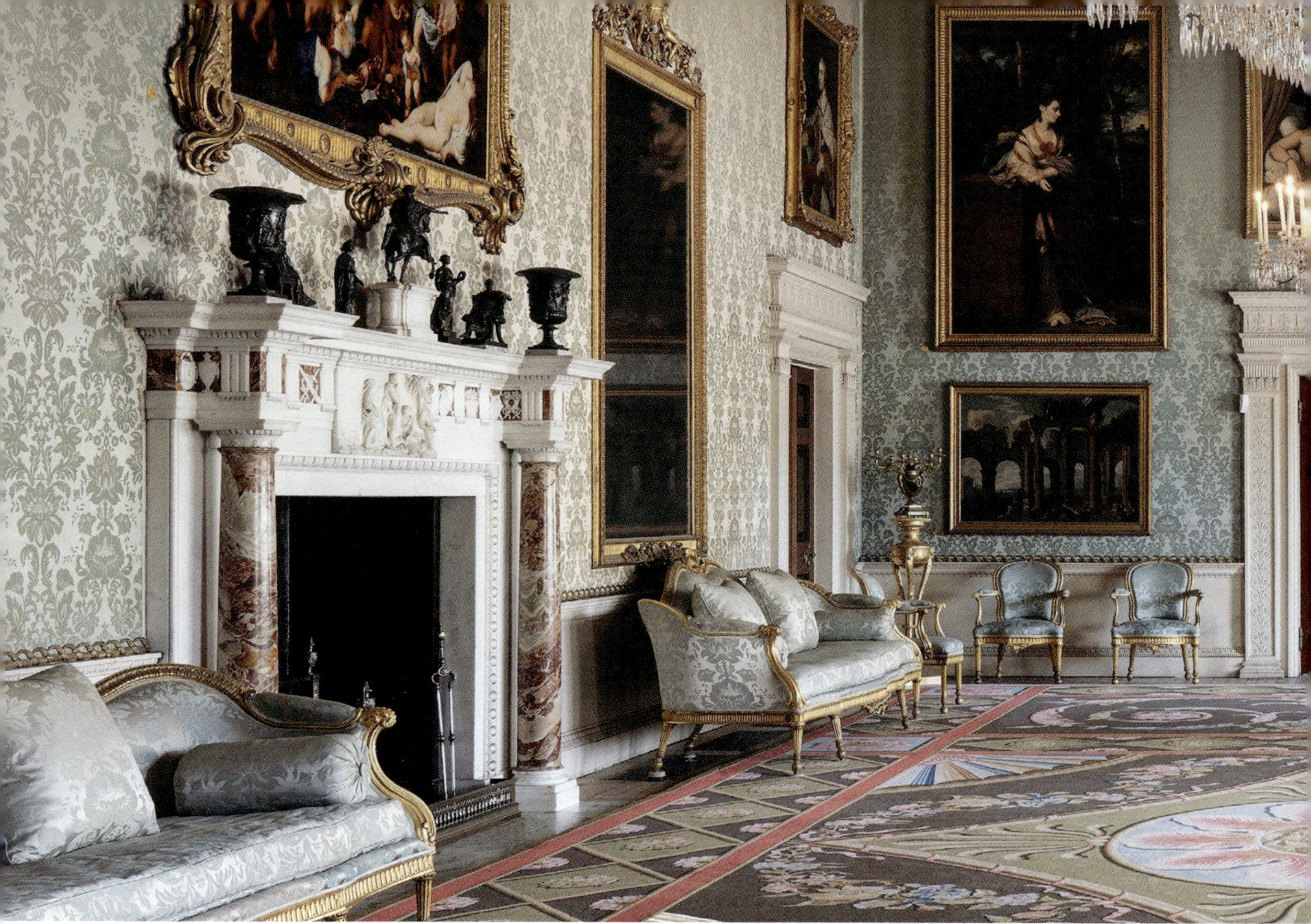

Reweaving a Spectacular Carpet

Axminster Carpet

Saltram, Devon

For the first time in more than 40 years, visitors can enjoy one of Britain's finest early Georgian interiors just as its designer Robert Adam intended. Measuring 44¼ × 19½ feet (13.5 × 5.9 metres), the Saloon carpet at Saltram may not quite have been a hidden treasure,

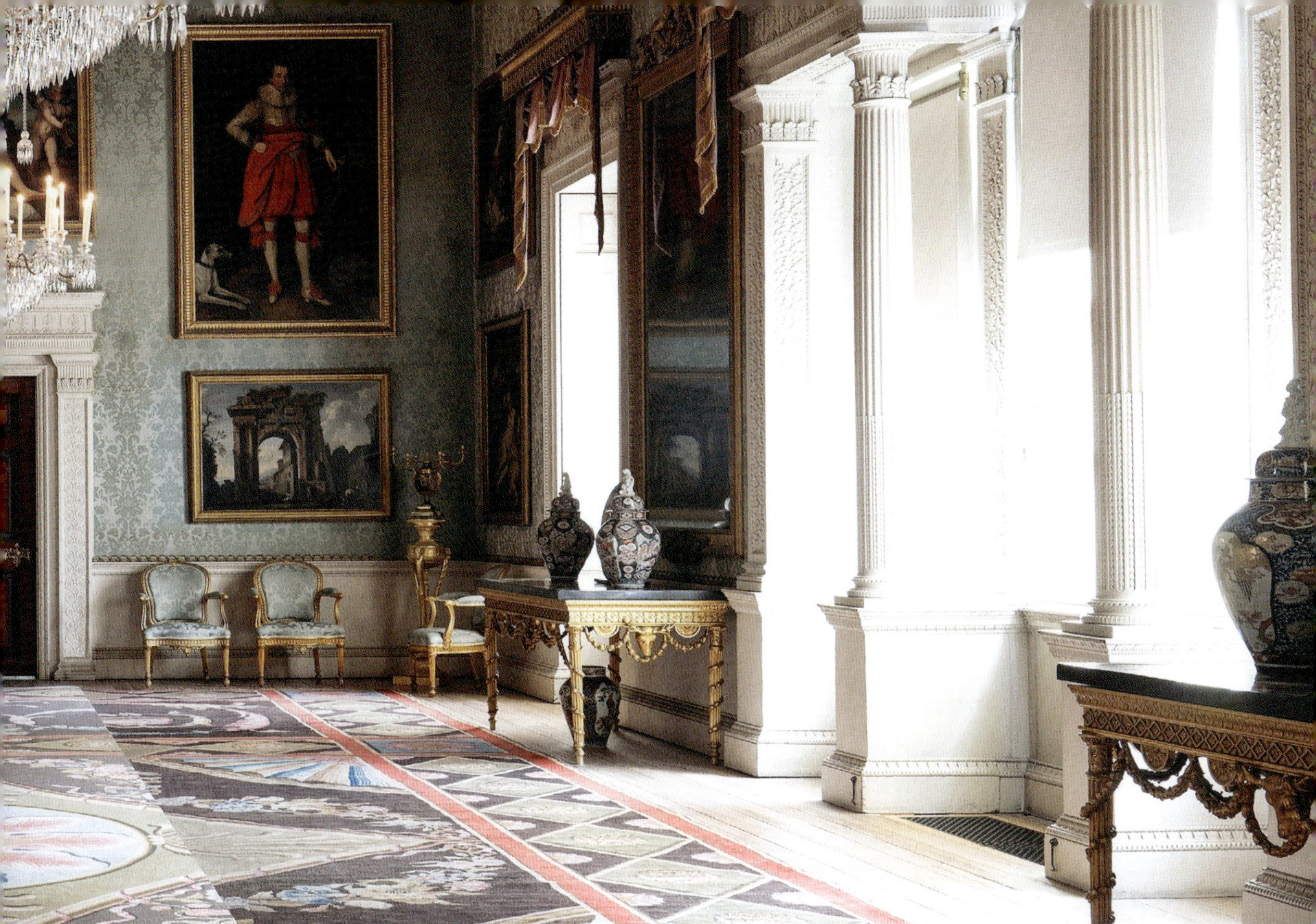

but for four decades part of the carpet's design had remained hidden to visitors – either partly rolled up or covered with a protective drugget across the middle – as they marvelled at this sumptuous space. Now they have the opportunity to fully appreciate this exquisite floor covering, described as the most important in the National Trust's care.

During the eighteenth century, Saltram was transformed from a substantial seventeenth-century house to a magnificent Palladian mansion. A number of the rooms were designed by Neo-classical architect Robert Adam. For those with the means, he was the go-to designer of the Georgian era, and Saltram's owners approached him not once but twice to remodel the estate's original residence.

^ Robert Adam was both an architect and interior designer whose schemes unified walls, windows, fireplaces, furniture, fixtures, fittings, ceilings and carpets.

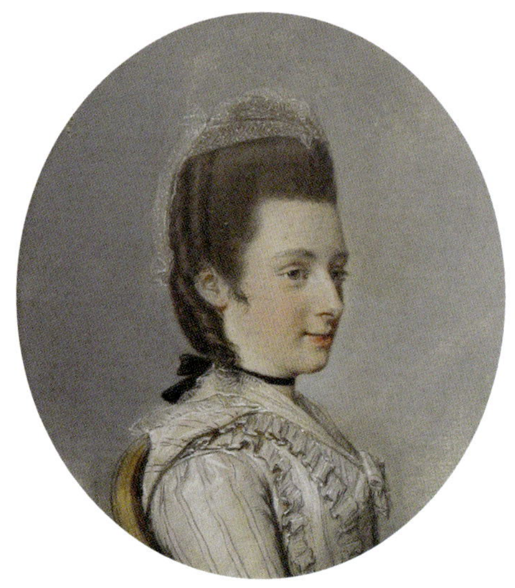

^ Theresa Parker is credited with making Saltram the most impressive country house in Devon.

The present building was begun by John Parker, a Devonshire landowner, and completed by his son, also John, who served as Member of Parliament for two local constituencies before being raised to the peerage as 1st Baron Boringdon. The Parkers had attained a certain standing in society, but much of the credit for what Saltram became – described by the architectural critic Pevsner as 'the most impressive country house in Devon' – must go to their wives.

The combined wealth of Catherine Poulett and her husband John Parker I funded the initial remodelling, which was then continued after his lifetime by his daughter-in-law, who is credited with making Saltram one of the finest houses in South West England. Her name was the Hon. Theresa Robinson and she was the daughter of the English Ambassador to the Habsburg court in Vienna. Born in Continental Europe and given a traditional aristocratic education, she would have seemed rather cosmopolitan compared with her Devon neighbours, and perhaps also in contrast to her husband. While John Parker II was keen on outdoor pursuits and also had an interest in politics, Theresa set about applying their significant wealth to transforming the interiors of her new home, and procuring a fine art collection.

In their bid to make Saltram the most fashionable place around, Theresa and John worked closely with Adam, who commissioned the best designers and makers: furniture from Thomas Chippendale, ceiling plasterwork by Joseph Rose, paintings by Antonio Zucchi and candelabra by Matthew Boulton. Theresa would also have acquired ceramics from Josiah Wedgwood. Everything about Saltram, both inside and out, was designed to impress; reception rooms were key, however, and most impressive of all was the Saloon. As property curator Zoë Shearman explained: 'The great houses of the eighteenth century were visible

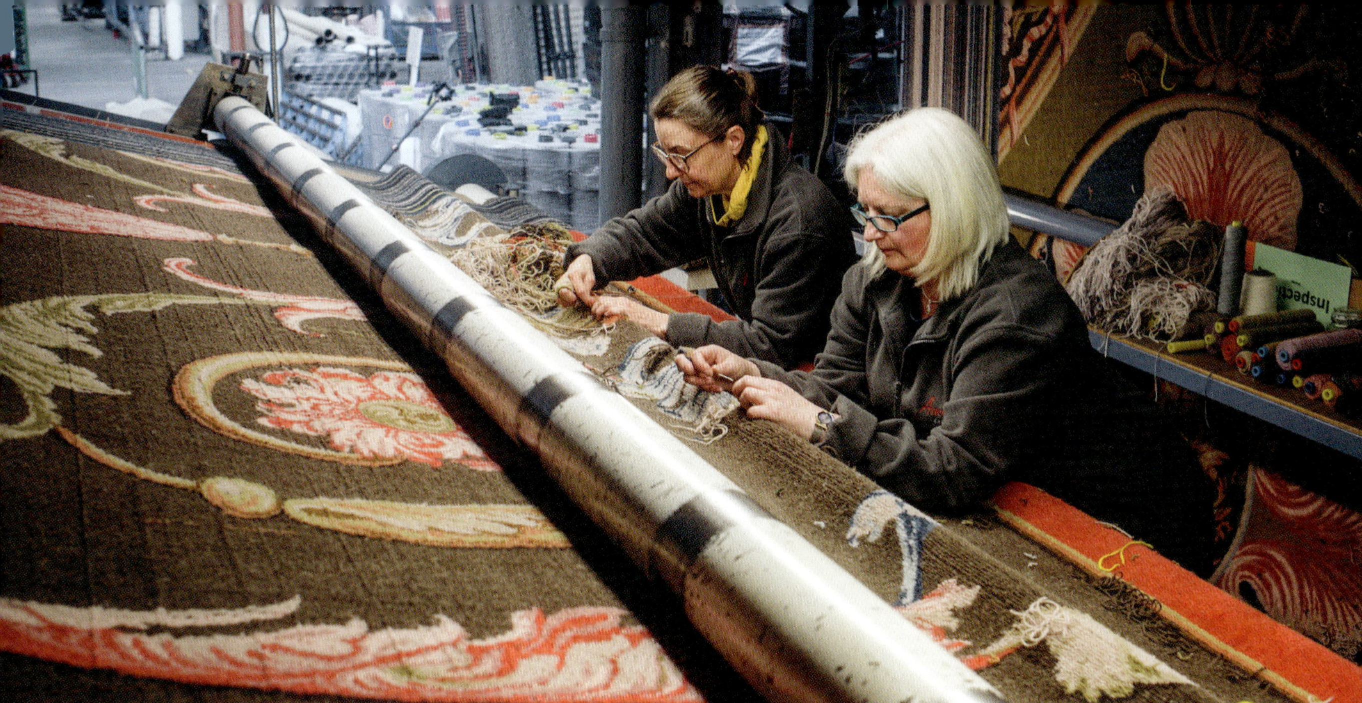

expressions of wealth, power and prestige. A main part of the role of a mistress of the house was to oversee its design and decoration. In this way, they would aid their husband's climb through social and political ranks, while moulding the house to their own taste.'

In Adam interiors, all the furnishings were considered together to create a unified and harmonious design. Robert Adam designed virtually every aspect of the Saloon, from the ceiling, windows, mirrors and side tables, to the door handles, bringing together the finest artists and craftspeople to ensure all the elements worked together as a coherent theme. This floor-to-ceiling approach resulted in perhaps the room's most spectacular feature – the large and lavish carpet, designed by Adam to echo the ceiling and knotted by hand at Thomas Whitty's factory in Axminster, Devon. Zoë elaborated: 'The design is very intricate; we think it was made by around seven people, probably Thomas Whitty's wife and his children. They hand-knotted the carpet, sitting alongside each other with the carpet hung from the ceiling, working to Adam's design that may have taken over a year to finish.'

Keen to show this masterpiece off to visitors – as Theresa and John would surely have wanted – but at pains to protect it, the National Trust

^ The loom took nearly two years to build and the weave almost two months to complete.

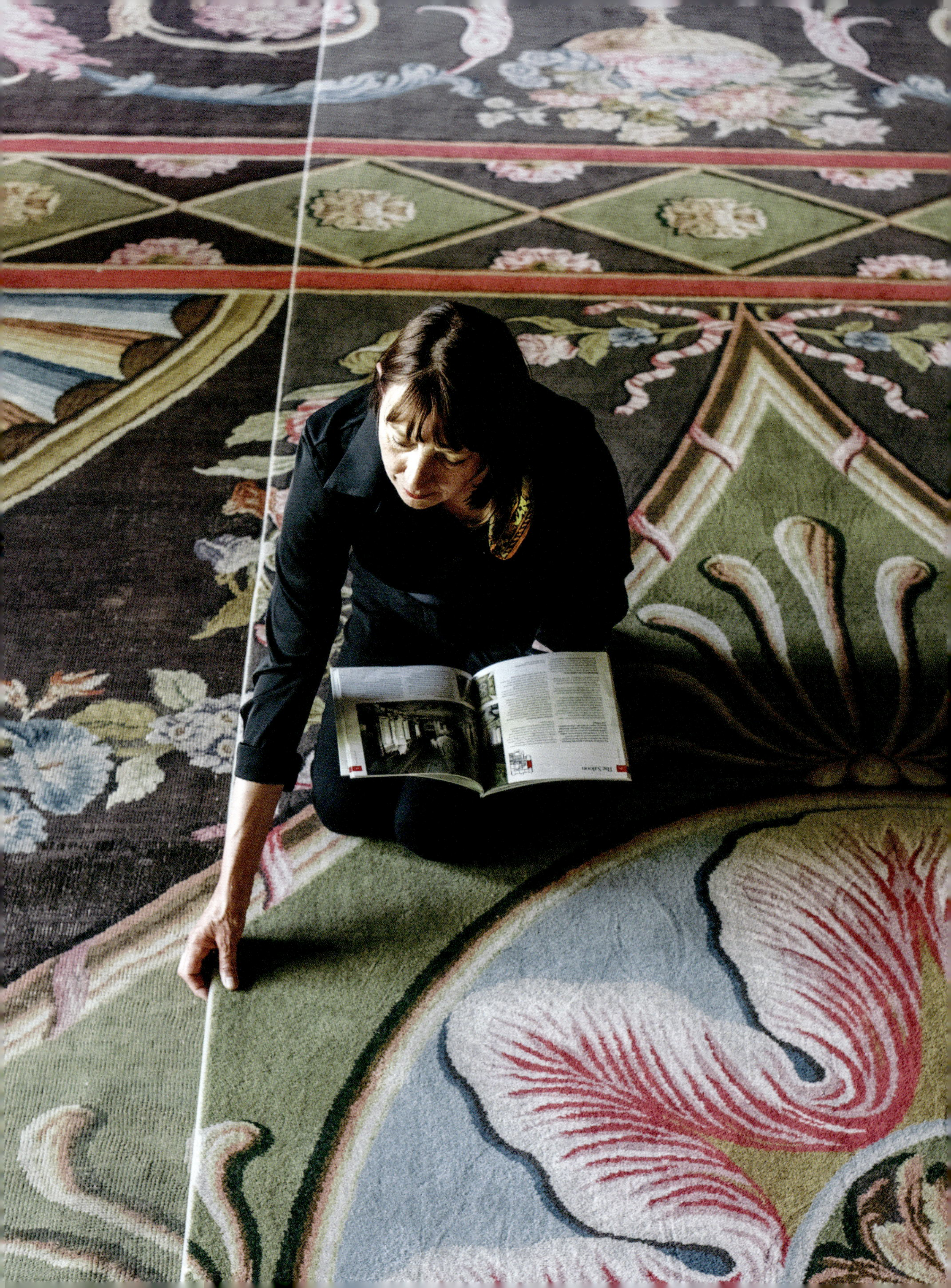
The Saloon

embarked on an ambitious project to replicate this weave. Fortunately, the Axminster factory is still going strong and this is where the 15-foot (4.6-metre) loom was built, making it the largest eight-pitch mechanical loom in existence. Pitch is a term that describes the number of holes per square inch. It is this that defines the quality of a woven carpet and naturally Axminster used the highest pitch – eight columns across and 10 rows down – providing 80 holes per square inch to weave the yarn through.

Begun in 2022, this replica is the most complicated weave Axminster have worked on and, they believe, ever attempted. The construction of the loom took 20 months. The design of the carpet was so intricate, however, that machines alone were not up to the task. The six-week weave involved 22 thread colours and required over 96,000 changes of bobbin (the cylinder on which the yarn is wound).

While the weave was underway, the original carpet received a thorough but careful clean, during which a discovery was made that threatened to cause major alarm among the house staff: the carcass of an unidentified insect. A country house sitting above an estuary can expect to receive some flying visitors of the insect kind, and the majority of these are harmless. However, there are some that can strike fear in those who care for the National Trust's collections. When you are looking after the Trust's most significant carpet, the very last thing you want to find is evidence of carpet beetle (*Anthrenus verbasci*) – an infestation of larvae feeding on natural fibres can spell disaster for carpets. However, staff are knowledgeable about and alert to the dangers, and closer examination of the carcass in question revealed it to be a harmless earwig.

In 2024, the replica was installed over the top of the 250-year-old historic carpet, ready to receive the first guests in many years who could walk across Adam's design, seeing how it mirrors the design of the ceiling above their heads, and appreciating it just as he would have intended – as a fully cohesive and immersive scheme.

< Spot the difference. The original Axminster carpet woven in around 1770 with the new, protective replica overlaid.

Skills and Techniques

The Pests That Test the National Trust

Only very few of our insect species pose threats to the contents and fabric of the properties looked after by the National Trust, but when they establish themselves, they can cause irreversible harm. Those who look after the collections of the National Trust prefer to take a preventative approach, to avoid, in the first place, damage that cannot always be successfully repaired. Key to that are vigilance and knowing what to look out for. While historic houses represent a veritable feast for these pests, they can occur in any interior, so here are the three key offenders, how to spot them and what to do to prevent and treat infestations.

The common clothes moth (*Tineola bisselliella*) is exactly that and is found in historic collections and at the back of wardrobes everywhere. The

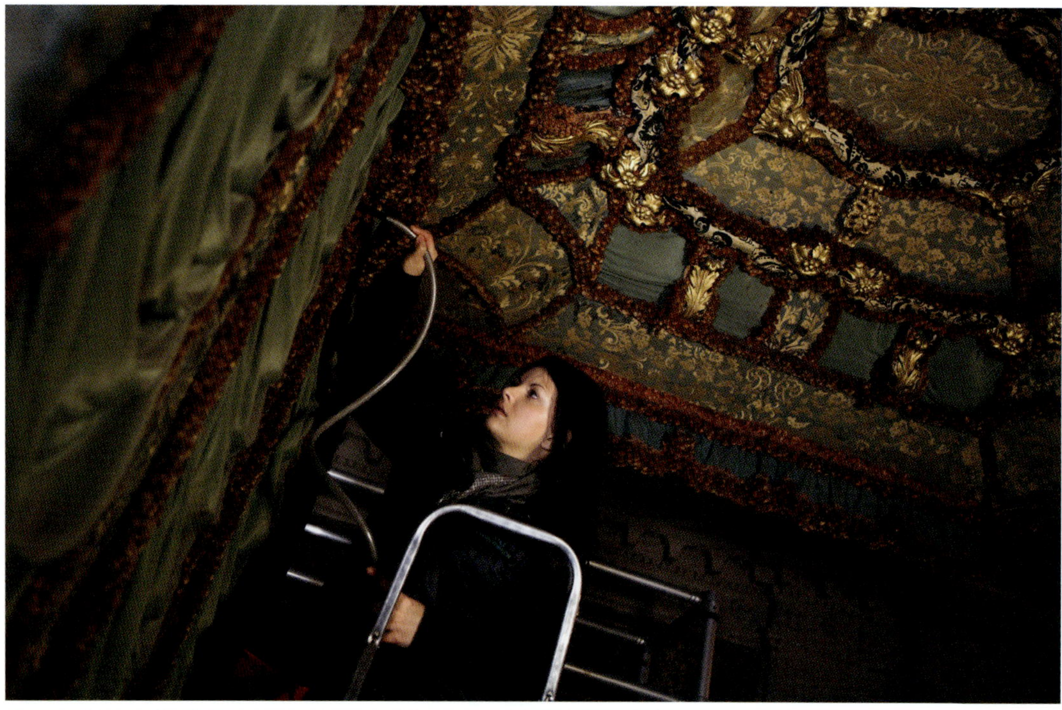

larvae feed on animal fibres, especially wool, fur, silk, feathers, felt and leather, leaving ragged patches in their wake. They can cause most damage when left undisturbed, so if you are able to wash or dry clean your garments before packing them away and periodically take them out, it's less likely you'll retrieve them shot through with holes. If you do discover a jumper with a hole in it, put it in a plastic bag and leave it in your freezer for about 14 days. This will kill any remaining eggs invisible to the naked eye and capable of surviving a low-temperature wool cycle wash.

Silverfish (*Lepisma saccharina*) thrive in damp conditions and eat starches and protein-rich items, so will feast on the fabric, glue and dyes found in many of the National Trust's historic wallpapers (see pages 77–78). Kitchens and bathrooms, with their high levels of humidity, are also appealing to these creatures and prone to infestations, so a good and simple deterrent is ventilation. If it seems an infestation has taken hold, there are some interesting natural remedies you can try. Silverfish hate the smell of citrus, cinnamon and lavender, all of which are readily available as essential oils. Also, cedar oil and shavings repel silverfish, as does the smell of cucumber; just leave some peel in the affected area.

The larvae of carpet beetles (there are various species, but a regular offender is the varied carpet beetle, *Anthrenus verbasci*) will munch their way through not only carpet, but also upholstery, curtains, clothing and any animal-based material. Carpet, however, is what they are particularly partial to, as populations do best when they are undisturbed, which is more likely to be an area of floor with low footfall than sofas that are sat on or curtains that are drawn. So regular vacuuming is the best preventative measure.

In the houses of the National Trust, moths, silverfish and other pests benefitted from the reduced disturbance and light levels that resulted from the Covid restrictions of 2020–21. When the houses reopened in May 2021, visitors returned and helped to drive down populations. And similarly in our own homes, we're more likely to push the vacuum cleaner around and get busy with the duster if we're expecting company. So, in summary, the best prevention is having visitors!

< A conservator using a small vacuum cleaner to remove dust from hangings around a state bed at Knole in Kent, where King James II is thought to have slept.

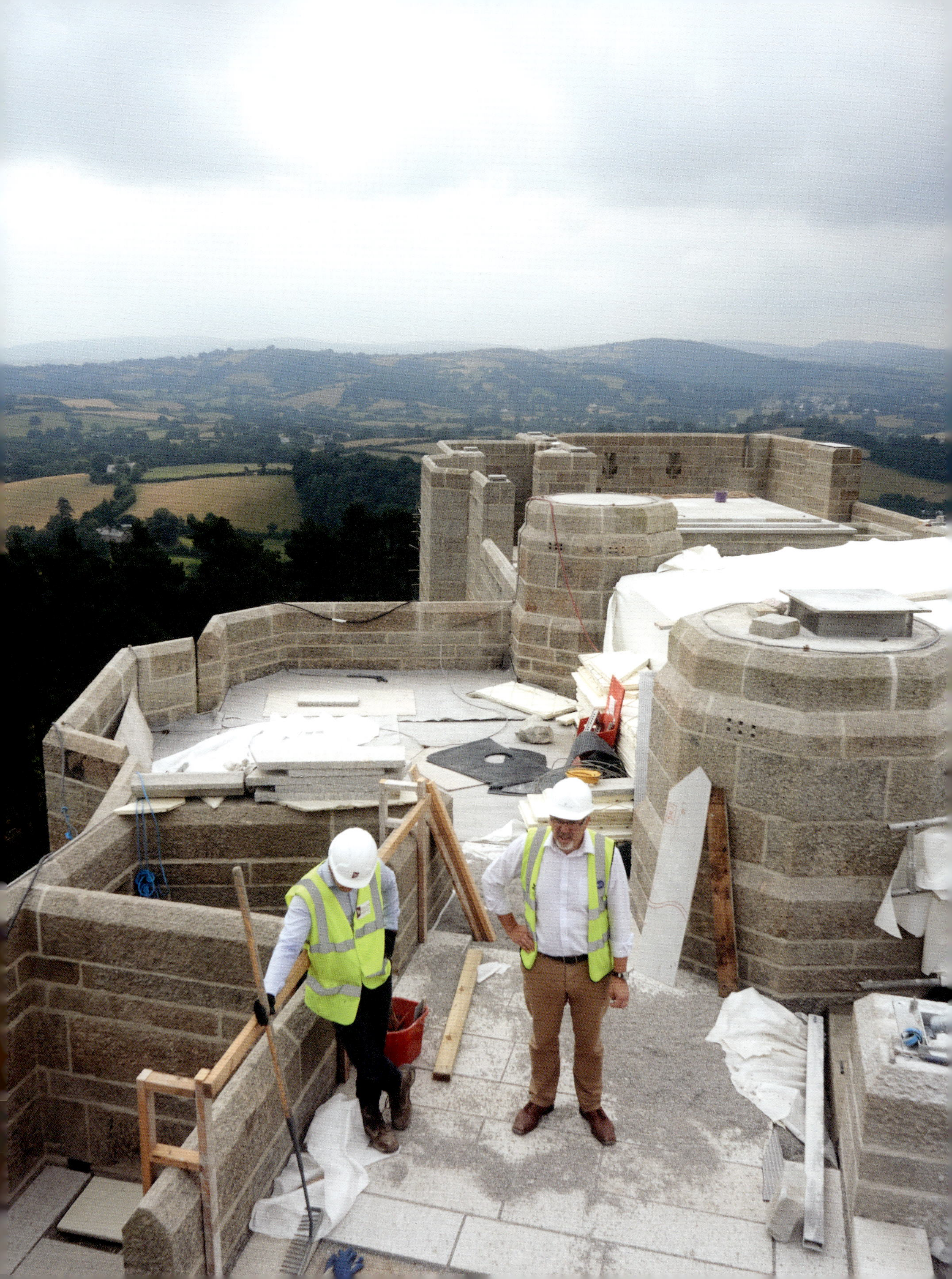

Fortifying a Castle Against the British Weather

Flat Roof

Castle Drogo, Devon

Castle Drogo is unique on many counts. Constructed between 1911 and 1931, it was the last castle to be built in England, and it is thought to be one of the last buildings in the world to be constructed entirely of granite. It has every appearance of an impregnable fortress on the outside – working portcullis, arrow slits, battlements – but the interior afforded its residents every luxury and modern convenience, including a custom-built kitchen, working telephones and electricity generated by hydro-turbines in the valley below.

Castle Drogo was designed by architect Edwin Lutyens as he was reaching the height of his career, although the overall style and various details of its construction were not his choices, but those of his client. The client was Julius Drewe, self-made businessman, entrepreneur and founder of Home and Colonial Stores, once one of the UK's largest retail chains. Money he had, but ancestry and a baronial home he did not, so he asked Lutyens to create one for him.

Lutyens struggled with the brief, privately writing: 'I do wish he didn't want a castle but just a delicious loveable house with plenty of good large rooms in it.' However, the result was declared a success, with the

< Castle Drogo's elevated position overlooking Dartmoor has the benefit of breathtaking views but the drawback of exposure to the elements.

noted architectural critic Christopher Hussey proclaiming: 'The ultimate justification of Drogo is that it does not pretend to be a castle. It is a castle, as a castle is built, of granite, on a mountain, in the twentieth century.'

Castle Drogo provides a unique perspective on so many things – the view from the roof spectacularly illustrates how defiantly it stands apart from anything around it – and its social backdrop was like nothing that had gone before. The castle's construction began before the horrors of the First World War could ever have been imagined and ended in their aftermath, providing a fascinating historical context. For what was built and for the times the people involved in its construction lived through, Castle Drogo is of enormous significance. This, together with the building's status as a Lutyens masterpiece, makes it unsurprising that Castle Drogo was the first twentieth-century building to be acquired by the National Trust.

Even before the building was finished, the ambitious, medieval-style flat roof requested by Julius Drewe was leaking.

That was in 1974, and ever since the National Trust has had the challenge of caring for an extremely large and complex building without architectural precedent. The castle's location provides an additional challenge – high on a rocky outcrop, making the most of Dartmoor's views but suffering the worst of its weather.

There is much to contend with, then, but by far the most problematic area of the building has been the roof. Even before the building was finished, the ambitious, medieval-style flat roof requested by Julius Drewe was leaking. Lutyens was aware of this and did attempt to seal the roof by using asphalt. A relatively new and untested material at the time, asphalt does provide a good initial seal, but temperature change over time can cause cracking and general deterioration. After the sun comes the rain, and Dartmoor experiences plenty of that.

In 2013, after around 100 years of water ingress, leaks and damage, a conservation project was started that would take nine years and cost £15.5 million to complete. An area roughly equivalent to two football pitches

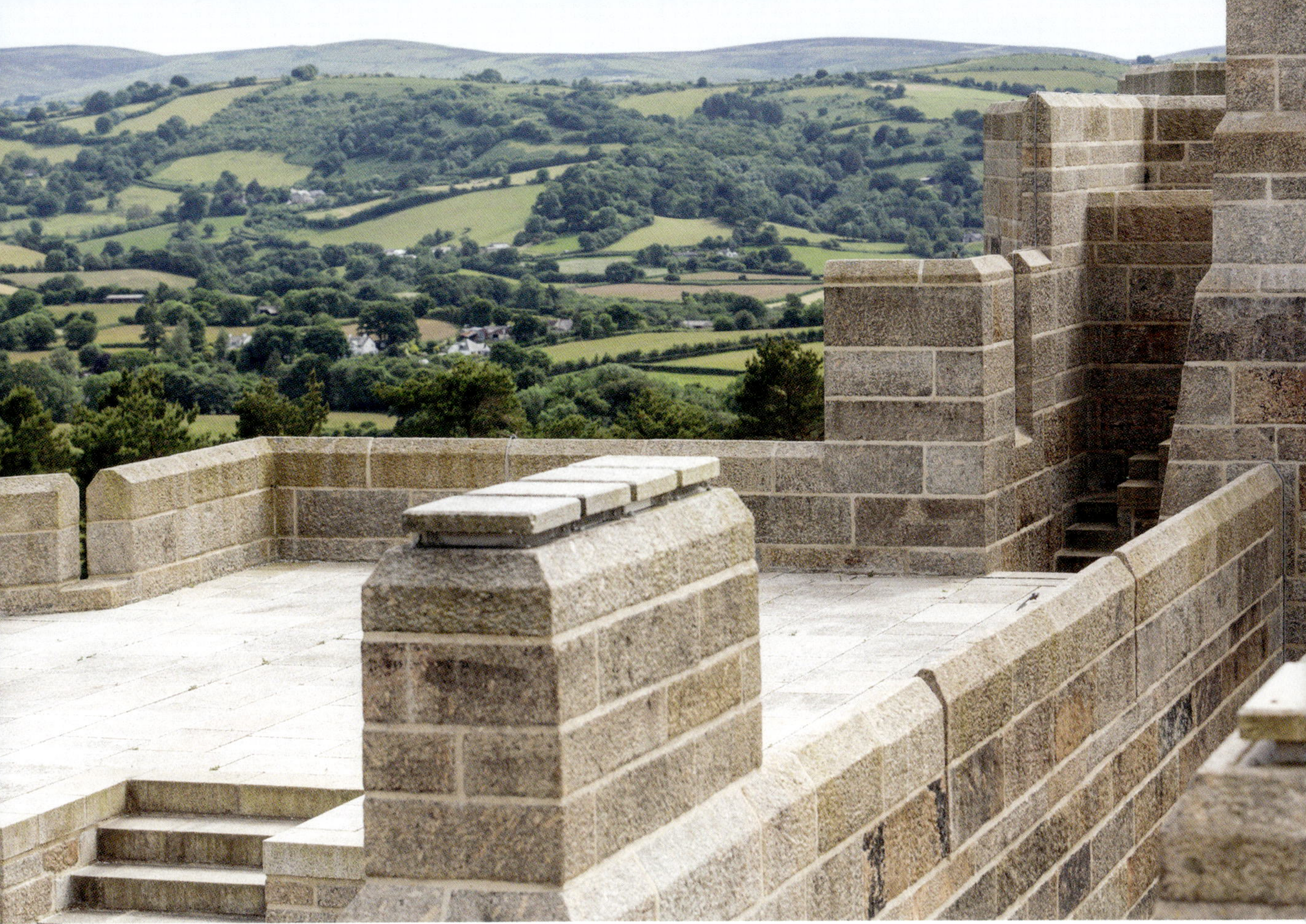

^ The finely finished appearance of Castle Drogo's masonry is the crowning glory of a roof that is finally weather-tight.

needed to be waterproofed, but before the high-tech, two-layer membrane roof system could be installed, 3,500 granite blocks, weighing anything up to 1.4 tonnes each, had to be removed and then reinstated. To complicate matters still further, many of the blocks had been laid out in a specific pattern when the castle was built, and are consequently unique. Each block had to be numbered and sorted so that it could be returned to the correct position. To expose every section of the roof, entire battlements and large sections of the castle walls had to be dismantled and rebuilt.

To repair the walls, the existing mortar needed to be raked out and repointed with a lime mortar. In all, 37 miles (60 kilometres) of new pointing was required. Tim Cambourne, senior project manager, observed: 'The granite being very hard, it's very unforgiving. The slightest

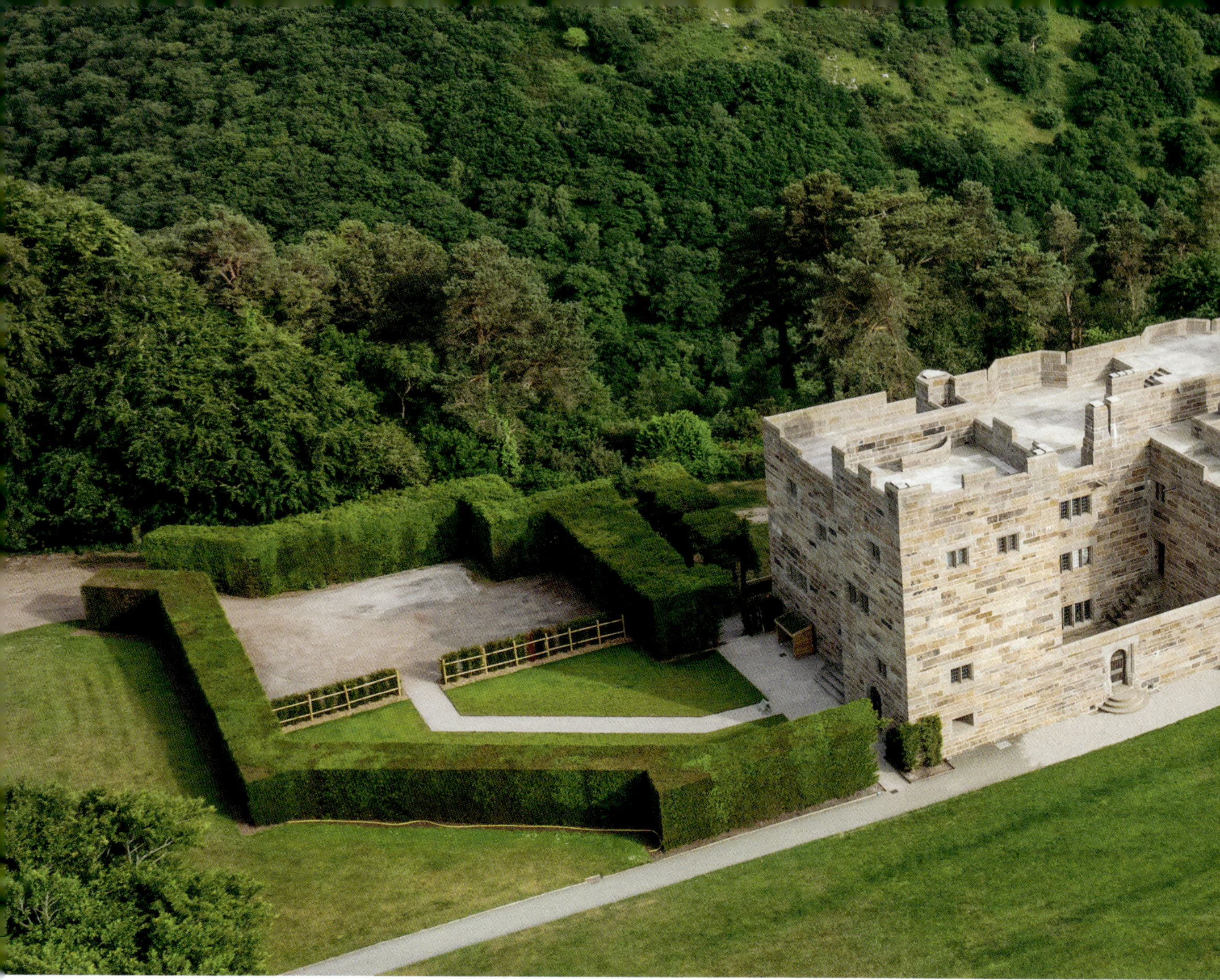

^ Castle Drogo's conservation project lasted nearly a decade and saw 3,500 granite blocks and nearly 1,000 windows reinstated.

crack in the mortar or a gap anywhere, because of the severity of weather we get here, it will drive water through.'

It was found that the windows, too, were letting in water. The linseed oil putty holding them in place had failed and had to be replaced with modern silicone sealant. Another detail that Julius Drewe had specified, to keep the façade more castle-like, created additional problems: he didn't want his castle to have window sills, which would have helped to direct water away from the windows. So, to help protect the building from water damage, a total of 913 windows had to be removed, refurbished and resealed.

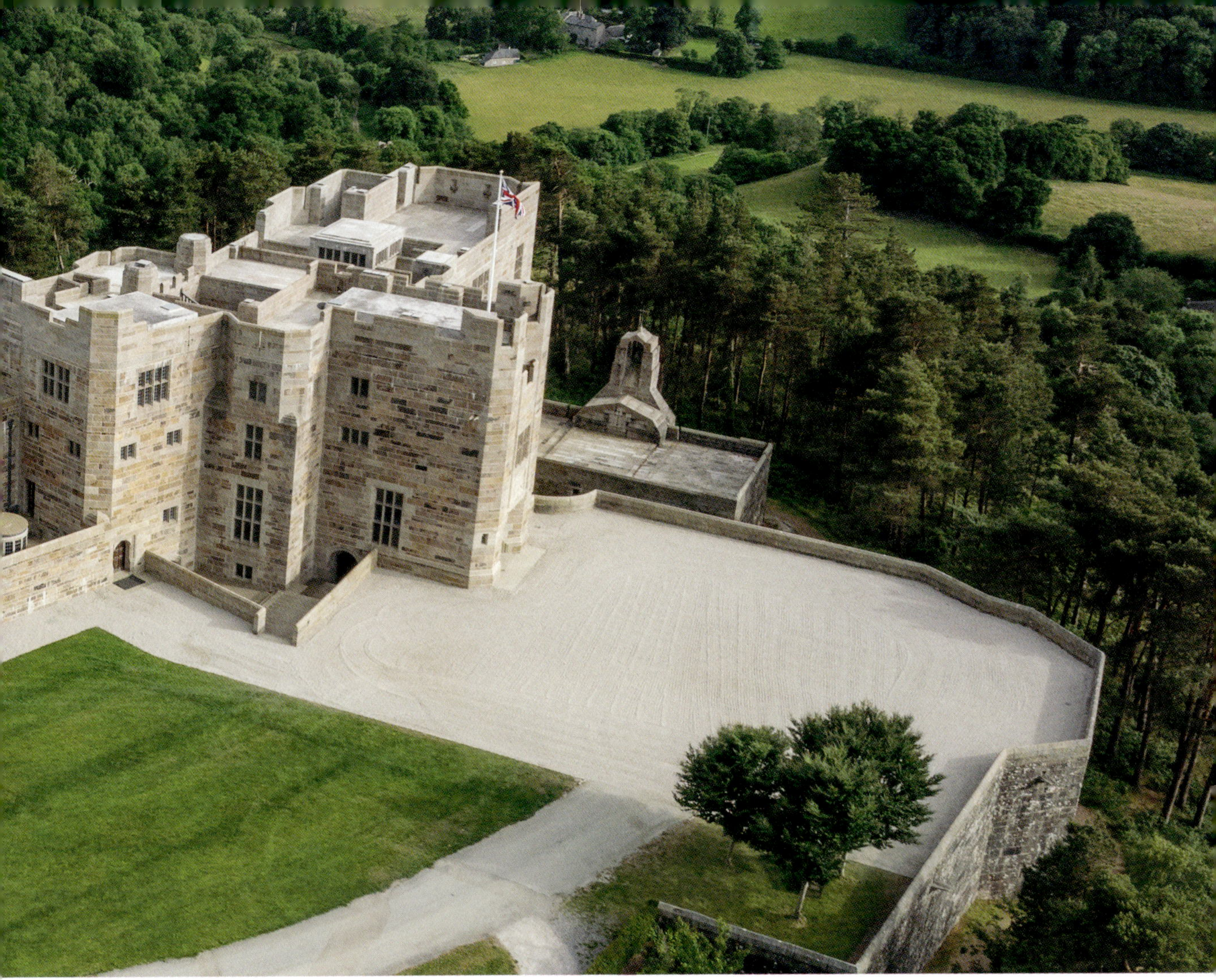

The scale alone amounted to an immensely challenging conservation project, but then there were additional factors, such as contending with the elements – a number of storms, with a particularly powerful one buffeting the works during the winter of 2014/15 – and the matter of a global pandemic in 2020/21.

When the scaffolding finally came down in 2021 Castle Drogo was revealed in all its glory, not as good as new but infinitely better. Heather Kay, Castle Drogo's general manager, said: 'This has been a huge undertaking and marking the project's completion is a moment to celebrate the dedication and commitment of all involved. The castle is regarded as a masterpiece of twentieth-century architecture and its future has now been secured.'

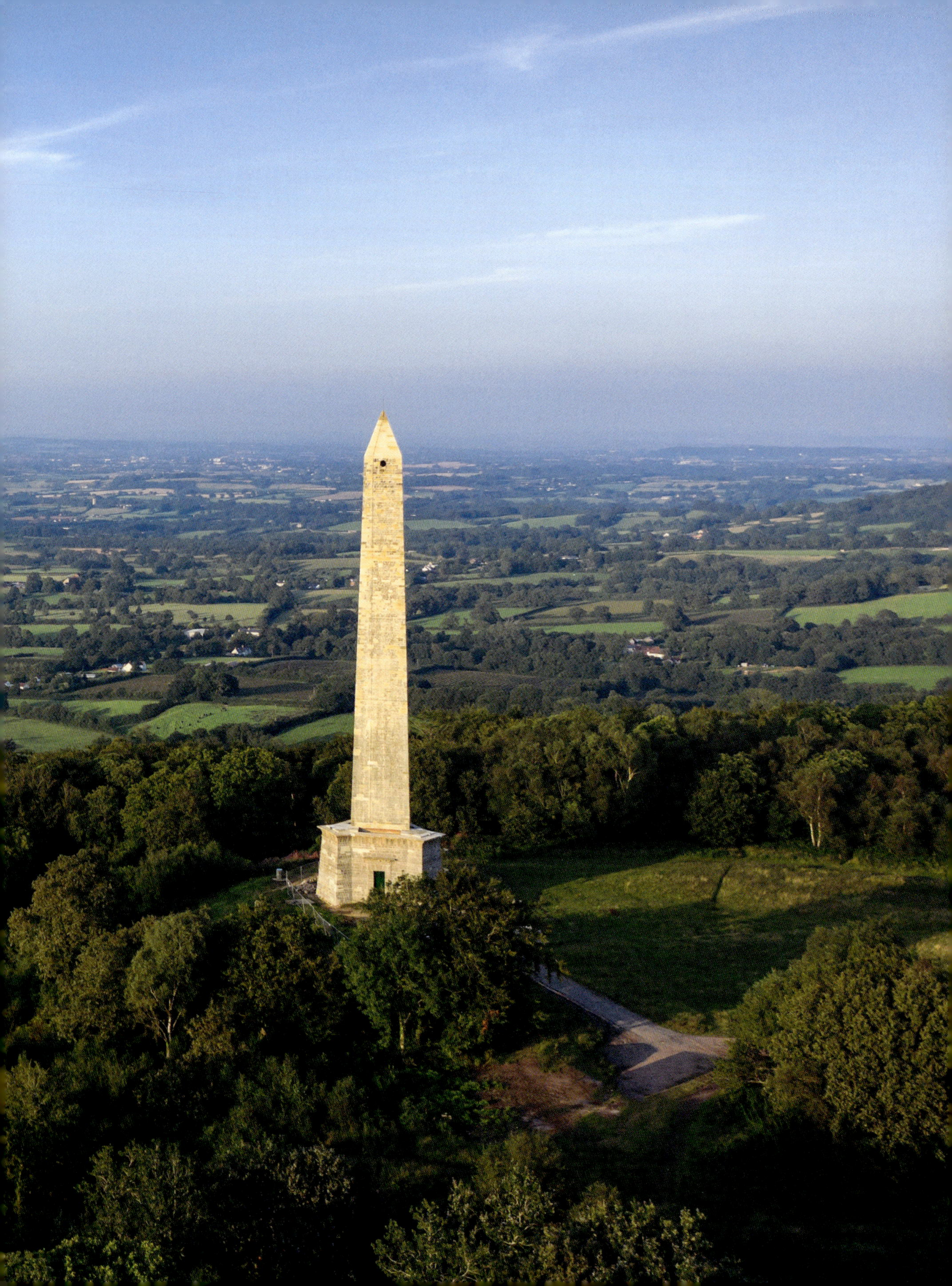

Restoring a Memorial to a Past Protector

The Wellington Monument

Somerset

Driving south down the M5, a few miles after Taunton, the Wellington Monument heaves into view. From that distance, it manages to appear simultaneously graceful and imposing, perhaps due to its beautiful rural setting in the Blackdown Hills, whereas the majority of military monuments are found in cities. Seen from a distance, it stands as proudly and resolutely as you would expect of a structure dedicated to martial success, but at close quarters the amount of conservation that has been required becomes apparent, in part due to its exposure to the elements, in part due to the problems encountered during its construction.

Many monuments were commissioned following the Duke of Wellington's victory over Napoleon's forces at the Battle of Waterloo in 1815. Most of these took the form of statues, which you'll find scattered around the UK with a concentration in London, where, too, you'll find the Wellington Arch on Hyde Park Corner.

Among these various commissions there was not one but two obelisks funded by donations, although only one was originally intended to take this shape. One stands in Dublin, birthplace of Arthur Wellesley, 1st Duke of Wellington, the other in Somerset, close to the town of

< Building of the Wellington Monument began soon after the Battle of Waterloo and 200 years later it is at last structurally safe and sound.

Wellington. Arthur Wellesley's connection with Somerset came about when he was offered a peerage in 1814, while he was busy commanding forces against the French. It's said he delegated the matter of the title to his brother, who chose the manor of Wellington as, first, it was available and, second, it resembled the family name.

Designed by Sir Robert Smirke, the obelisk in Wellington's place of birth stands 203 feet (62 metres) tall, making it the largest obelisk in Europe. The obelisk in Wellington's old manor is 174 feet (53 metres) high, making it the tallest *three-sided* obelisk in the world. (For completeness and for fact fans, the biggest obelisk in the world is the Washington Monument in Washington D.C., at a colossal 554 feet/169 metres.) That the Somerset monument holds a world record is more noteworthy when you consider that its eventual form was the result of financial shortfalls and design concessions.

The idea to erect a monument to the Duke of Wellington was first raised in 1815, soon after his most famous victory. A public fundraising campaign was set up to pay for it; then in 1817 a competition was held to find its designer, which was won by architect Thomas Lee Jnr. His design was for a triangular pillar that would be surmounted by a massive cast-iron statue of the Duke. The obelisk's design was unusual in that it was to be constructed from a facing of ashlar blocks rather than being shaped as a single stone monolith. All of this would be supported by a plinth, which would incorporate three cottages for occupation by three veteran soldiers, and be surrounded by cannons captured at Waterloo.

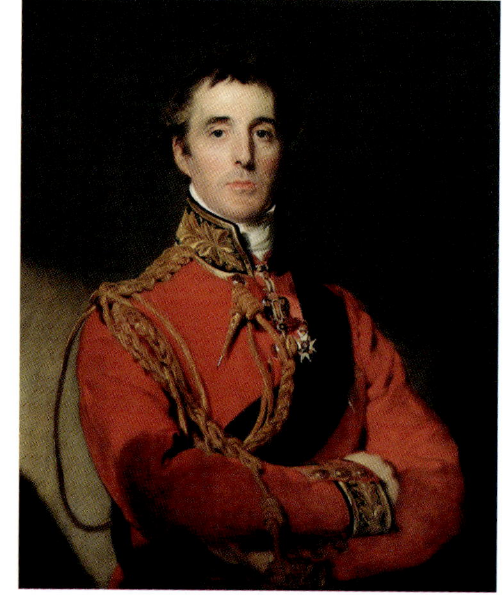

^ The Duke of Wellington, or Arthur Wellesley.

However, only months after work began on this ambitious design, funds ran out, with the triangular pillar having reached just 46 feet (14 metres)

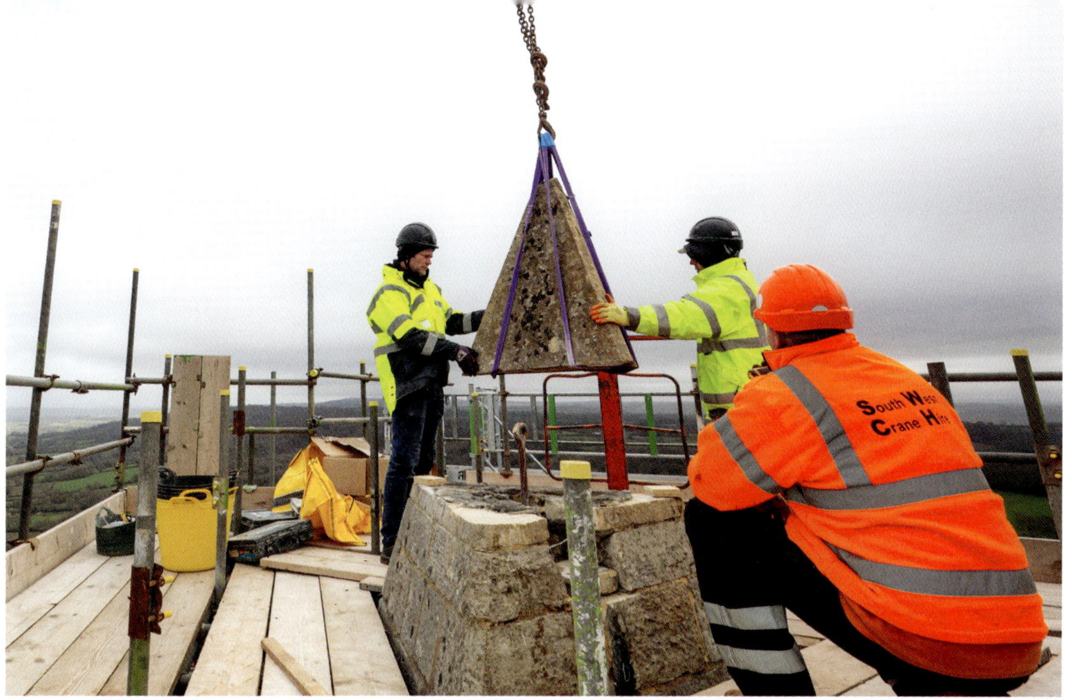

^ The final piece of the pyramidion is manoeuvred into position.

in height. Perhaps related to fluctuating public opinion of the Duke himself, enthusiasm and support for the project subsequently waned, and funds were not provided for its completion. The statue was never commissioned and work on the monument was abandoned.

In 1846, the monument suffered at least one lightning strike, causing significant structural damage and a fear that it was a danger to the public. The death of the Duke in 1852 led to revived interest in the project, and the following year local architect Charles Giles submitted a detailed report on the monument, in which he made recommendations for its repair and completion to a simpler design, without the terminal statue. Bath-based architect Henry Goodridge was then selected to produce that design. The monument was thus transformed from a statue-bearing pillar into an obelisk, complete with pyramidion (the triangular section at the top). Giles may have been responsible for the completed monument as we see it today, but he could not prevent it, decades later, from falling again into disrepair. By the 1890s, the local press was describing the monument as 'dilapidated', and in 1892 it was repaired, the plinth rebuilt and the obelisk raised to its current height. Since the monument came into the care of the National Trust in 1933, it has required regular renovation and repair.

By 2007, the monument's condition had deteriorated to the point it had to be closed to the public, and specialists were brought in to identify the structure's frailties. Perhaps owing to the fact that construction of the monument had taken place in fits and starts, and the shortage of funds may have forced certain compromises, major structural discrepancies were detected, with the top third found to be in the worst condition.

The estimated cost to carry out all necessary repairs was over £3 million. Much of the original funding for the monument had come from local sources, which is another reason why money often ran short, but in 2018 the National Trust launched a national appeal to help fund its full repair. This also received significant local input. Lasting three years, the project has seen the Wellington Monument restored not to its former glory – its original construction being somewhat below par – but to better condition than ever before.

Helen Sharp, the National Trust's project manager said: 'This has been a huge undertaking and to see it completed is a special day for us and the people of Wellington. A glance at the monument shows the extent of new stones which have had to be added – 1,508 in total, all of which had to be hand-tooled by qualified masons.'

In acknowledgment of the support the restoration had received from the public, when work was completed in 2021, the National Trust invited visitors and those who had a connection with the place the opportunity to leave a memento at the monument. Many letters, photos and poems from the local community and further afield were received, all of which were placed along with visitors' and supporters' memories inside the monument.

In 1815 the Wellington Monument was conceived as a way for the public to give thanks for their safekeeping; now, more than two centuries later, the monument has cause to thank the public for saving it.

> More than 1,500 stones had to be removed and their replacements hand-tooled by masons, leaving the monument not as good as new but better.

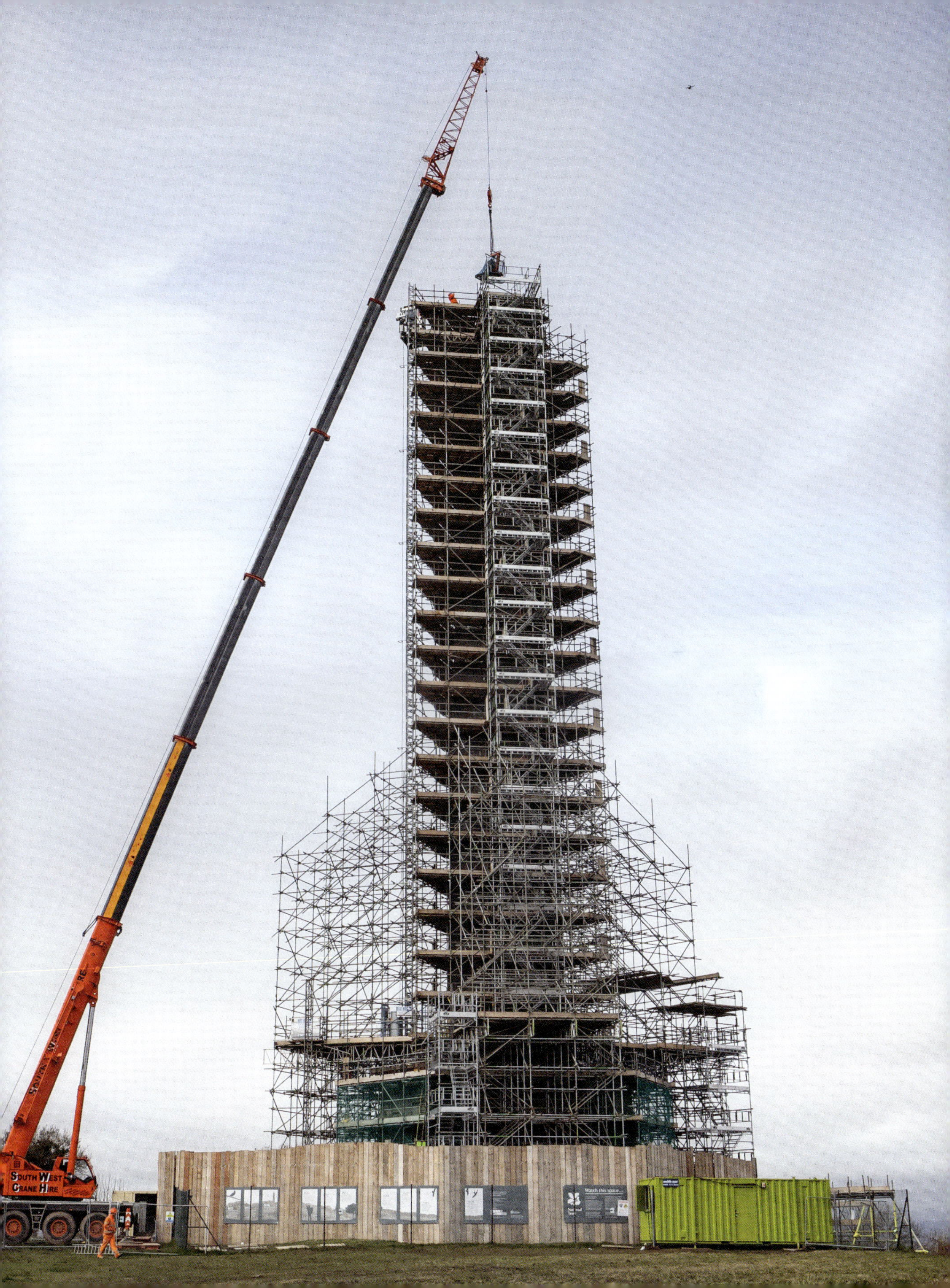
SOUTH WEST
CRANE HIRE
Watch this space...

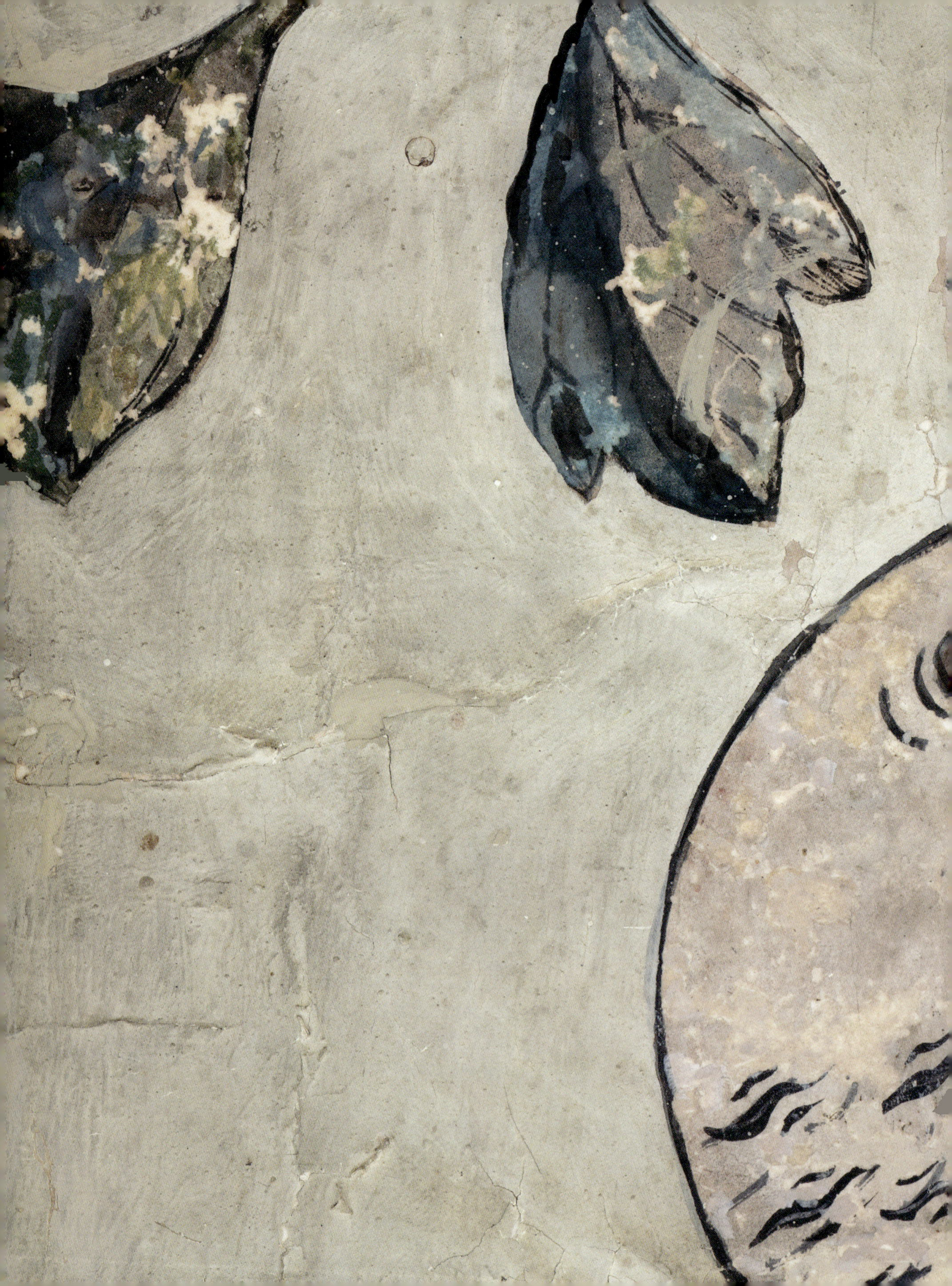

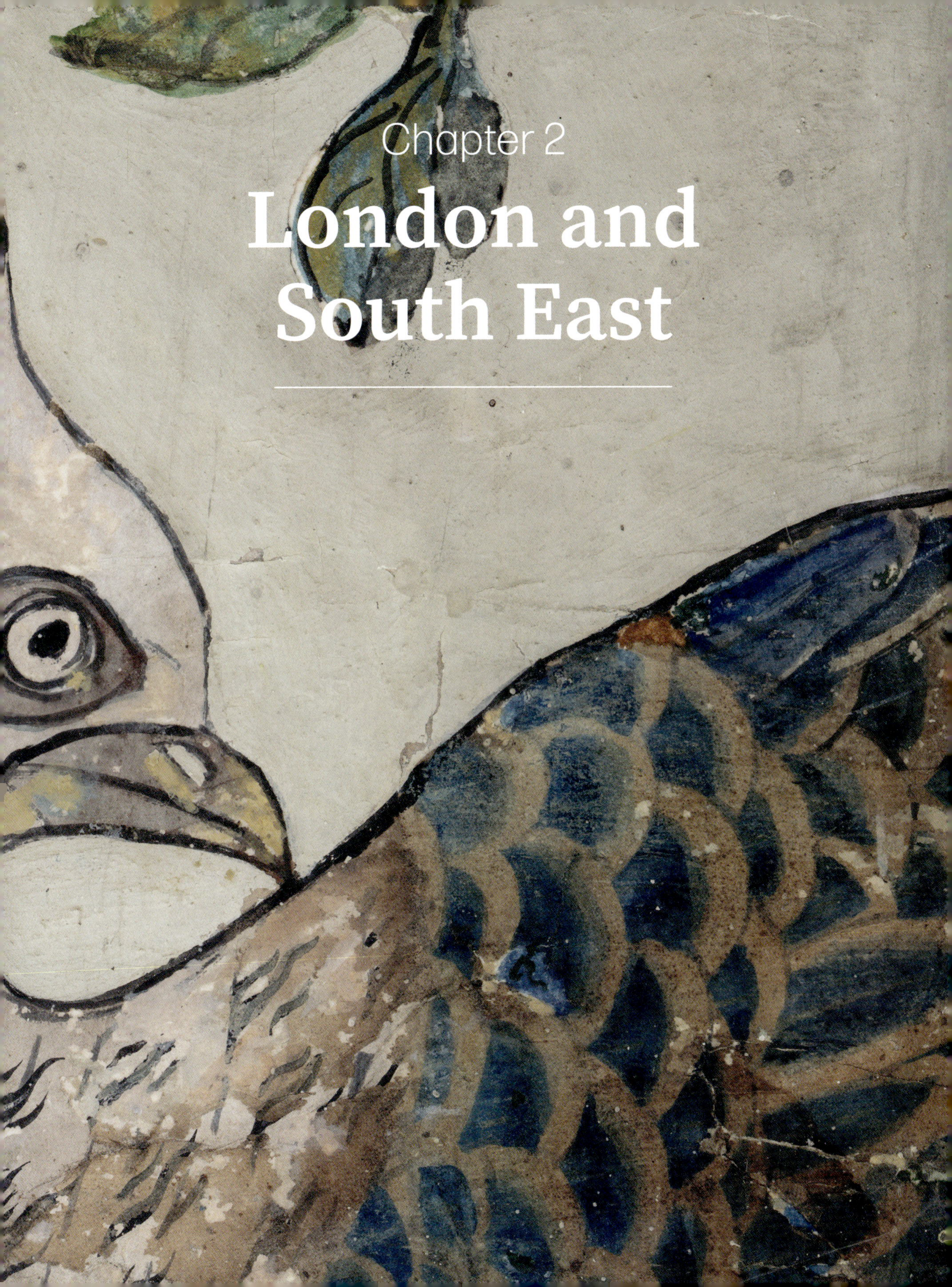

Chapter 2

London and South East

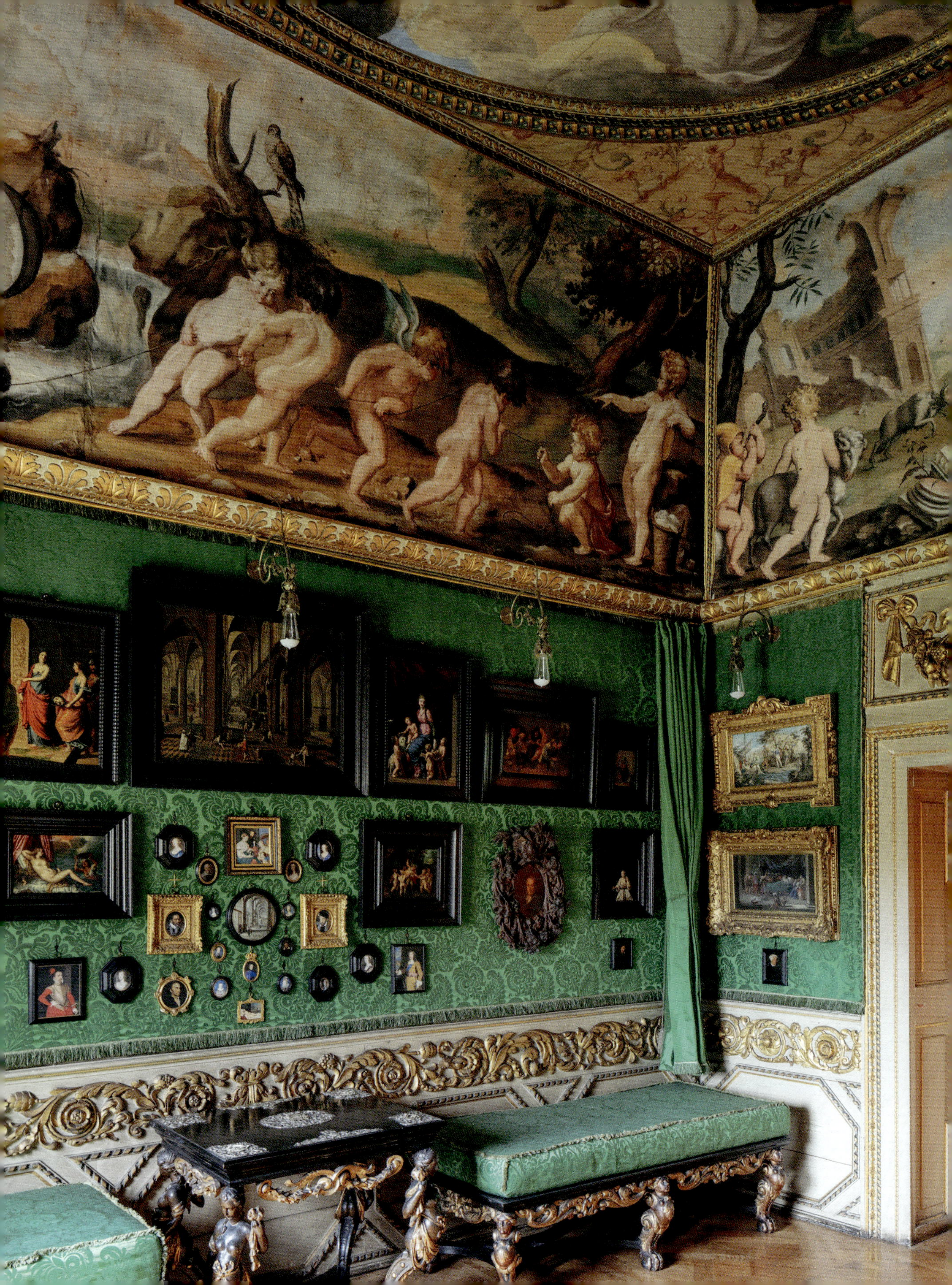

Seeing the Ceiling Anew

The Green Closet

Ham House, London

This fine, red-brick house has stood on the banks of the River Thames since 1610, when it was completed for Thomas Vavasour, who had been Knight Marshal to James I. By 1626 another courtier, William Murray, lived at Ham House. He was similarly well connected, having been educated by his uncle alongside James I's successor, Charles I. Murray and Prince Charles remained close into adulthood. Charles I made his childhood friend a Groom of the Bedchamber and granted him the lease on Ham House.

As the home of a courtier, Ham House needed to not only convey its owner's status but also afford private spaces where confidential conversations concerning matters of state could take place. Murray made a number of improvements to Ham House, installing the grand cantilevered and carved Great Stairs, remodelling the Long Gallery and adding the Green Closet.

The Green Closet served the two aims of the house beautifully. This small chamber, accessible from the Long Gallery, would only have welcomed those who were most intimately acquainted with, and useful to, Murray. Once inside, they would have marvelled at their host's taste and his private collection of miniatures and Dutch paintings. The room

< The Green Closet, largely unchanged since 1672, was designed as a jewellery box of a room in which to display the owner's most prized possessions.

was hung with green silk damask, which it is to this day, though the present hangings are copies.

Murray went to great lengths to impress his guests with his cabinet room, said to be modelled on Charles I's own 'Cabbonett Room' at Whitehall Palace. Murray used it to display his most prized possessions and had it decorated by master craftsmen. What we see today is largely unchanged since 1672, when a doorway into the North Dining Room was created. Given that its inspiration at Whitehall was consumed by fire and Whitehall Palace demolished in 1698, we are extraordinarily fortunate that this room is so little changed, making it a very rare survival of a room in the style of Charles I's court.

Such rarity means that every item in the room, and the very material of the room itself, must receive the utmost care and attention. Its size makes the task somewhat easier, however, and when the time came for the ceiling paintings to be cleaned, this small room became the scene of a large-scale conservation project. Larger objects that could be moved were moved, walls (with the miniatures *in situ*) and surfaces were covered and protected, and a scaffold was erected in an operation that could be compared to hoisting the sails of a ship in a bottle.

The ceiling paintings are the work of German-born painter and tapestry designer Franz Cleyn, and are thought to have been painted between 1637 and 1639. Their subject matter is classically inspired – there are goddesses and cornucopia, cherubs and nymphs, and ruins in an Arcadian landscape. The presence of satyrs and a vulnerable-looking Venus over the fireplace confirm this as a chamber that was designed with male users in mind. Also, there are depictions of goats locking horns, perhaps a fitting metaphor for the heated discussions that may have taken place in this room.

Any painting that is nearly 400 years old will have suffered from the ravages of time, but these are especially delicate given that they are tempera paintings on paper laid down on linen. Tempera, also known as egg tempera, is a painting medium that has been in use for thousands of years, consisting of pigments mixed with a water-soluble binding agent,

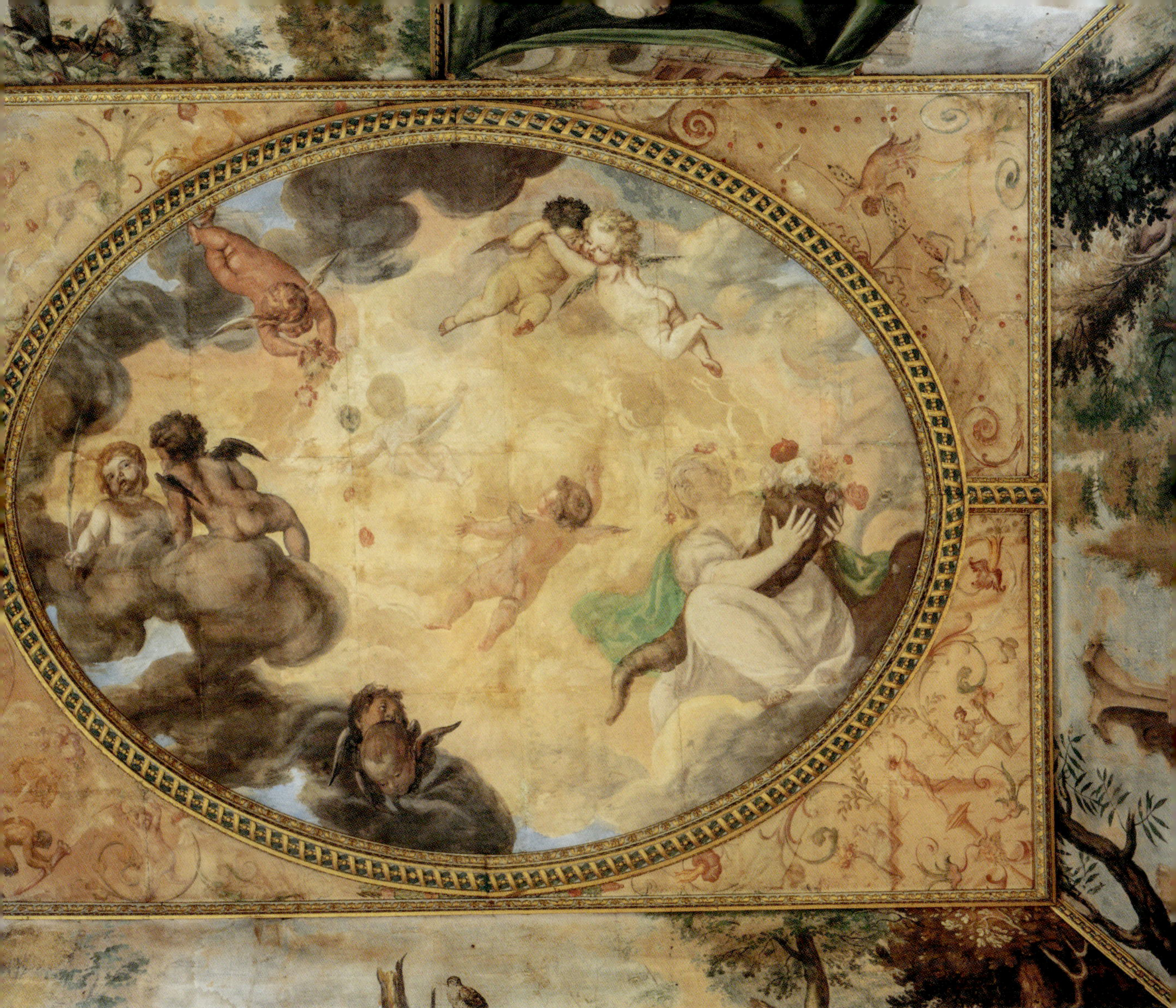

usually a glutinous material such as egg yolk. Perhaps surprisingly given the medium's organic components, tempera paintings are very long-lasting, and examples from the first century AD still exist. It wasn't until after 1500 that it was superseded by oil painting. As tempera has to be applied in thin, semi-opaque or transparent layers, it has the advantage of

^ The ceiling of the Green Closet, painted by Franz Cleyn in the style of Raphael, depicting the goddess Flora reclining with cupids among the clouds.

being fast-drying, which would have suited Franz Cleyn when working on such large compositions at height. Tempera paint can't be applied in thick layers as oil paints can, so it doesn't achieve the same colour saturation – but it holds its colour over time, whereas the pigments in oil paints can degrade, turning yellow and becoming transparent with age.

While tempera has its own unique set of characteristics that are distinct from those of oil, the two mediums can and do work together. In fact, egg tempera is used as a retouching medium by some conservators when working on oil paintings, though resin is the more common choice due to its reversibility and slower drying time. This was the approach adopted by the National Trust's conservators on Cleyn's ceiling paintings.

The Green Closet was never designed to be widely accessible and, to this day, the number of visitors to this room has to be limited. But part of the work of the National Trust's conservators and curators, in addition to ensuring the continued survival of such rarities as the Green Closet and its contents, is to make history more visible. So in this case, where it's difficult for visitors and students to get close to the room's paintings, the post-conservation photography – an essential part of any such project – is especially valuable.

The ceiling paintings of the Green Closet now dazzle more brightly than they have in a very long time, and images of these conserved pieces are available to viewers all over the world.

> Containing so much of its original furnishings, décor and art, the Green Closet at Ham House is a wonderfully preserved example of a room in the style of Charles I's court.

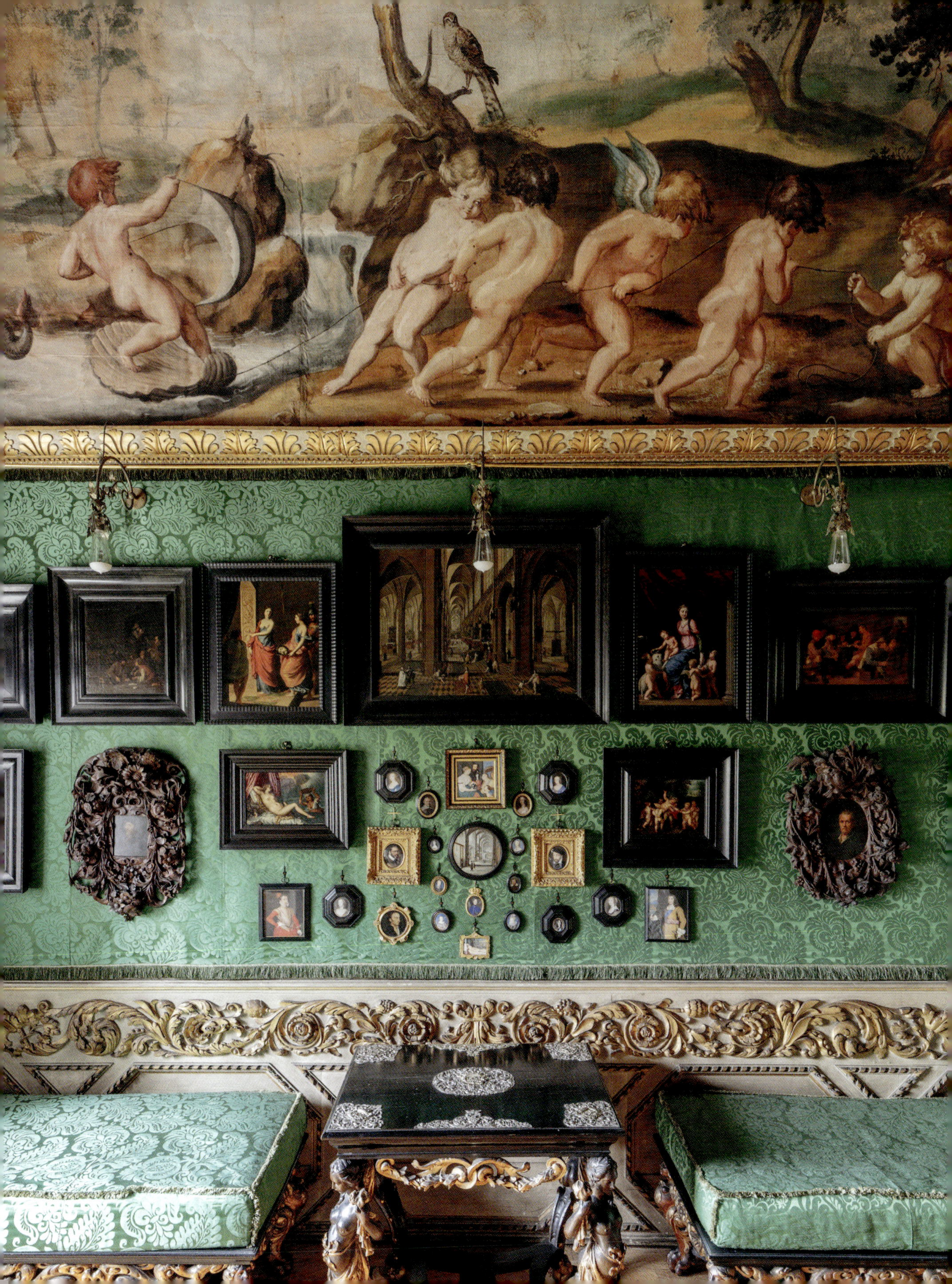

The Woman Behind the Statue

La Baccelli

Knole, Kent

The life-size statue, *La Baccelli*, that reclines seductively at the foot of Knole's Great Stairs, demands to be admired, so it may be surprising to learn that at some point in the late eighteenth century she was banished to the upper reaches of the house. You might assume this was prudishness for her naked form in rumpled bedsheets, both of which are captured in plaster in exquisite detail, but perhaps it was more to spare the feelings of John Frederick Sackville's new wife, as *La Baccelli* had been modelled on his one-time mistress, the renowned dancer Giovanna Zanerini.

This statue was commissioned by Sackville, the 3rd Duke of Dorset, it is thought from Giovanni Battista Locatelli, in 1778. At this time the Duke was a bachelor, so there was no great scandal in his having affairs with women. Indeed, high-ranking men were expected to take lovers and the Duke certainly collected a few – the Prime Minister's mistress Anne Parsons, the Countess of Derby and Lady Elizabeth Foster, who was also the mistress of the 5th Duke of Devonshire – but his longest relationship, one that lasted over a decade, was with Giovanna. However, she was far more than one among a long list of mistresses. Just as her statue has been returned to public view, so should her reputation as a talented woman in her own right.

> Much more than a mistress, Giovanna Zanerini was a celebrated dancer and key player in the development of ballet as an art form distinct from opera.

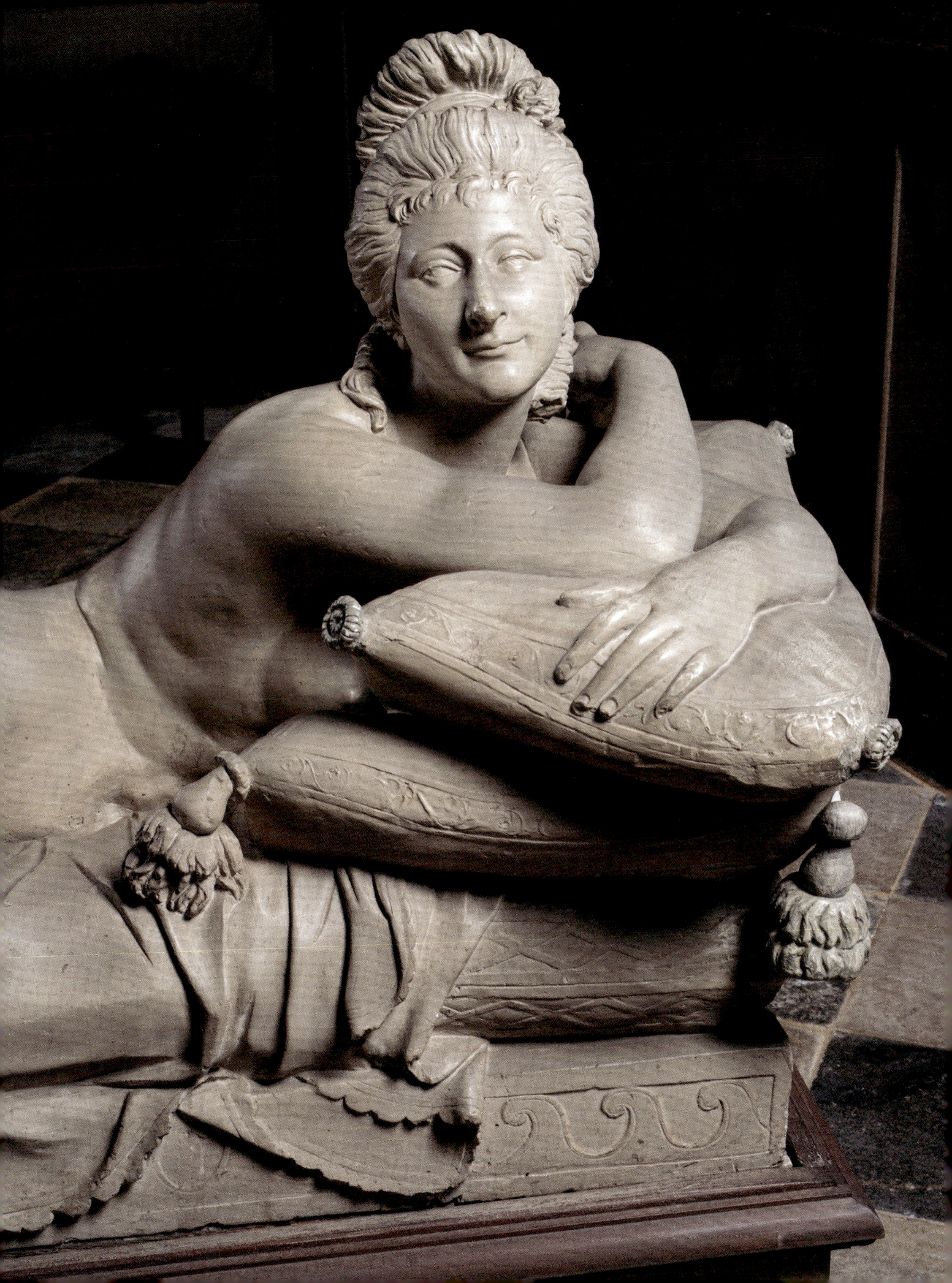

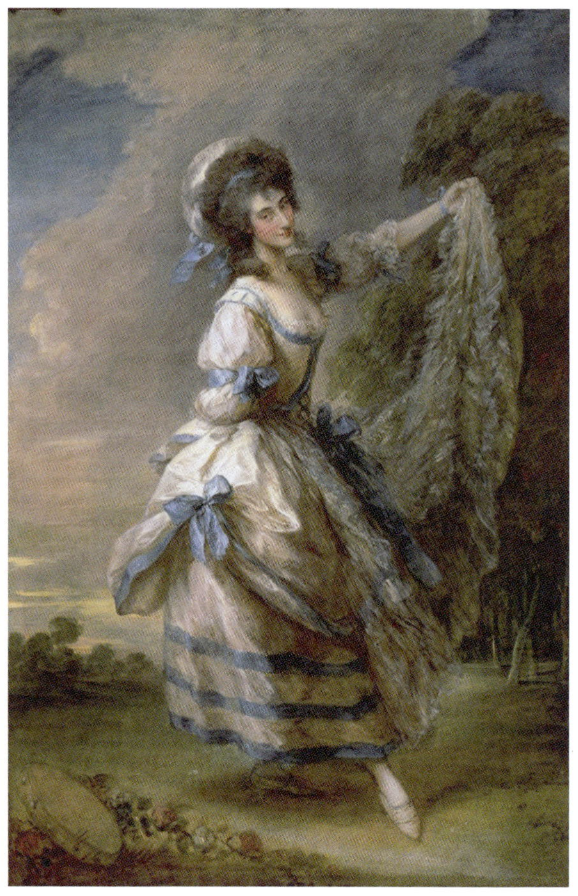

^ The 3rd Duke of Dorset commissioned this portrait from Thomas Gainsborough in 1782 when Giovanna's career was at its height.

Using her mother's name Baccelli, Giovanna was the principal ballerina at the King's Theatre in Haymarket. This was at a time when ballet was establishing itself as its own art form, separate from opera, and Giovanna was one of its leading lights, who caught the eye of the Duke soon after her debut in 1774.

He commissioned this statue in 1778 and, by the following year, both she and the statue that captures so vividly her physicality and sensuality had taken up residence at Knole. She was openly acknowledged to be the Duke's mistress but, whether it was due to the fact that such affairs were commonplace in these circles or her talents as a dancer were far more noteworthy, the press made little of the relationship. One of the papers that regularly reported on her career, the *Morning Post and Daily Advertiser*, reviewed a performance in 1777 by saying: '... we believe no theatre, not even Paris, ever saw two such serious dancers performing on the stage together, as Madame Simonet, and Mademoiselle Baccelli; the pas de deux between them excels almost any thing we have seen.'

Giovanna was clearly delighting audiences and impressing critics alike, but she was absent from the stage for much of 1779. Her return to performance in January 1780 was greeted rapturously by the *Whitehall Evening Post*: 'The dances, particularly the second and the last, were well devised, and executed in a masterly manner by the principal dancers,

Just as her statue has been returned to public view, so should her reputation as a talented woman in her own right.

Mad. Simonet, Mons. Favre Guiardele, Mr Slingsby, Signora Tantini, and Mad. Baccelli. The latter was received, for her first time this season, with that enthusiastic applause which is so flattering to the performer, when, as is here the case, it is founded on the strictest justice.' No mention was made of her having given birth to a son the previous year.

To receive such praise on her return to the stage after having a baby must have been both a source of pride and relief to Giovanna – that her professional life and not her personal life remained the focus of the press's attention.

Giovanna lived at Knole with the Duke and their son, John Frederick Sackville, in a suite of apartments. We know this from an account written by Fanny Burney, satirical novelist, diarist and playwright, who visited Knole in 1779 and expressed frustration that certain rooms were off limits: 'We were prevented from seeing the library, and two or three other modernised rooms, because Madlle. Baccelli was not to be disturbed.'

It seems contradictory that the Duke should grant Giovanna such privacy in their living arrangements, and yet that such a sensual portrayal of her should be placed in full view of every visitor to Knole. If he had installed it in his private apartments, it might have been a wealthy man celebrating the physical beauty of his partner and mother of his son. If he had instructed the

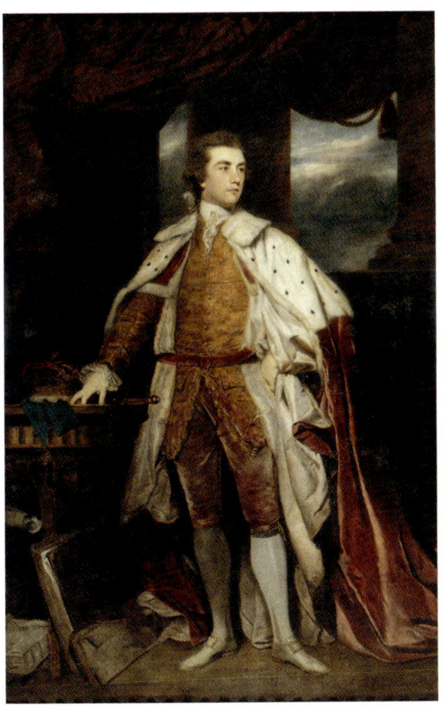

^ The 3rd Duke of Dorset was an ardent supporter of the contemporary arts. A close friend of Joshua Reynolds, he acquired many of his paintings, of which this portrait was the first.

sculptor to model the body on Giovanna's but make the facial features less recognisably hers, it might have been a work of art with a personal meaning to the Duke that wasn't public knowledge. After all, the statue's composition is a knowing reference to an ancient marble sculpture called the *Sleeping Hermaphrodite* – a statue that from the back resembles the form of a female nude but at the front pronounces itself male – so the Duke was prone to a private joke.

La Baccelli is a wonderfully executed piece of sculpture, but one wonders about the motivation for placing this intimate piece on prominent display. Perhaps the Duke was keen to show off the allure of his famous lover to all his friends; maybe Giovanna felt empowered by the statue – she would certainly have posed for it and presumably agreed to where it was placed in the house. Their relationship lasted over 10 years and apparently ended amicably. It's thought that it was the horror of the events of the French Revolution unfolding in 1789, when the Duke was His Majesty's ambassador in Paris, that made him consider his family responsibilities and the need to produce an heir. The Duke married the following year, and at some point *La Baccelli* was relocated, to 'the Top of the Stairs, next [to] the Wardrobe', according to an inventory dated 1799, in which she's referred to as 'A Naked Venus'.

Following their separation, Giovanna received a pension from the Duke and she left their son to be brought up and educated by him. He sadly predeceased his parents in 1796, possibly succumbing to yellow fever while serving with the army in the West Indies. Giovanna died in 1801, her death reported in the 9 May 1801 edition of the *Morning Chronicle*: 'Madame Baccelli, who for so many years distinguished herself as one of the most fascinating dancers that ever appeared on the Opera stage, died at her lodgings in Sackville Street on Thursday morning, after a most lingering and painful illness, which she bore with the most exemplary resignation, and with that sweetness of temper which rendered her so attracting in the days of youth and beauty.'

If those words sound like the kind of platitudes you'd expect in such an announcement, consider Giovanna's will, in which she left to a former servant at Knole, who came to live with her towards the end of her life

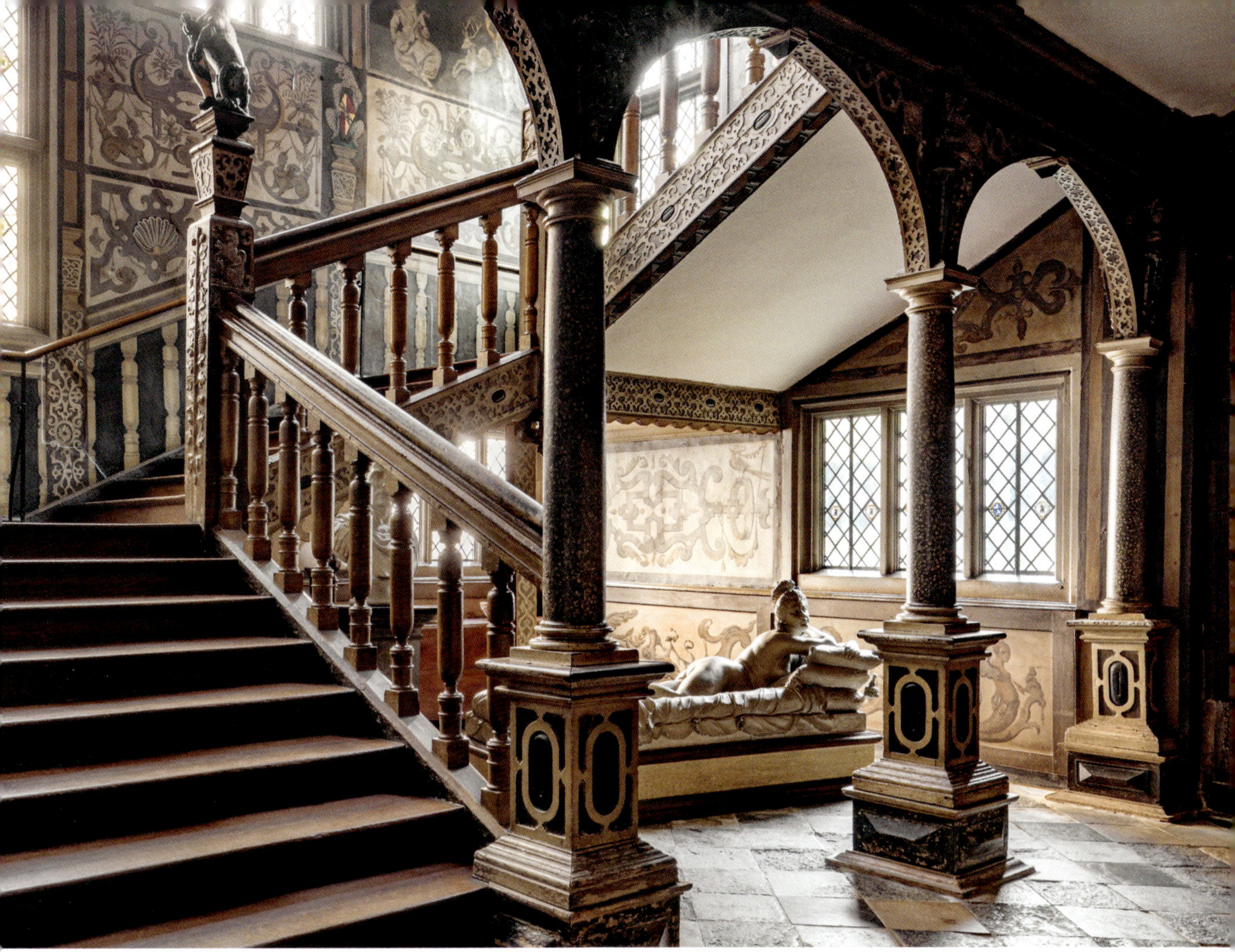

in Sackville Street, all of her clothes, an annuity of £25 a year, and 'my Metal Watch & Chain, & my Birds Cage, to take care of the Birds that are in it, and then sell it'.

Sometime after the 3rd Duchess's residency at Knole, *La Baccelli* was returned to her place at the foot of the stairs. Whether due to age or excessive handling, she recently required consolidation to old repairs which had come loose. A hairline crack appeared, appropriately, in her hair, and in one of the pillow tassels. *La Baccelli* is now fully conserved and, with our improved understanding of who the woman behind the statue really was, Giovanna's reputation is also now far better presented.

^ *La Baccelli* fully conserved and restored to her position at the foot of Knole's Great Stairs.

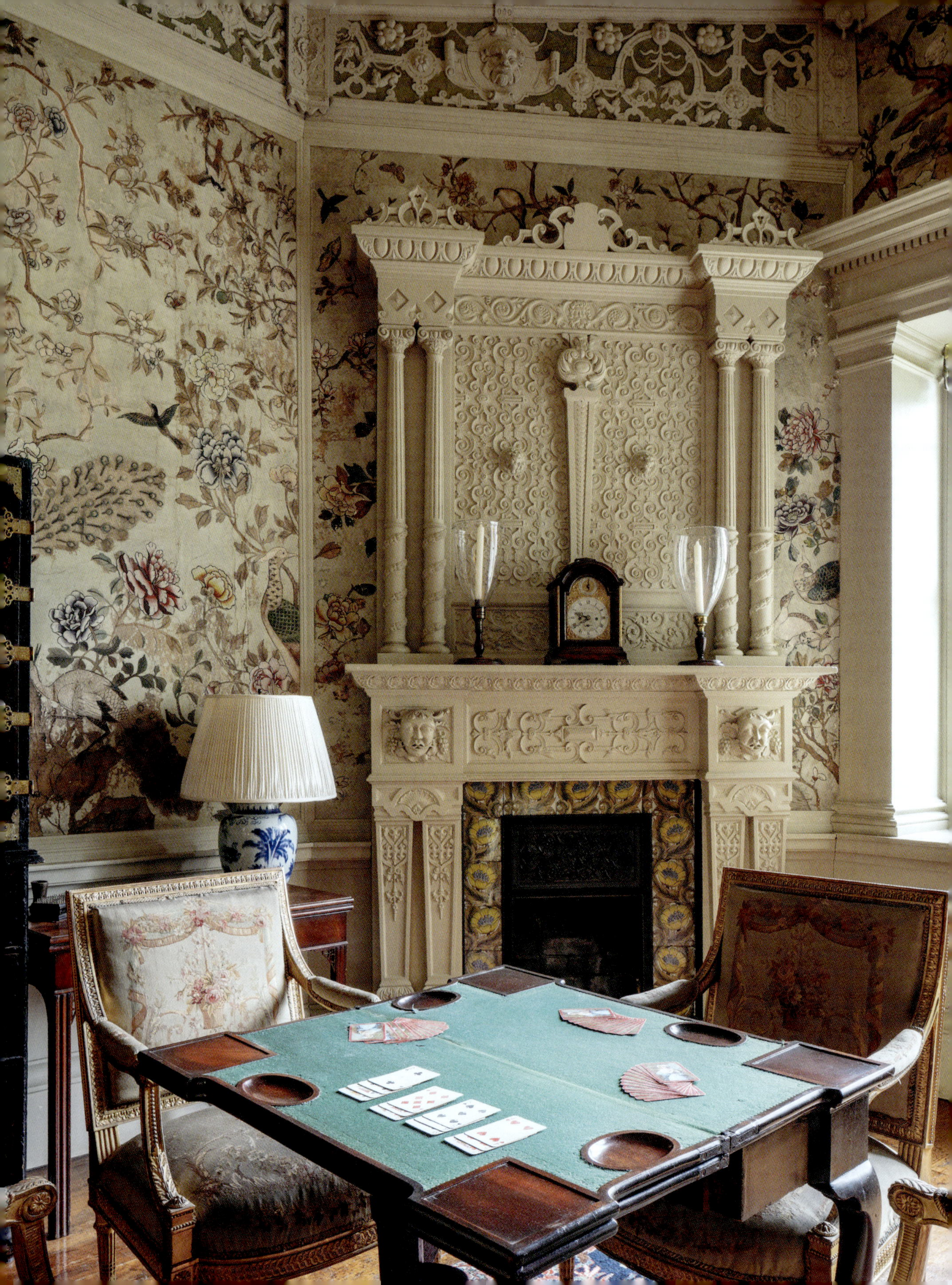

Fending off a Damaging Infestation

Chinese Wallpaper

Ightham Mote, Kent

Ightham Mote is the country's most complete medieval manor house, dating back to around 1320. As you'd expect from a house of such antiquity, there is layer upon layer of occupation history, from medieval knights and Tudor courtiers through to Elizabethan spies and high-society Victorians, all leaving traces of their time here. There are chimney pieces carved in the ornate Jacobean style, windows inspired by Renaissance architecture and eighteenth-century interior design that reflects the early days of British expansionism. The unique collection that has resulted presents a challenge to those whose job it is to conserve what's here, making sure all those layers of history are respected.

As you cross the cobbled bridge over the moat, you can almost see those jousting knights and royal courtiers sporting doublet and hose, but step inside the Drawing Room and you enter a completely different world. It's a world of elegance and femininity, much of which derives from the beautiful, sinuous depictions of birds, butterflies, flowers and trees that cover the walls. But as well as having this delightful visual impact, Ightham Mote's wallpaper is exceptionally precious.

It was made in around 1750, its age alone making it a rare survivor. Chinese wallpaper was at that time a highly fashionable form of interior decoration in Britain, but fashions come and go and paper is susceptible to so many environmental threats, as we shall see.

< Georgian elegance in a medieval moated manor house.

The appetite for Chinese art and design developed in the early seventeenth century, when maritime trade was bringing Asian goods to the British Isles in substantial quantities. Along with the bulk imports of tea, porcelain and silk, there was a smaller but steady supply of Chinese luxury goods. By the early eighteenth century these included paintings and prints that fashion-conscious owners of country houses used to decorate screens, panels over doors and fireplaces, or had pasted onto walls in a kind of collage. Such was the appetite for this that, by the 1740s, Chinese workshops were producing pictorial wallpapers specifically for the European market.

Ightham Mote's wallpaper is therefore one of the earliest surviving examples of Chinese export wallpaper. Until recently it had been assumed that it was entirely hand-painted, but new research and closer inspection has revealed tiny, tell-tale breaks in the black outlines. This suggests that

∨ As well as genuine Chinese wallpaper, the Drawing Room includes pseudo-Asian touches such as Delft blue and white earthenware and an English japanned clock.

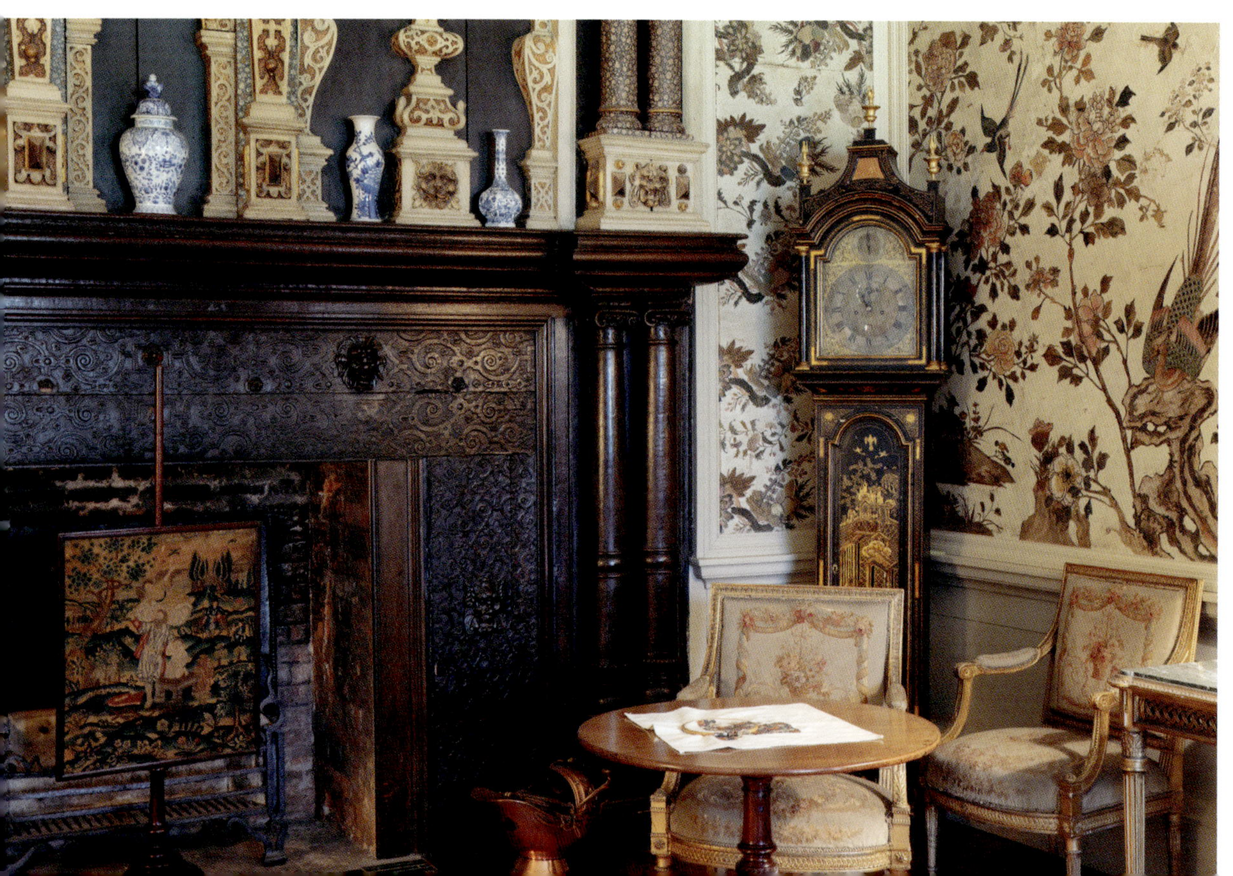

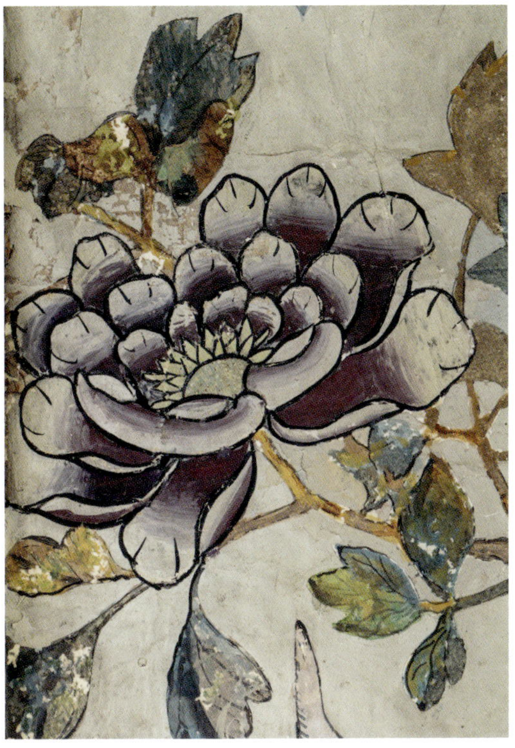

∧ Ightham Mote's wallpaper was mostly block-printed with additional detail painted by hand.

designs were printed using woodblocks, but the colour, background and additional details were painted by hand. Further investigation revealed that some of the sheets in the wallpaper at Ightham Mote were printed from the same blocks used to make wallpaper at Felbrigg Hall, Norfolk, and others featured patterns also found in a French *château*, a German *schloss* and an Italian *castello*.

These papers, dispersed throughout Europe, adorned their respective walls, most of them succumbing to changing fashions, fire and demolition. But a few survived. Their continuing survival requires a watchful eye against a variety of environmental factors, such as damp and insect infestation. These two are often jointly present, as was the case at Ightham Mote.

When a section of paper in a corner of the Drawing Room was showing signs of accelerating deterioration, paper conservator Louise Drover was brought in to identify the cause. Sure enough, she detected both damp and indications of a silverfish infestation. These moisture-loving insects are partial to paper as well as starch, found in the adhesive, and protein, present in the paint pigments, so were thriving in this section of wall, slowly devouring the paper.

Once the damaged strip of paper was peeled away, the wall could be inspected by National Trust architect Stuart Page. The cause of the damp in the wall had to be identified and rectified before the paper could be rehung. It transpired that mortar joints around the window in the Renaissance style had failed, letting in water. The application of lime mortar without and lime plaster within ensured that, once dried

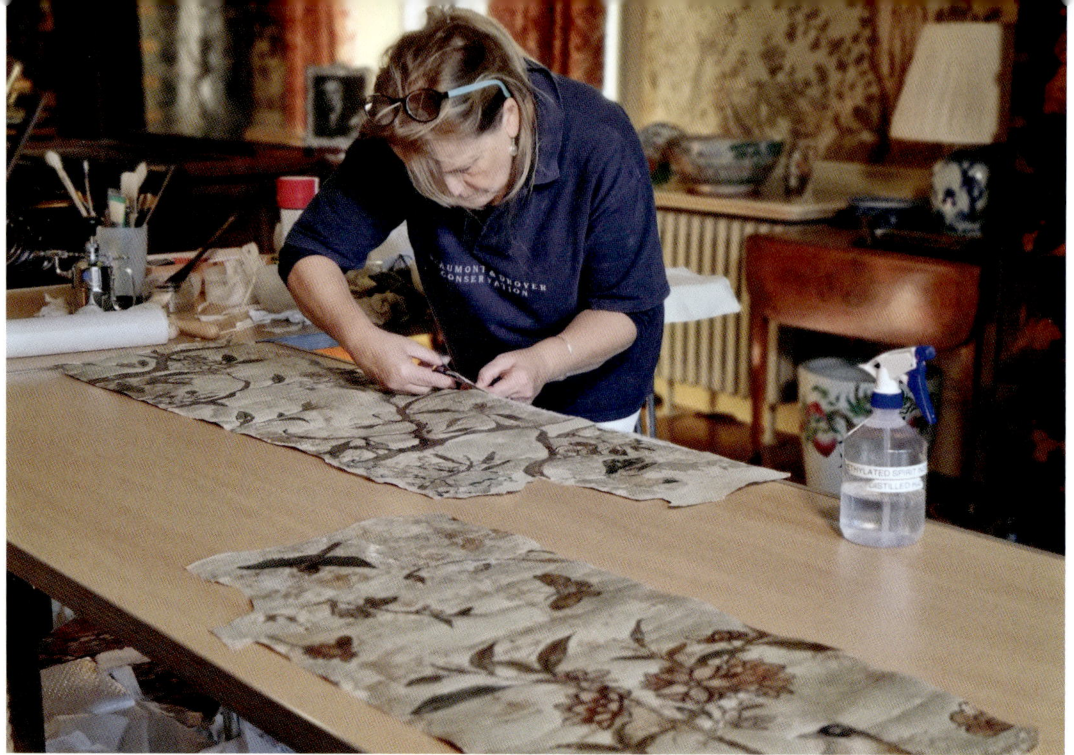

out, the wall would remain dry and unwelcoming to silverfish.

The rehung paper could then be conserved in position – a painstaking process when you consider its intricate details and many colours. But conservators love a challenge – and consequently their jobs. In Louise's words: 'You almost hold your breath, particularly if you're retouching tiny areas. I actually love the retouching process. It's the home straight in a way, and the whole story of the paper comes back to you. I love it.'

The rehung paper could then be conserved in position – a painstaking process when you consider its intricate details and many colours.

When caring for the properties and collections of the National Trust, peeling back the layers can yield some exciting discoveries as well as some troubling ones. But understanding and responding to both make the work of curators and conservators endlessly satisfying.

^ Paper conservator Louise Drover bending to her task of repairing sections of wallpaper damaged by damp and silverfish.

> No longer being devoured by silverfish, Ightham Mote's wallpaper is now simply a feast for the eyes.

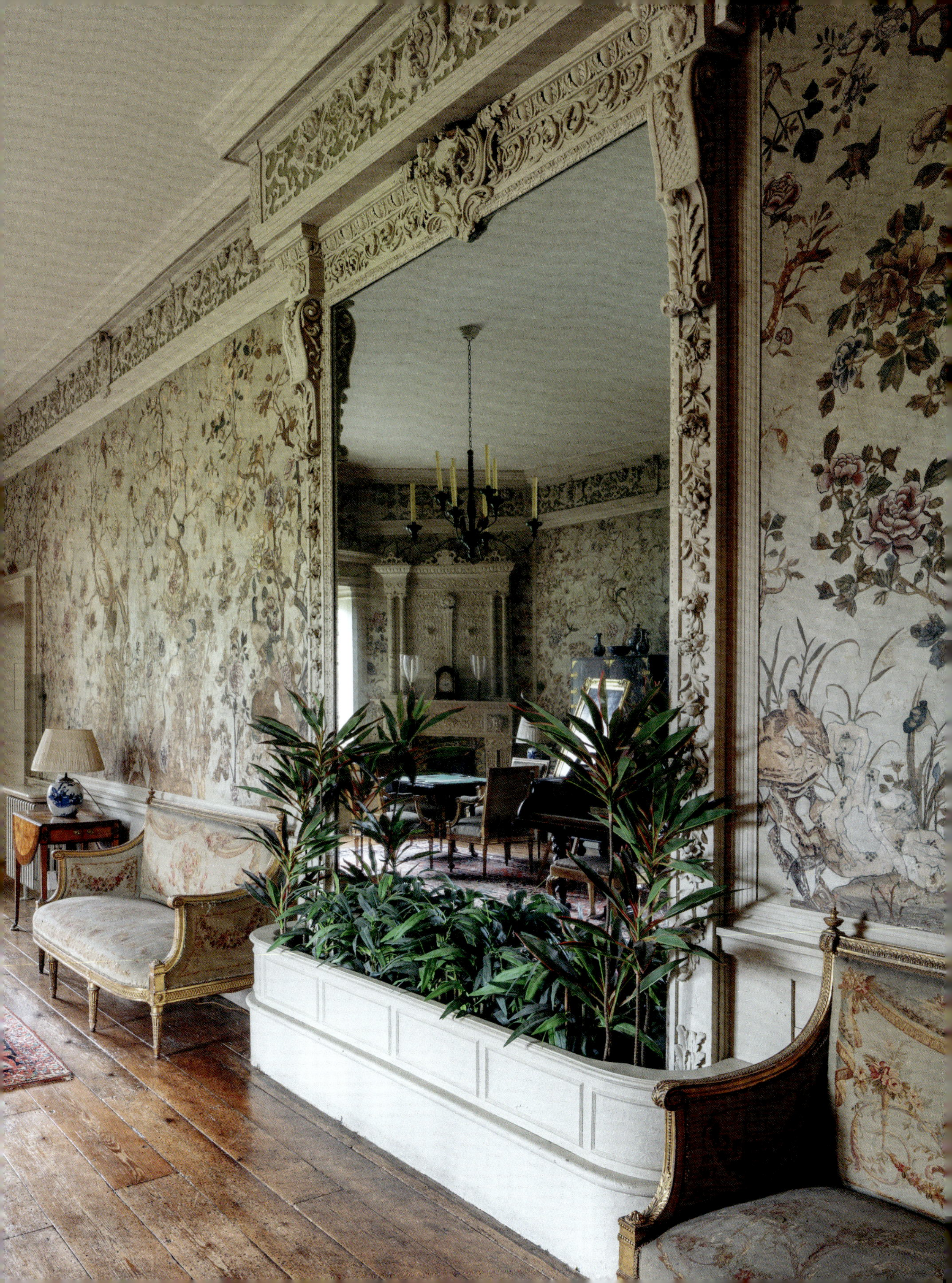

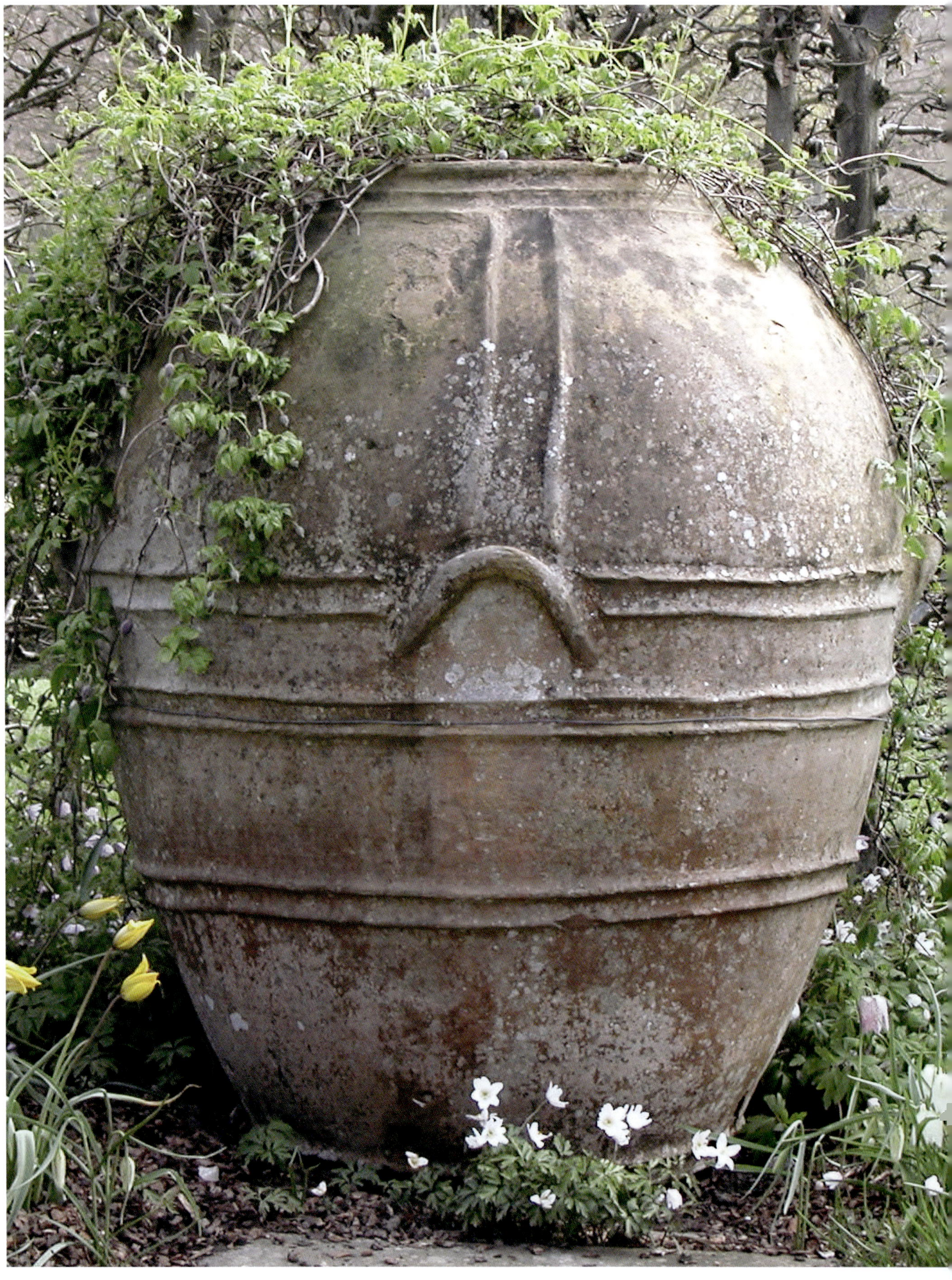

Conserving the Vision of an Unorthodox Gardener

Vita Sackville-West's Clematis Pot

Sissinghurst Castle Garden, Kent

In 1930, Vita Sackville-West and her husband Harold Nicolson moved to Sissinghurst. Of aristocratic stock, Vita had by that time made a name for herself as a successful author. Her parents were Victoria and Lionel Sackville-West, 3rd Baron Sackville, and she was their only child, but her gender had prevented her from inheriting the ancestral home at Knole on her father's death in 1928. To be passed over in this way, for no reason other than ancient custom, was something she bitterly resented. However, being a woman of both words and action, Vita determined to redress this imbalance and, barred from inheriting Knole, resolved to find a place to call her own.

Though Sissinghurst was a ruin when Vita and Harold bought it, just fragments of an Elizabethan mansion with a range of buildings, a tower and land full of debris, the property was found to have once belonged to one of Vita's ancestors. Its history and state of romantic ruin inspired Vita to do something truly spectacular here. She created her own ancestral home and a garden that became world-renowned. In 1938, Sissinghurst was opened to the public and Vita was lauded as a garden designer as well as a writer. In 1947 she began a weekly column in *The Observer* called 'In Your Garden' and in 1948 she became a founder member of the National

< Vita Sackville-West kept detailed plant lists which tell us this *Clematis alpina* has been growing in this pot since 1959.

Trust's garden committee. And all this she did without having had any formal horticultural training. Here was clearly a woman of redoubtable determination, who followed her own path and would never concede to any sort of societal constraint or expectations.

Because Vita didn't subscribe too closely to the accepted ways of doing things, she allowed herself to experiment at Sissinghurst. Working in a traditional setting against the backdrop of a historic building, she developed new approaches. For example, here at Sissinghurst she innovated single-colour planting schemes. She divided up the space into a series of distinct and defined areas – the White Garden, Rose Garden, Orchard, Cottage Garden, Nuttery and so on. This was something that Major Lawrence Johnston had done at Hidcote, but Vita apparently had had no contact with the reclusive major. She also laid out her garden with discovery and exploration in mind, leading and directing the visitor's attention. All these elements introduced by Vita at Sissinghurst are now standard principles of garden design.

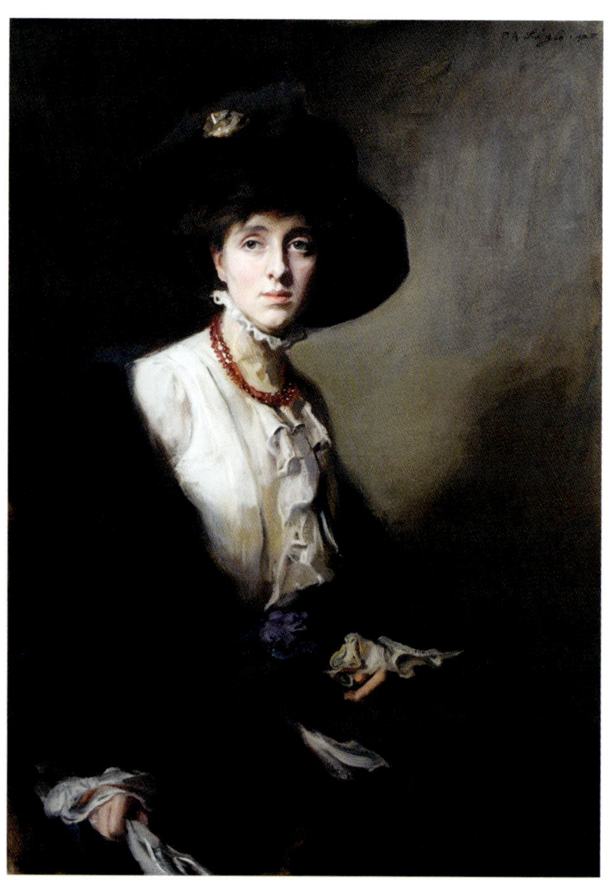

∧ A romantic depiction of Vita the author, painted by Philip de László.

Another case in point is the clematis in a pot on the Lime Walk. The creative but methodical Vita kept detailed plant lists and one such catalogue dated to 1959 includes mention of a *Clematis alpina* trailing out of a large Grecian-style pot. Anyone who has grown or who has attempted to grow a clematis will know that these

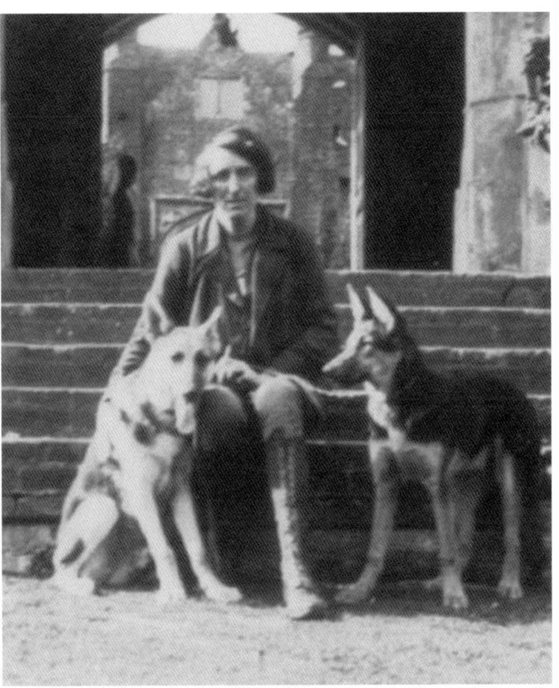

^ Vita on the steps of Sissinghurst Tower with her German Shepherds.

plants are traditionally regarded as climbers that require some sort of support or structure to grow on or through. Vita, however, was not overly concerned with tradition and frequently rejected the customary way of doing something if she thought there was a better alternative. She had fallen foul of inheritance customs and resolved to find her own solution. She married Harold despite her parents' objections to his lack of wealth and status. The couple were married for nearly 50 years and had two children, though theirs was an open marriage with both pursuing same-sex relationships. While Vita's marriage arrangements aren't directly relevant to her skills as a garden designer, it demonstrates her practical approach to life and determination to be true to her feelings.

Because what Vita created at Sissinghurst is so very personal and unique to her, it is essential that the work of today's gardening team remains true to her vision. So when the clematis, thought to be growing in that position since 1959, and the pot, thought to be anything up to a hundred years old, were both showing signs of deterioration, considered conservation was required.

First, head gardener Troy Scott Smith had to carefully extricate the clematis. For such an established plant, the system of roots below soil level was found to be worryingly small – a sure sign of a plant in distress. The clematis was given some intensive care and nourishment in Sissinghurst's greenhouse, while the terracotta pot was taken away in several pieces to Cliveden Conservation's workshop in Buckinghamshire.

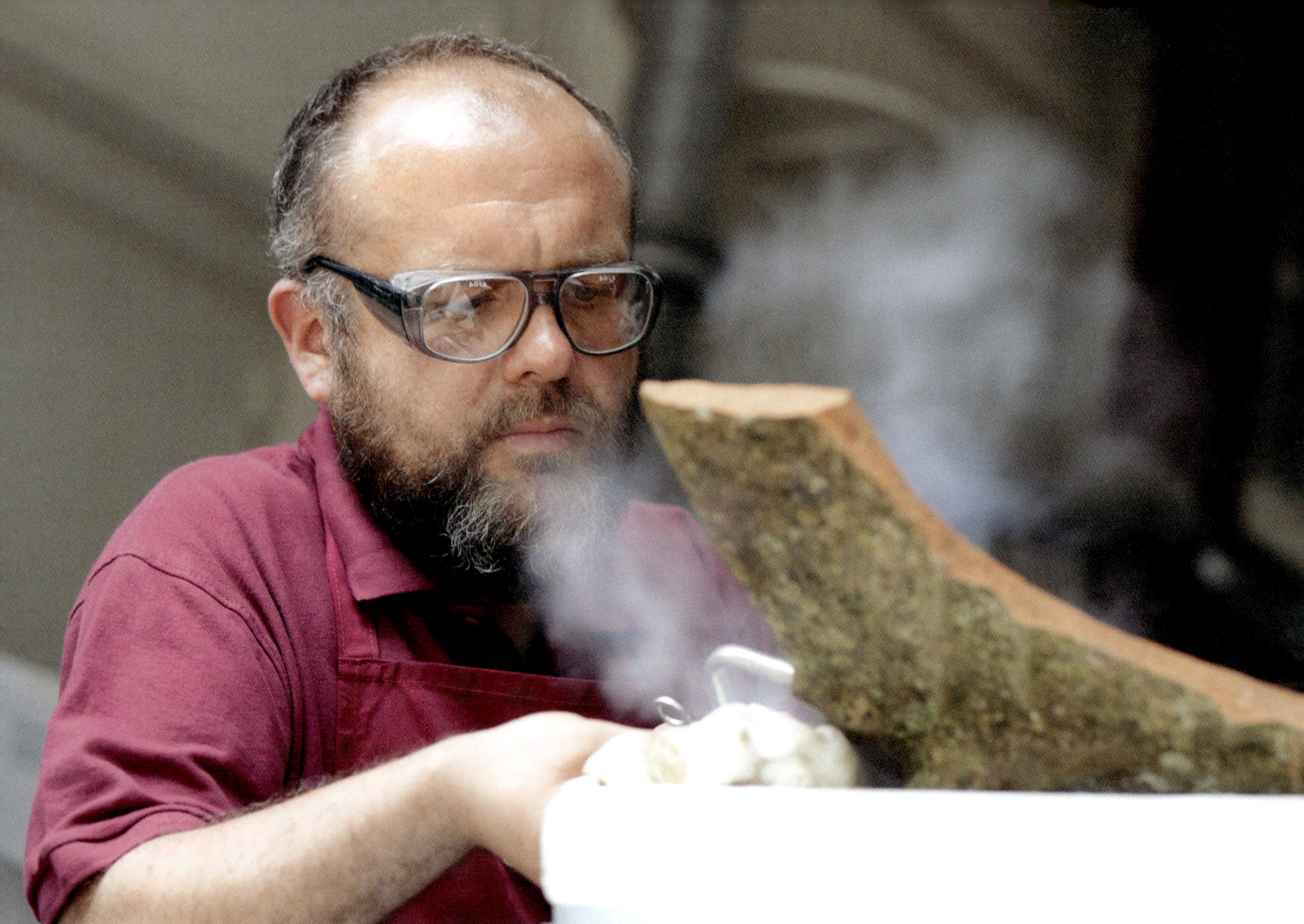

^ Stonework conservator Kris Zykubek removing all the surface material required to make a good repair but ensuring character remains.

There, stonework conservator Kris Zykubek applied himself to the task of cleaning and repairing the pot. A certain amount of algae, lichen and moss needed to be removed to make surfaces sound for repair, but not so much as to spoil the character of a century-old pot. After painstakingly patching areas that were completely absent, putting all of the pieces back together again and rendering the joins invisible, the pot that was returned to Sissinghurst wasn't as good as new – it was better. With all the patina of age, it now has the integrity of being whole once more and the addition of reinforcing bars to ensure Kris's repairs withstand the winter frosts.

The clematis, now enjoying a new lease of life, was returned to the spot Vita and Harold had picked out for it and is allowed to trail freely, not a support in sight other than the watchful eye of Sissinghurst's gardeners. But this was much more than the rejuvenation of a plant and the restoration of a pot. Family photos suggest that pot was a feature of which Vita was particularly fond. In one image, her infant son sits on the floor in front of the pot, seemingly transfixed by an insect; in another, her most famous lover, Virginia Woolf, stands somewhat coyly behind it. The same pot, but two different sides of Vita, and following conservation, it will remain testament to her and her vision for many more years to come.

∨ Restored to the Lime Walk once more, this trailing clematis speaks to the free-spirited and unconventional woman who planted it over 60 years ago.

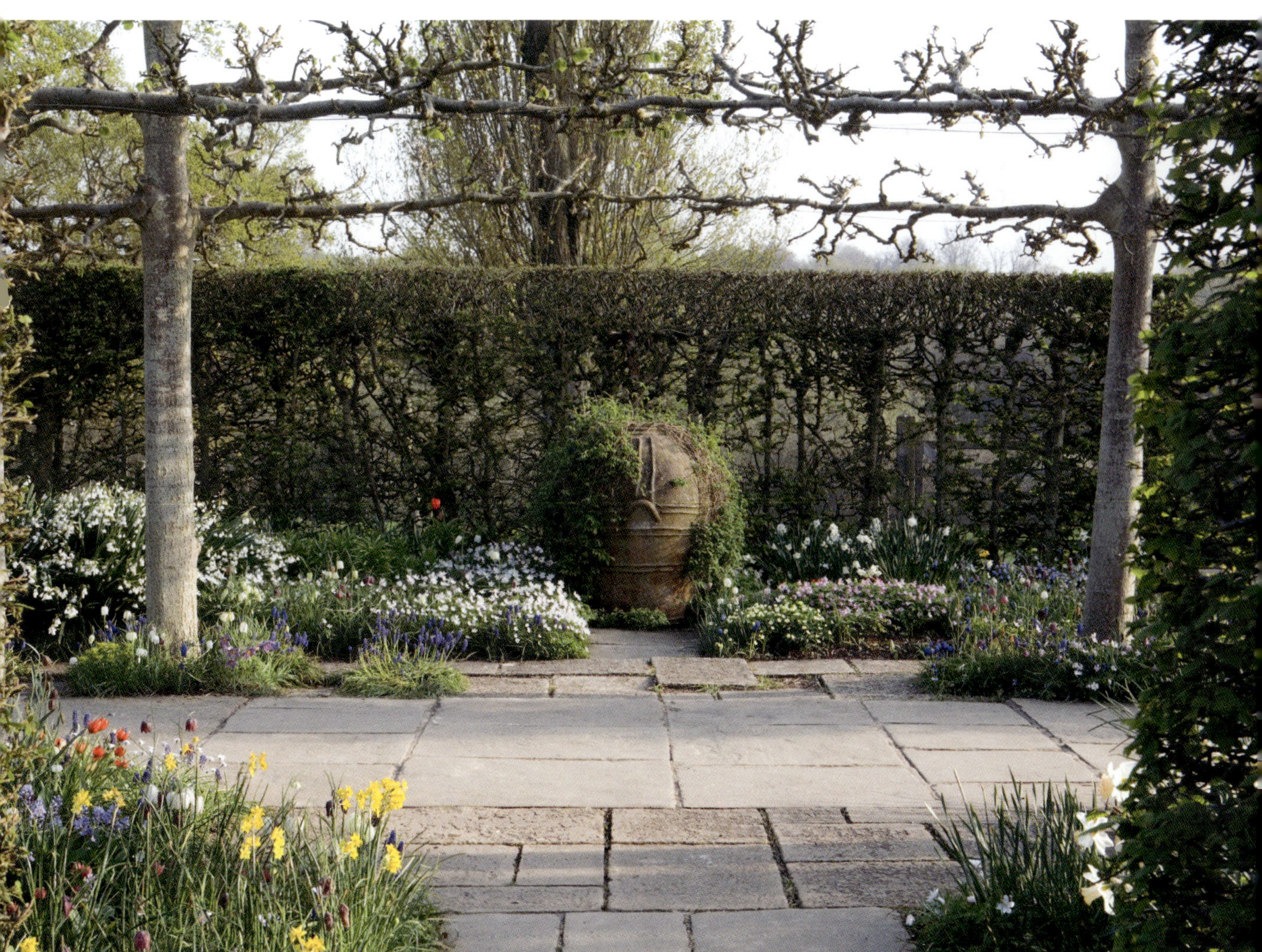

Restoring a Famous Writer's Desk

Henry James's Secretaire

Lamb House, East Sussex

When on the hunt for hidden treasures, you might think a secretaire is a promising place to look. However, the name of this type of furniture doesn't derive from secrets but from the French *écrire*, meaning 'to write'. Known as a *secrétaire à abattant* or *secrétaire en armoire*, it is a tall piece, composed of a chest of drawers topped by a cabinet. Part of this cabinet is fitted with small drawers, cupboards and pigeonholes behind a hinged, falling front, which, when flat, forms a writing surface.

Being both stylish and practical, secretaires first appeared in the UK in the 1600s. They gained in popularity during the eighteenth century and by the following century they were essential items in middle-class interiors. They possessed a constrained beauty, with finely polished surfaces to draw out the grain, or skilful marquetry to delight the eye. They also showcased the owner's intellectual activities, with a design structured around reading and writing, including numerous drawers for storing letters and journals. And finally, they were economical in terms of the space they occupied, if you lived in a town house rather than a country mansion.

Our secretaire resides in Lamb House, in Rye, East Sussex, the former home of author Henry James. By the time he moved to Lamb House, in

> The desk area of Henry James's secretaire with letters and personal items that once belonged to the famous author.

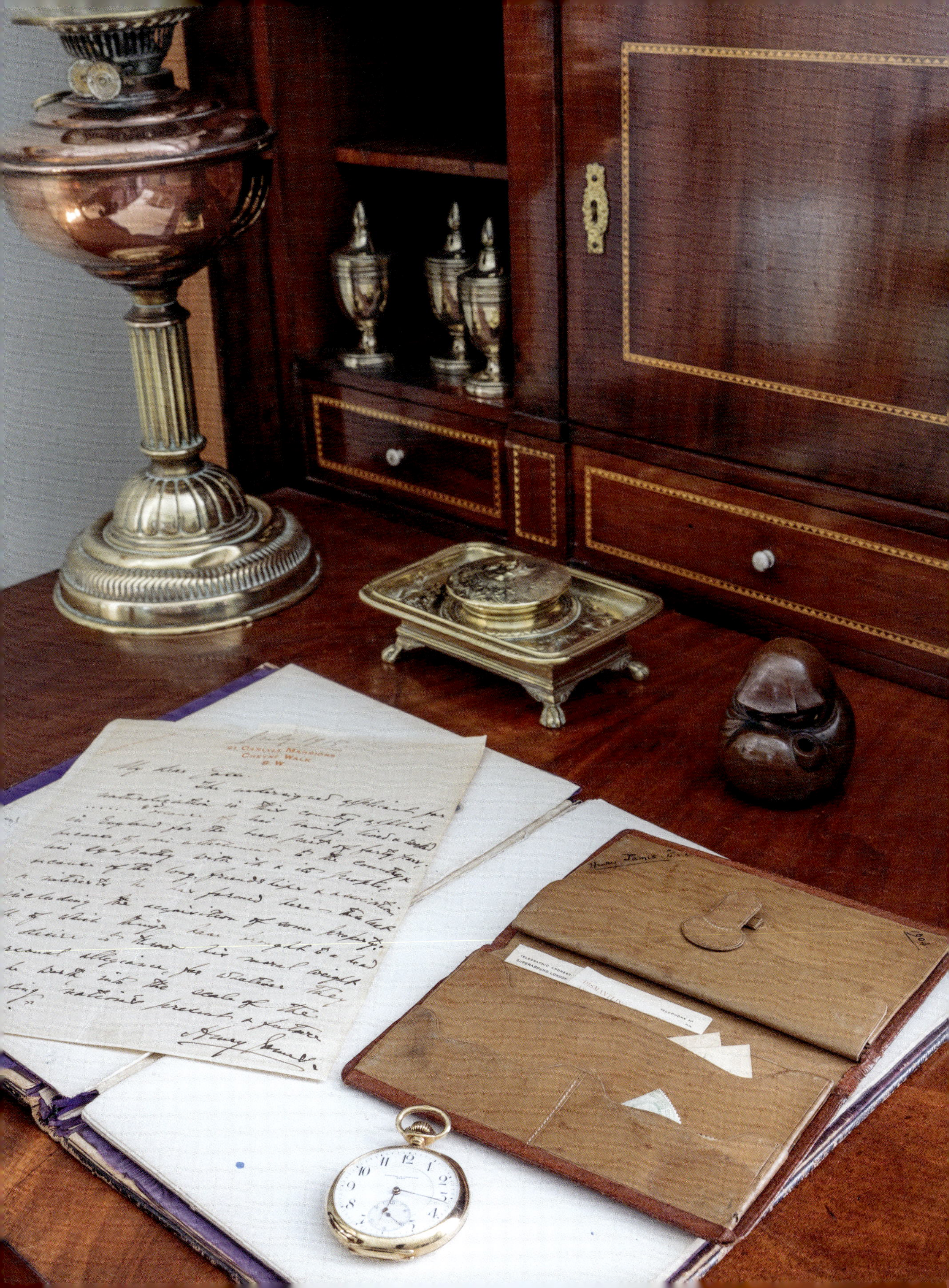
21 Carlyle Mansions
Cheyne Walk
S.W

1898, James had achieved success with works such as *Daisy Miller*, *Washington Square*, *The Portrait of a Lady* and *The Bostonians*. If a theme is apparent here, it's because James drew on his experiences and observations as an American living in England, writing about the social mores and foibles of the two nationalities and the occasional cultural clash between them. His writing career was so long, however, that it passed through distinct phases: from what some consider his early 'potboilers' written for magazines; through the more dramatic works that were far less popular, depressing him immensely; to penning the horror novella *The Turn of the Screw*, and his final works that followed the inner lives of his characters, making him a master of the 'stream of consciousness' style of writing. For his contribution, he was nominated for the Nobel Prize in literature three times.

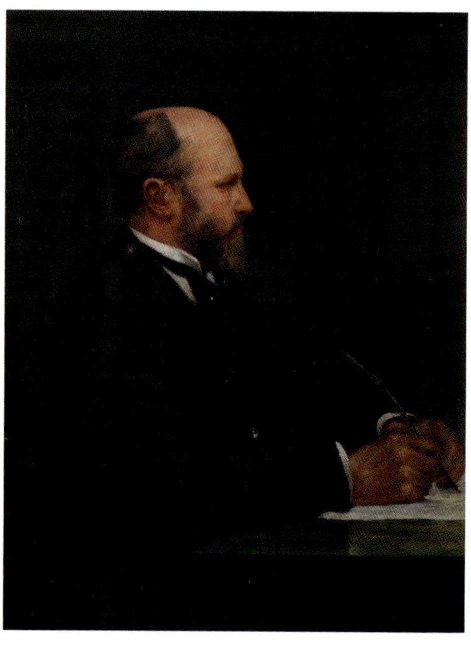

^ Henry James painted by Sir Philip Burne-Jones in 1894.

> Lamb House was once a hub for the country's literary establishment.

So, of all the secretaires in middle-class abodes up and down the country, this one stands taller than most. But being culturally significant has made it no less susceptible to wear and tear. Over time, its veneer and hinges suffered splits, requiring it to be removed for a full inspection and assessment of all necessary repairs. This was made all the more pressing following the discovery of damp in a section of plasterwork close to where the secretaire stood in the Green Parlour at Lamb House. Further inspection revealed that, internally, this wall had been replastered in the twentieth century using cement – a common practice at the time – but which has since been found to allow water to become trapped. This was further compounded by the presence of yet more cement in the pointing of this south-west facing wall that receives the worst of the weather.

The affected area of plaster had to be removed and a substantial amount of pointing scraped out, ready for the reapplication of a lime-

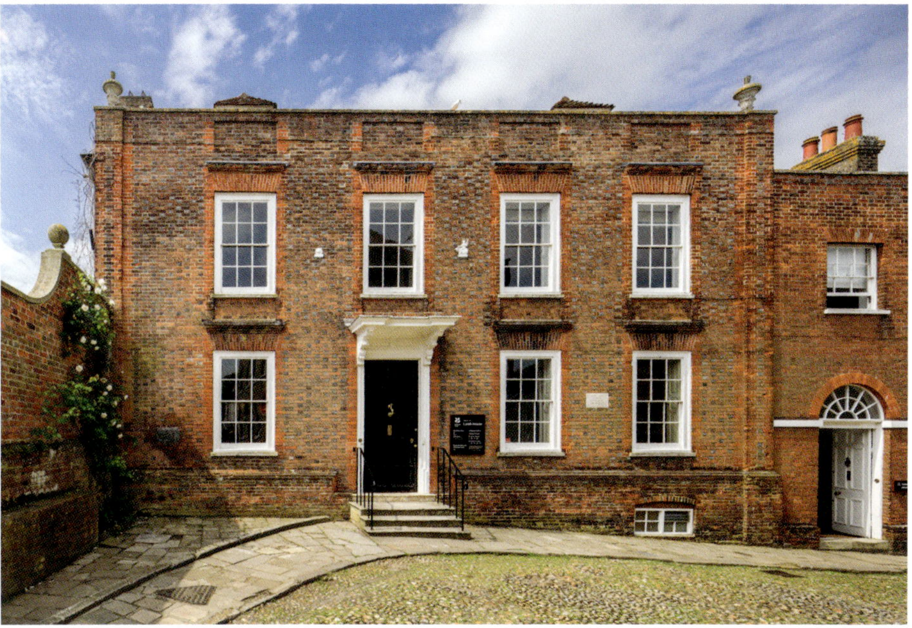

based equivalent that allows the free movement of moisture. This is a lengthy process, as the internal exposed brickwork behind the plasterwork must be allowed to fully dry out before replastering, and three coats of lime plaster are usually required with drying time in between.

National Trust Regional Conservator Siobhan Barratt was tasked with taking the secretaire apart in order to fully understand how this complex item was originally made. This process yielded an unexpected discovery. The front door key to Lamb House was found in a compartment at the back of the desk. Presumably this had been a spare, squirrelled carefully away until required and then entirely forgotten about – something to which most of us can relate.

Once conservation treatment was complete and the Green Parlour damp-free, the secretaire was returned to its original home, a home that was presented to the National Trust in 1950 by the widow of Henry James's nephew, Henry James Jnr., 'to be preserved as an enduring symbol of the ties that unite the British and American people'. There is of course much at Lamb House that speaks to the time of this famous American author, but a writer's desk has an additional eloquence over other everyday items. Its conservation ensures the continuation of his story.

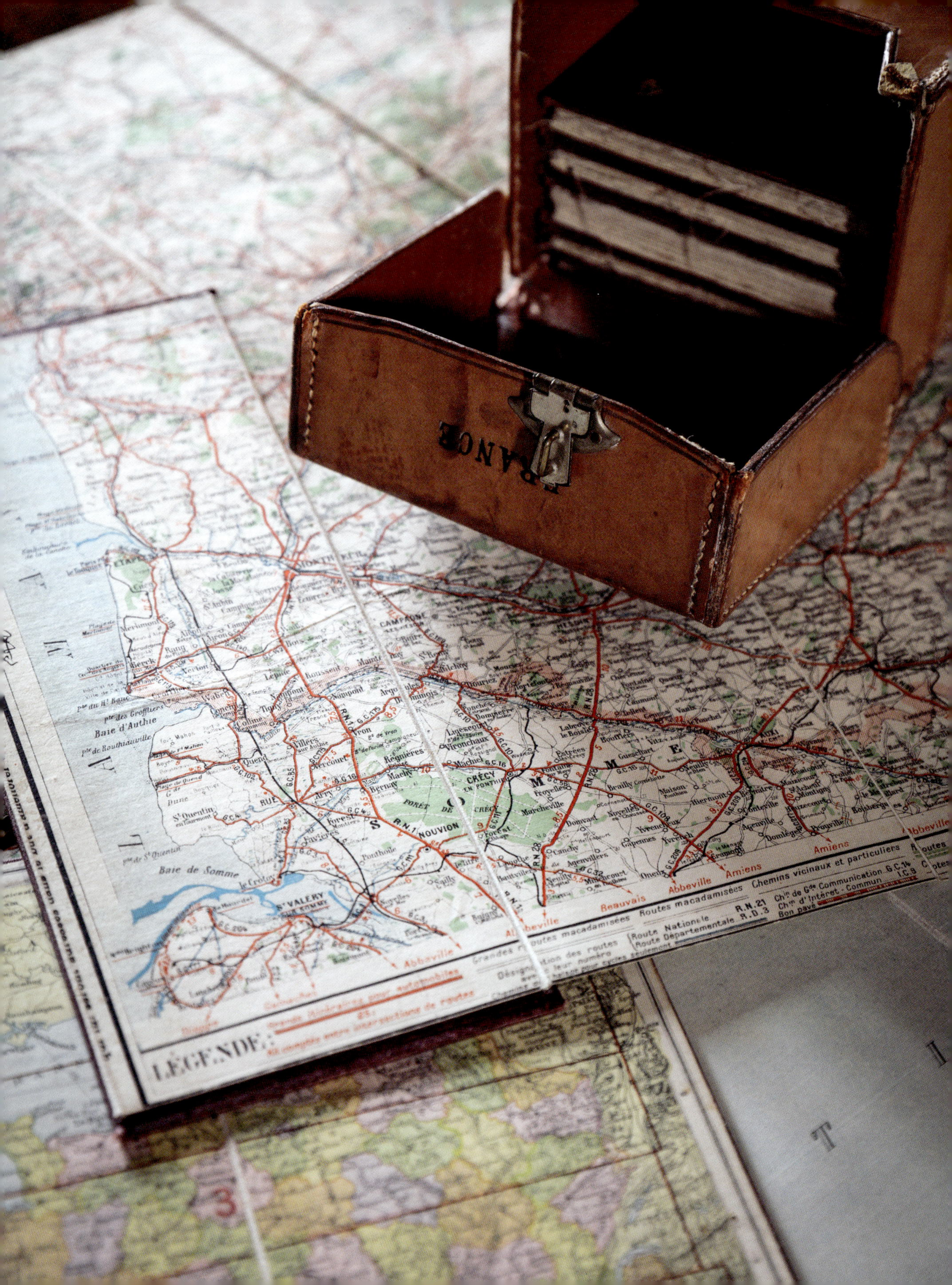
FRANCE
LÉGENDE:
Baie d'Authie
Baie de Somme
ETAPLES
RUE
CRÉCY
NOUVION
FORET DE CRÉCY
S^T VALERY
Abbeville
Amiens
Beauvais
Chemins vicinaux et particuliers
Routes macadamisées
Route Nationale R.N.21
Route Départementale R.D.3
Bon pavé
Désignation des routes

Preserving the Memories of a Lost Generation

Rudyard Kipling's Maps of Northern Europe

Bateman's, East Sussex

A journey across the High Weald takes us from the home of one author whose focus was the West, to that of another who was famously inspired by stories from the East. Henry James and Rudyard Kipling were contemporaries – James was a couple of decades older – but more than that, they were friends – James gave away Kipling's wife Carrie when the two were married in London in 1892.

Rudyard Kipling is credited with a great many works of fiction, but perhaps none is better known, and more loved, than *The Jungle Book*, published in 1894. By the time the Kiplings moved to Bateman's in 1902 with their two young children, Elsie and John, Kipling was probably the most famous author in England. They were straightaway smitten with Bateman's, Kipling writing of it: 'We have loved it ever since our first sight of it … We entered and felt her Spirit – her Feng Shui – to be good. We went through every room and found no shadows of ancient regrets, stifled miseries, nor any menace, though the "new" end of her was three hundred years old … A real house in which to settle down.'

< These century-old maps bear markings that tell the story of a famous writer and his wife who used them in the search for their lost son.

It is indeed a beautiful building, of soft, warm sandstone on the outside and oak beams and panelling on the inside, but the Kiplings' response may have been more than a question of aesthetic appeal. Their eldest daughter, Josephine, had died of pneumonia in 1899, aged just six. Bateman's offered the family a place where they could heal. It was the family's much-cherished home right up until Carrie's death in 1939, three years after her husband's. Bateman's was left to the National Trust in Carrie's will, and today the National Trust shows it as the Kiplings would have known it, letting people see something of the life of a world-famous author, but also that of the family that lived here. Some of the items on display help visitors to reflect on the work Rudyard Kipling published, his writing desk covered in an author's accoutrements, while others tell a much more personal story.

The Kiplings suffered a second bereavement in 1915, when their son John, like so many other young men, was killed in the First World War. During his very first engagement of the war, at the Battle of Loos, John went missing and was presumed dead. Both parents were devastated, but his father perhaps especially so, as it was he who,

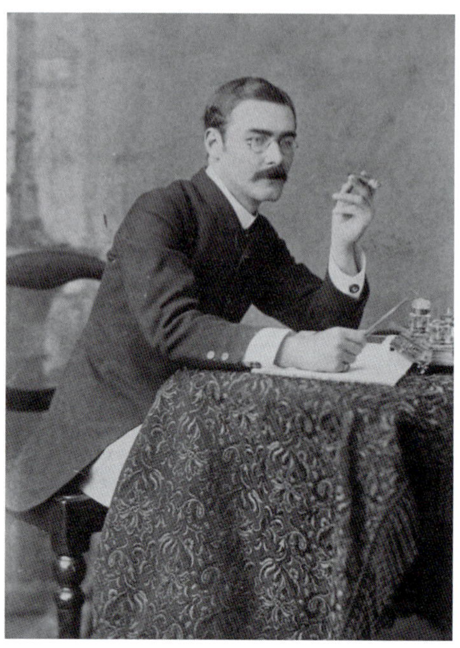

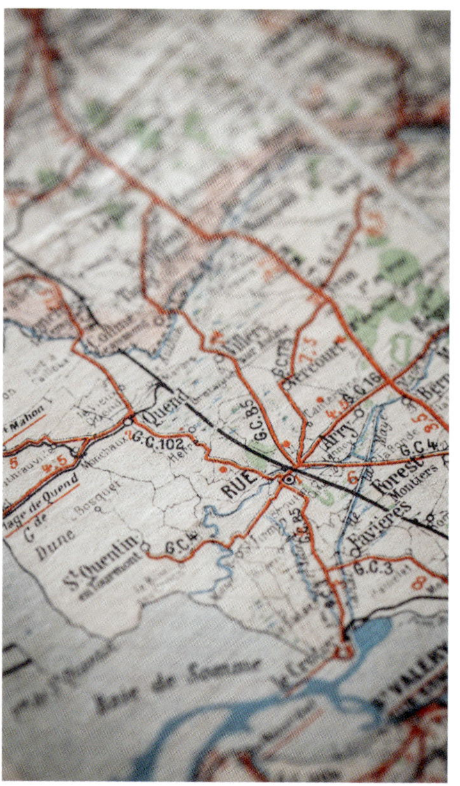

^ Rudyard Kipling photographed in the 1880s when he was living and working in India.

> Rudyard and Carrie used these maps as they scoured northern France for clues.

under great pressure from his son, had used his influence to arrange a commission in the Irish Guards after John's initial application had been turned down due to poor eyesight. Rudyard and Carrie were desperate to find their son's resting place, and they made frequent visits to France after the end of the war, looking for their son or clues as to what might have happened to him. In a leather travelling case on a shelf in Rudyard Kipling's study is a tightly packed bundle of cardboard-bound folding maps. One of these appears more used than the others and is speckled with dots of ink. It's thought that these were the places that the Kiplings visited in their search for the grave of their missing son, marking them off as they went.

A set of well-preserved maps that is over a hundred years old, presented in their original leather carrying case, has an intrinsic value. But one such as this that speaks of such a personal and profoundly sad experience, an experience that, more tragically still, was shared by millions of families during and in the aftermath of the First World War, has a particularly poignant significance.

Because of the way in which they're stored, these paper maps need to be regularly taken out of their cases and unfolded, allowing air to get between their leaves, and for a close inspection, checking for signs of mould or other damage. When National Trust Regional Conservator Siobhan Barratt was asked to come to Bateman's to clean and assess the maps, she had no idea of the story behind them. Of course, every item worked on by a conservator is approached with sensitivity, but the knowledge that these maps were used by grieving parents searching for their son's last resting place changed the way Siobhan looked at them. In her words: 'Suddenly Kipling isn't this author who wrote *The Jungle Book* and all the other stories; he's a father looking for his lost son … I think the maps are a really good way in to telling the stories of the people who lived there. If they weren't there, the house wouldn't be the same.'

Certainly, sharing the story of these maps makes for a far more poignant reading of some of Rudyard Kipling's most famous words from the poem 'If': 'Yours is the Earth and everything that's in it, / And – which is more – you'll be a Man, my son!'

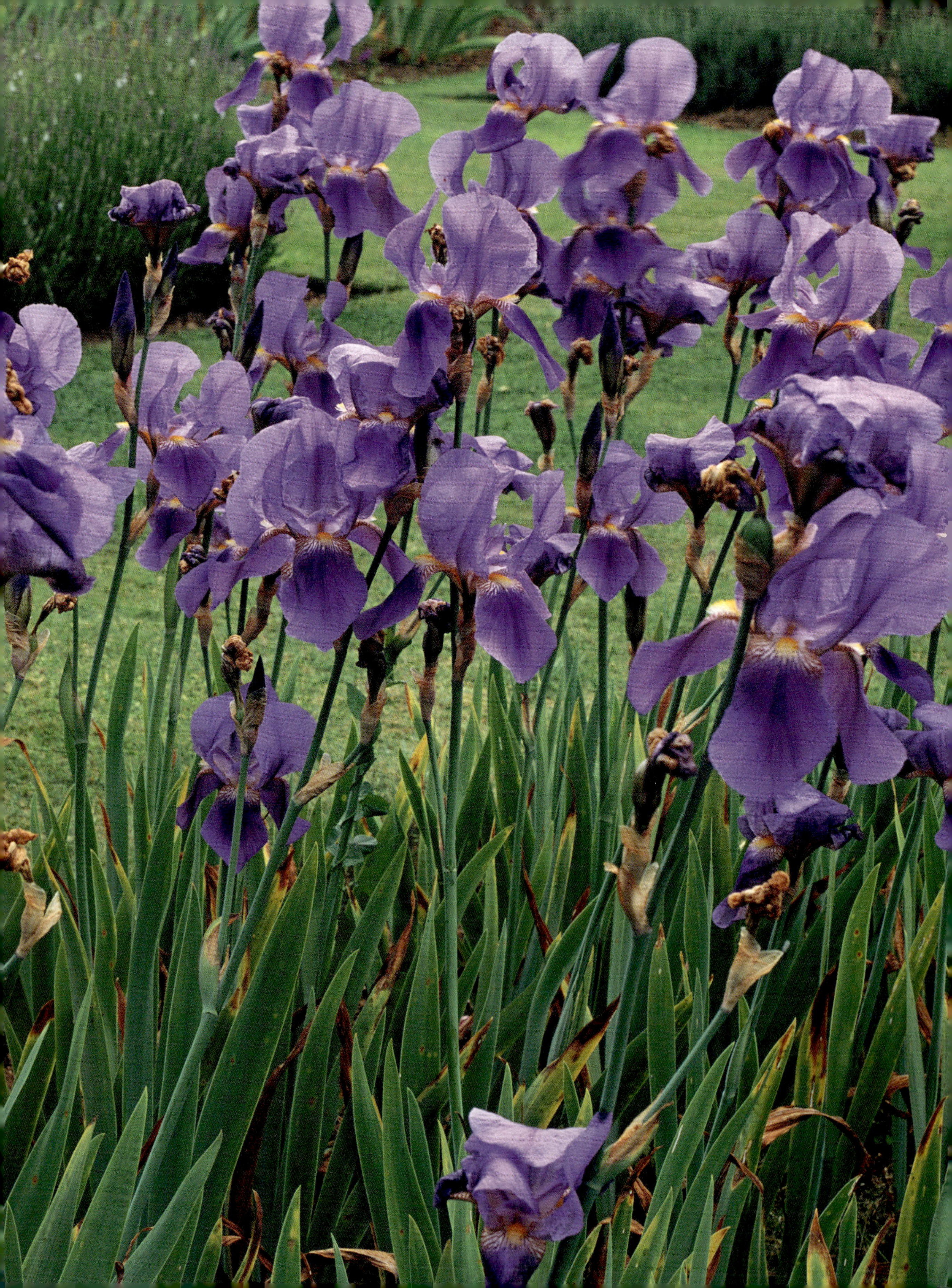

Keeping a Botanical Collection True to Its History

Lady Churchill's Irises

Chartwell, Kent

At Sissinghurst (see page 81) we encountered perhaps the best example of living history that you can find within the collections of the National Trust. It is something very special indeed to be cultivating the same plant that was tended by one of our predecessors, more thrilling still when that predecessor has played a significant part in our history. At Chartwell, too, you can delight in the sights and the scents of the plants personally selected by the former owners of this country house overlooking the Weald of Kent. Indeed, it was these views that drove a man to purchase the property, without his wife's knowledge and neglecting the fact that more renovation was required than the couple could really afford.

That man was Winston Churchill, and he bought the house in 1922. His wife Clementine had at least seen the property and initially liked it, remarking: 'I can think of nothing but that heavenly tree-crowned hill', but her feelings towards it later cooled. However, as history would prove, Winston was not a man who gave up on anything, and so, in the same week that Clementine gave birth to their fifth child, he went through with the purchase. In an effort to assuage his wife's anxieties, Winston wrote to her, saying: 'My beloved, I beg you not to worry about money,

< Clementine Churchill was very involved in the planting at Chartwell and had a particular penchant for bearded irises.

or to feel insecure. Chartwell is to be our home [and] we must endeavour to live there for many years.'

And that they did, for over 40 years, until Winston's death in 1965. Chartwell provided them with a safe haven during his long and tumultuous political career, and in return Winston and Clementine, each in their respective ways, poured their creativity into the house and garden, turning it into a much-loved family home.

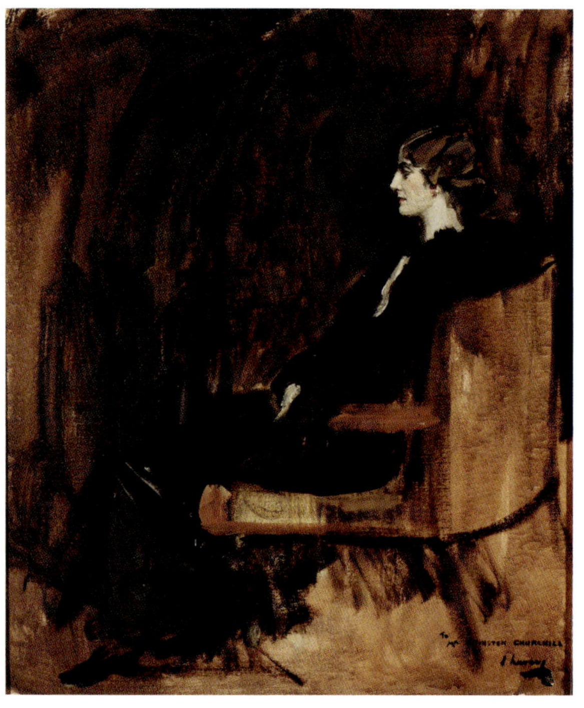

^ Clementine Churchill, later Baroness Churchill, by Sir John Lavery.

Drawing another comparison with Sissinghurst, where Vita Sackville-West honed her skills as a garden designer, Winston personally oversaw the landscaping of the grounds at Chartwell, and some areas he actually built with his own hands. Two-times Prime Minister, Winston Churchill was also a skilled and largely self-taught bricklayer, as evidenced by Chartwell's Walled Garden.

Clementine also contributed to some of the landscaping decisions at Chartwell. She made numerous visits to the Chelsea Flower Show where she admired displays created by nurseryman Col. Gavin Jones. In 1948, Jones transferred the rock garden he had created for Chelsea to Chartwell, and installed it free of charge. However, it was with the planting that Clementine was most concerned.

Breeding irises became a popular pastime among the leisured classes in the 1920s and 1930s, and Clementine was a particular fan of bearded irises. Consequently, the Churchills gave the 260-foot (80-metre) border below the main terrace wall almost entirely over to irises. Here the soil is poor, stony and particularly dry owing to its exposure to the sun.

Bearded irises (*Iris germanica*) thrive in these conditions, compared to their moisture-loving cousins often found in or around ponds (such as *I. pseudacorus* or *I. laevigata*). Over time, Clementine built up an unusual and varied collection. Planting lists from the 1930s and 1940s include the varieties 'Lord of June', 'Grace Sturtevant' and 'Mrs Alan Gray'. Another variety known to have been enjoyed and grown by Clementine is 'Corrida'. A description in a plant catalogue from 1926 reads: 'Its flowers are darker blue than those of that excellent standard variety, and some English landscape architects place "Corrida" at the head of the list of blue Irises for landscape work. I am glad that I have enough stock of it that I can afford to sell it at a popular price.' Popular it may once have been, but it is no longer commercially available. So, keeping history alive in this case poses a number of challenges to the gardening team at Chartwell, who have to combine the principles of conservation *and* horticulture.

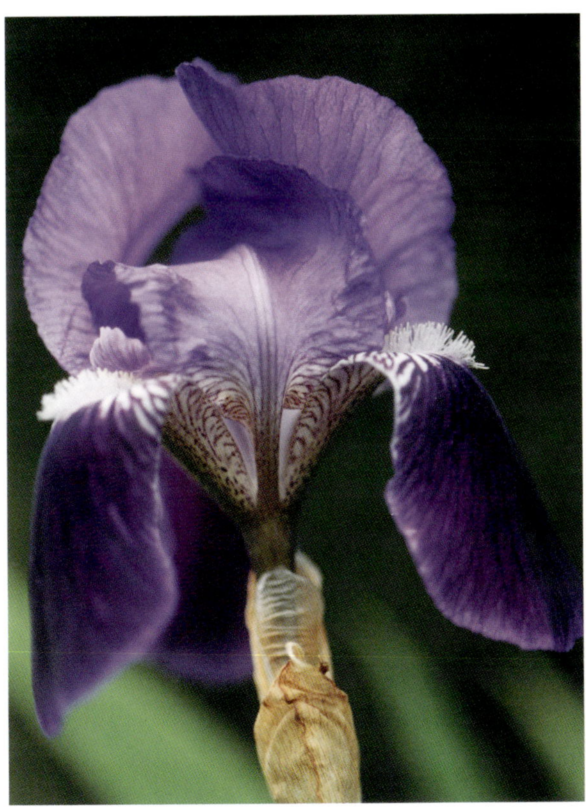

^ The tall stems of bearded irises bear large, showy flowers in all colours from white to black and many combinations of blue, yellow, orange, purple and pink.

Although lovely in bloom, irises have a relatively short flowering period. They can also become congested and are prone to a number of diseases, so their care requires specialist knowledge. As the irises in Lady Churchill's Iris Walk have particular significance, given the person who initially developed and curated the collection, every effort is made to keep the planting scheme as true to the original as possible. In this, of course, Chartwell's gardeners

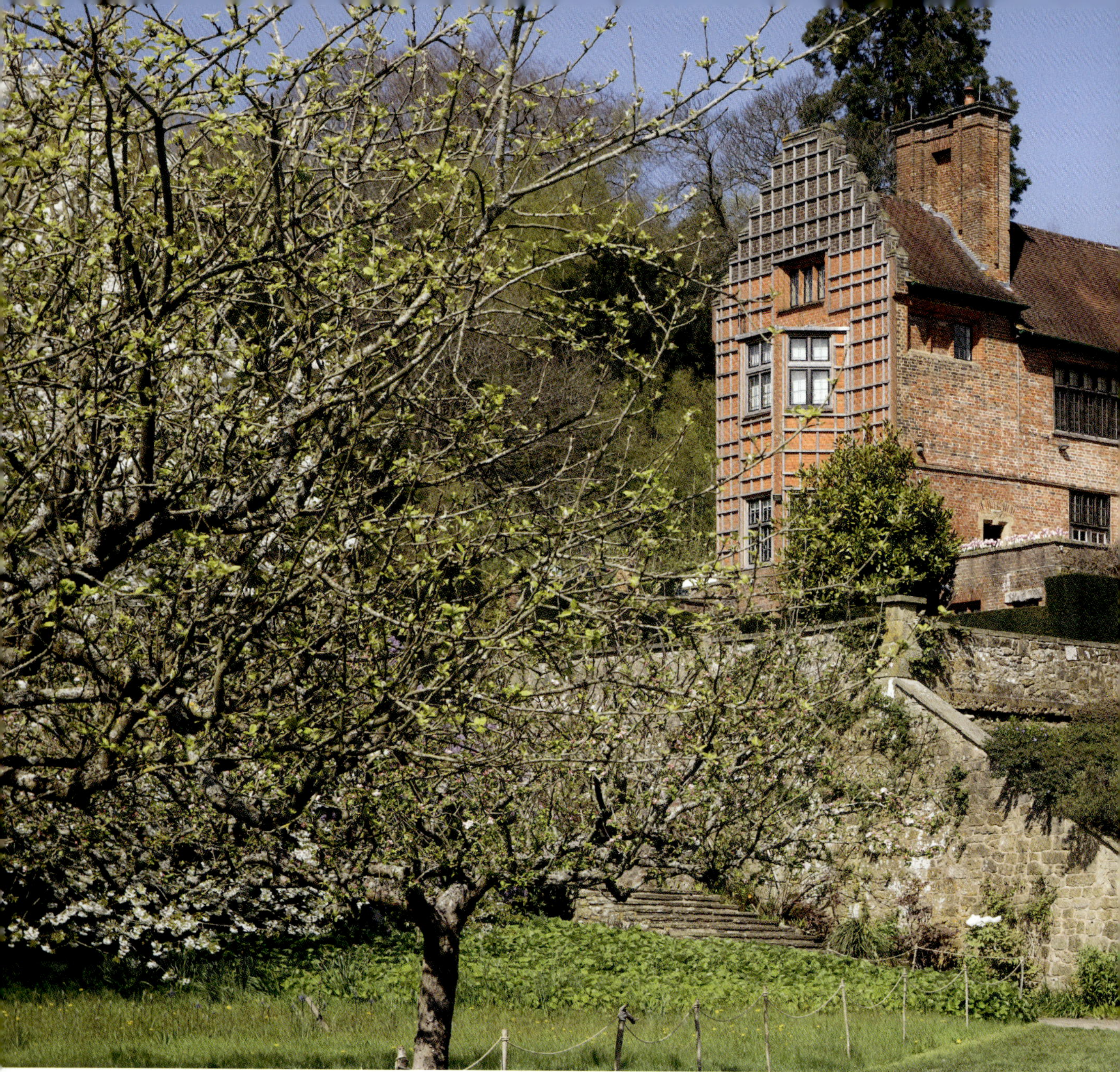

are aided by having access to the many other gardens in the care of the National Trust, including those at nearby Polesden Lacey and Sissinghurst.

Once Chartwell's team had sourced all the varieties they could and had drawn up a plan, the planting could begin. But in order to extend interest beyond the short flowering period of the irises, they have been combined with other plants offering contrasting foliage, colours

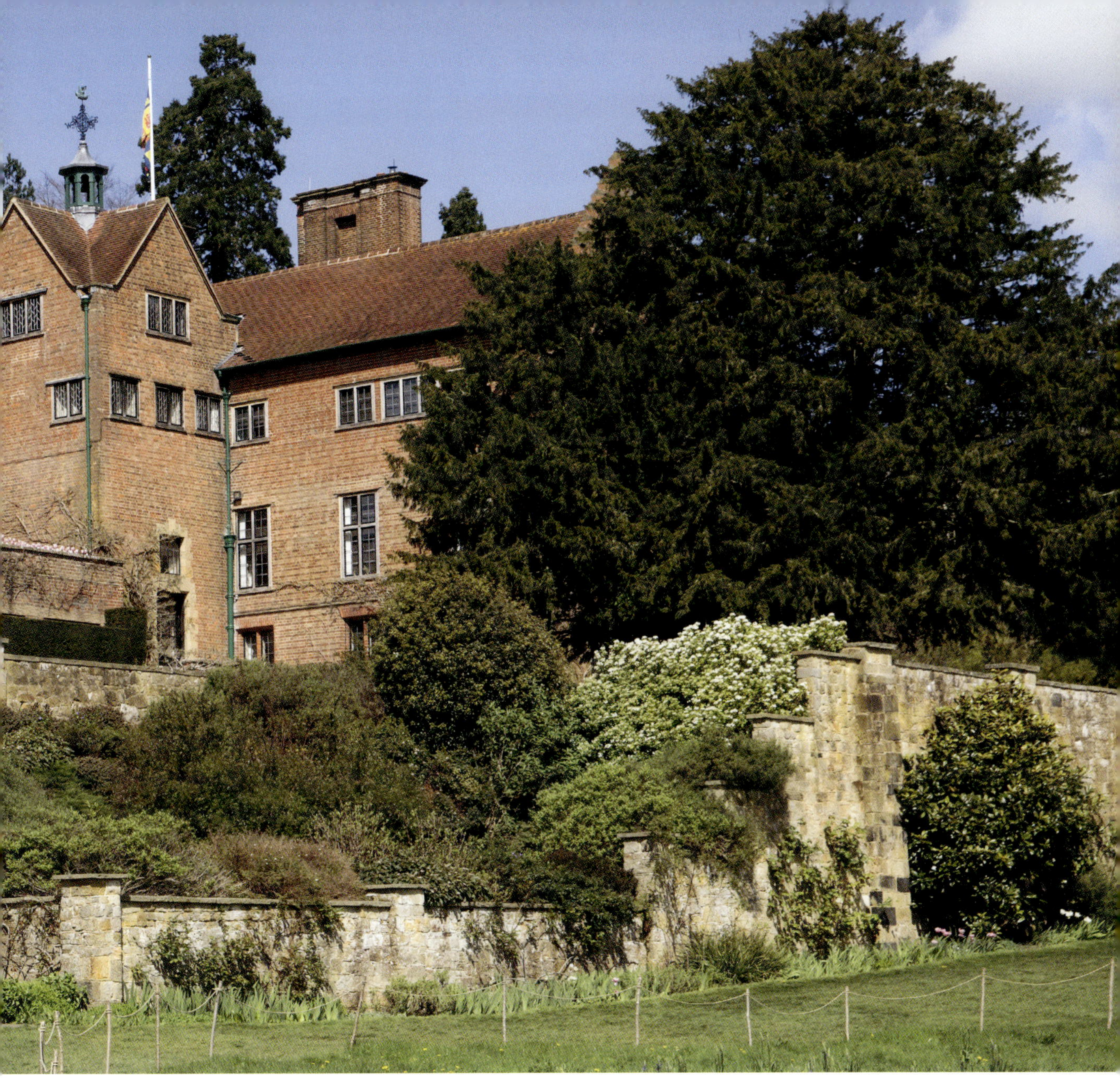

and textures. This ensures that Lady Churchill's Iris Walk looks lovely throughout the summer and, vitally, maintains that link to all the summers the Churchills enjoyed at Chartwell.

^ Chartwell was the Churchill family's home from 1922 up until Winston's death in 1965. In that time, Winston and Clementine developed the garden and wider landscape to their own, very personal design.

Treasured Gifts

Margaret Greville's Objets d'Art

Polesden Lacey, Surrey

At Polesden Lacey you will find a remarkable collection of precious objects, in a veritable jewel box of a house. Renovated in anticipation of entertaining royalty, by the architects responsible for remodelling The Ritz hotel in London, Polesden Lacey was the country retreat of Margaret Greville. Here she played host to such glittering guests that Polesden Lacey became the go-to destination for the wealthy and influential.

In 1942, after decades of entertaining, Margaret left Polesden Lacey, together with a treasure trove of paintings, furniture, ceramics, books, silver and one of the UK's largest groups of Fabergé objects in a country house collection, to the National Trust. The dazzling interiors of the house are as flush with social history as with glittering treasures. Margaret had such riches and influential friends that she bequeathed most of her jewellery to Queen Elizabeth (later the Queen Mother), all of which remains in the possession of the royal family and makes regular appearances at weddings and state events.

The head-turning opulence at Polesden Lacey can make it easy to miss some of its daintier treasures, no less valuable for their diminutive size. But these items are carefully catalogued and photographed by the National Trust, and so we can put a metaphorical eyeglass over them here.

Take Margaret's Fabergé collection, for example. These elaborate, jewel-encrusted creations were first produced as gifts and keepsakes that

> Polesden Lacey has one of the country's largest collections of *objets de vertu* (as in 'virtuosic'): small luxury items made with the finest materials by the most skilled craftsmen.

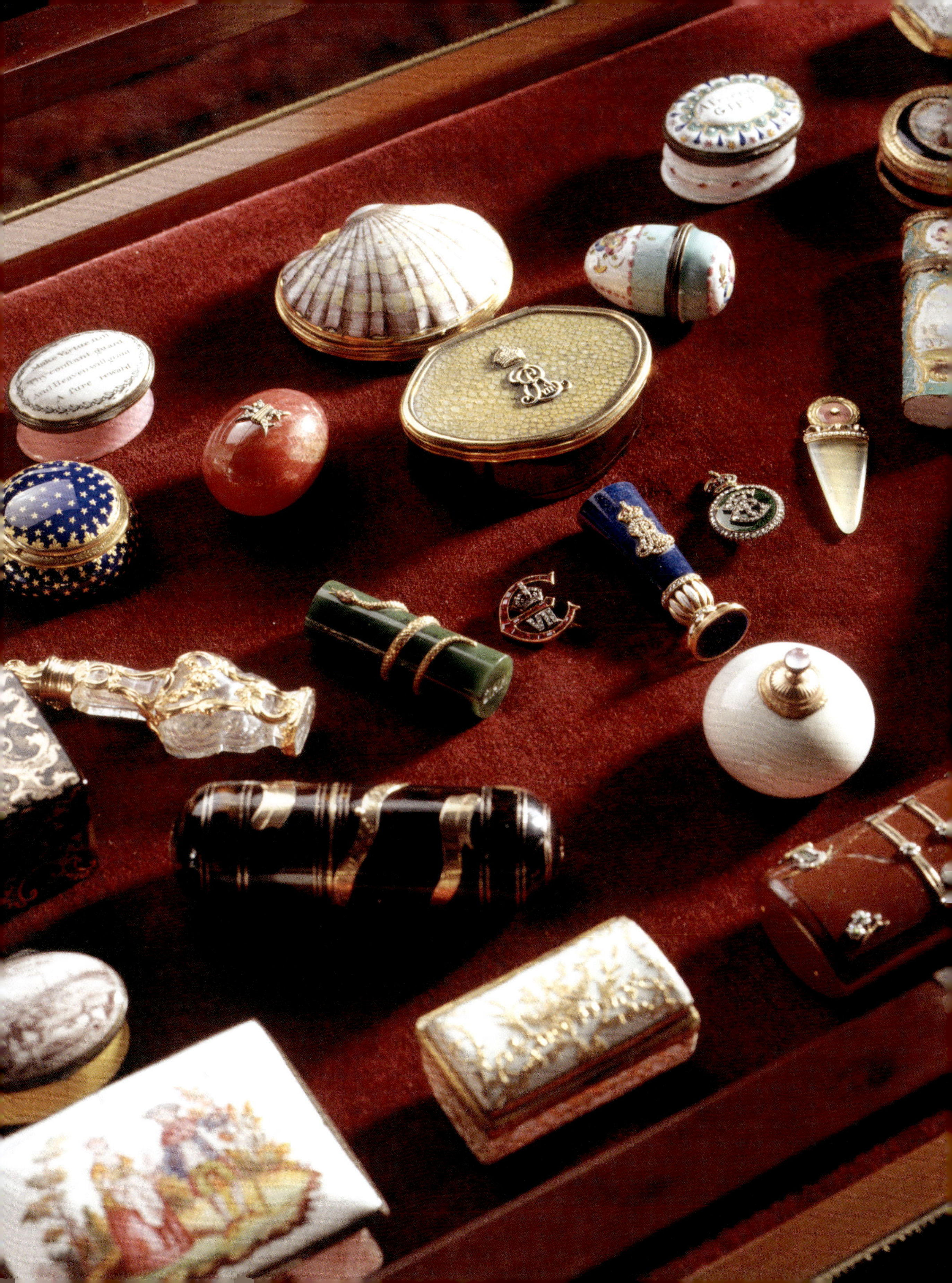
Make Virtue ſtill
Thy conſtant guard
And Heaven will grant
A ſure reward

circulated in the Russian imperial court. By the early twentieth century, the House of Fabergé was Russia's largest jewellery firm employing some 500 craftsmen and designers, with flagship stores in Moscow, Odessa, Kiev and London. At the time that Margaret was aspiring to throw the final word in house parties, it was seen as the ultimate luxury brand. But these weren't ornaments to buy for yourself; these were bought to be given to people, and, once received, were a token of affection to treasure and show off. They were a form of social currency that flowed only in the highest circles. Margaret made purchases at Fabergé's London shop 31 times according to the sales ledgers. Her collection at Polesden Lacey comprises no fewer than 12 exquisite creations firmly attributed to Fabergé, including a jade frog with diamond eyes gifted to her by a Russian Grand Duke.

The egg pictured here, in its original velvet- and satin-lined case, is made from polished rhodonite – a mineral that can range in colour from pink to deep red. The egg opens horizontally and is decorated with a rose-cut diamond clasp in the shape of a snowflake, symbolising winter giving way to spring.

While the egg's donor is unknown, we do know the provenance of the oval tortoiseshell snuff box, pictured opposite. It bears the cypher of King Edward VII in silver, but the absolute giveaway is the handwritten note inside – 'From King Edward 7th June 1909' – the date of Margaret's

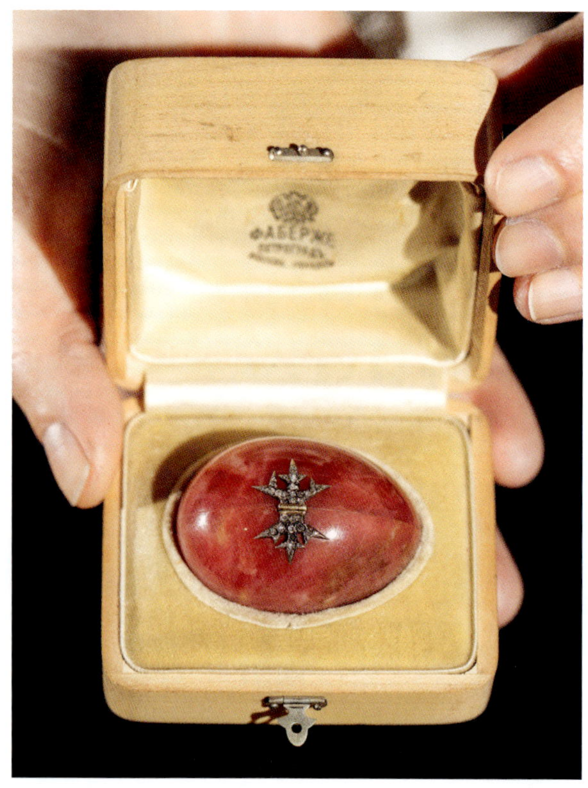

^ This Fabergé egg of rhodonite was made around 1914. Rhodonite can be found in many locations around the world but only in small quantities, making it highly prized.

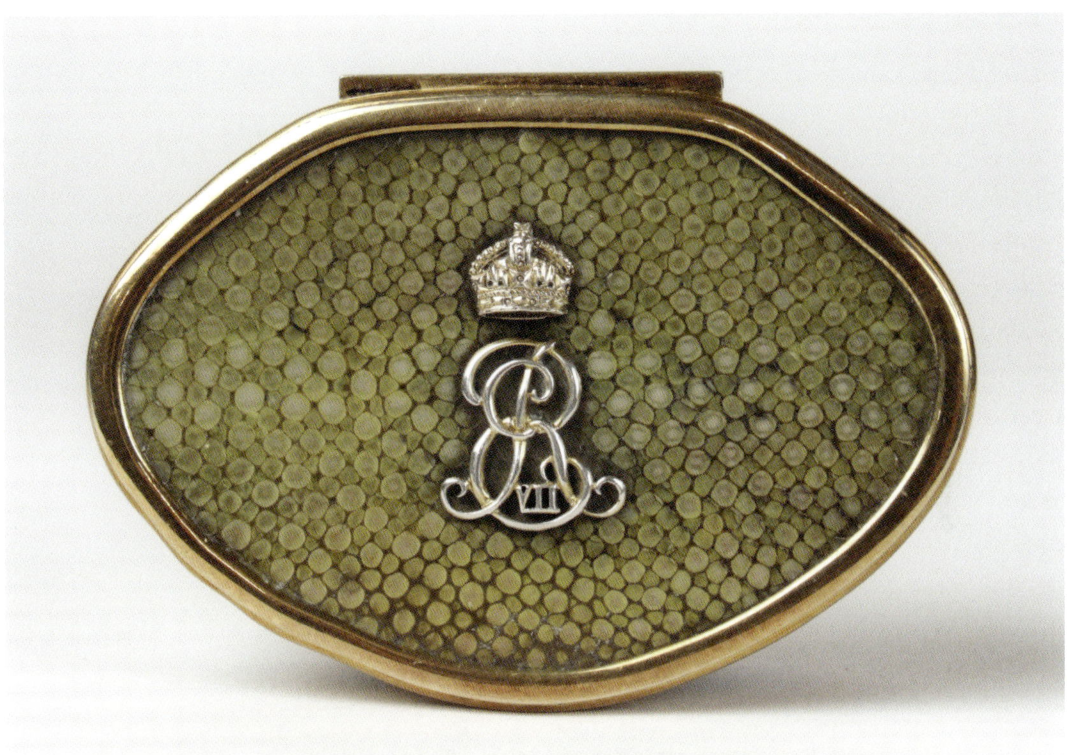

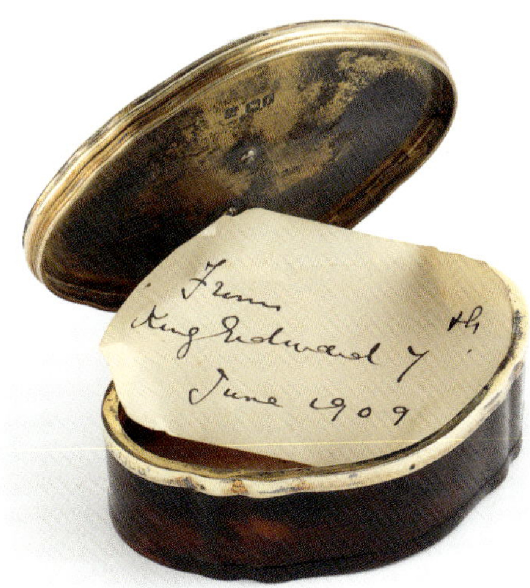

^ A handwritten note from King Edward VII to Margaret Greville.

inaugural house party at Polesden Lacey, at which King Edward VII was its guest of honour.

Margaret also counted Queen Mary, wife of George V who succeeded Edward VII, as a close friend. A blue enamel box with stars and fleurs-de-lys in gold was a gift from Queen Mary, a small trinket but, given by a queen to a brewer's daughter, it was surely a prized possession. For what this extravagance and glitz belie are the origins of the woman who presided over Polesden Lacey and all its treasures. Again, you need to look beyond the ostentation to discover details you might otherwise miss.

Margaret Greville was born Margaret Anderson, though her father was in fact William McEwan, the founder of McEwans beer. The man named as her father on the birth certificate was a brewery employee, who happened to have the same surname as Margaret's mother, Helen Anderson. McEwan directed him to pose as the baby's father when registering the birth, as no one would question that the two were married, thereby saving Helen's reputation.

So, it was a somewhat complicated start to life for Margaret, but wealth, and the influence it brings, can smooth over almost every social wrinkle. William McEwan made a fortune from brewing, but also served as a member of parliament for Edinburgh Central and funded the construction of McEwan Hall at the city's university. He saw to it that his daughter, who became his sole heir after he and her mother finally married when Margaret was 21, received the best education and moved in the highest circles, preparing her for a life of wealth and influence.

In 1891, aged 27, Margaret married Ronald Greville, son of the 2nd Baron Greville. This match was the making of what Polesden Lacey would become, with Margaret as the lavish hostess and Ronald as a member of the Marlborough House set, the social circle around the future King Edward VII.

Margaret purchased Polesden Lacey under her own name, using funds from her father. She had already established herself as a society hostess, but clearly aspired to entertaining on a grander scale. To make all the improvements Margaret wanted, affording her guests every luxury and modern convenience and creating rooms such as the Saloon, took time.

Sadly, Ronald would not get to

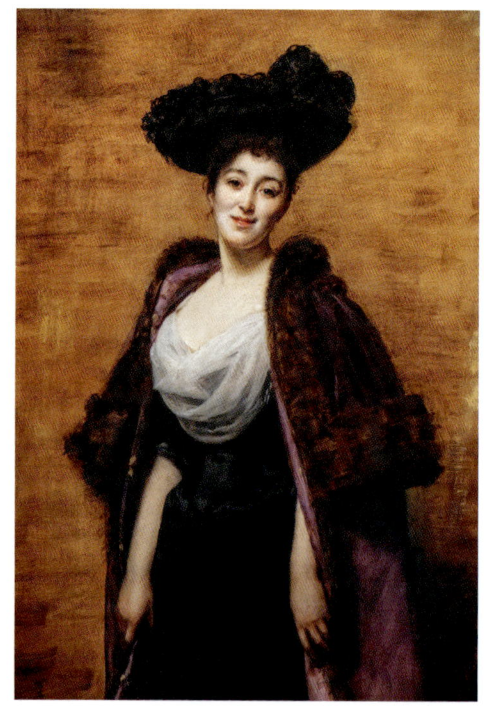

^ Margaret Greville, painted by Émile-Auguste Carolus-Duran.

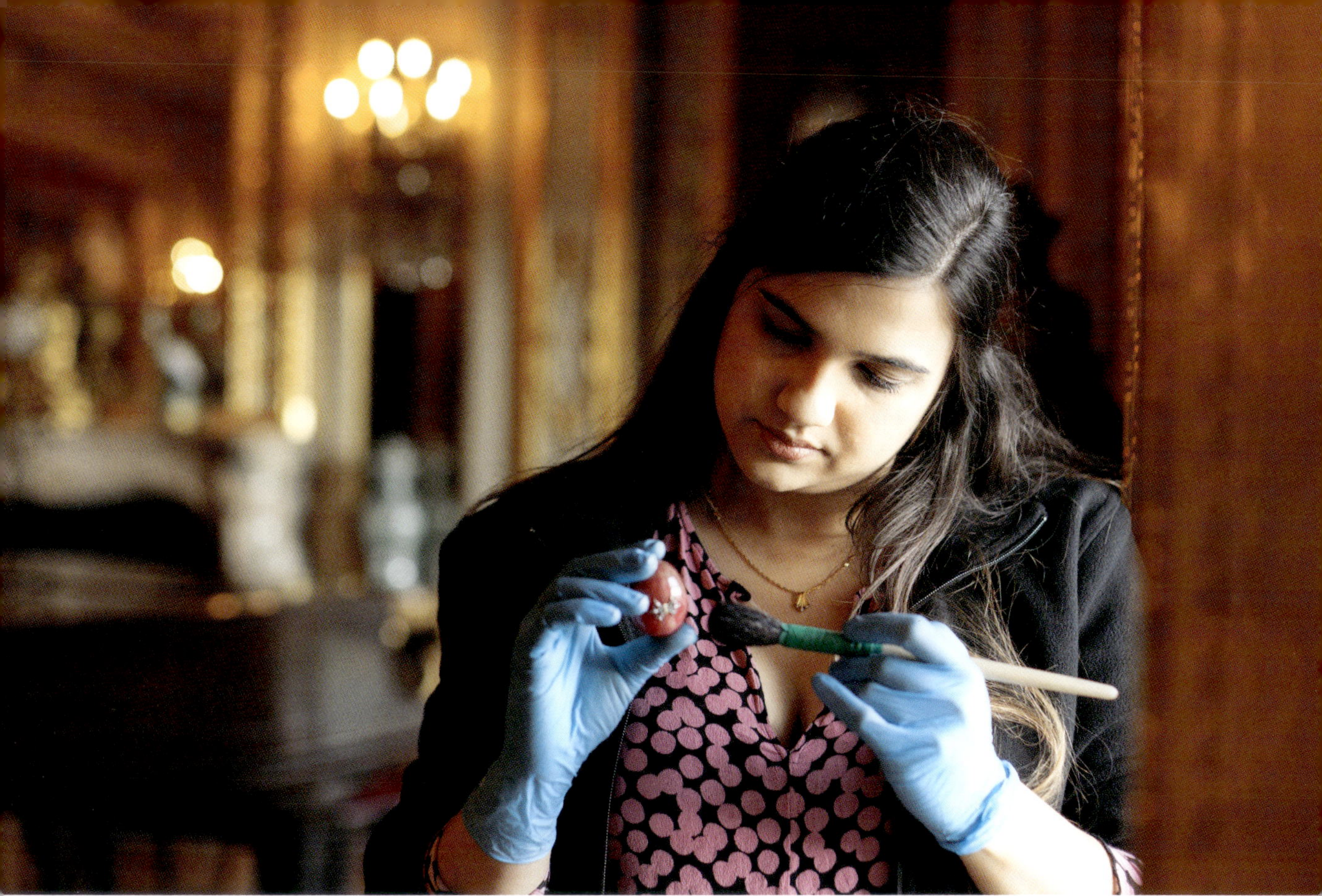

^ Naomi Kulasingham, Collections and House Manager, cleans the rhodonite Fabergé egg, known as a bibelot, from the Old French *beubelet* meaning 'trinket' or 'pretty thing'.

experience any of this, as he died from pneumonia in 1908 aged just 43, the year before the renovations were completed. Margaret never remarried, though she received proposals, perhaps because she was busy focusing on social and political networking, and developing her collections.

Margaret clearly had friends and a great many acquaintances. Opinions on her character varied, but Queen Elizabeth, later the Queen Mother, who inherited the bulk of her jewellery in 1942, described her as 'so shrewd, so kind and so amusingly unkind, so sharp, such fun, so naughty.' What is undeniable is that she was extraordinarily good at what she did, and her gift to the National Trust – in her words 'for the largest number of people to have enjoyment thereof' – suggests a generous host indeed.

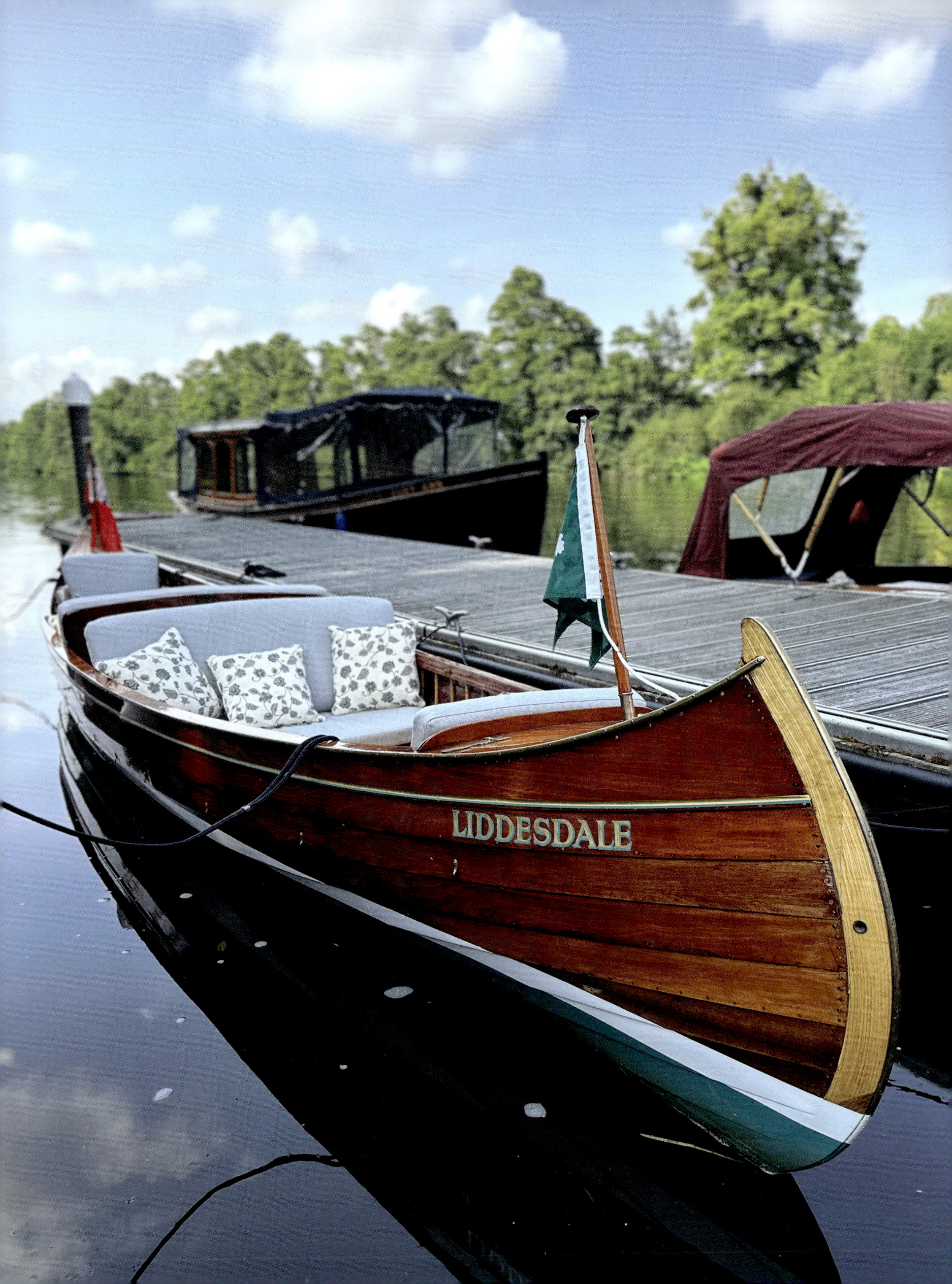
LIDDESDALE

Keeping Lady Astor's Boat Afloat

Liddesdale Electric Canoe

Cliveden, Buckinghamshire

When the Duke of Buckingham built a mansion at Cliveden in the 1660s, it was designed to provide escapism and splendour. Today the house, the third on the site, operates as a luxury hotel, and the gardens and woodlands as one of the National Trust's most popular visitor attractions, so that offer very much continues. If you've breath left after seeing the Italianate entrance front of the house, designed by Charles Barry in 1851, the rest will be taken away when you look out over the Parterre to the River Thames. This has always been a place devoted to pleasure, and down on the river, the well-to-do with little to do but enjoy themselves have whiled away many an hour.

Snippets of 8mm home movie footage dating from the 1920s and 1930s show Cliveden's owners and their friends generally messing about in boats, paddling Canadian canoes and enjoying time aboard *Liddesdale*. This 25-foot (8-metre) electric-powered wooden canoe represented the height of luxury and cost more than a typical house at the time.

Waldorf and Nancy Astor were the last owners of Cliveden, which had been a wedding gift to them from Waldorf's father, William Waldorf Astor, an American millionaire and anglophile. Nancy was an American-born socialite, who in 1919 gained the distinction of being

< This 25-foot (8-metre) electric-powered canoe was commissioned by Nancy Astor and became her favourite among a variety of pleasure craft.

the first woman to sit as an MP in the House of Commons. First visiting England in 1904 with her son from her first marriage, Nancy was a puzzle to some, as she acquired a reputation for having a wicked turn of phrase in conversation. For instance, when she was asked by an English woman, 'Have you come to get our husbands?' her reply was, 'If you knew the trouble I had getting rid of mine!' On the other hand, she was devoutly religious and almost prudish in her behaviour.

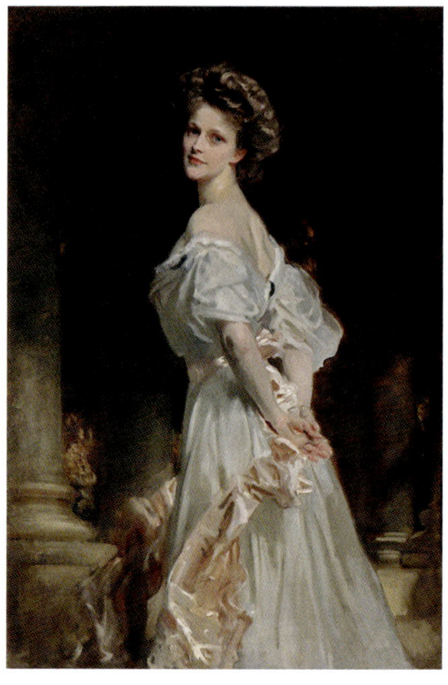

^ Nancy Witcher Langhorne, Viscountess Astor, MP, by John Singer Sargent, RA.

During Waldorf and Nancy Astor's time, Cliveden was a centre of political, literary and artistic society. Nancy set about making Cliveden *the* destination for the wealthy and powerful, and established herself as the consummate hostess, as she entertained guests such as Winston Churchill, Franklin D. Roosevelt, Mahatma Gandhi, George Bernard Shaw, Rudyard Kipling and Charlie Chaplin, to name a few. However, it was not only the rich and famous who were welcomed to Cliveden.

During the Second World War Nancy had a hospital built in the grounds at Cliveden for injured Canadian soldiers. Recuperating men were allowed to enjoy the grounds, including spending time on the river. Also during the war, in 1942, Waldorf and Nancy presented the estate to the National Trust, but kept the house for the duration of their lives. After their son's death in 1966, the Astor family moved out, selling some items in the process, *Liddesdale* among them. However, she remained in the area and in the 1990s – by which time the house was operating as a luxury hotel – she was bought and returned to Cliveden Reach to take hotel guests on trips along the Thames between Cookham and Boulter's Lock.

> The finishing touches are applied to *Liddesdale*, getting her ship-shape before taking to the water once more.

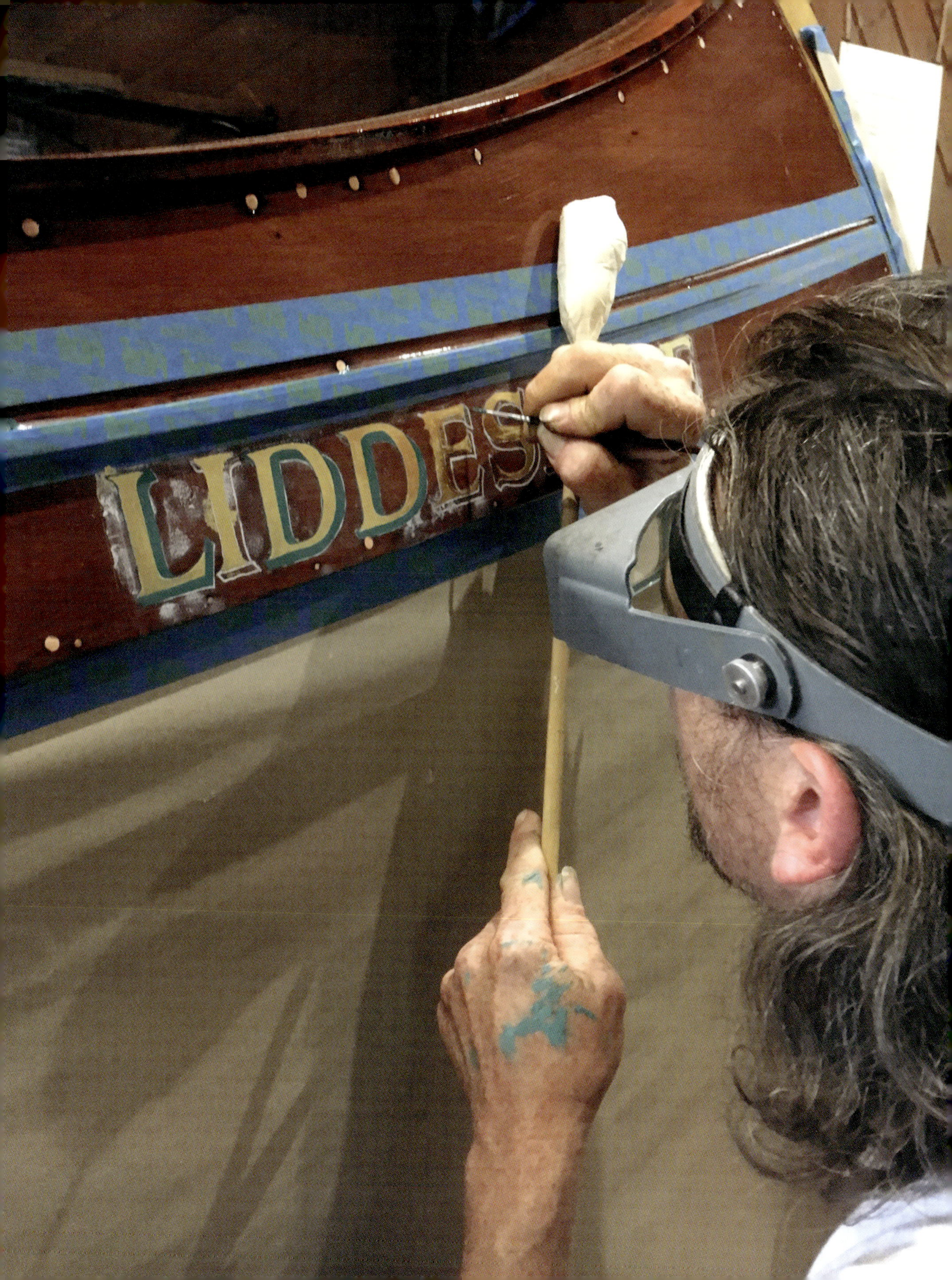
LIDDES

Liddesdale plied the waters below Cliveden for many years, evoking some of the leisure and luxury enjoyed by the Astors and their guests, but she was not wearing well. By 2016, she had fallen into disrepair and was acquired by the National Trust.

As the only electric canoe in the Trust's collection, her restoration was a unique opportunity. John Hartley, formerly one of the National Trust's furniture conservation advisers, is also a specialist in classic boats. He approached the International Boatbuilding Training College at Portsmouth, who introduced him to boatbuilder Seb vanden Bogaerde. After two years of fundraising and research, the restoration could begin, and Seb and his team moved into Cliveden's boathouse and began stripping away the old layers of paint and varnish. While much of the timber from below the waterline was rotten and had to be replaced, all the mahogany above the waterline was original and intact. Paint samples provided evidence of her original colour scheme.

The restoration of *Liddesdale*'s power system also needed its own specialist. In the 1920s, there were over 400 electric boats registered on the Thames, with 36 charging points between Teddington and Lechlade. One of the legacies of this popularity is the Thames Electric Launch Company. The canoe is a rare survivor, but the knowledge and skills behind the

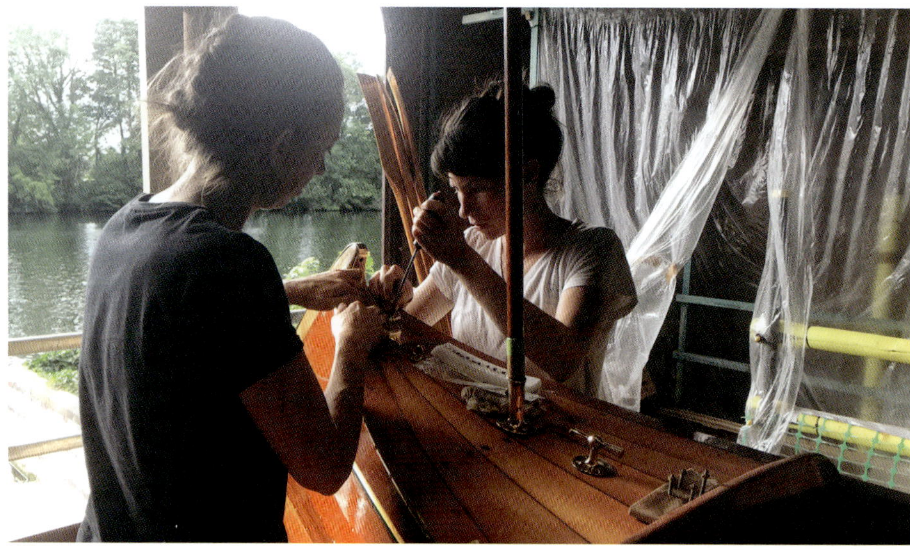

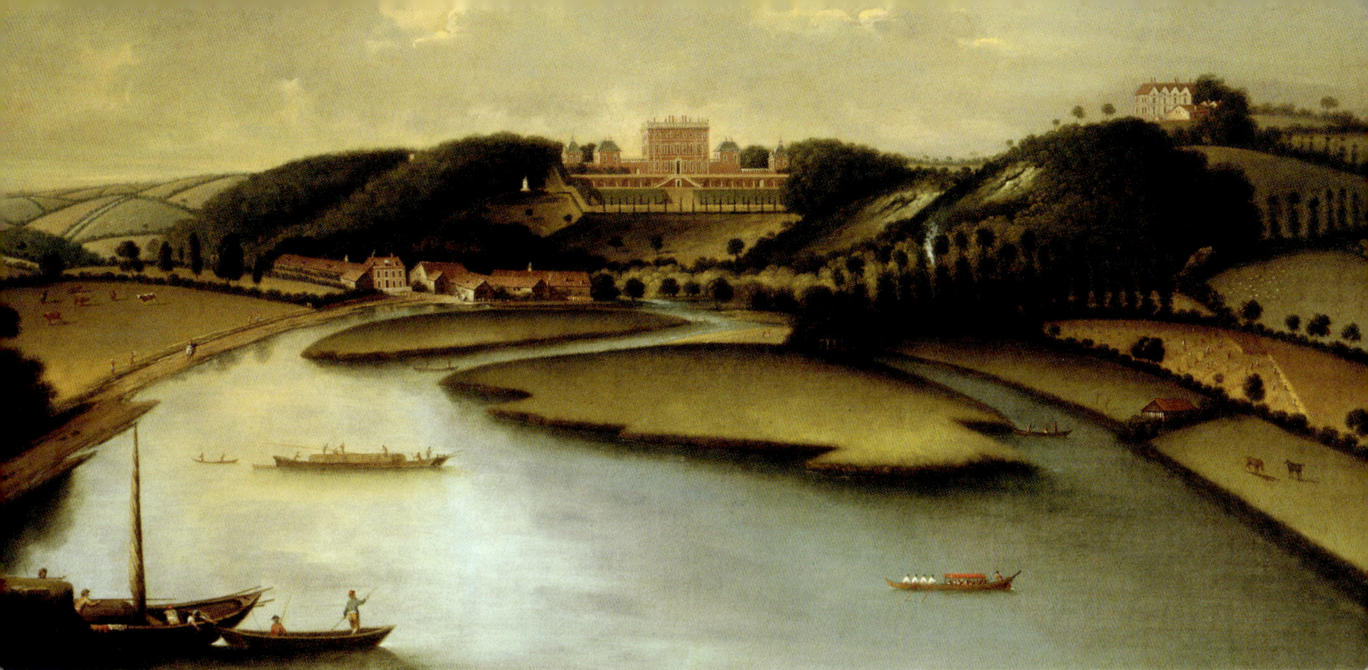

restoration continue to be passed on. Emrhys Barrell, Managing Director, explained why the boats were once so popular: 'Electric power in pleasure boats dates back to the early 1880s as an alternative to steam engines, which had a habit of splattering a lady's finery in soot. The technology leapfrogged early petrol engines, which could never be relied on to start. By contrast, electric boats were clean, quiet and even in those days could run for six hours or more on one charge.'

The people who enjoyed cruising along the river in electric vessels did so in comparative tranquillity, without having to raise their voices over the sound of a steam or petrol engine. It's strange to think that a form of transport that was so popular a century ago was so much cleaner and greener than what replaced it. *Liddesdale*'s restoration is timely not only in terms of her own continued survival but also as an example of a sustainable way of powering us over our waterways.

Liddesdale is relaunched every spring, plying the stretch of water below Cliveden, much to the enjoyment of the pleasure seekers who continue to come here.

< Becci Haigh and Laura Christie, part of Seb vanden Bogaerde's boat-building team, refitting *Liddesdale*'s original bronzework.

^ An eighteenth-century view of Cliveden from the Thames, attributed to William Tomkins.

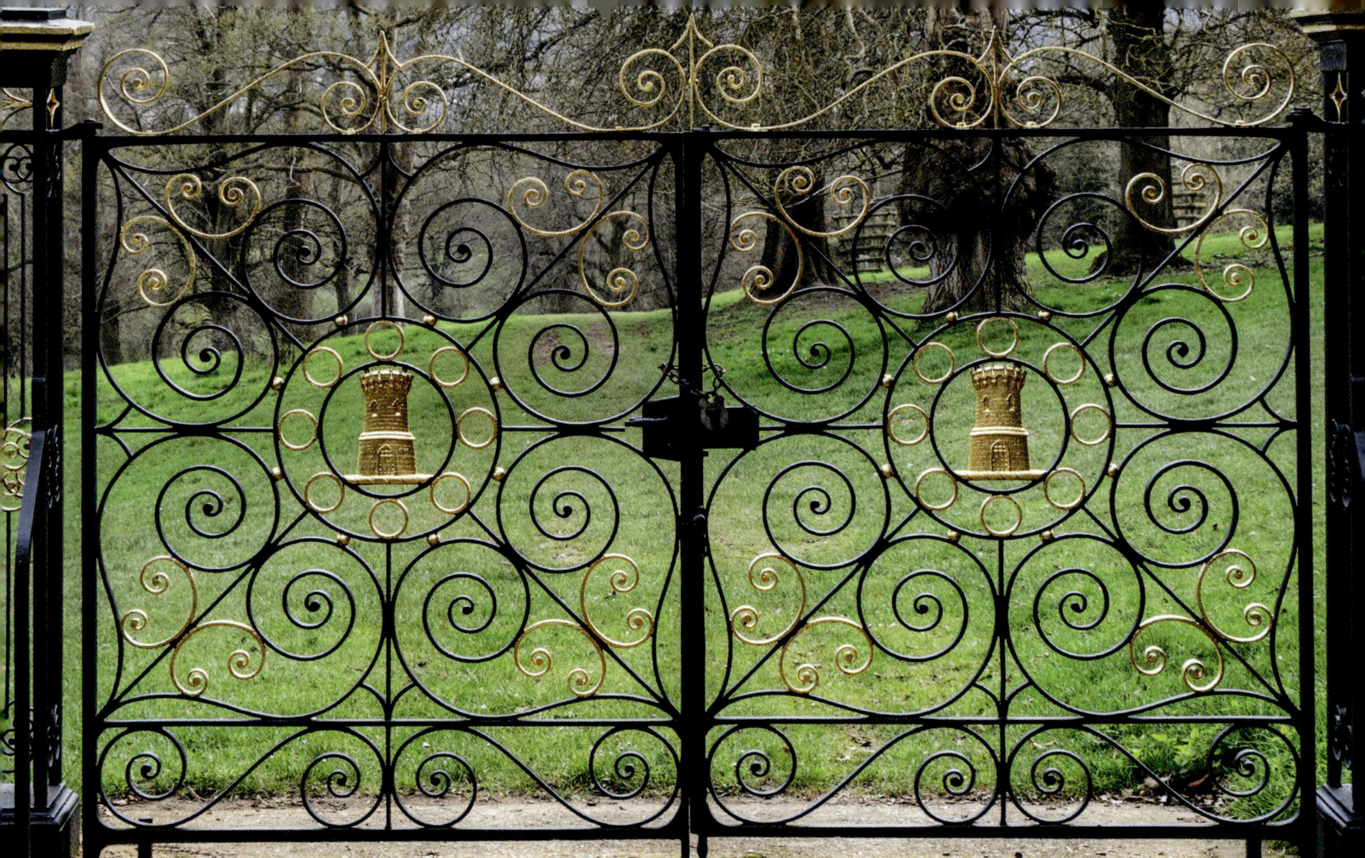

Making an Entrance

Benjamin Disraeli's Castle Gates

Hughenden, Buckinghamshire

A little over 10 miles (16 kilometres) north of Cliveden is another political stage set. Benjamin Disraeli bought Hughenden when he was 43 years old and a backbench Conservative politician. Disraeli served Queen Victoria, so a good few years before Nancy Astor entered parliament in 1919, but he and Nancy had something in common – they both entered English politics as outsiders. Nancy was an American who came from new money; Disraeli was born Jewish and into the middle classes. Nancy made her mark by dazzling and devastating her opponents in turn with her charming personality and forceful nature; Disraeli perceived that cultivating the correct image was essential to political advancement, or climbing 'to the top of the greasy pole' as he put it.

Take his purchase of Hughenden. To achieve this, Disraeli had to borrow the equivalent of £3.5 million in today's money. But he knew that if he wanted to advance in the Conservative Party, a country house and a county constituency were considered essential. Thankfully, his acquisition paid off. In the 1847 general election, he stood, successfully, for the Buckinghamshire constituency. The following year he completed the purchase of Hughenden. He had set the scene for his political ambitions beautifully. In his grand country manor, he couldn't be taken for anyone other than a leader in waiting.

< The gates Benjamin Disraeli had commissioned to announce his status to all who entered, now restored once more.

∨ Benjamin Disraeli, painted by Sir Francis Grant PRA in 1852 when Disraeli became Chancellor of the Exchequer.

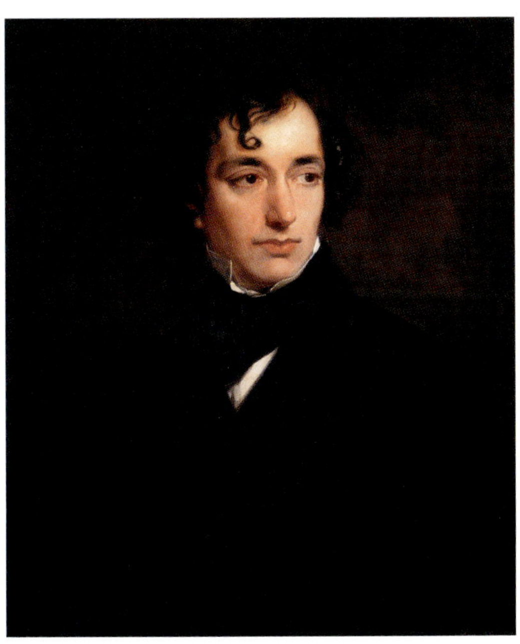

In 1852, he served as Leader of the House and as Chancellor of the Exchequer. His main impediment to power was Edward Smith-Stanley, Earl of Derby, who was (and remains) the longest-serving leader of the Conservative Party. It took a particularly nasty bout of gout to force his retirement, allowing Disraeli his first, albeit brief, tenure as Prime Minister in 1868. Queen Victoria, whom by then Disraeli counted as a friend, wrote to her daughter: 'Mr. Disraeli is Prime Minister! A proud thing for a man "risen from the people" to have obtained!' He had to wait another five years for his second, but this time full, term as Prime Minister.

Disraeli had begun his political career as an outsider and had ascended as far as it was possible to go. He had created a powerful political persona, which is proudly on display at Hughenden. Not so long ago, however, there was a forgotten corner of Hughenden that was of great importance to Disraeli and that, like the man himself, had to bide its time before resuming centre stage.

Standing in the place that once served as the main entrance to Hughenden are two stately piers, between which hang wrought-iron gates bearing symbols that were deeply meaningful to Disraeli, but which, by the early 2020s, were showing signs of age. When the entrance to Hughenden was relocated in the twentieth century, these gates fell out of use. Over time, the layers of paint that had been applied, obscuring the Victorian scheme, started to flake, exposing the iron beneath to the elements.

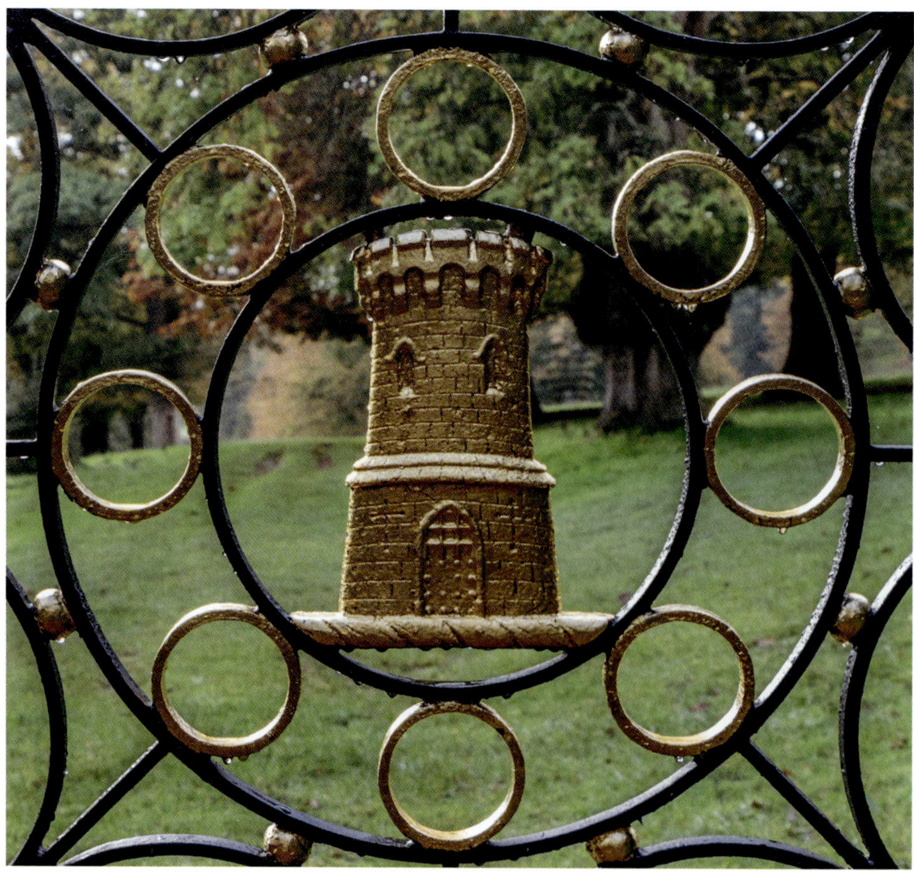

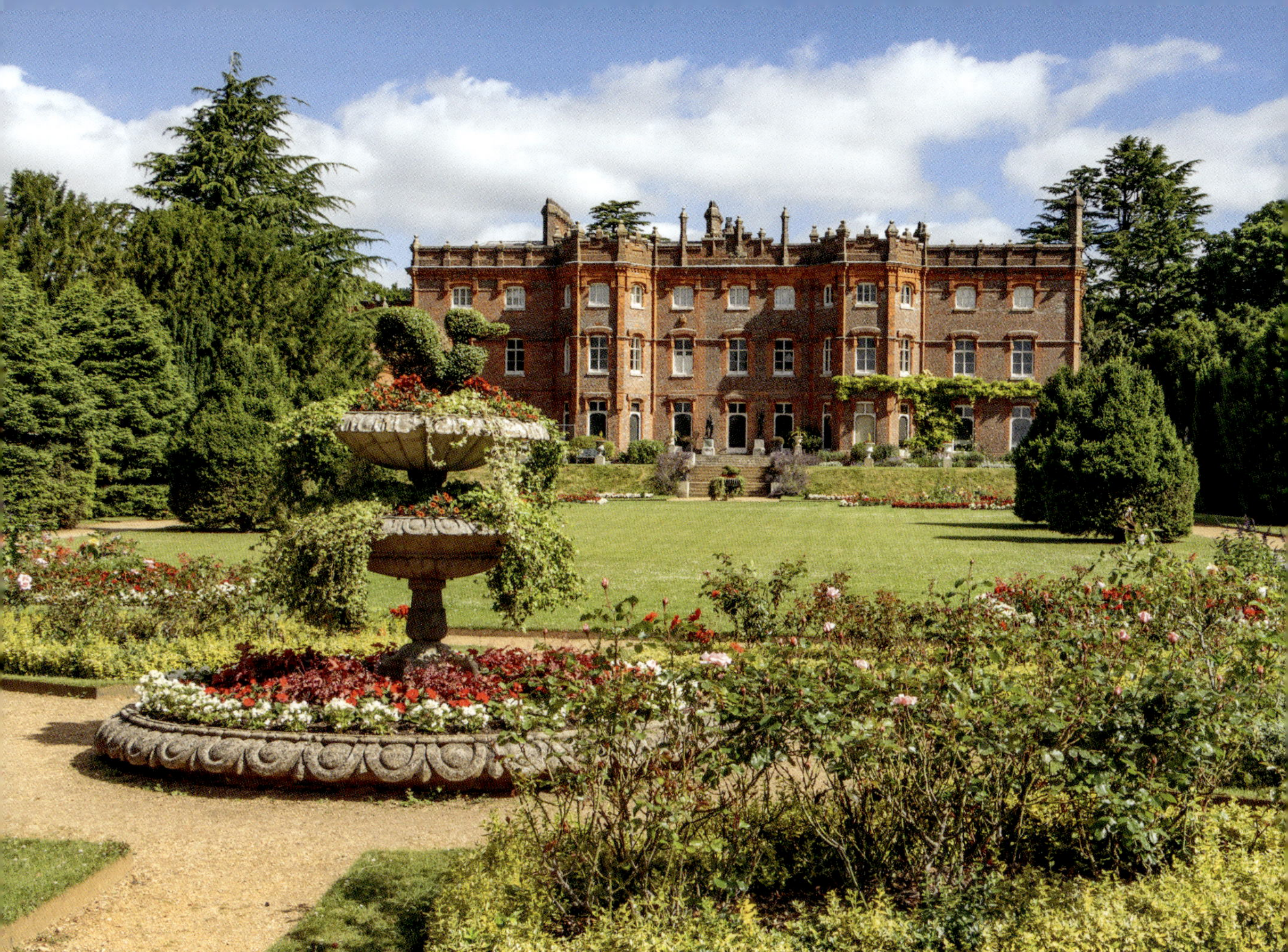

The central motif of the gates, the castle, is taken from the coat of arms that Disraeli created for himself, again to support the idea of him as a member of the land-owning establishment. As Rob Bandy, Collections and House Manager, explained: 'He was very particular with this way of accessing the property. It was like a grand reveal just at the last minute, and that's what he liked. This motif is the castle element from the top of his coat of arms. A little subtle nod to the aristocratic Spanish/Jewish lineage that he told everyone that he came from.' Given the visual impact the gates would once have had and their intended significance, restoration was about much more than making good.

< The gates' castle motif was from a coat of arms Disraeli himself devised.

^ Hughenden was vitally important in consolidating the political persona Disraeli sought to portray.

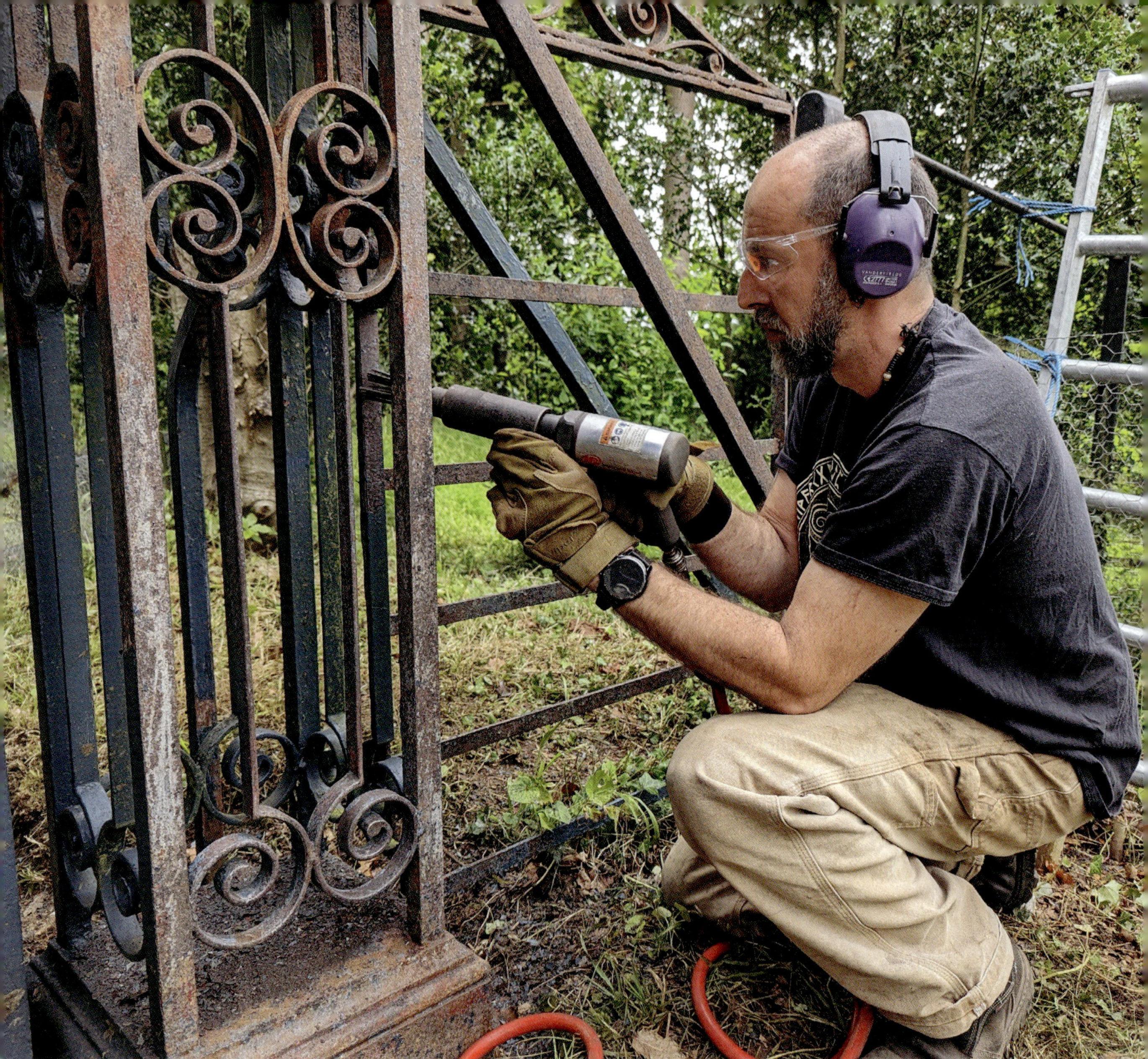

^ Blacksmith David Gregory debriding decades of corrosion and flaking paint before restoring the gates to their original splendour.

The task of their restoration fell to blacksmiths David Gregory and Matt Spinks. The traditional image of a blacksmith is someone in a forge, red-faced and sweating, while they beat things into shape with a hammer, but when metal has been left to the mercy of the elements for over a century, it needs far more careful treatment. A blacksmith will employ as much attention to detail and problem-solving in a restoration project as any other craftsperson. As David said: 'I'm a practical person. I love making things. I like taking broken things and repairing them. And it stands a good chance to outlast anyone who's ever heard of me.'

David and Matt's first job was to remove the more recent paintwork while trying to retain whatever original Victorian paint they could. As they began to clean the worst-affected areas, it became clear that the gates were in a more precarious state than first thought. They were receiving the attention they needed in the nick of time, but difficult decisions still had to be made. As David put it: 'In metalwork, the trick is knowing when to stop and take stock of where you're at. We often have this trade-off between preserving the original historic ironwork and making it functional. The paint is failing now. And it's causing corrosion. If the rust doesn't have the ability to just fall off, it piles up and it causes quite a bit of damage. On these gates, this is clearly happening.'

The central motif of the gates, the castle, is taken from the coat of arms that Disraeli created for himself, to support the idea of him as a member of the land-owning establishment.

After repeated rounds of careful brushing, filing and cleaning, the Victorian paintwork, long hidden from view, was uncovered. It was colour-matched and the gates and piers were restored to their original scheme and weather-proofed once more. The final task was to gild the gates, to give them the dazzle Disraeli would have known. Guided by a black-and-white photograph from the 1930s, and references in account books from the 1860s, David carefully applied 24-carat sheets of gold leaf to certain sections and to the central castle motifs.

The result is truly a transformation, from a somewhat forgotten and forlorn corner to a gateway proudly proclaiming that a man of great significance once lived here. Disraeli was so careful to manufacture and maintain his image that it is only fitting that the National Trust continues to uphold those standards at Hughenden.

Skills and Techniques
Heritage and Rural Skills

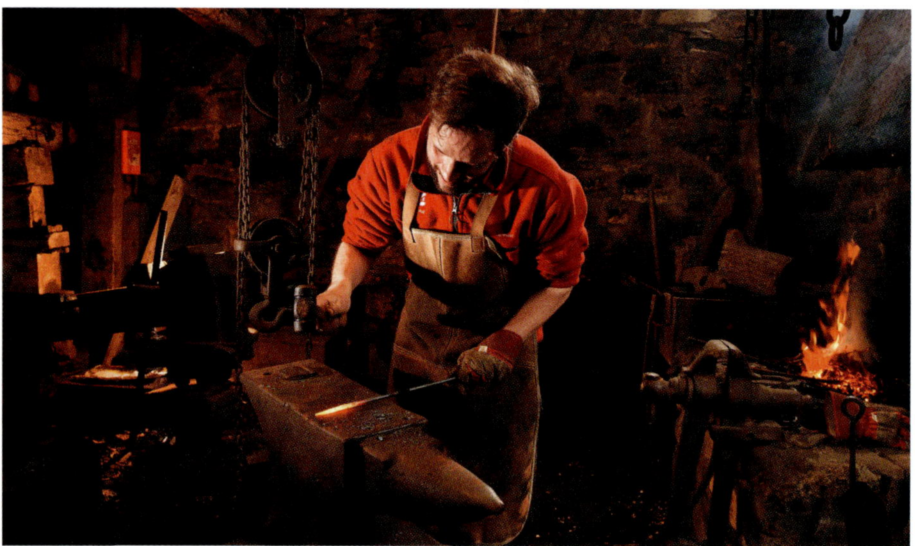

The number and variety of objects looked after by the National Trust is difficult to fathom. These objects are fascinating for what they tell us about their former owners, but can pose a challenge when they're in need of repair. Fortunately, the National Trust has a repository of expertise and knowledge equal to that challenge and has taken deliberate measures to ensure the preservation of skills that might otherwise have been lost.

Across the UK, traditional building techniques and rural crafts are in decline – the very skills that ensure the survival of the buildings and collections looked after by the National Trust. It's estimated that around 25 per cent of the country's building stock predates the First World War, and therefore requires traditional building techniques to maintain it.

The National Trust's Buscot and Coleshill Estates in Oxfordshire comprise over a thousand buildings and structures – cottages, a pub, a village hall, churches and tea rooms – of traditional construction. Most of these were built before the nineteenth century and some, such as Coleshill's twelfth-century church, are ancient. In 2017, Christian Walker, the general manager of the two estates, needed repairs to be made to a historic roof but, being unable to find the relevant skills locally, had to import specialist lead workers from Europe. This identified both a problem and an opportunity, so six years later the National Trust opened the Heritage and Rural Skills Centre in Coleshill, providing a learning hub where these traditional crafts can be learned, practised and passed on.

Here experienced craftspeople teach construction and crafting methods to professionals and amateurs alike. Some of these techniques have remained unchanged for generations, whereas others have been adapted, employing new, more sustainable materials that offer better efficiency and longevity, and have generally reduced environmental impact. Keeping these skills alive ensures the preservation of a part of our history, but the idea here is not to be backward-looking and nostalgic. Innovation can also play a part in how we safeguard cultural and artistic legacies for future generations.

The villages of Buscot and Coleshill and the surrounding patchwork of fields occupy an extremely picturesque part of the country and are strongly evocative of bygone traditions and ways of working. But the connection is more than scenic, as the villages in this area were for a while the centre of the Arts and Crafts movement in the second half of the nineteenth century. The honey-hued buildings of the Cotswolds were a far cry from the soot and the grime of the rapidly industrialising cities, and communities of craftspeople answered that cry.

In Buscot church you'll find stained glass designed by William Morris, a leading figure in the movement, who lived nearby at Kelmscott Manor in Oxfordshire. So it's a bit of a coup to be able to learn how to make stained glass not only using techniques that would have been familiar to William Morris, but also in buildings he would have known.

In addition to stained-glass making, there are regular courses in blacksmithing, willow weaving, wood carving, knife making, glass painting, block printing and lime plastering. There are certainly skills enough to keep the Buscot and Coleshill Estates looking their best and, once learned, those skills can travel far and wide, keeping age-old traditions alive.

< At Finch Foundry, Devon – the last working water-powered forge in England – you'll find a complex of ancient buildings and machinery but also a place where a suite of heritage skills is preserved.

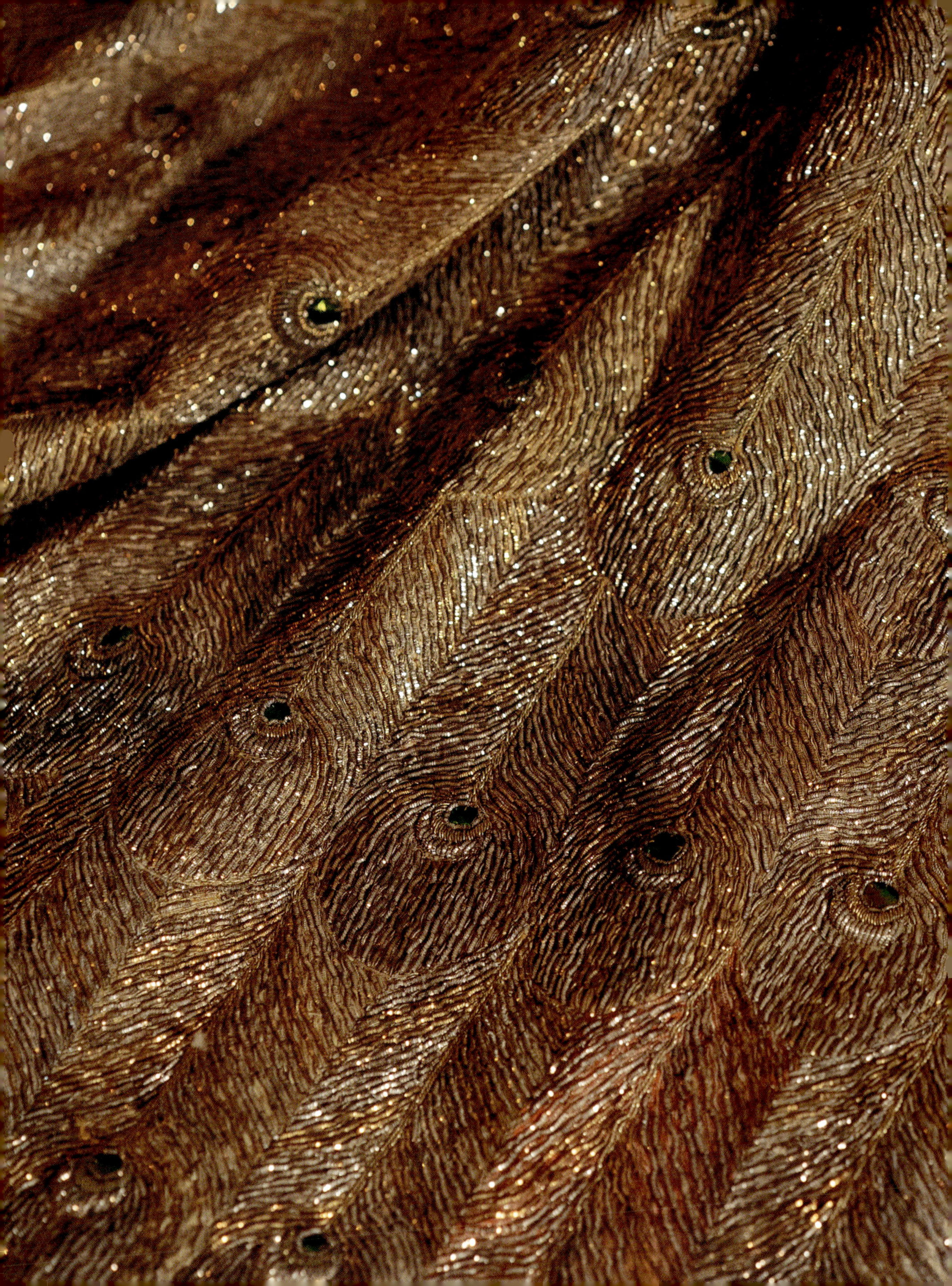

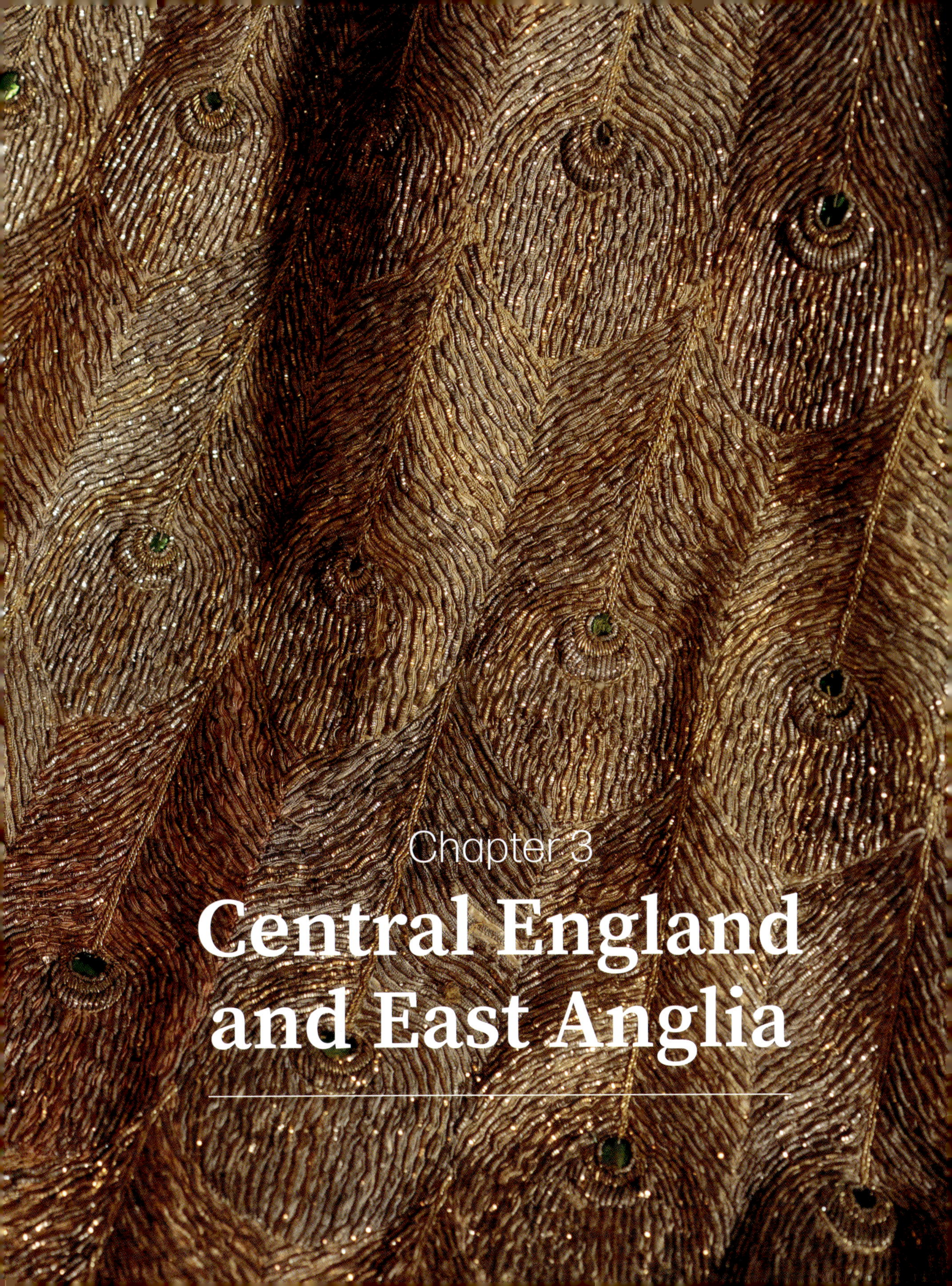

Chapter 3

Central England and East Anglia

Getting Up Close to a Tintoretto

The Wise and Foolish Virgins

Upton House, Warwickshire

Upton House does harbour some secrets. They are not especially closely guarded secrets, and National Trust staff and volunteers at the house would be only too happy if they were more widely known.

Upton is a fine country house and boasts a beautiful garden. Certainly, both reward a visit, but time and time again visitors are surprised to find that Upton is home to one of the finest art collections in the country. Alongside Old Masters, there are paintings by George Stubbs, Hieronymus Bosch, El Greco and Canaletto, to name but a few.

This collection was assembled by Walter Samuel, 2nd Viscount Bearsted, son of the founder of the Shell Transport and Trading Company. Walter worked for the family business and served as the company's chairman from 1921–46, these years mostly coinciding with his ownership of Upton House. When his father died in 1927, Walter became Lord Bearsted and in the same year bought Upton to be used as a weekend retreat for leisure and entertaining. Over 21 years he adapted the house, creating a series of galleries to showcase his collection, which he left to the National Trust in 1948.

Lord Bearsted also served as chairman of the board of trustees for the National Gallery, a trustee at the Tate and chairman of the Whitechapel

> Conservation and scientific analysis revealed intriguing secrets about changes made to the painting.

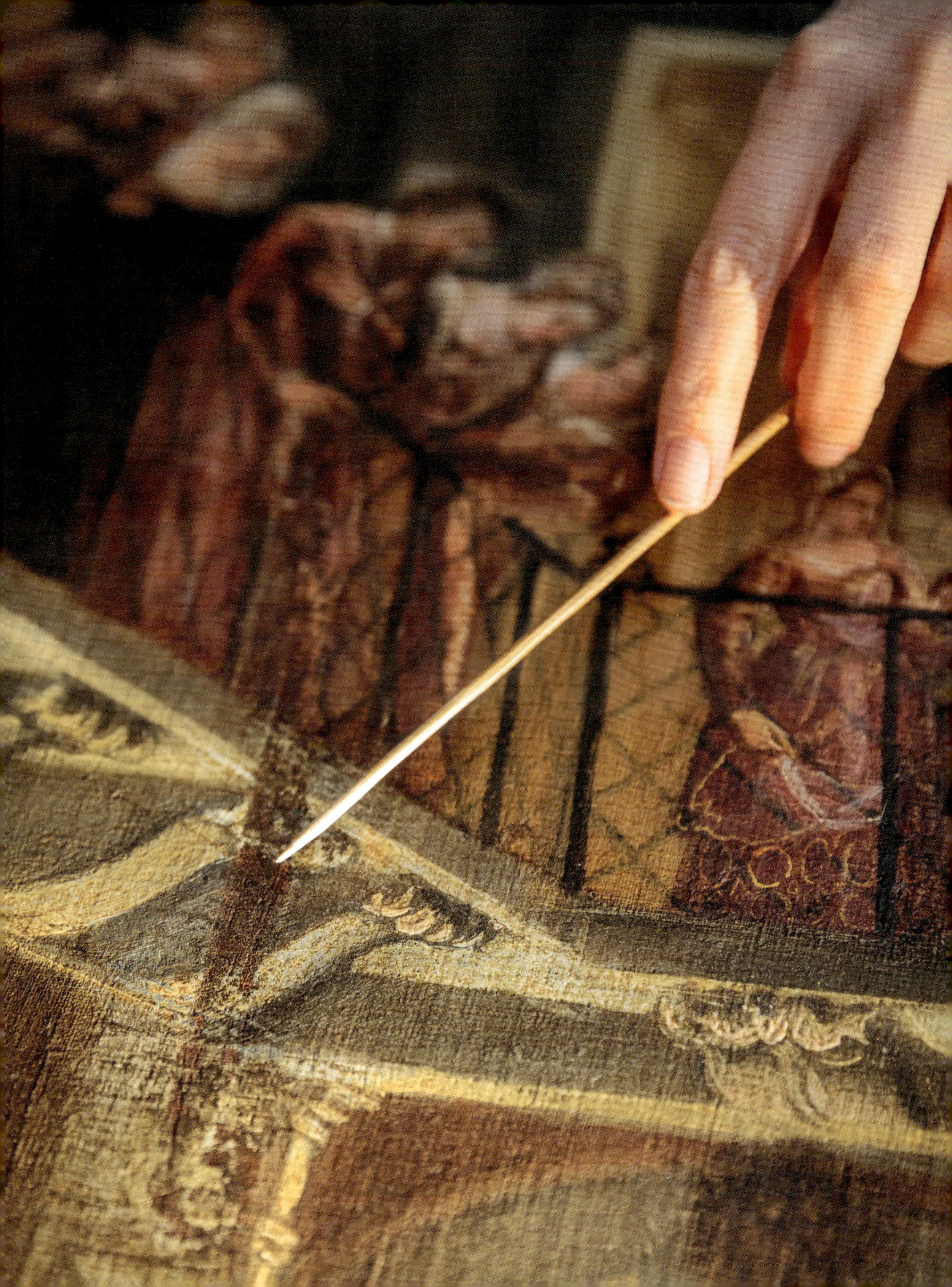

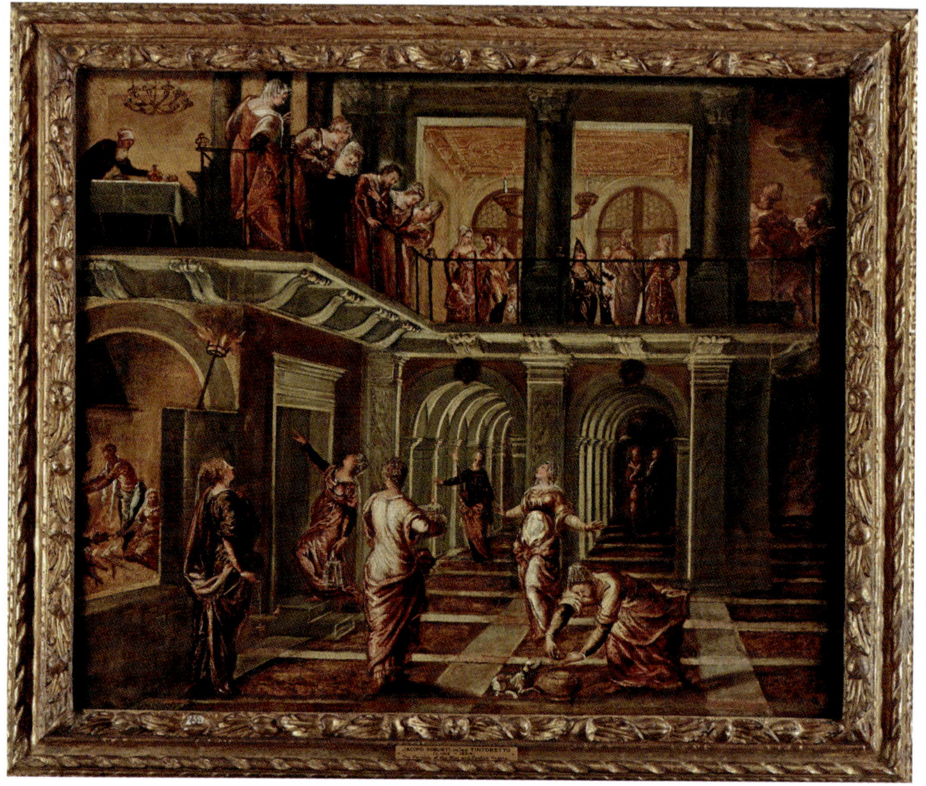

^ *The Wise and Foolish Virgins* was painted by Jacopo Tintoretto in c. 1546.

Gallery. His knowledge of art, along with the contacts he made in the art world, helped him amass his personal collection.

When *The Wise and Foolish Virgins* by Tintoretto came on the market in 1939, Lord Bearsted was advised to buy it by Horace Buttery, a picture dealer and restorer. Buttery wrote that '... experts on Venetian painting have all been enthusiastic about this picture – a recent discovery of mine – as an important unrecorded early period work. The picture is beautiful in colour – rosepink, grey and gold – and the subject is amusingly treated.'

Lord Bearsted followed Buttery's advice and bought the Tintoretto, which he hung in a prominent position in the picture gallery he'd recently had converted from a squash court. Over time the image began to darken, the painting's colour and depth having become compromised by layers of discoloured varnish. Visitors would walk past without even noticing it.

Given Tintoretto is especially known for a richness of palette – and that is what caught Buttery's eye – for one of his works to go unnoticed in this way would not do, and so in 2022 it was sent away for conservation.

Tintoretto's real name was Jacopo Robusti, but he gained the nickname on account of being the son of a dyer, or *tintore*, making him 'little dyer'. His childhood being imbued with colour, it is little wonder he grew into a painter who was confident and skilled in using a diverse palette. Furthermore, being a Venetian painter active in the sixteenth century, Tintoretto had access to a particularly wide range of quality pigments. This was because, at the time, Venice was a very important centre of trade, and its links across Europe, Asia and the Middle East meant that pigments were available that were not easily accessible to painters elsewhere.

Some of this rich palette was still present in Upton's Tintoretto, but under layers of discoloured varnish and later restorers' overpainting. At the Royal Oak Foundation Conservation Studio at Knole in Kent, these were carefully removed to give a truer sense of the painting's original colours and improve its perspectival depth.

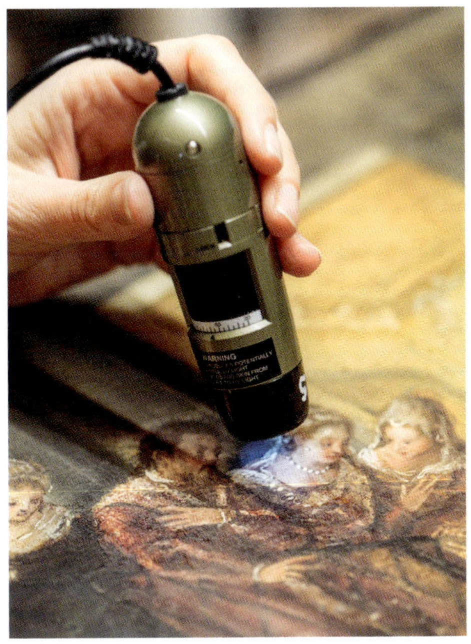

^ Scientific and technical analysis allows conservators to see elements invisible to the naked eye.

As Buttery observed, this was an early work by Tintoretto, thought to have been painted around 1546. Tintoretto revisited the parable of the wise and foolish virgins and another version of the painting thought to be from around the same date exists in the Museum Boijmans Van Beuningen in Rotterdam. This was naturally an invaluable reference to the conservators working on Upton's Tintoretto, but it also aided some intriguing discoveries.

In the Rotterdam version, Tintoretto included scrolls with writing on them, which act like speech bubbles. Before conservation cleaning, no such scrolls were obvious in the Upton version and it also has a wrought-iron balcony whereas the Rotterdam version's balcony is of stone. When conservation scientists X-rayed the Upton Tintoretto, the subsequent image showed two dark lines that corresponded to the position of the scrolls in the Rotterdam version. After cleaning and the removal of later restoration overpaint from these areas, it became apparent to the naked eye that two scrolls had indeed at some point been scraped out of the painting.

It wasn't possible to say for sure whether this was done by Tintoretto or at a later date, perhaps by a dealer who thought the piece would be easier to sell without them. Doctoring a Tintoretto seems scandalous to us, but it is the likelier scenario as an artist such as Tintoretto wouldn't have left the change visible. This presented conservators with a dilemma. Do they paint the scrolls in, as this is likely how Tintoretto intended the painting to look? Do they retouch the areas to make all evidence of the scrolls and their removal disappear, which is how Lord Bearsted would have understood the painting? Or do they leave gaps where the scrolls once were, which accurately shows the history of the painting but mars its appearance?

The decision was taken to retouch the painting as if the scrolls had never been there, as to paint them in would have been a major compositional intervention and it's not known with certainty that Tintoretto didn't remove them himself. Influencing that decision was evidence uncovered by X-ray that Tintoretto did indeed change his mind about the painting's composition: in an early sketching the balcony appears to be of stone, similar to that in the Rotterdam version.

Scientific analysis has revealed layers within the painting previously invisible to the human eye. While this has presented conservators with difficult decisions to make, they can base them on more evidence than has ever been previously available and this has helped restore the work to a version both Tintoretto and Lord Bearsted would have recognised.

> Paintings conservator Sarah Maisey has the responsibility and privilege of conserving a work by one of the great Italian Renaissance painters.

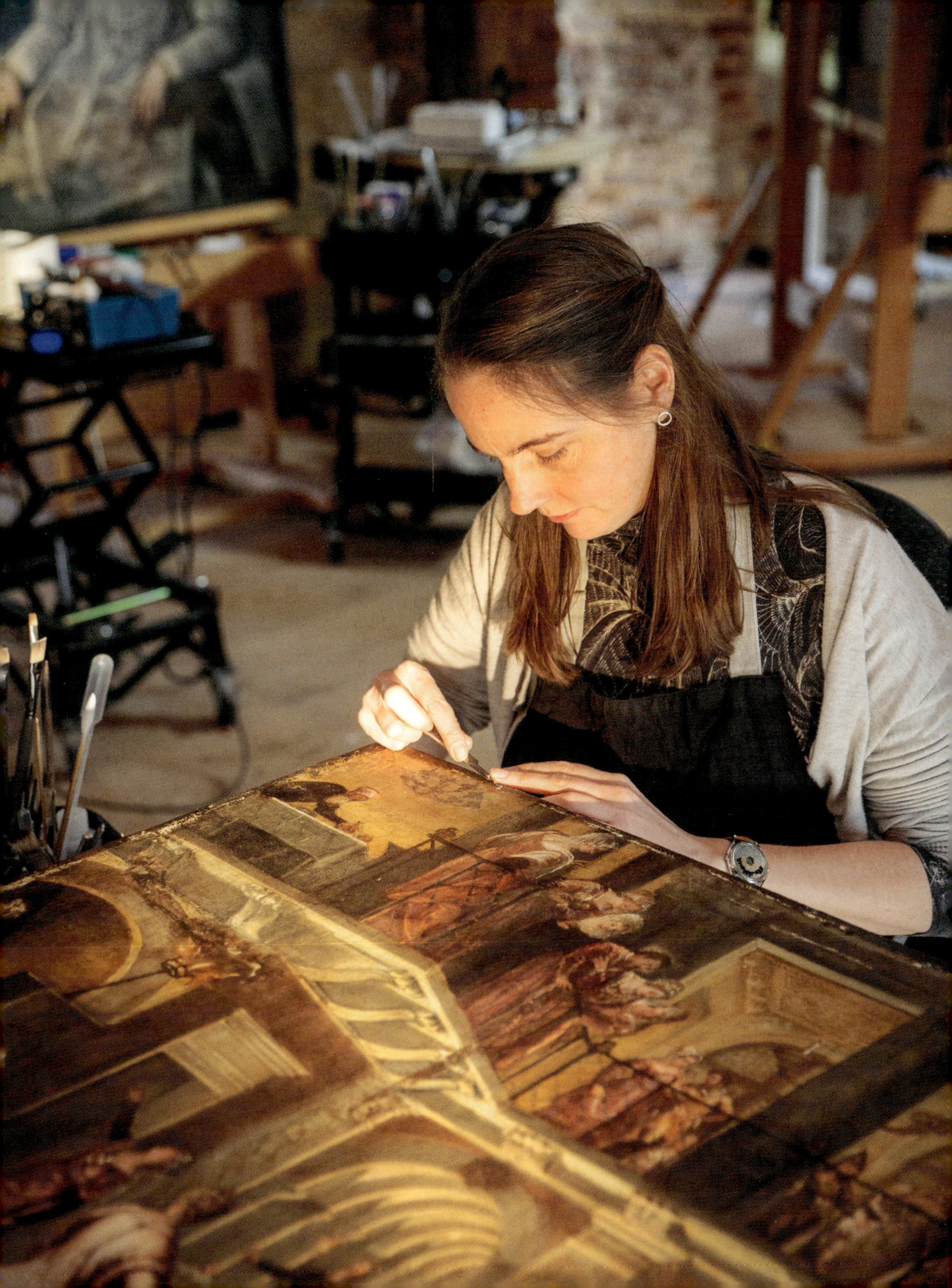

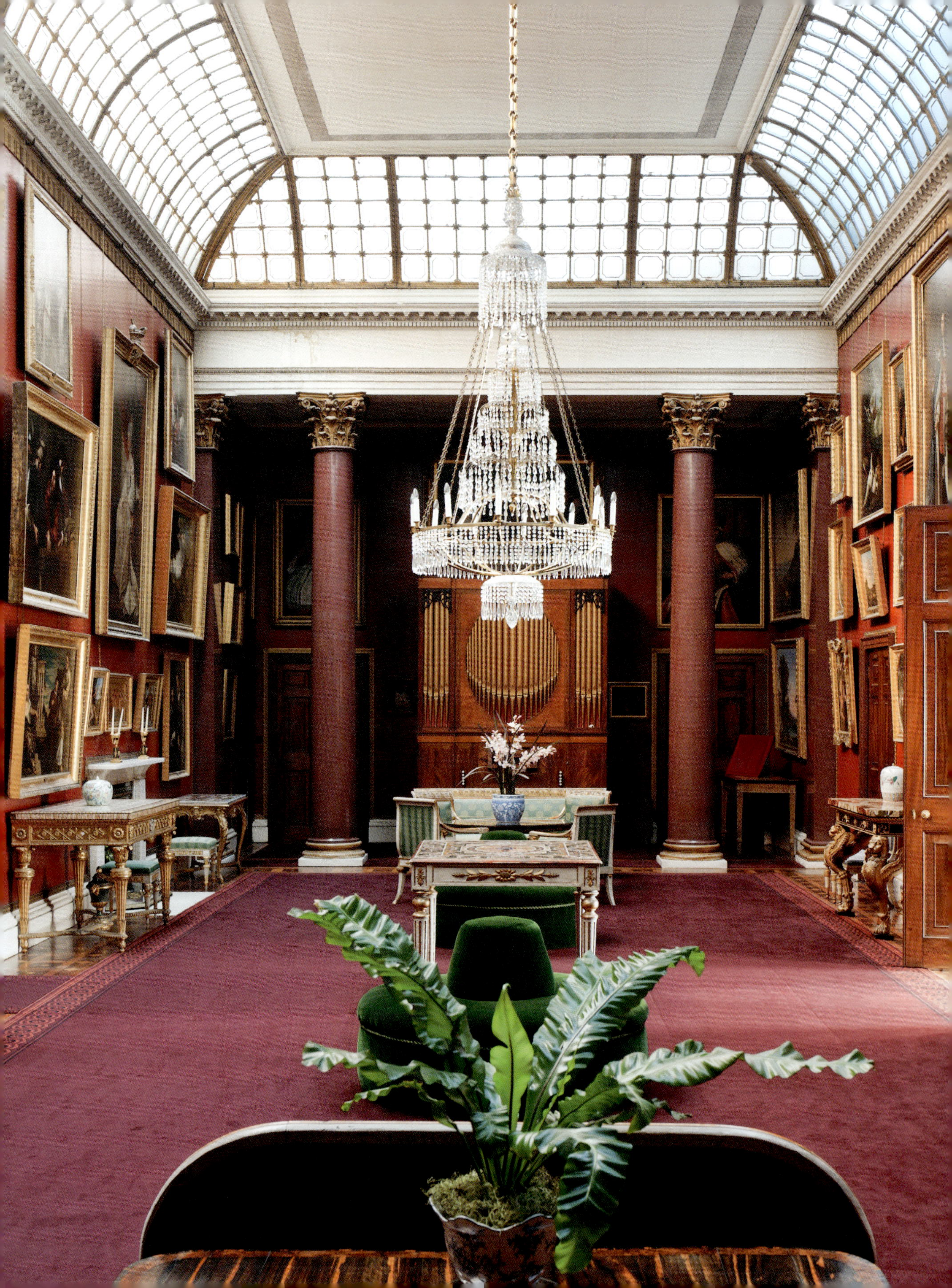

Raising the Roof

Picture Gallery

Attingham Park, Shropshire

Attingham Park was built towards the end of the eighteenth century for Noel Hill, 1st Baron Berwick. It's in the Neo-classical style, exemplified by the soaring columns on its entrance front that broadcast wealth and taste, like architectural exclamation marks. Some have criticised its proportions, however, finding the façade too tall or the columns too thin. Elsewhere in the mansion, architectural ambitions were stretched to their limits, resulting in something just as spectacular but flawed.

Thomas, 2nd Lord Berwick, came into his inheritance in 1789 at just 19 years old. Like most young English aristocrats, he embarked on his Grand Tour to immerse himself in the art, antiquity and architecture of Europe and particularly of Italy. It was usual for these young men to return laden with souvenirs, and Thomas, with his recently inherited wealth, amassed quite a collection. His weakness for picture-buying meant that on his return to Attingham he had to commission a new picture gallery to house his art, which involved removing the original staircase.

He chose the prominent Regency architect John Nash to design the gallery, as well as a grand staircase, and the location chosen for this architectural glory was at the centre of his mansion. That presented Nash with a problem: the brief was to design a gallery that would show his client's art collection to best effect, but as it was a completely internal space without windows, how could it be lit sufficiently? Fortunately,

< Located in the heart of the mansion, the Picture Gallery is lit from above by its extraordinary curved roof of cast iron and glass.

Nash's client had a very generous budget, which allowed him to be quite experimental. His proposed solution, however, was not without risks.

The Picture Gallery has, since its completion in 1807, been lit from above through a curved roof of cast iron and two layers of glass in an early attempt at double glazing. Providing innovative top-lighting, and one of the first uses of cast iron in a domestic building, the Picture Gallery was flashy but flawed. It leaked from the moment it was built.

In 2012, the National Trust embarked on a major project to repair the damage done to the fabric of the building by years of water ingress, to conserve the original decorative scheme and, above all, to construct a protective new roof of glass and steel over the whole of the original Nash roof. The secondary roof, composed of 64 panes of glass and weighing 20 tonnes, was installed at a height above the original that allows access to the historic roof for cleaning and maintenance.

Over three years, the Picture Gallery was emptied of its paintings and furniture, and an internal scaffold platform assembled to allow contractors and conservators access to every inch of the Picture Gallery roof. Helen Royall, who worked on the project, said: 'There have been some unique moments, from the crane lifting the steel beams and glass panels, to visitors being able to climb up high and go on scaffolding tours.'

Allowing an up-close and personal view of the subject and uncovering previously unknown information are twin benefits of any conservation project, in addition to extending its life span. The remarkable decorative scheme of the Nash staircase, for example, has undergone careful conservation now that it too is protected by a new, secondary roof, and in-depth study of it has revealed some amazing details.

The upper half of the staircase walls are fluted plaster to mimic pleated drapery, painted bright vermilion red, while the lower half features a paint effect in imitation of porphyry stone. With a name derived from the Latin for 'purple', the colour of Roman nobility, porphyry was Imperial Rome's most prestigious material, and was used for columns, busts and other

> The bold scheme of the Nash staircase uses fluted plasterwork resembling pleated drapery and colours associated with the nobility of Imperial Rome.

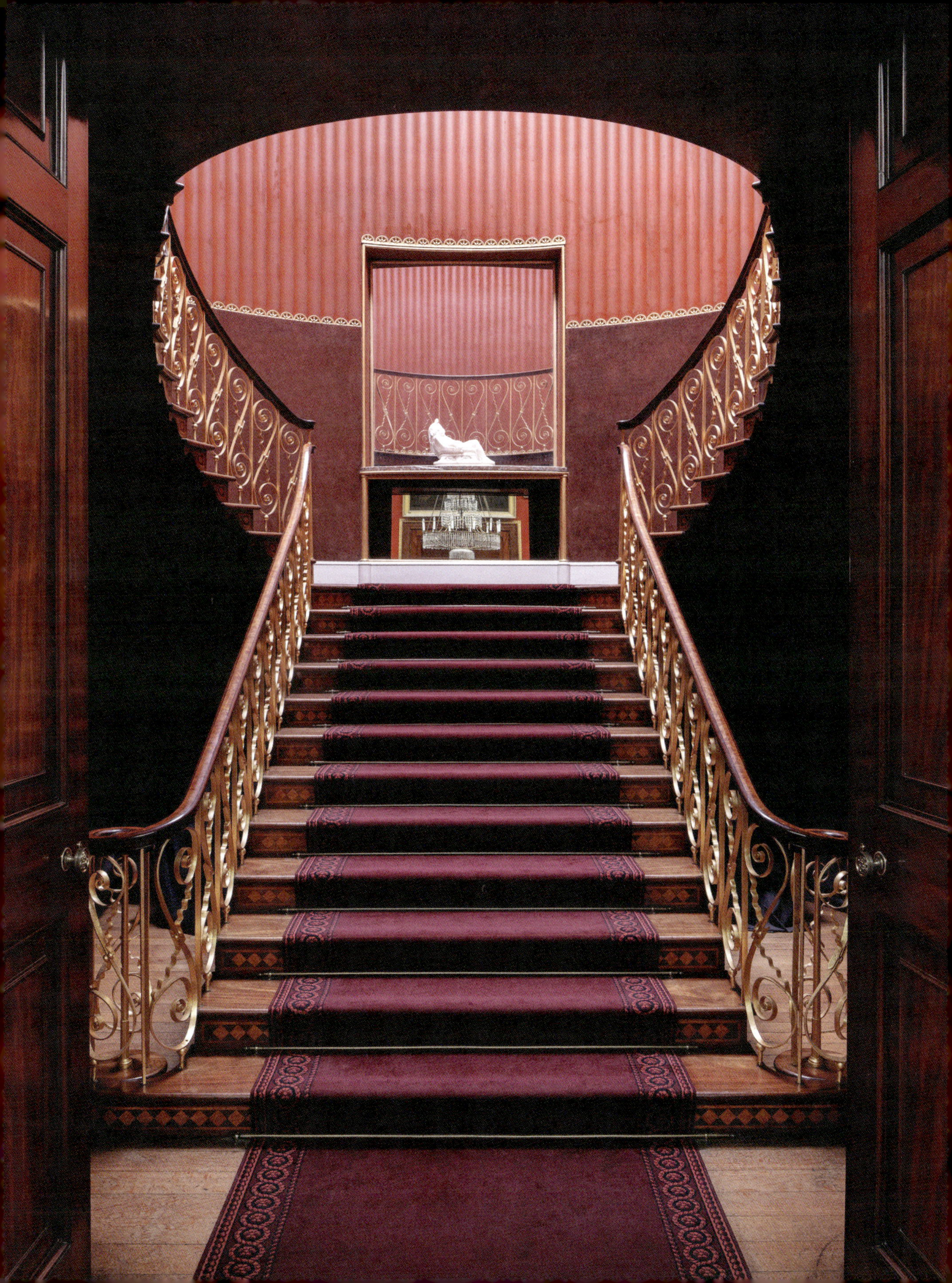

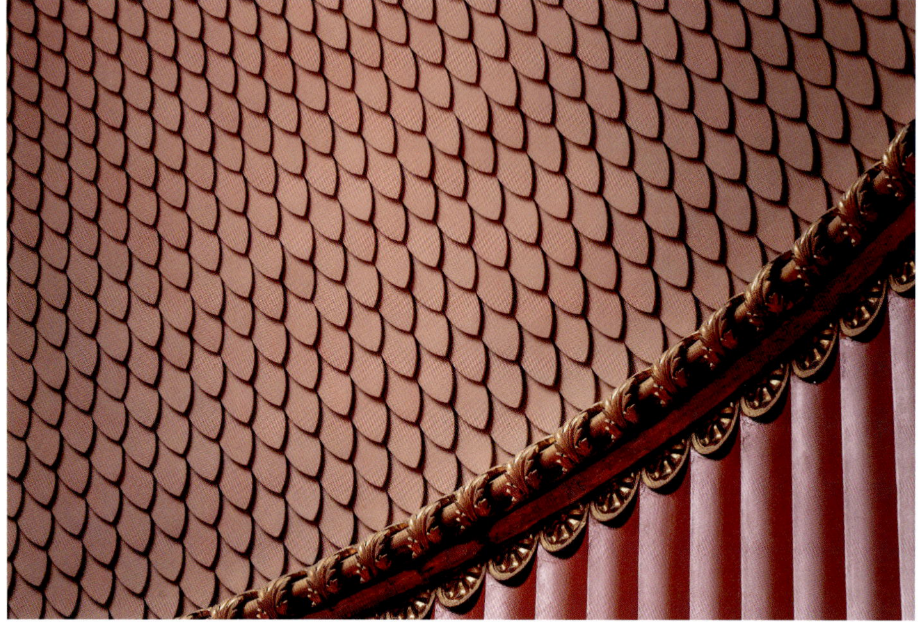

objects. The staircase's sumptuous decorative scheme, enhanced by rich gilding, becomes yet more intricate as you travel upwards.

The domed ceiling, topped with a painted glass lantern, is covered in thousands of tiles laid in a 'fish-scale' pattern that flows down and around, creating a dynamic texture. As a part of the John Nash roof conservation project, this 'fish-scale' ceiling has been closely studied. It comprises 11,550 tiles, made of plaster and individually cast in moulds. The size of the tiles in each row was precisely calculated, as they fit exactly around the inside of the dome, with the same number of tiles in every row, and the tiles becoming gradually smaller the further up you go. Twelve different-sized moulds were used to produce 12 different-sized tiles: the smallest tiles are 1⅜ inches (3.5 centimetres) high and make up the two uppermost rows; the tiles then increase in size by ⅛ of an inch (0.3 centimetres) every few rows, until you get to the largest tiles in the bottom row that are 2¼ inches (5.7 centimetres). The precision of the design and the skill in the

^ The 'fish-scale' plaster tiles on the domed ceiling gradually reduce in size as they go higher.

> The dome's decoration comprises 11,550 tiles, all now conserved.

craftsmanship are eye-watering, and are an example of the costly building work and expenditure that ultimately led to the 2nd Lord Berwick's financial ruin.

Examination of the 'fish-scale' tiles also revealed that their original colour had been overpainted. They started out light pink – or salmon pink, appropriately enough – and this colour has since been reinstated.

Now that the entire decorative scheme of the Nash staircase has been restored, it is possible to bask in the glorious effect that the 2nd Lord Berwick intended. Additionally, the soaring magnificence of the Picture Gallery, crowned by the heavens, is all the better for keeping out unwanted elements of the British weather.

The 2nd Lord Berwick's extravagance did finally force him to hold a number of auctions to pay off debts, but his legacy lives on at Attingham, in the imperial Roman heart of his mansion.

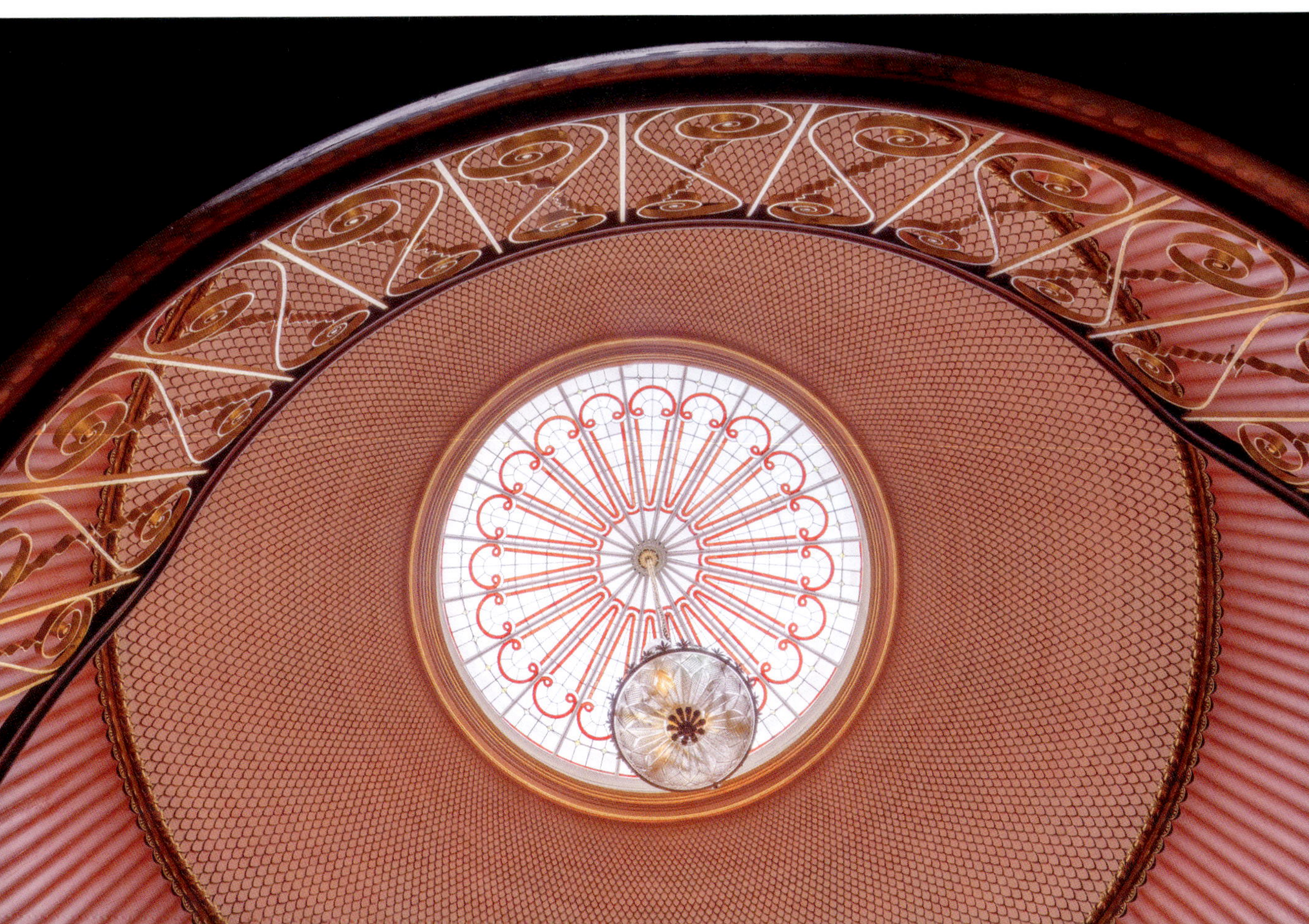

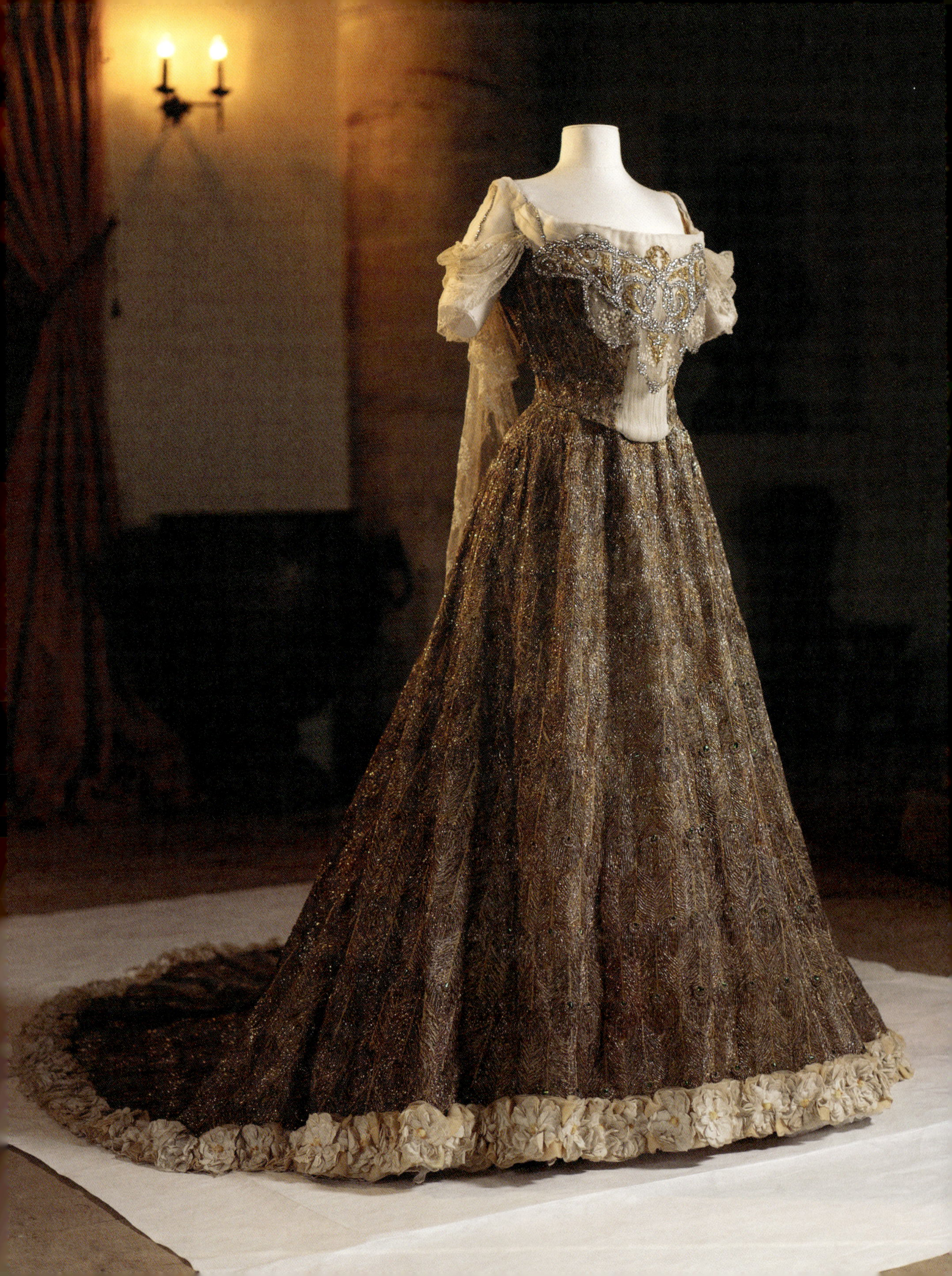

The Secret Language of Fashion

Mary Curzon's Peacock Dress

Kedleston Hall, Derbyshire

Kedleston Hall has been the seat of the Curzon family since the twelfth century. The current house was largely constructed in the 1760s, and was gifted to the National Trust in 1987 following the death of Richard Curzon, 2nd Viscount Scarsdale.

Nathaniel Curzon, 1st Baron Scarsdale, had Kedleston Hall built to dazzle but also to make a political point. A Tory politician, he needed his country mansion to outshine that of neighbour and political rival, William Cavendish, 4th Duke of Devonshire, who lived at Chatsworth. The pursuit of beautiful things and political advancement were twin obsessions of the Georgian era, and would continue to be so in the Victorian period that followed.

This dress made for Mary Curzon, the wife of George, 1st Marquess Curzon, is another example of a beautiful item making both a visual impact and political statement. George was made Viceroy of India in 1899, when Queen Victoria was also Empress of India. When she died in 1901, she was succeeded by Edward VII. The enthronement of the new Emperor of India was marked in Delhi by a week-long celebration organised by the Viceroy and attended by governors, maharajas, princes and nobles. This grandest of gatherings was known as a durbar. The Mughal Empire ruled over much of South Asia from 1526 until 1857 and used the Persian term 'Darbar' to refer to their

< Lady Curzon's Peacock Dress combined European fashions and dress-making techniques with Indian motifs and craftsmanship.

own court. This term was adopted by Curzon as a means of legitimising British imperial rule in South Asia.

The Delhi Durbar of 1903 took place in January, the coolest month when the average temperature is in the mid-teens on the Celsius scale, so the dress Mary Curzon wore to the State Ball wouldn't have been entirely impractical. It was naturally highly fashionable, but there were other important considerations at play. The fabric, for instance, was one traditionally worn by Mughal court rulers and the design used the motif of a peacock feather, which is an important Hindu symbol, particularly associated with Lord Krishna and the goddess Saraswati. Attendees at the ball would have noted the use of the peacock on her dress.

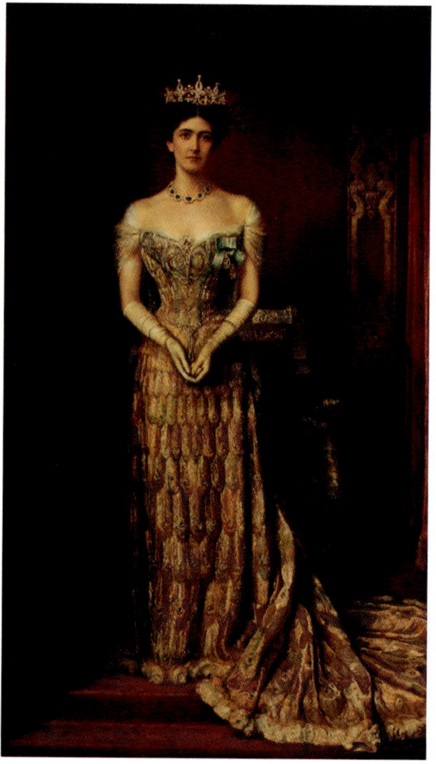

^ The posthumous portrait of Lady Curzon in her famous Peacock Dress, painted in 1909 by William Logsdail.

This motif may not just have been about the visual appeal of a familiar symbol. The room at the Red Fort in which the State Ball was being held once housed a peacock throne. This had belonged to the emperor Shah Jahan in the seventeenth century and was removed when the Mughal Empire fell to invaders in 1739. Mary Curzon's dress referenced the throne, suggesting the Vicereine and her husband the Viceroy as the representatives of a legitimate empire.

The dress is in two pieces, bodice and skirt, but it is so heavily hand embroidered in silver and gold that it appears as one. The heavy and elaborate metal embroidery, in a style known as zardozi, was created at the well-known workshop of Kishan Chand in Delhi. Brilliantly executed are the iridescent 'eyes' of the hundreds of interlocking peacock feathers, each of them made from the wing cover of a real beetle. Using beetle wings for decoration or to embellish textiles can be traced back to Mughal India, where such was the demand that beetles were farmed for the purpose.

> Each one of the iridescent 'eyes' of the hundreds of interlocking peacock feathers is made from the wing cover of a real beetle.

Once the dress panels were embroidered, they were sent from India for the dress to be constructed at the workshop of fashion designer Jean-Philippe Worth in Paris. A lace panel, embellished with diamanté, gilded metal spangles and threads, was added to the bodice with additional lace to hang from the shoulders, and the hem was finished with a circle of white silk roses. The House of Worth was the premier haute couture name of the day that every society woman in the Western world aspired to.

Again, there are conflicting optics at work. There is of course the glitz and glamour of French fashion houses and then there are the hours and hours of manual labour in the workshops of Delhi to bring together such

∨ The skirt of Lady Curzon's dress is a complex creation of gold and silver embroidery, beetle-wing cases and white silk roses.

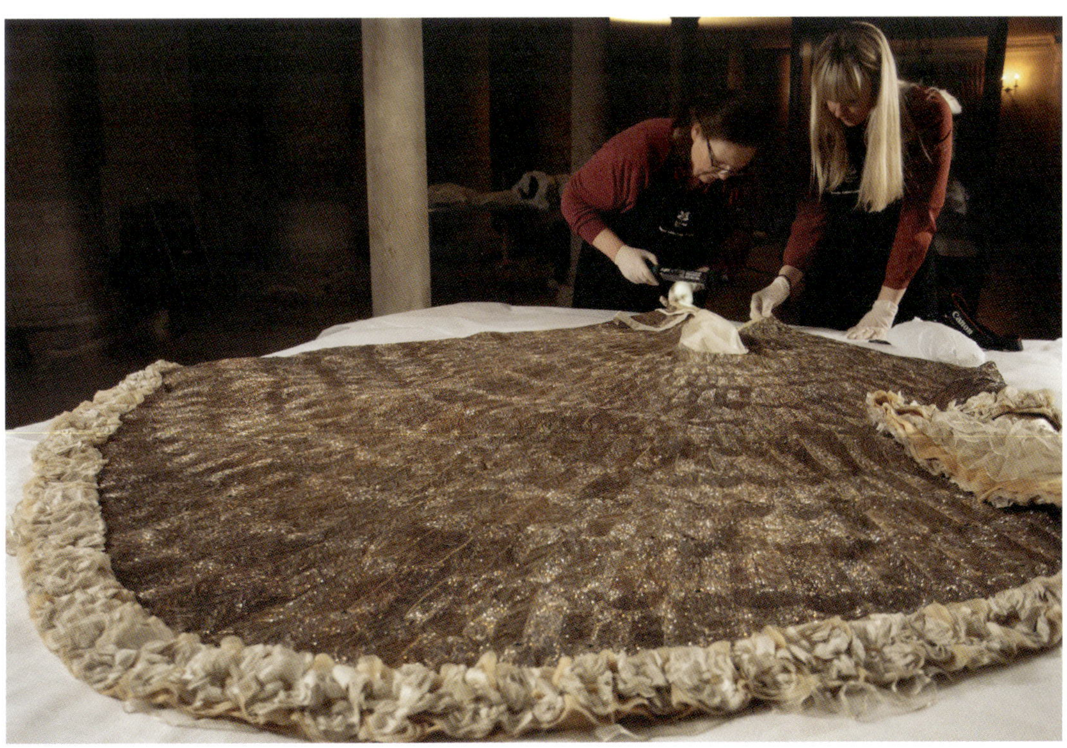

a display of power and prestige. Just as the durbar was intended to present a visual sense of continuity, aligning British rule with Indian courts of the past, so Mary Curzon's dress was designed to combine the best of Western aesthetics with Indian arts and crafts.

It was certainly a hit with the world press, and Mary Curzon was marked out as a leader of style in much the same way that the young Princess Diana caught the world's attention in 1985 when she danced with John Travolta at the White House in a midnight-blue velvet dress by Victor Edelstein. And just as that look is one that is immortalised in the record of iconic images of Princess Diana, Mary Curzon's Peacock Dress is forever associated with her. It is known that she wore the dress at least once more after the 1903 Delhi Durbar and that it was altered to accommodate a change of figure. She gave birth to her third daughter in 1904, but a miscarriage a short time after led to a near-fatal infection. It was this illness that resulted in her early death in 1906 at the age of 36. In 1909 William Logsdail painted her posthumous portrait, based on the official photograph taken of her at the Delhi Durbar. She is depicted full length and wearing the Peacock Dress. It is assumed that Logsdail was given access to the dress to capture its style and colour.

The National Trust is fortunate enough to be able to display the dress, as it was gifted to HM Government by Mary's daughter, Lady Alexandra Metcalfe, in lieu of inheritance tax. But to continue to show it to best effect, conservator Rosamund Weatherall had to intervene to address lots of small areas of damage, such as snagged threads, tears in the more delicate fabrics and loosening of some of the appliqué items. The dress was sufficiently famous that much had been written about how it was made – it had been part of an exhibition at New York's Metropolitan Museum of Art in 2004 – but even so there were some things about the dress that took Rosamund by surprise, such as the true colours of the embroidery (now faded) that were revealed when examined using a digital microscope, suggesting the makers' original intention was to capture the iridescence of the peacock feathers. Another unexpected discovery was that the dress had pockets! As the dress has been altered since Mary Curzon's time, conservators have been focusing on restoring

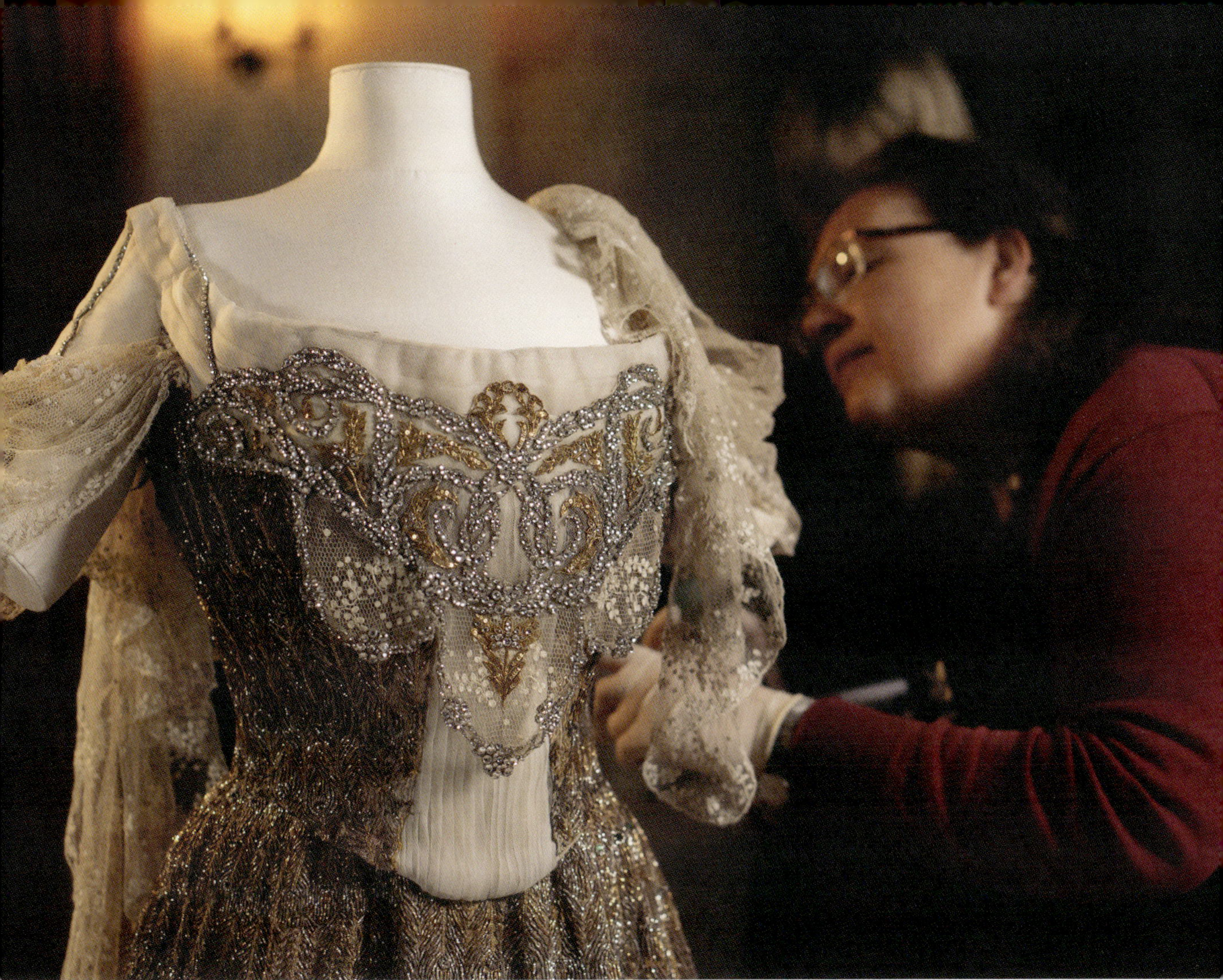

^ The Peacock Dress once again dazzles as it did at the Delhi Durbar of 1903.

the dress to its appearance during her lifetime, using Logsdail's painting as a guide.

While conservators have been poring over every stitch, curators have been assiduously scrutinising and examining the Peacock Dress and its historical context, making sure that its future presentation and interpretation are as fully researched and culturally inclusive as they can be.

As it waits to go back on show in a specially designed display case, it is hoped that the Peacock Dress will turn heads once more, while also inviting new ways to evaluate historic items.

Finding Lost Fossils

The Geological Gallery

Biddulph Grange, Staffordshire

Hidden away in a leafy Staffordshire valley is one of the most idiosyncratically designed gardens you can find anywhere in the world. In fact, when you've found it, you can stay right there and continue your travels around the world, at least as imagined by the garden's creator, James Bateman. In the words of head gardener Paul Walton: 'When you visit Biddulph, you can head down into Italy, through to China, and out past Egypt … We have a journey round the world each day.'

James Bateman inherited a fortune from his grandfather and used it to pursue his two chief interests: botany and religion. At Biddulph he created a labyrinthine garden covering 20 acres (8 hectares) with distinct areas between the hedging – imaginative and playful, if not historically and topographically accurate. You can visit an Egyptian pyramid in the Staffordshire Moorlands, a Victorian vision of China and an imagining of a Himalayan glen.

Bateman filled his garden with specimens collected from all around the world and he also sponsored some expeditions to Mexico and South America. He was particularly fascinated by orchids and published books on the subject. He became an accepted expert on this group of plants, and corresponded with contemporary scholar and naturalist Charles Darwin.

When Bateman sent Darwin some Madagascan orchids in 1862, he included a specimen of *Angraecum sesquipedale*, a beautiful, white, star-shaped orchid with a nectary – the tube that supplies the nectar – around

> James Bateman opened his Geological Gallery to the public in 1862 at a time of great debate around the origins of life on Earth.

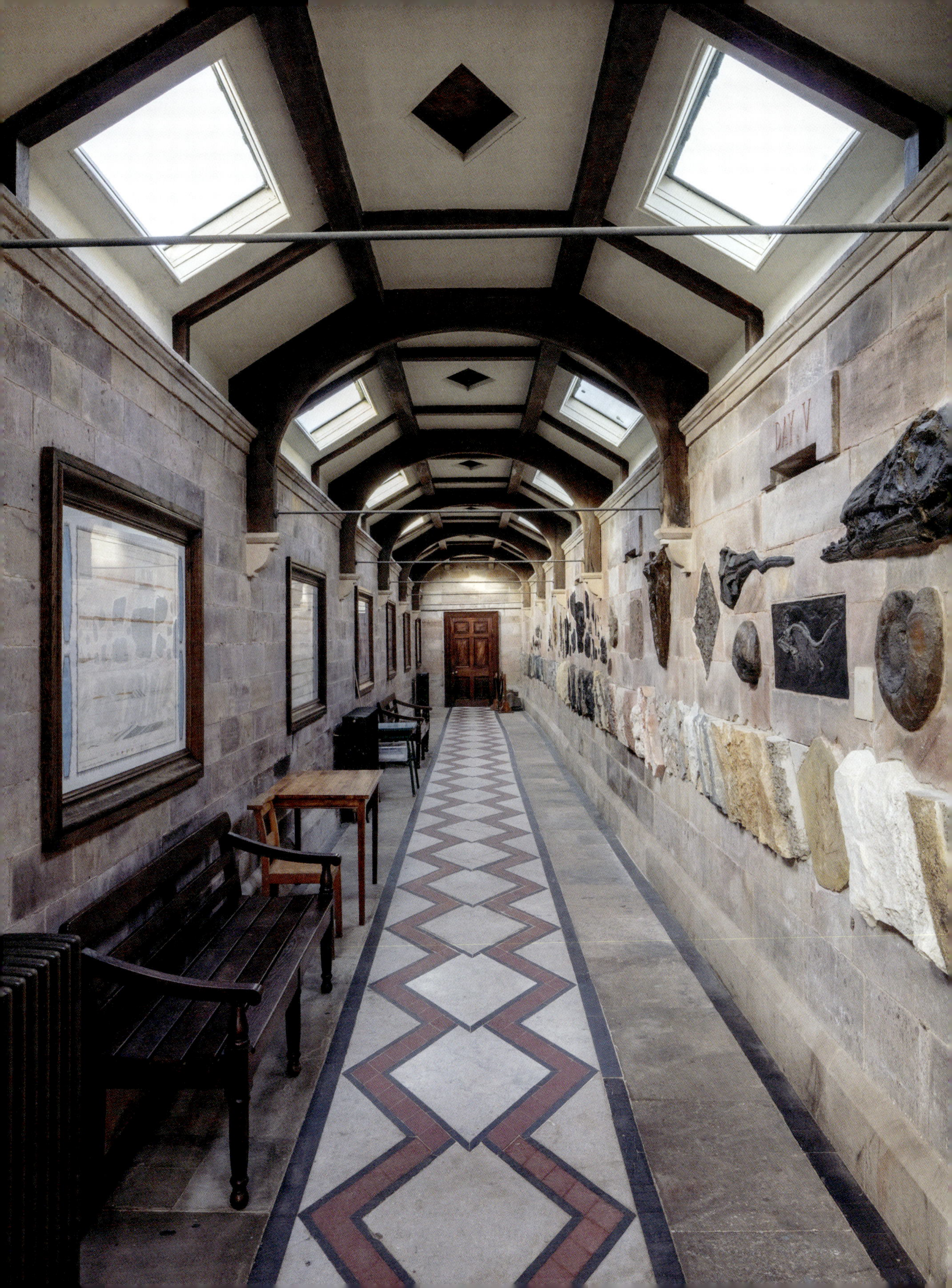
DAY V

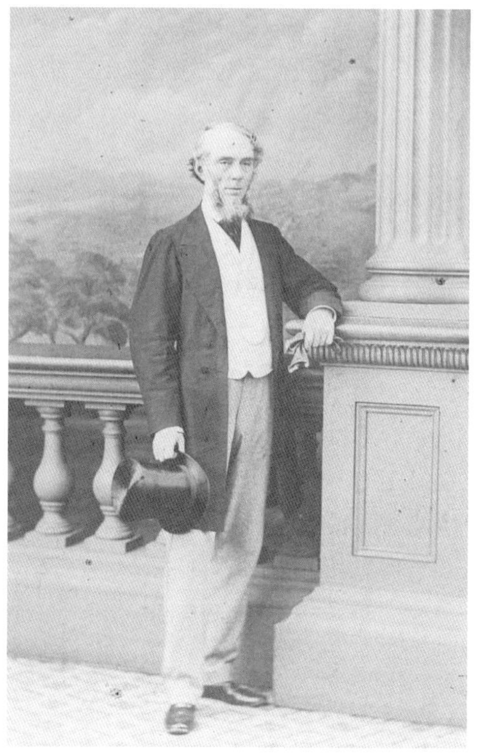

^ A studio photograph of James Bateman taken around 1870.

12 inches (30 centimetres) long. Darwin concluded that this flower could only be pollinated by a creature with a proboscis of a similar length, that had evolved alongside the flower. In 1992, around 130 years after Darwin's prediction, a hawkmoth with a proboscis in excess of 8 inches (20 centimetres) was discovered feeding on the flower. So, this exchange of specimens between Bateman and Darwin resulted in a helpful cross-pollination of ideas, but in other matters of natural history the men were very divided.

When Darwin published *On the Origin of Species* in 1859, it split the scientific community of the time, with many struggling or refusing to accept our shared ancestry with apes and Darwin's lack of a role for God in the creation of the Earth and all living things. As Bateman was one of those who struggled to accept Darwin's conclusions, the gallery was his attempt to reconcile the physical evidence of the evolution of species as preserved in the fossil record with his religious beliefs. Work on the Geological Gallery at Biddulph began in 1858 and it opened in 1862.

The Victorian visitor entered the Gallery up steep stone steps to be presented with a collection of South American and Roman marble and terracotta artefacts, which collectively tell the story of God creating Adam, Eve and life on Earth. The route would then have led on through a doorway into a long gallery around 100 feet (30 metres) long. On one wall were mounted a series of fossils, grouped into 'days' to correspond with the six days of the creation of life on Earth, as laid down in the Book of Genesis, with primitive invertebrates created on Day I and mammals on Day VI. Running underneath the fossils are rock strata, laid out according to the plan of 'the father of English geology', William Smith. The fossils above correspond with the rock strata below, so Day III displays ferns and plant fossils with coal-bearing rocks from the Carboniferous period beneath them. On the facing wall, oak frames hold information to aid the study of the Gallery, including geological maps and horizontal sections and tables of minerals. The seventh 'day', when God was supposed to have rested, leads visitors out to the garden itself, where Bateman ensured that there were no 'man-made' hybridised plants.

After its unveiling, the popularity of the theory illustrated by the Gallery waned. Bateman left Biddulph in 1868 and the property was sold three years later. When Biddulph Grange became an orthopaedic hospital in 1922 the Gallery was slowly converted into use as a storeroom and overspill mortuary.

It wasn't until the 1970s that the importance of the Geological Gallery was recognised as a representation of the point in history in which it was created. Dr John Stanley of Keele University found the

∨ According to the Bible, on the fifth day of creation, God created aquatic animals and flying creatures; here the display includes an icthyosaur (an aquatic reptile) and fragments of a pterosaur (a flying reptile).

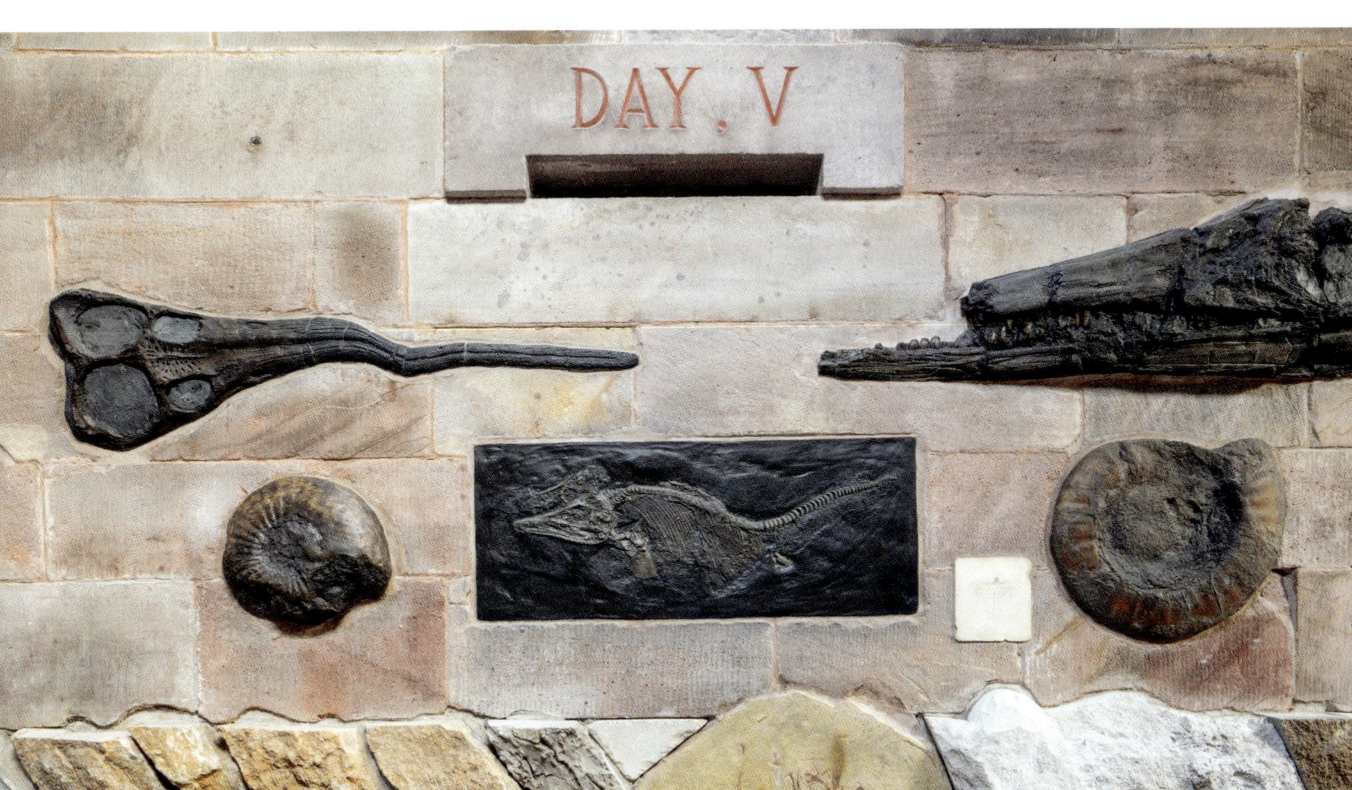

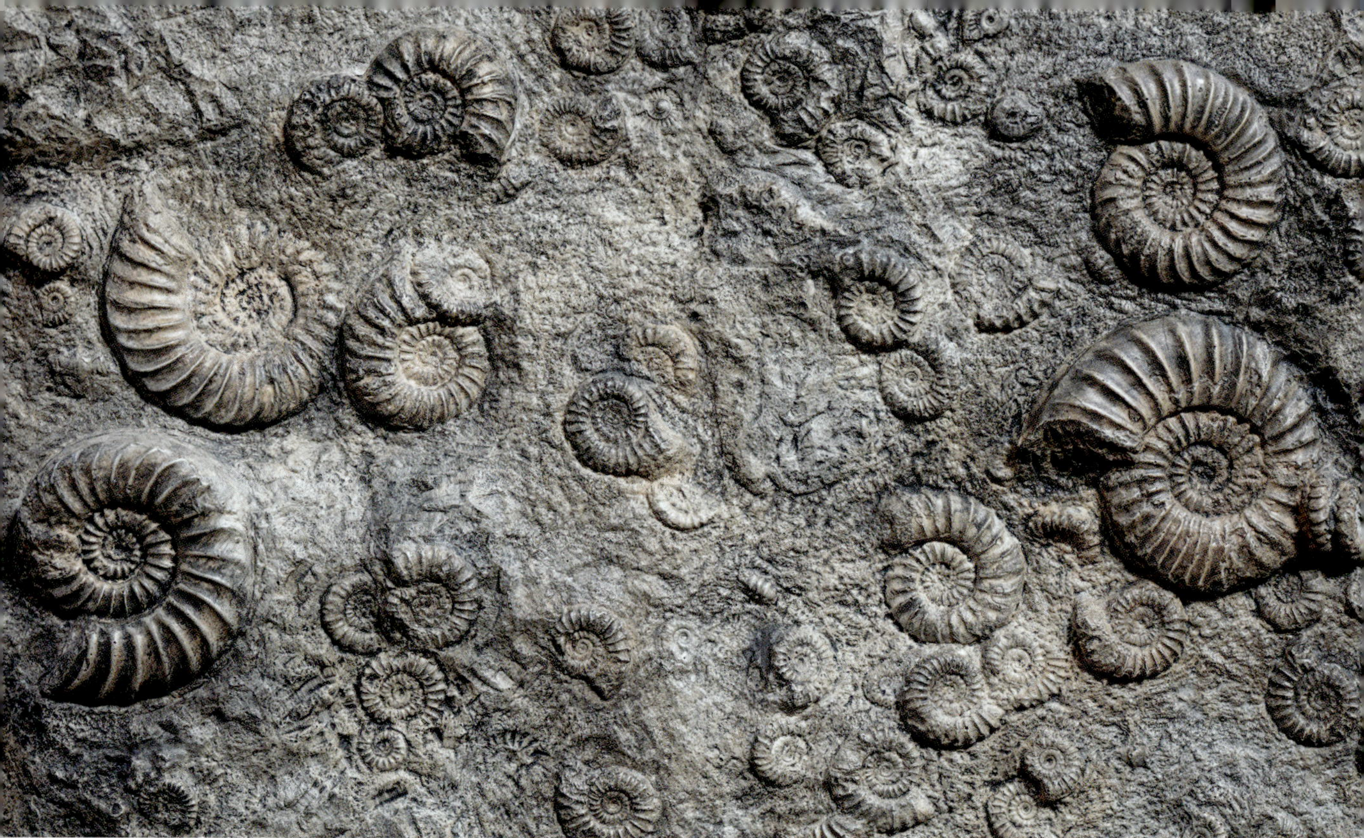

^ Perhaps the most widely known fossil, ammonites were cephalopods that lived during the Jurassic and Cretaceous periods, an interval of about 140 million years.

Gallery in a dilapidated state with most of its fossils missing. The few that were left were taken to the university for use in the adult education department and were kindly donated to the National Trust when funding for the Gallery restoration project was secured.

In 2012, the National Trust, having acquired the gardens in 1988, began the job of restoring Bateman's vision. Over the next five years, the remaining few fossils were subject to careful cleaning and conservation, and while replicas were made of the missing fossils, the recesses in which the originals and copies were to be displayed had to be stabilised, as did the entire Grade I-listed building. This included resolving major structural issues as well as replacing original tiles and stonework.

Work on the fossils, both on the originals and on the casting of replicas, required specialist help of the type not usually within the National Trust's repertoire. As palaeontological conservator Nigel Larkin said: 'I normally work in museums. Here I am at a National Trust property and that's unusual. You don't normally find geology and fossils like this at a National Trust property, but this is a unique space.'

While digging out old mortar from the recesses, Nigel was also digging for clues. In some, he was able to make casts of imprints left in the old mortar before removing it, so he could determine the type of fossil that would have been held there. In Day II, a piece of rock had been left behind when a particularly large fossil was removed; this was examined under a microscope in search of nannofossils (fossils of minute planktonic organisms) to identify where in the world the missing fossil came from. As so often in conservation, a good amount of detective work was also required. A total of 63 missing fossils had to be deduced, their replacements carefully researched to ensure they originated from the correct geological age and from sites that would have been known about in the 1850s. Specimens were then borrowed from museums for casting.

Conservation projects of a space as unusual as this one are few and far between, requiring diverse skills, but the National Trust has the additional and invaluable resource of its volunteer workforce and external volunteer partners. At Biddulph, the project benefitted from the contributions of many volunteers, including Barbara Kleiser, a geographer with a specialist interest in historical geology, and historian Kevin Dale. The largest input on the restoration of the Gallery, and without whom the restoration would not have taken place, came from Professor Hugh Torrens and Dr Ian Stimpson of Keele University, who mapped out the rock strata and did extensive research work.

By April 2017, all of the recesses created in the wall of the Geological Gallery by James Bateman were filled. Replicas were also made of the 10 fossils that were original to the Gallery, including the 50-million-year-old turtle fossil thought to have been given to James Bateman by Richard Owen, the palaeontologist who gave us the word 'dinosaur' and who was the driving force behind the creation of the Natural History Museum.

Bateman's Geological Gallery was designed as a tool to educate visitors about the then-new science of geology. Today, open to a curious public once more, it stands as a record of a time of fervent theological and scientific debate.

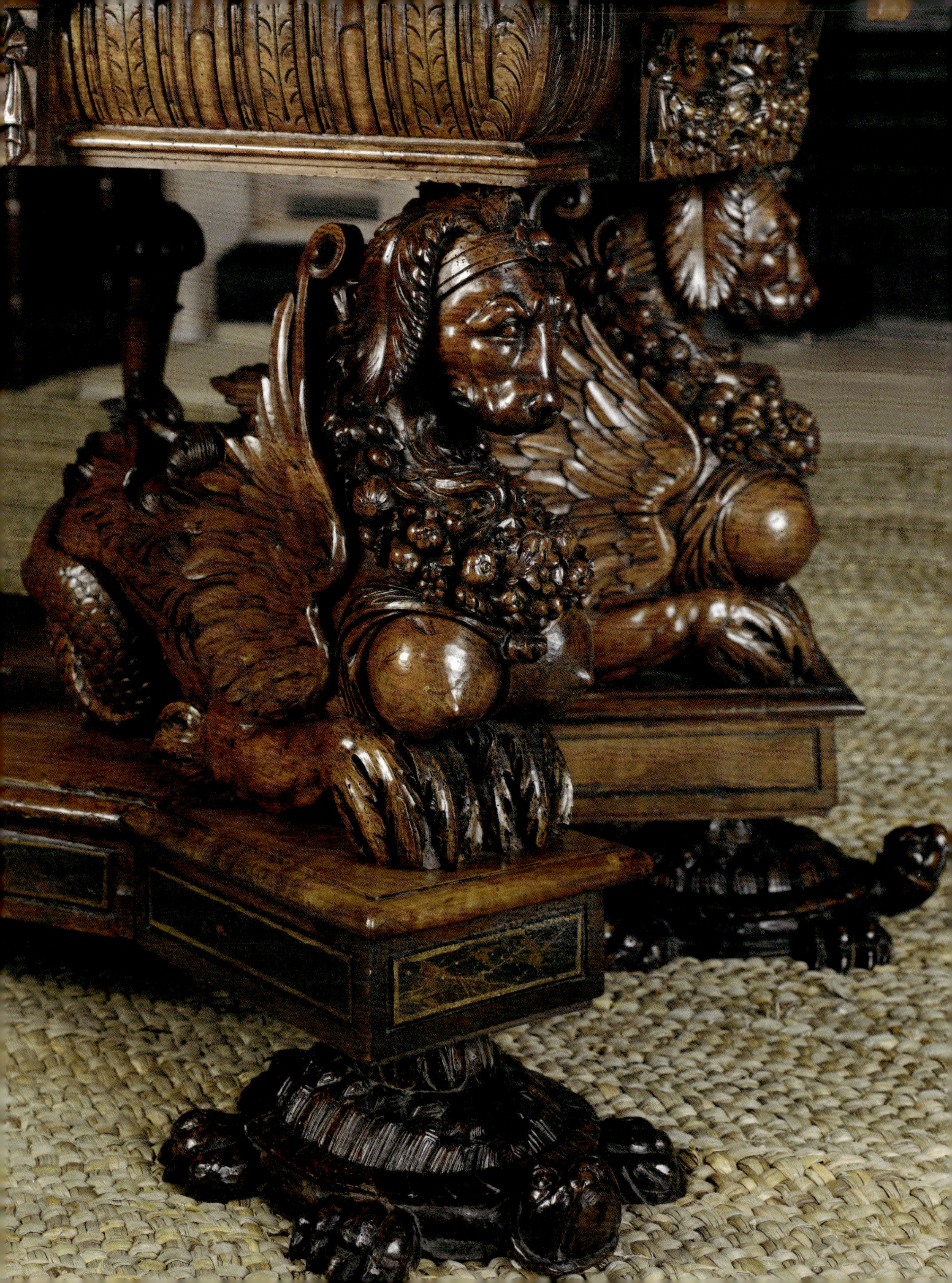

Getting an Elizabethan Masterpiece Fit for Tour

The Sea-Dog Table

Hardwick Hall, Derbyshire

The ambition behind Hardwick Hall, the glittering Elizabethan mansion that was the creation of Bess of Hardwick, is clear for all to see. Featuring conspicuously large and numerous windows, it gave rise to the saying, 'Hardwick Hall, more glass than wall.' After Queen Elizabeth I, Bess of Hardwick was one of the wealthiest women in England. She filled her head-turning home with suitably eye-catching treasures, and so it is conceivable that she would have approved of items from her collection travelling to the other side of the world to be marvelled over in world-famous art museums.

One of the items to tour America – firstly the Metropolitan Museum of Art in New York in autumn 2023, and then the Cleveland Museum of Art and the Fine Arts Museums of San Francisco in 2024 – was the Sea-Dog Table. Probably made in Paris in the 1570s after designs by Jacques Androuet du Cerceau, it is regarded as one of the most important examples of sixteenth-century French furniture in Britain. From its Paris workshop, it is possible the table went to Chatsworth, where Bess lived with her fourth husband, George Talbot, 6th Earl of Shrewsbury. When the couple separated in the mid-1580s, it is assumed that this

< Made in the 1570s, the Sea-Dog Table is considered to be one of the most important examples of sixteenth-century French furniture in Britain.

much-prized piece was kept by Bess and later moved to her new home, Hardwick Hall. There it has resided for four centuries, evidently well cared for by a succession of owners.

Due to its long association with Hardwick Hall, so expressive of the Elizabethan era and the powers that were, the Sea-Dog Table was for a time mistaken as a reference to the Elizabethan Sea Dogs. These were mariners of renown authorised by Queen Elizabeth I to raid England's enemies, which they did during times of both war and peace from 1560 to the queen's death in 1603. Notable Sea Dogs were Francis Drake and Walter Raleigh. While their exploits would have been well known and widely talked about at the time this table was made, the name is entirely coincidental. This is a French table after all, so it seems highly unlikely that its maker would have been celebrating English mariners. France's alliance with Scotland and specifically Mary Queen of Scots, whom Elizabeth had beheaded in 1587, ensured enmity between the two nations while she reigned.

The exquisitely carved creatures on this mostly walnut table were likely inspired by a taste for the grotesque among the courtly circles of sixteenth-century France. And when you study them more closely, it soon becomes clear that the sea-dog designation doesn't quite cover it. The faces are canine, but the ears and paws are formed from acanthus leaves, then there are feathered wings that give way to scaly tails, and garlands of intricately carved fruits rest on prominent breasts.

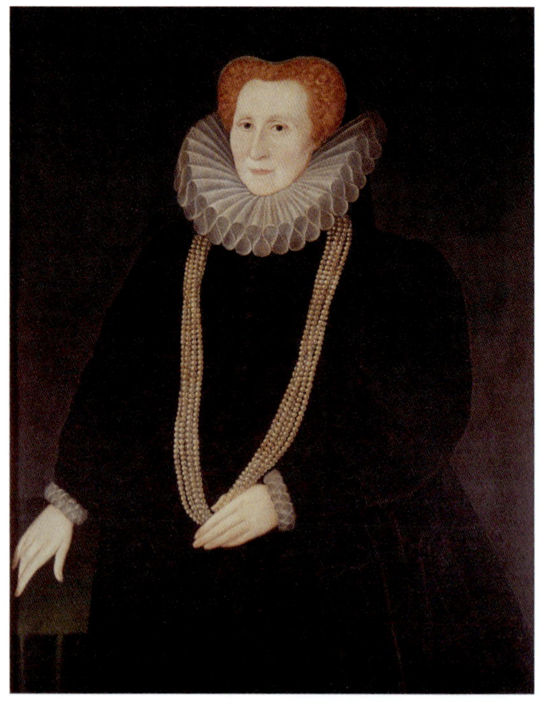

^ Elizabeth Talbot, Countess of Shrewsbury, also known as Bess of Hardwick.

Before the table could depart for its US tour, it needed to be carefully inspected and any areas of vulnerability identified and rectified. This was the

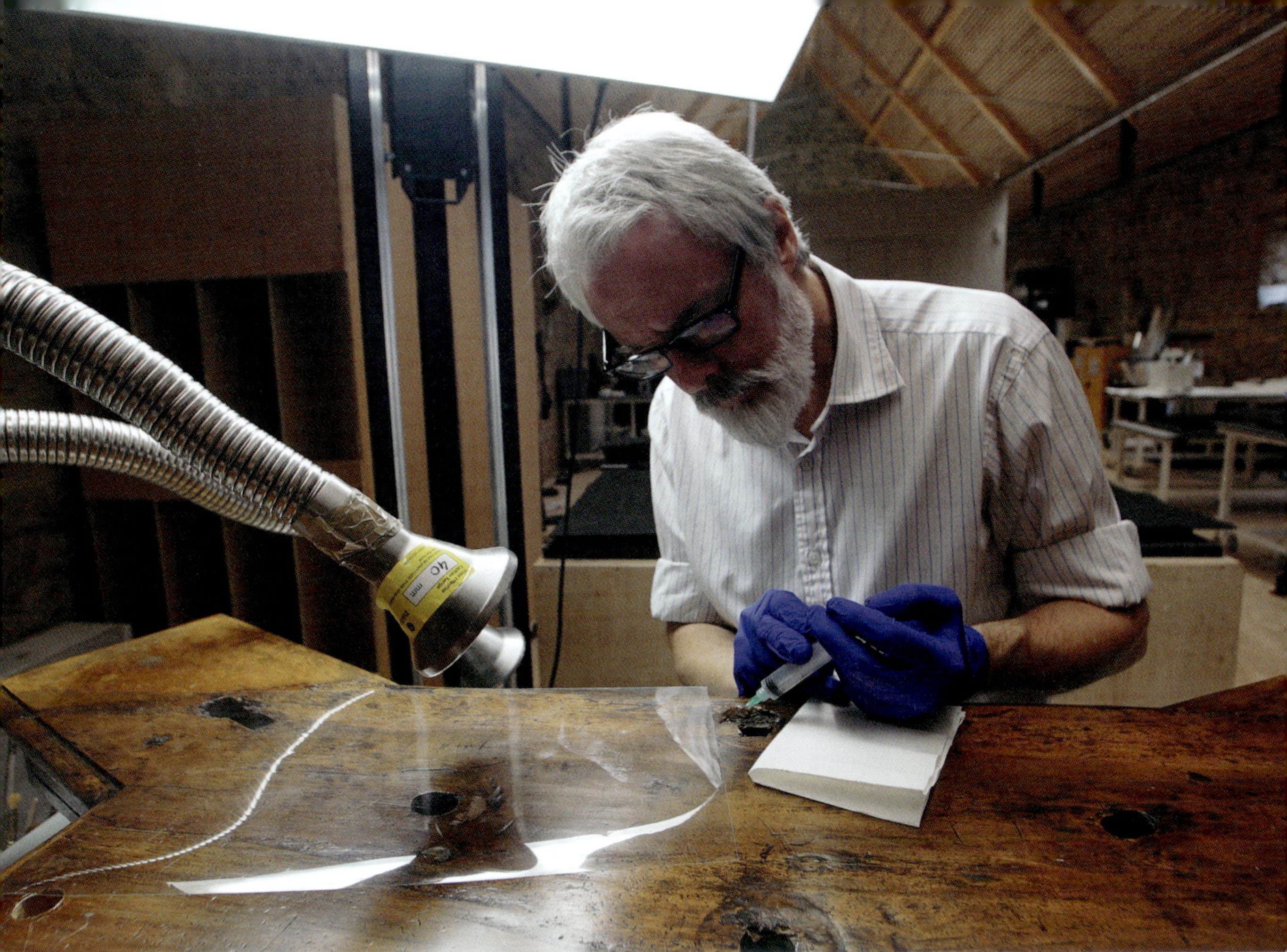

^ Senior Conservator for furniture and frames, Gerry Alabone, treating an area damaged by a historic infestation of woodworm.

'For it to still be almost entirely intact is quite remarkable, and it's only happened like that because it's been cared for over hundreds of years.'

task of Senior Furniture Conservator Gerry Alabone, who confirmed the overall condition of the piece: 'For it to still be almost entirely intact is quite remarkable, and it's only happened like that because it's been cared for over hundreds of years.'

However, the care the table has received was not enough to prevent, at some point in its exceptionally long history, an infestation of woodworm. Woodworm describes the wood-eating larva of many species of beetle, of which the most prevalent in the UK is the common furniture beetle

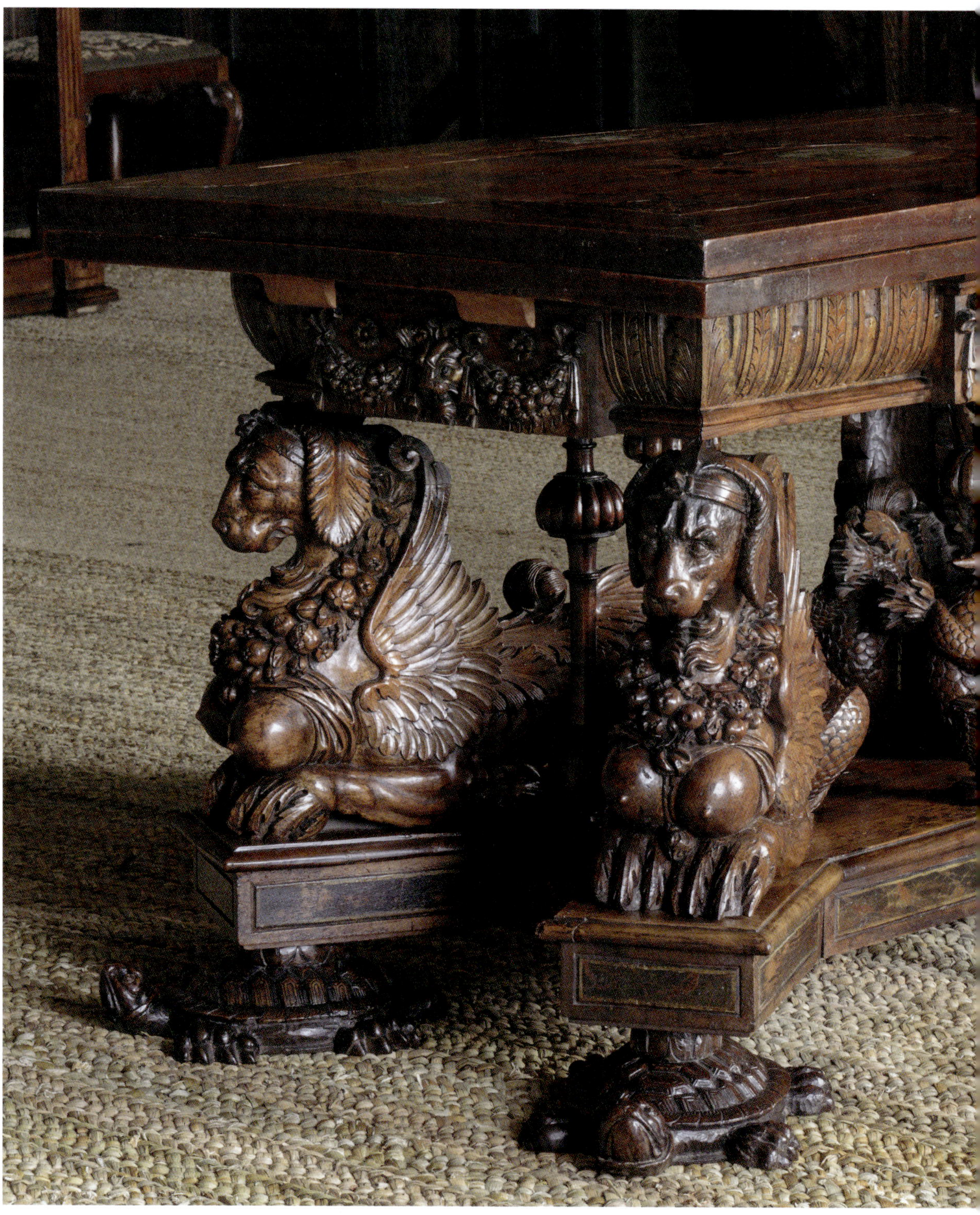

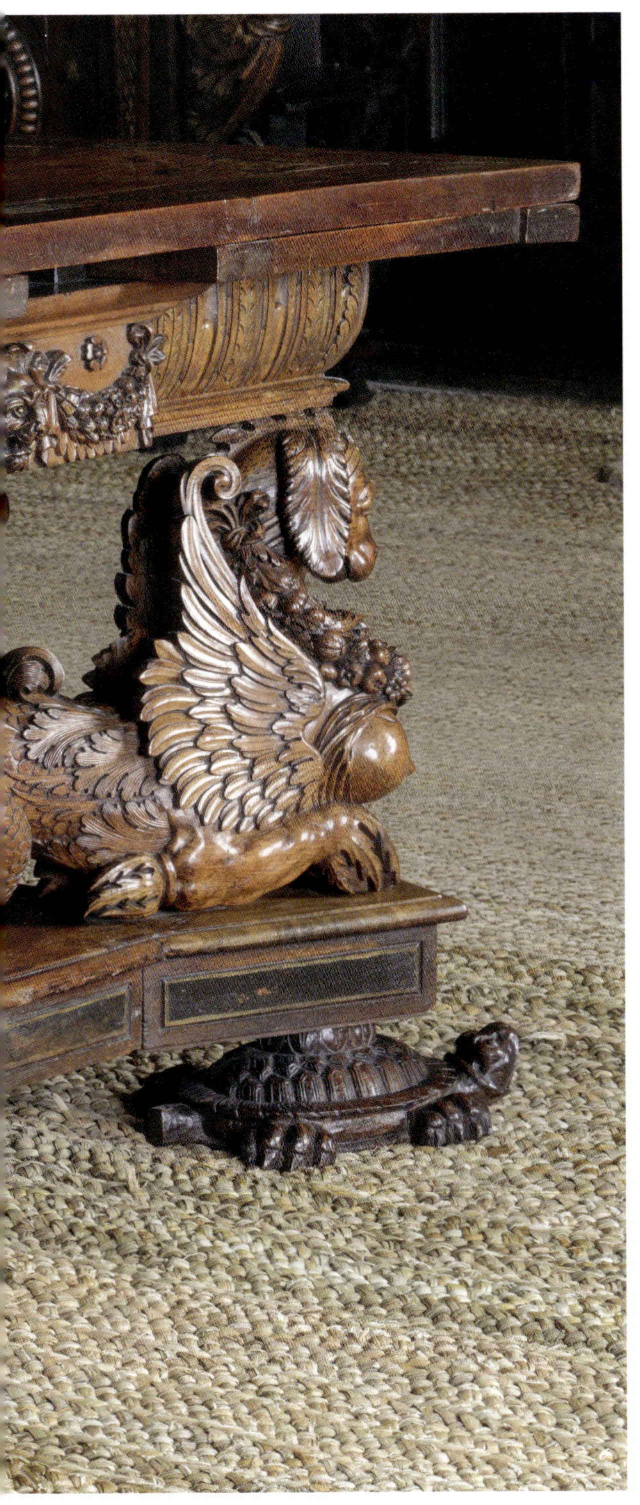

(*Anobium punctatum*). The superficial damage to wooden furniture – those tell-tale holes – are seen only after the larvae have eaten their fill, reached the next stage in their lifecycle and bored their way to the surface to take flight. In the case of Hardwick's Sea-Dog Table, the most concerning areas of damage were found to be in the dogs' heads, revealed by X-rays taken in the Royal Oak Foundation Conservation Studio at Knole in Kent.

These hollowed out areas were at risk of collapse and so Gerry had to intervene. Using a hypodermic needle and surgical precision, he introduced an acrylic resin that gently flooded and filled the tunnels left by the historic infestation. When the X-rays and Gerry's physical examination of the patient confirmed the operation had been a success, the table was declared fit to travel. A relieved Gerry said: 'It's been a very special piece to work on. It's been great to feel part of a continuum of treatment.'

< After conservation, the Sea-Dog Table travelled to North America to delight museum-goers in New York, Cleveland and San Francisco.

Skills and Techniques
The Secrets of Saving Textiles

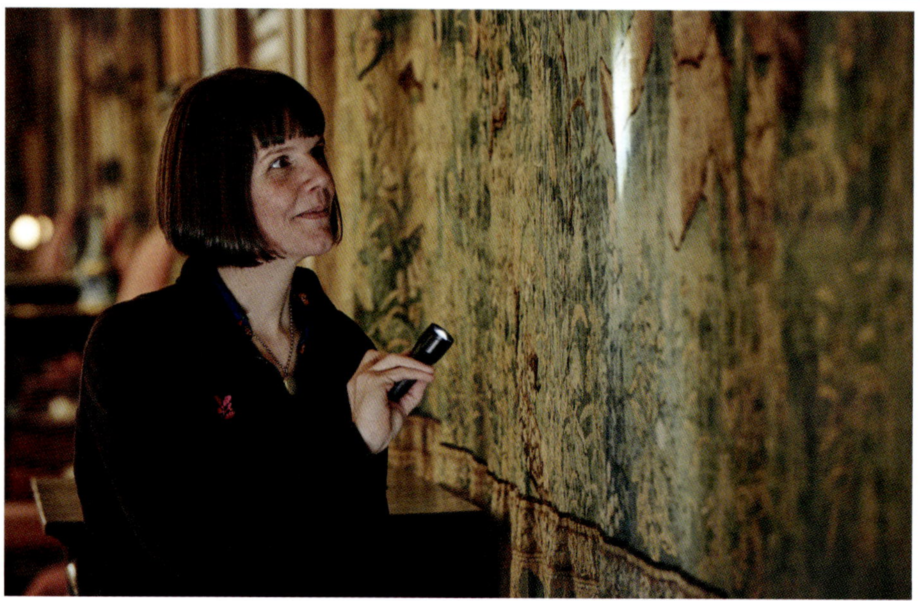

Since 1976, the National Trust has had a specialist textile conservation studio, which now operates from a converted barn on the Blickling Estate in Norfolk. Here a team of 13 highly trained textile conservators tend to objects that find themselves in need of a little extra care and attention. As a national facility, it receives every type of textile imaginable – and some surprises. When you think of textiles at National Trust properties, you might think of the large-scale wall hangings and tapestries found in many country houses, and state beds draped in delicate fabrics, often centuries old. But when you consider that the Trust's textile collections number over 150,000 individual items, the conservators at Blickling can expect anything and everything to come through the door. Here is a tiny selection of completed projects that hints at that variety.

First, the National Trust's longest-running conservation project, which saw Hardwick Hall's 13 Gideon Tapestries taken down one by one from 1999 and rehung over a period of 24 years. These tapestries measure 20 feet (6 metres) in height and, when all hung together, 230 feet (70 metres) in length. Woven in around 1578, they were the most expensive single purchase the immensely wealthy Bess of Hardwick (see page 147) made for her house. And that's where they have stayed, in the Long Gallery, since it was first decorated at the end of the sixteenth century. Four hundred years of dust, soot and general grime had to be removed and so the tapestries were sent to a specialist cleaning facility in Belgium. Once returned to the studio, many different conservators – it's thought around 30 over the course of the project – spent approximately 5,470 hours on each tapestry, supporting and repairing damaged areas using special stitching techniques. Then they re-lined and strengthened the hanging mechanism of each one.

By comparison, in 2020, the contents of dolls' houses from Uppark and Nostell were treated at the studio. Both houses date from the eighteenth century and are fine examples of grand mansions in perfect miniature. The dolls' miniature clothes are made with tiny stitching and Uppark's doll's house features a 'best bed', which has all the elements of a full-size bed, including valances, curtains and a headboard.

The studio has treated some surprising textiles from Snowshill Manor, Gloucestershire – which was the home of collector Charles Wade. A qualified architect, he bought and restored a sixteenth-century manor house in which he kept his varied collections of hand-crafted items. He even created his own coat of arms that bore the Latin motto *Nequid pereat*, 'Let nothing perish' (which, incidentally, might work rather well over the doors at the Textile Conservation Studio).

One of Wade's collections comprised suits of Samurai armour, which he displayed in their own room. Antique and perhaps battle-worn when purchased in the first half of the twentieth century, one of these suits of armour made its way to the conservation studio. It had various elements in need of repair – several areas of wear on the cotton and silk cords, braids and ties that went around the body, damaged silk brocade on a leather thigh guard and a broken silk thumb loop – all requiring a variety of individual practical conservation solutions. Having such variety in your work is surely a good thing, or put another way: 'It's all part of life's rich tapestry.'

< Property curator Liz Waring inspects the restored Gideon Tapestries at Hardwick Hall in Derbyshire.

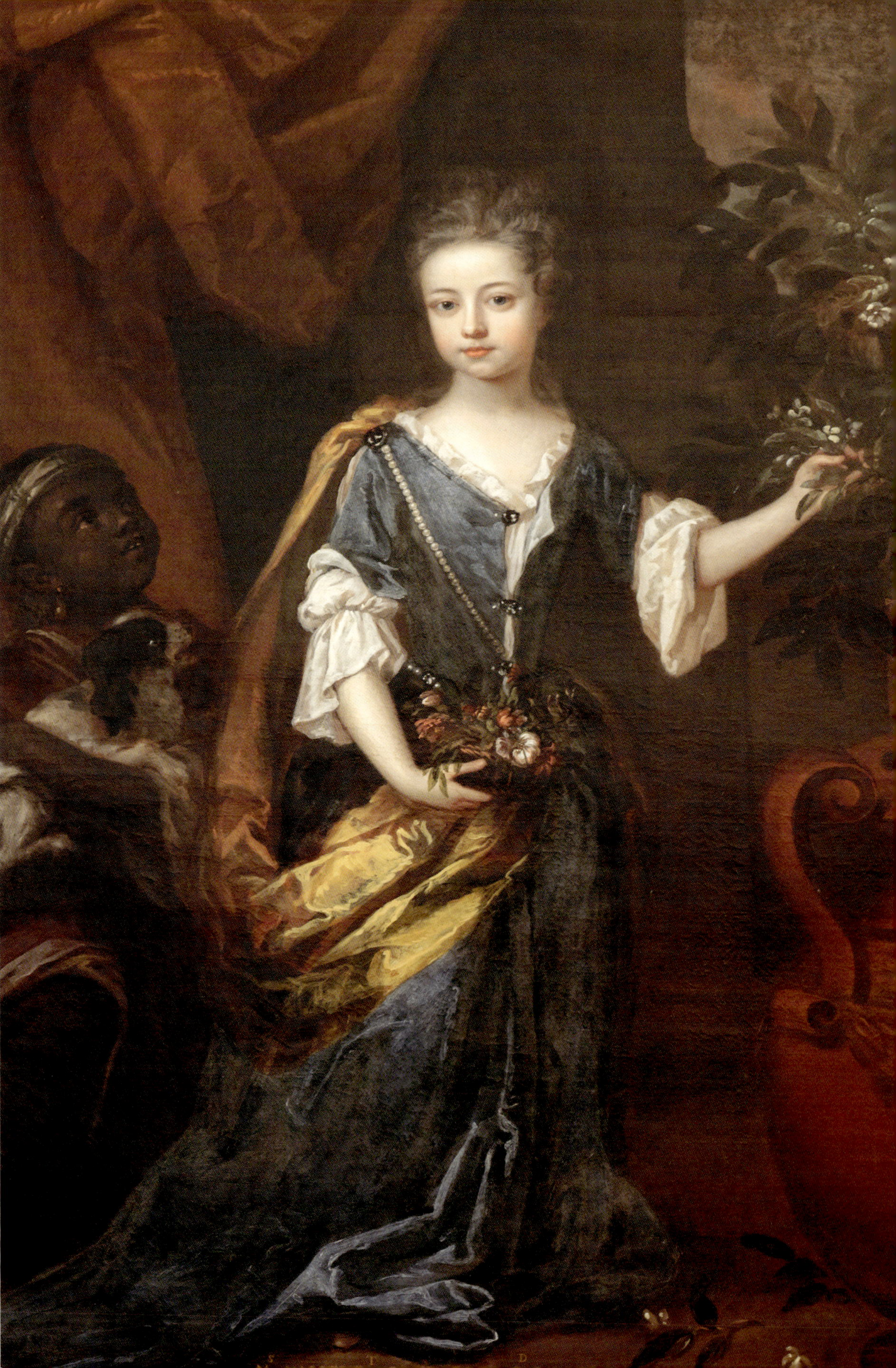

Shining a Light into the Shadows

Margaret Brownlow's Portrait

Belton House, Lincolnshire

For three centuries Belton House was the country seat of the Brownlows. This family of politicians and lawyers knew the importance of maintaining one's reputation in society, how to exert their influence and demonstrate their importance. What Sir John Brownlow, 3rd Baronet, and Lady Alice Brownlow commissioned has been described as the finest example of Carolean architecture (that is, built during the reign of Charles II, 1660–85) and the most complete example of a typical English country house.

Generations of the Brownlow family added to the impressive collections of art, silver and porcelain, commissioning and acquiring what was fashionable or what mattered to them, marking their lives and times by adding their portraits to those that had gone before. The Brownlows created the archetypal scene of English aristocratic domesticity and in their portraits had themselves depicted just as they wanted to be seen.

In the Saloon are the portraits of the seventeenth-century Brownlows, including the builders of Belton, Sir John and Lady Alice, and their daughter, Margaret. Margaret was around eight years old in 1695 when she sat for painter Henry Tilson and her portrait was placed over the mantelpiece, set in a surround of fine woodcarving. One inference from this is that this little girl was much loved, but this painting contained

< The conservation of Margaret Brownlow's portrait restored its lustre and also sought to bring out the detail of her attendant.

other details and another character largely obscured by dirt and degraded varnish, suggesting it had more stories to tell.

When the time came for the portraits to be cleaned and their condition assessed, the opportunity to gain a greater understanding of these works of art was exciting, especially in exploring their historic presentation and how these objects were used by the family. Yet as John Chu, Senior National Curator for Paintings and Sculpture, put it: 'Moving a 300-year-old painting is always a complex process; moving a painting which is still in its historic position is even more complex.'

In Margaret's portrait, smaller in stature, and perhaps even younger than her, is a child who is portrayed as her servant, obliged to carry her dog and who gazes at her as devotedly as her pet does.

By the 1690s England and Scotland were actively participating in the trade of enslaved people, but there are no records at Belton of any slaves, servants or attendants fitting a description of this child at the time this portrait was painted. However, enslaved people were often given new names and their ethnicity was not always a matter of record. Nonetheless, with no records to indicate the existence of this child in the Brownlows' service, the suggestion here is that this is not a depiction of an actual servant but is rather a symbol of power and status. From his knowledge of portraits of this period, John suspects that the child was painted from real life, possibly a model who sat for the portraitist Henry Tilson. John explained the appearance of imaginary enslaved people shown as servants in high-society portraits as follows: 'It's a fashion that we see emerging in Britain from about the middle of the seventeenth century. It would usually be something you would see in a portrait of a very prominent, aristocratic woman, so what the inclusion of this figure does is elevate her status to that level of society.'

Whether this child was real or not, the trade of enslaved people is an undeniable part of our history and entwined with the history of the country house in Britain. It's an area of study that Charlotte Holmes, Cultural Heritage Curator, has spent a great deal of time on, approaching it with both professional and personal interest: 'I do this work with [the] knowledge, that some of my ancestors were enslaved African people

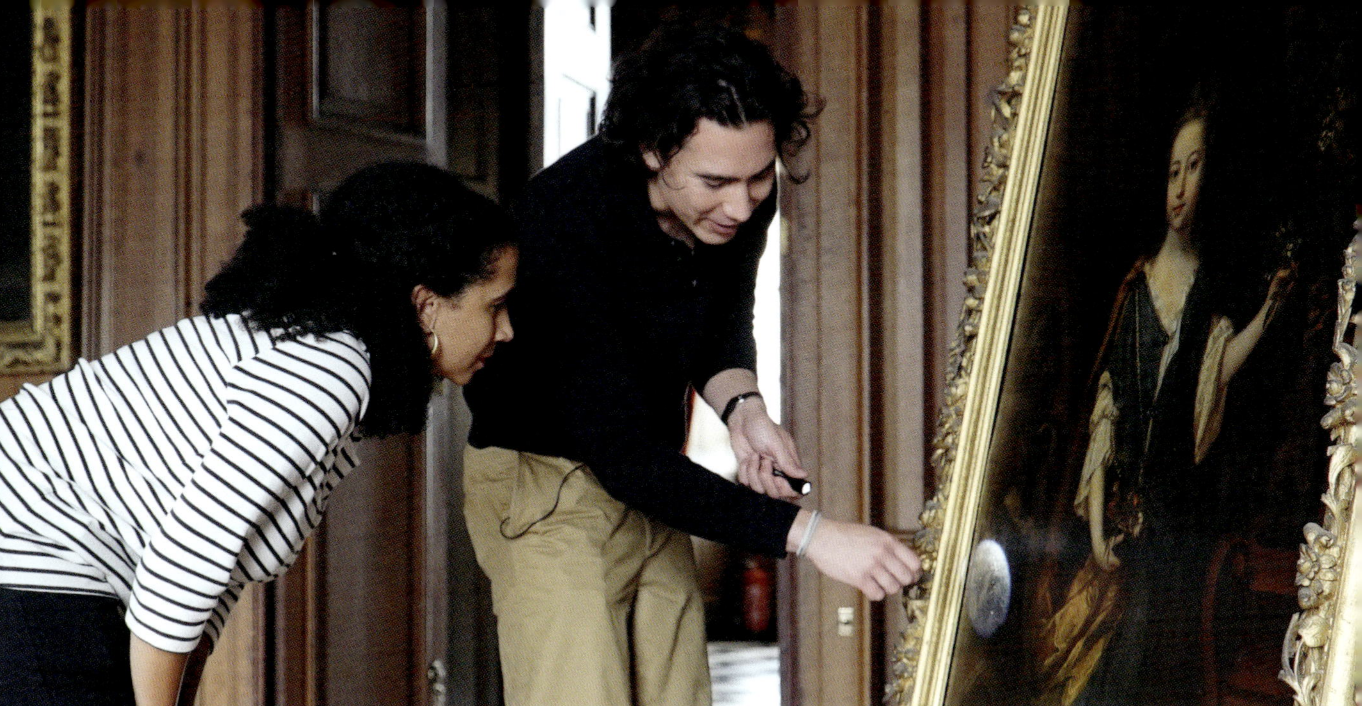

and seeing African people portrayed in a subjugated pose in the visual language of the country house is a really important thing to acknowledge. It's history, it's our past and it's here represented in our material culture.'

Responsible for bringing this child out of the shadows was paintings conservator Polly Saltmarsh. Her initial assessment of the portrait's condition suggested to her that it had been cleaned at least once in its past, although not the whole, as some areas were much darker than others. It seemed that some attempt had been made to clean the pale flesh of the young girl at the centre of the portrait, or as Polly put it: 'The easiest way to make a painting look better is to clean the lightest areas.' This left Polly with a great deal of work to bring all the painting's details evenly to the surface.

Because the painting had been cleaned so selectively, when the darkest areas containing the child and spaniel had their numerous layers of varnish removed and new varnish applied, they positively radiated out of the canvas. So while this child's identity remains a mystery, their presence and purpose can be considered now in greater detail.

^ Cultural Heritage Curator Charlotte Holmes and Senior National Curator for Paintings and Sculpture John Chu study the attendant's portrait for clues to their identity.

A Great Rarity Found Under the Stairs

Mezzotint by Christoph Le Blon

Oxburgh, Norfolk

Described by property curator Shona Johnston as 'a house of secrets', from the outside at least the hall at Oxburgh makes no bones about the aspirations of the family that founded it. The Bedingfelds built this fortified mansion, complete with a moat, in the fifteenth century, when they were rising stars of the Plantagenet court. Their Catholic faith, and refusal to renounce it when Henry VIII separated from the Roman Catholic Church in order to obtain his first divorce, put their social standing and their very lives in jeopardy. One of the secrets Shona references is the priest hole at Oxburgh, accessed through a concealed trapdoor in a lavatory, where priests could hide in the event of a raid. It is said to be one of the country's best examples.

Less well preserved but also, as it turns out, harbouring a secret beneath its darkened surface, is a picture that for years hung in a shadowy corner under the stairs. It was known to be a copy of a famous work by Flemish artist Sir Anthony van Dyck, the country's leading court painter in the seventeenth century. When its turn came to be sent away for conservation cleaning, this picture proved to be much more than had been assumed.

The image was copied from Van Dyke's original portrait of the eldest children of Charles I – the future Charles II, James II and Mary, Princess

> Many copies of this portrait of the eldest children of Charles I were made and hung in country houses but Oxburgh's proved to be something quite different.

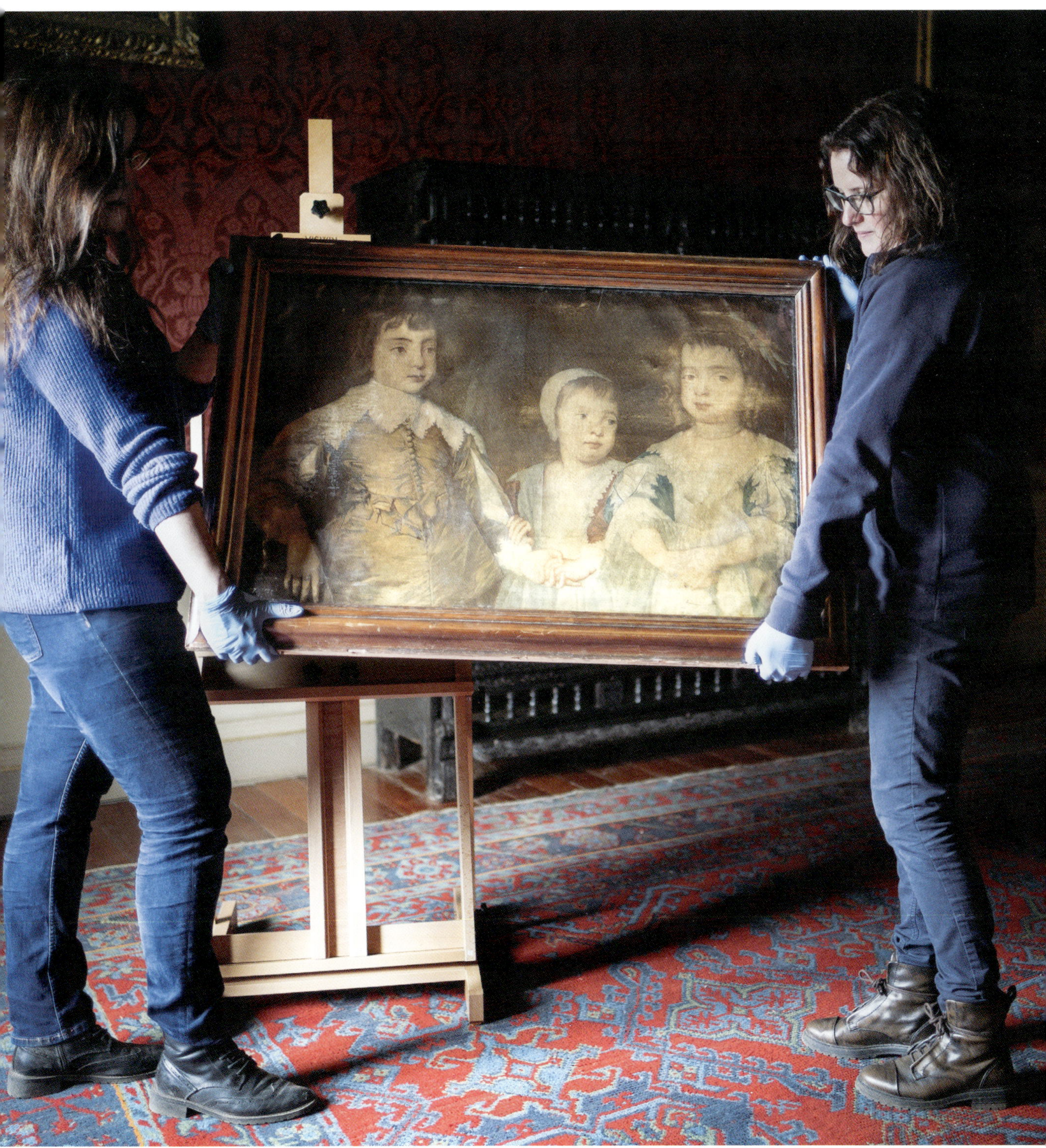

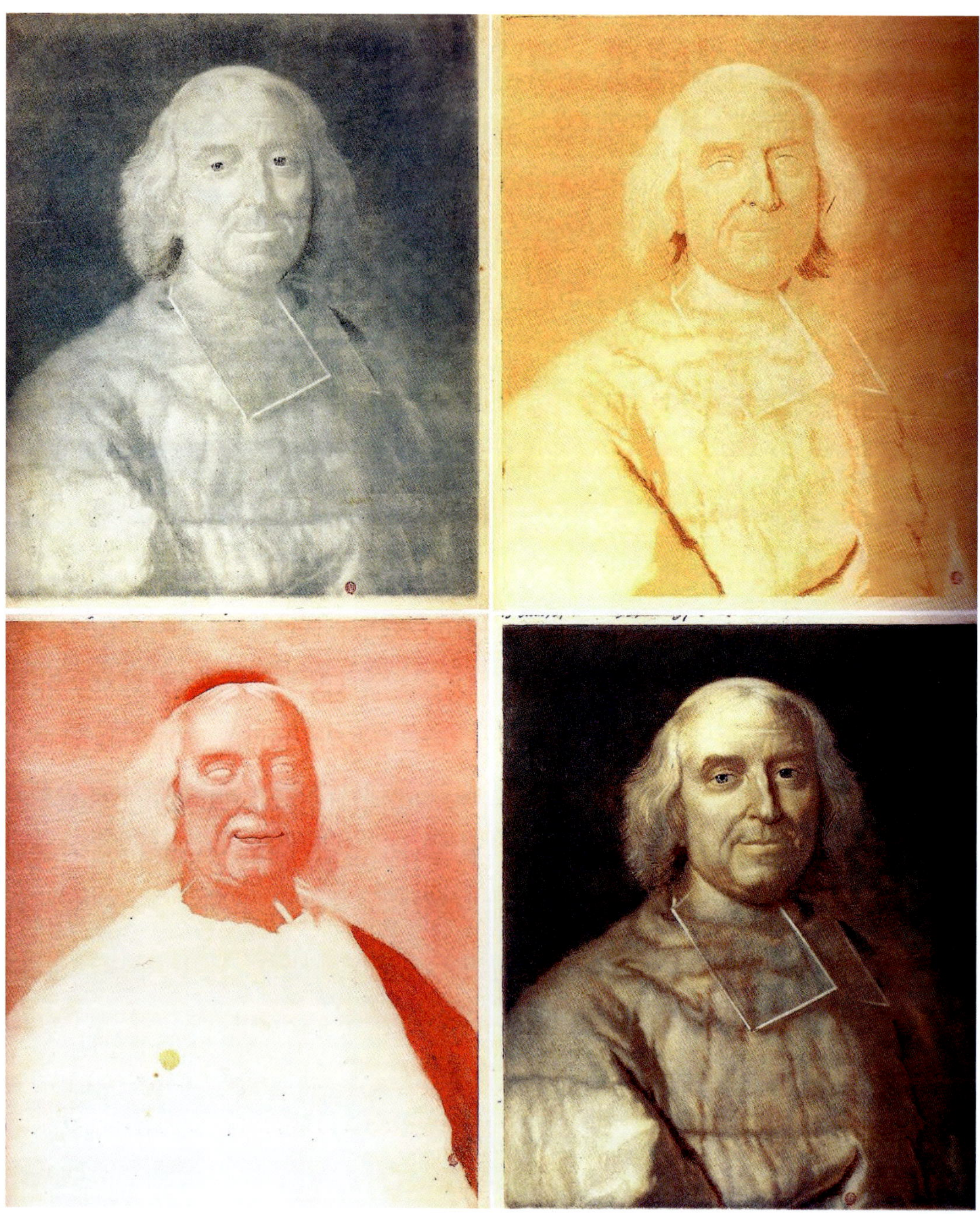

^ Jacob Christoph Le Blon's pioneering technique used separate prints of four plates in blue, yellow, red and black to make prints with a wide range of colours.

of Orange – and it had been assumed, beneath the heavy nineteenth-century varnish, to be oil on paper. That the portrait includes the future James II, the last Catholic monarch of Britain, would explain its significance to the Bedingfelds. Since the end of the Civil War in 1651, the Bedingfelds had proudly supported the fallen Stuart monarchy, both in exile and when restored to the throne. The painting was also important in its depiction of three Stuart monarchs; a complete set of Stuart portraits hung on the walls at Oxburgh, from Mary Queen of Scots to James II. But when this picture was sent to the Royal Oak Foundation Conservation Studio at Knole for the removal of that badly discoloured varnish and, it was presumed, a touching up of the oil painting beneath, conservators discovered the picture had greater significance still.

It turned out the picture was not oil on paper, but rather a rare, coloured mezzotint by Jacob Christoph Le Blon, inventor of three- and four-colour mezzotinting. In 1725, Le Blon asserted in his book *Coloritto* that any colour could be achieved by combining varying amounts of red, yellow, blue and black. When you consider that modern colour printing uses the CMYK model – cyan, magenta, yellow and key (black is the key colour in a print as, being darkest, it gives greatest definition and detail) – Le Blon's contribution to its development is clear.

The picture is known as a mezzotint, from the Italian *mezzo-tinto* meaning 'half-tone', as it was the first technique to create a range of shades between black and white without the use of lines, such as cross-hatching. It was invented during the seventeenth century and mezzotints remained monochrome until Le Blon developed a way of engraving three or four copper plates (one per printing ink) to make prints of paintings and portraits with a wide range of colours. The painting that this print was based on was in the possession of George I, who had granted Le Blon a royal warrant and a commission, thereby enabling access to the work.

Consequently, when the conservators at the Royal Oak Foundation Conservation Studio at Knole discovered what they had before them – not a copy in oil but a rare survivor from a key point in the history of printmaking – they were surprised and excited in equal measure. To put its rarity into context, it's believed that this print is only the fourth known example of Le Blon's *The Three Eldest Children of Charles I* to have survived into the twenty-first century. As it has been printed on paper it is exceptionally fragile.

> It had been assumed, beneath the heavy nineteenth-century varnish, to be oil on paper.

Paper conservator Nicholas Burnett was initially encouraged by the colours being so little faded, doubtless as a consequence of being tucked away in a dark corner protected from light for over a hundred years, and due to the thick layers of nineteenth-century varnish. However, examination of the paper revealed tears, creases, punctures and whole pieces missing. In his own words: 'It needs a bit of TLC but, wow, what a piece! Forty years I've been waiting to work on one of these.'

Before any repairs could be attempted, there was the matter of how much of the Victorian varnish it would be possible to remove.

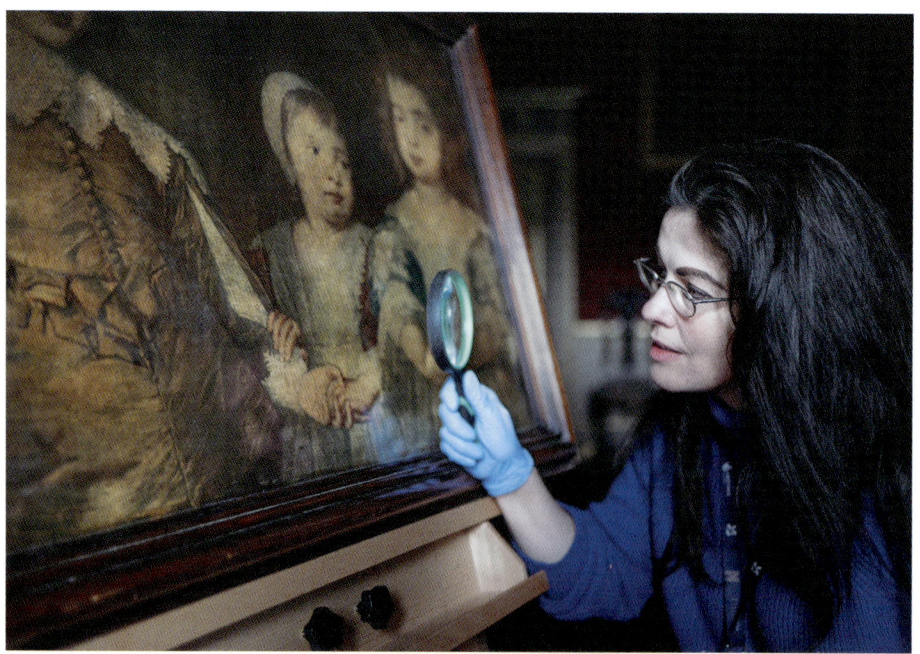

^ Ilana Van Dort, Collections and House Manager at Oxburgh, admiring the expert repairs made to this delicate and rare mezzotint.

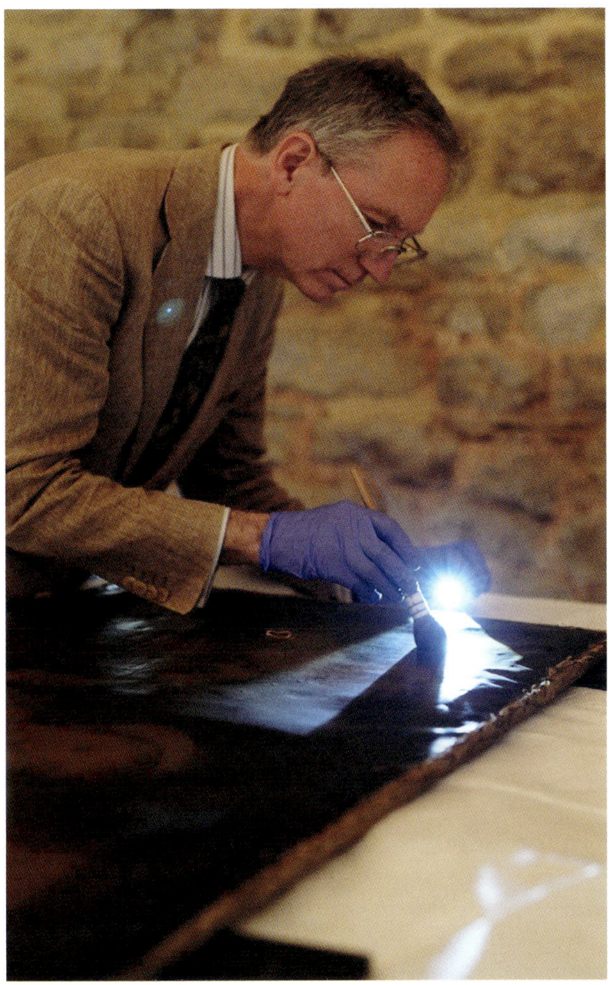

^ Paper conservator Nicholas Burnett fulfills a long-held ambition to work on a mezzotint by Le Blon.

Underneath was a thinner layer that appeared to have been applied by Le Blon himself, making the job of removing the top layer while keeping the original varnish doubly difficult. There being a large age difference between the layers, Nicholas hoped that a suitable solvent could be found – through careful testing on inconspicuous parts of the print – which would dissolve one but not the other.

When this proved unsuccessful, Nicholas had to try something different, using vapour rather than topical solvents. This atypical technique was successful in reducing the blanching and analysis confirmed the original hand colouring and varnish layers remained intact. This painstaking work allowed the dirt to be cleaned away and Charles I's children started to show themselves more clearly. Nicholas was then able to turn his attention to the tears and holes.

When the mezzotint was returned to Oxburgh, its resident and the sixteenth generation of Bedingfelds to live there, Sir Henry Bedingfeld, gave his verdict: 'It's lovely to have it back. You've done all this work on it and you've got rid of all the yellowness and filled up the holes. It's cleaner now and looks much more important too.'

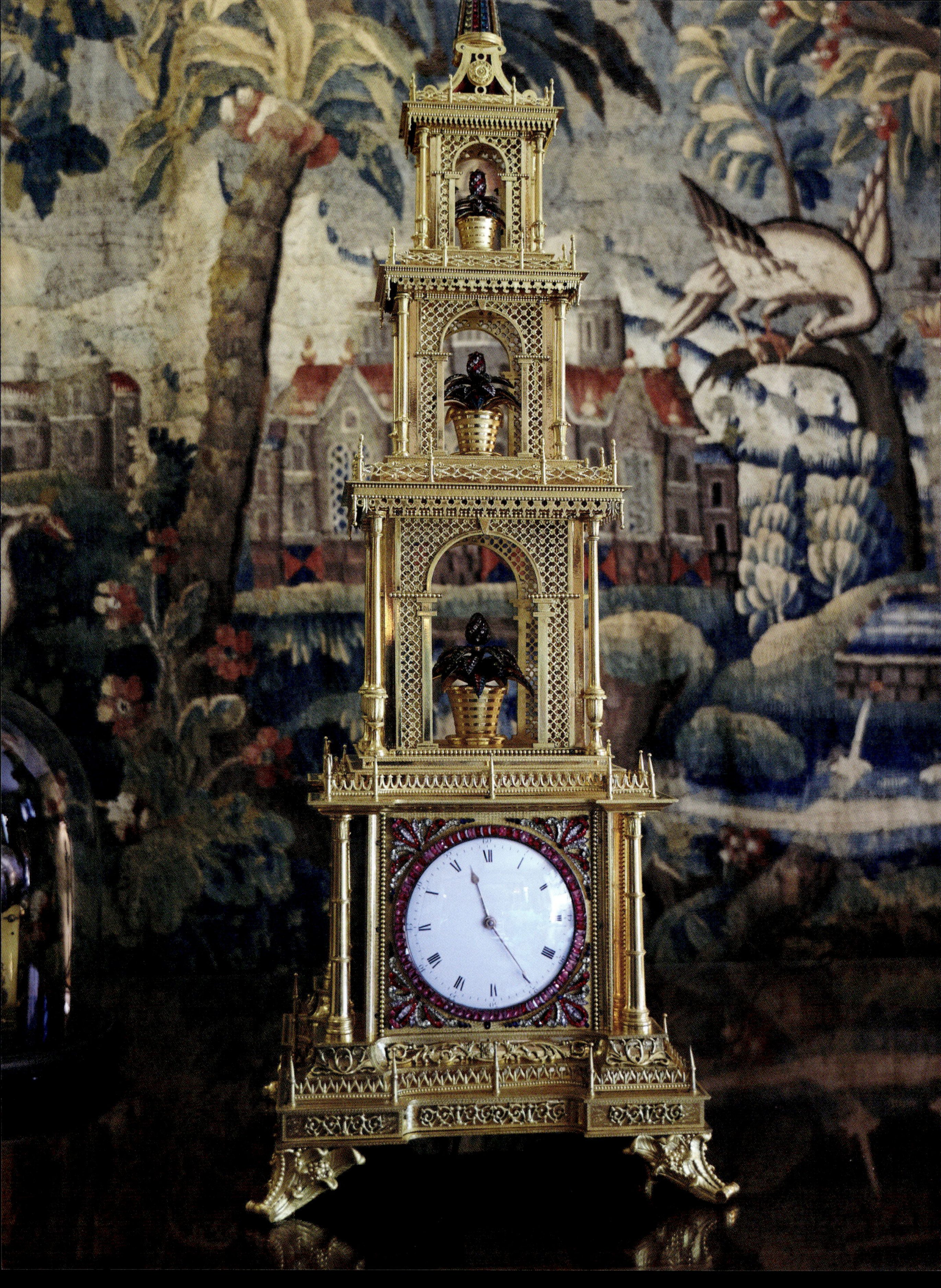

Restoring an Extraordinary Timepiece

Pagoda Clock

Anglesey Abbey, Cambridgeshire

Anglesey Abbey might, on first appearances, seem like so many houses that are looked after by the National Trust – an ancient ancestral home at the heart of an estate, full of the treasures and possessions accumulated by generations of the same family. That assumption may have been music to the ears of the last owner of Anglesey Abbey and the former owner of this timepiece.

He was Urban Huttleston Rogers Broughton (usually known as Huttleston), American-born but raised as an English gentleman. His father, also Urban, was a British civil engineer who had taken a job in the United States installing state-of-the-art hydro-pneumatic sewerage systems. While installing such a system for Henry Huttleston Rogers, oil tycoon and one of the world's wealthiest men, he met and married his client's daughter, Cara.

In 1912, by which time Cara had come into her very sizeable inheritance, the family of now four moved to England and their two boys were sent to Harrow. After school, Huttleston joined the 1st Life Guards cavalry regiment in the British Army, confirming in him a life-long love of horses. He and his younger brother Henry decided to start up a stud together, and in 1926 bought a farm close to the horse-racing town of Newmarket. At the same time, they came across a dilapidated

< Lord Fairhaven assembled a fine collection of clocks at Anglesey Abbey, of which the Pagoda Clock is a top-tier example.

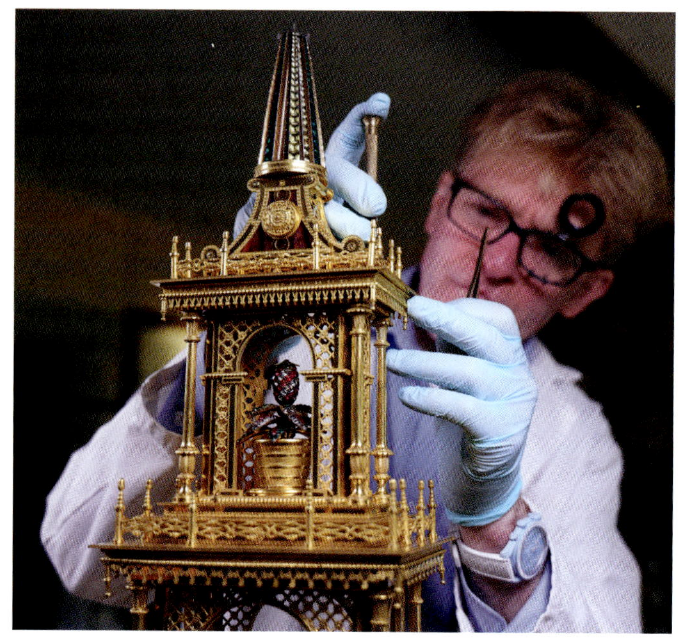

seventeenth-century country house built on the remains of a thirteenth-century priory, which they undertook to renovate.

Huttleston was just 30 when he arrived at Anglesey Abbey and for the next six years, with the enthusiasm of youth, a passion for British history and a large inheritance received in 1929 upon his father's death, he and his brother brought the Abbey back to life, creating an elegant country house while retaining a sense of its antiquity.

After his brother married and moved out, Huttleston – who had become Lord Fairhaven having inherited the peerage granted to his father – carried on with the alterations and additions necessary to accommodate his ever-expanding collection of books, pictures, furniture, tapestries, clocks and objets d'art. In all, he amassed almost 15,000 objects, not including books, that he effectively curated to give the impression of a house passed down through generations of the same family.

Lord Fairhaven clearly had a vision that he spent decades of his life realising, so understandably he was specific with his instructions when he left the Abbey to the National Trust. As Senior Collections and House Officer Katrina Dowman put it: 'Part of the agreement is that we are showcasing that way of life that he felt was quite quickly passing. [It's a] kind of lasting legacy for him.'

^ Intricate inside and out, the Pagoda Clock was a challenge undertaken by clocks conservator Matthew Read.

> Disassembling such a complicated timepiece requires a careful and methodical approach.

Within this curated time capsule, one of the glories of Lord Fairhaven's collection was, until it was recently repaired, a stopped clock. Of course, Lord Fairhaven being the collector he was, it's one of over 60 clocks at Anglesey Abbey that the Trust must try to keep ticking, but this one is something quite special. Known as the Pagoda Clock, as it takes the form of a tiered pagoda topped with an obelisk finial, it was made in London around 1800, probably by the clockmaker John Mottram. Much of the clock is made of ormolu, or gilt metal, embellished with enamelled panels and jewel-like coloured glass. To top it all, it has pineapples in pots on each of the tiers, which, when the clock is working, move up and down and spin to a tune played on 12 bells every three hours. This flamboyant clock was originally made for the Chinese imperial court, where there was a taste for luxury timepieces.

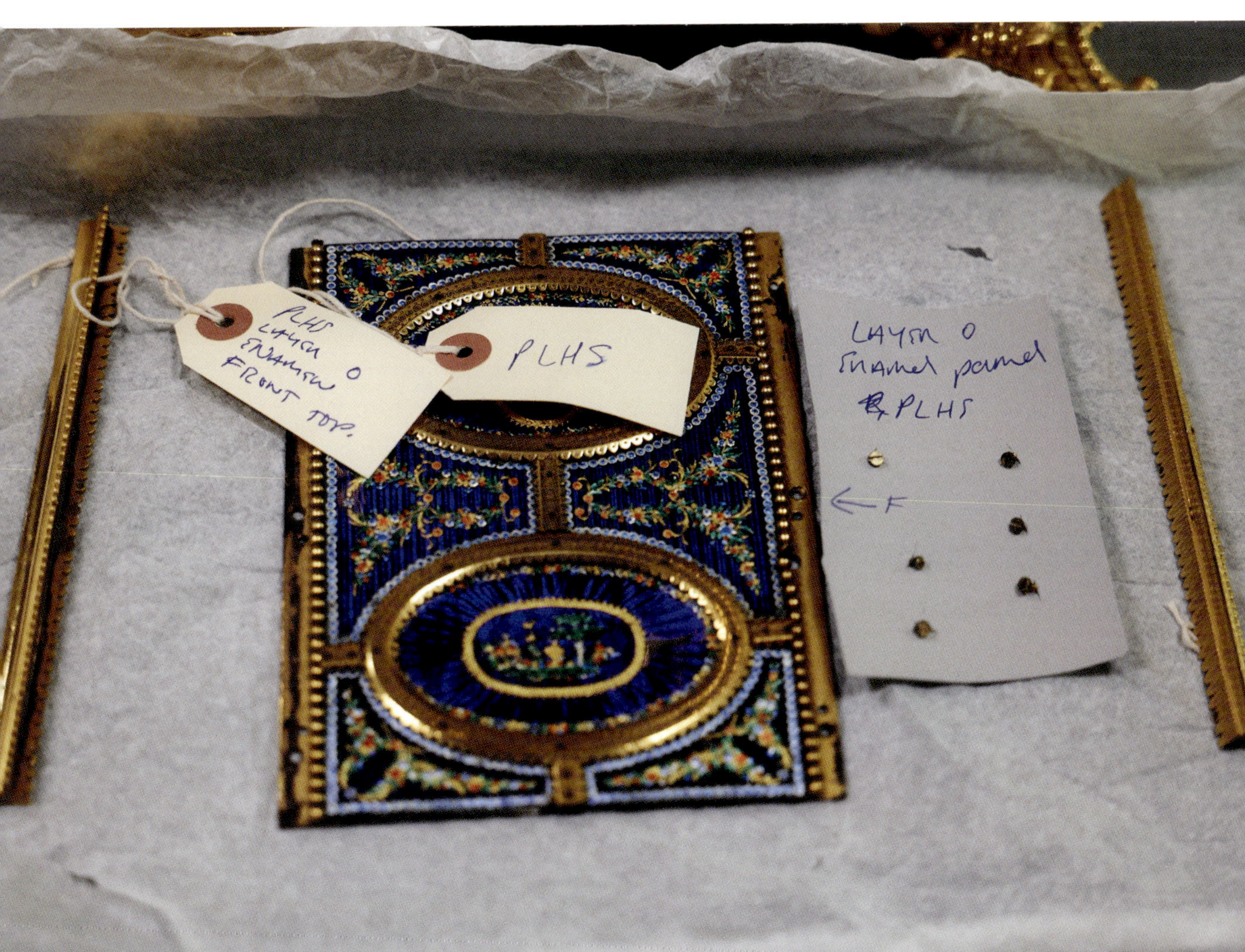

Clocks conservator Matthew Read took up the challenge of getting Lord Fairhaven's showstopper of a clock going again. But if the exterior decoration of the piece is eye-watering in its precision detailing, it is nothing compared with the complexity of the inner workings. To work out what had caused it to stop, Matthew had to disassemble the mechanics, wash, dry and re-lubricate them before piecing everything back together again. There is of course a process, but there is also a sense of voyaging into the unknown. As Matthew said: 'We've got no instruction manual; it wasn't in the nature of clockmakers to write things down. It was all very secretive.'

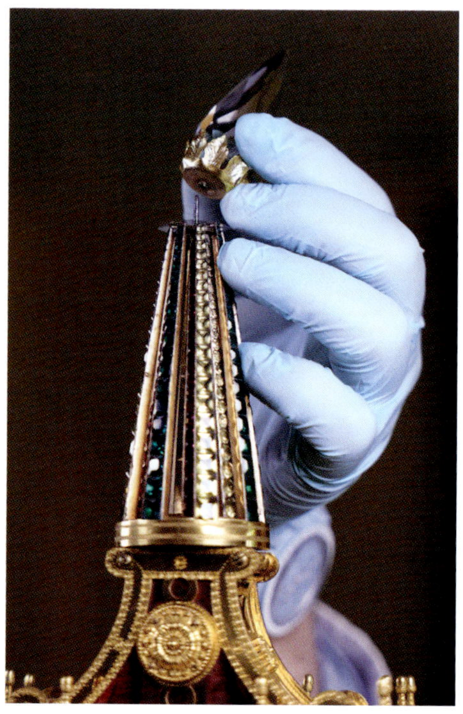

^ The obelisk finial that tops off the extraordinary decoration of this gilt metal and enamelled musical tower clock.

After spending days methodically taking the timepiece apart, cleaning and replacing pieces as he went, before finally putting the Pagoda Clock back together again, Matthew's moment of truth approached. The movement mechanism was clearly working again – an encouraging sign – but the failure of just one out of hundreds of parts could see those pineapples staying firmly in their pots. Waiting for any stopped clock to chime after a long period of silence is going to cause breath to be held, and as the house team assembled in front of the clock shortly before midday, it must have been an extremely anxious wait for Matthew.

Visitors today will find that it was worth the wait, however, as the Pagoda Clock once again joins the chorus of ticks and chimes at Anglesey Abbey.

> One of the three jewelled pineapple plants that lift from their pots and rotate as the clock chimes.

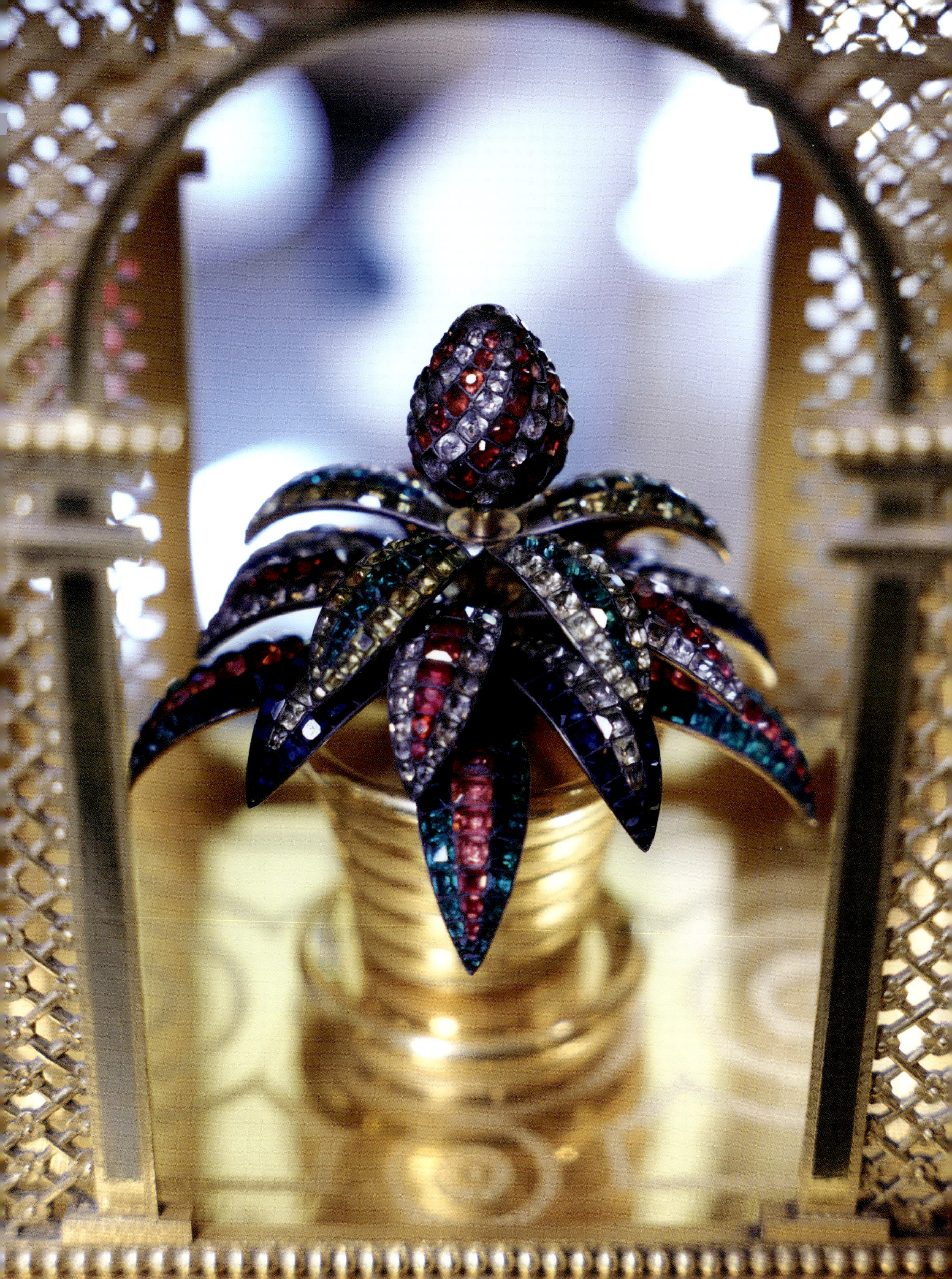

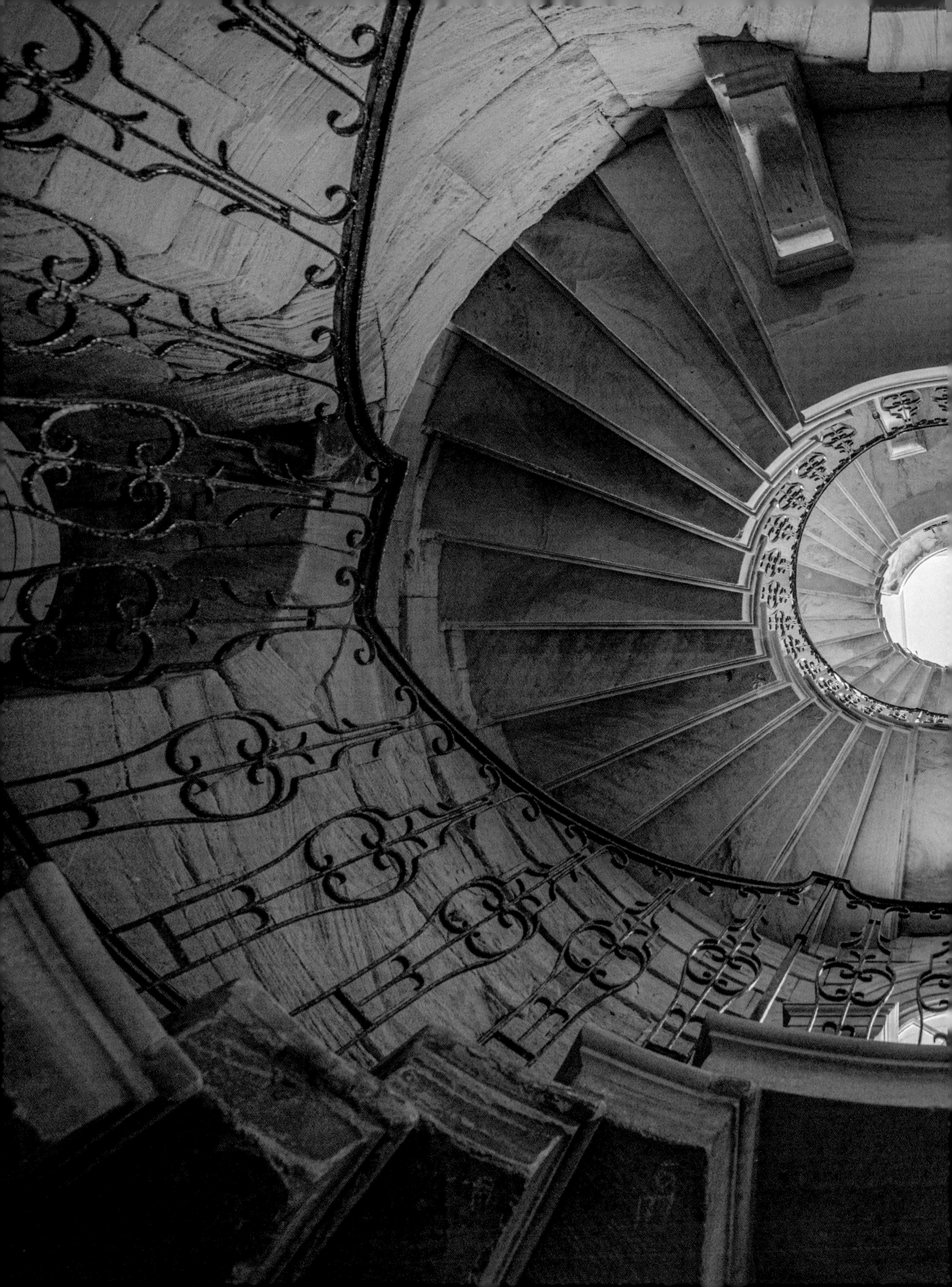

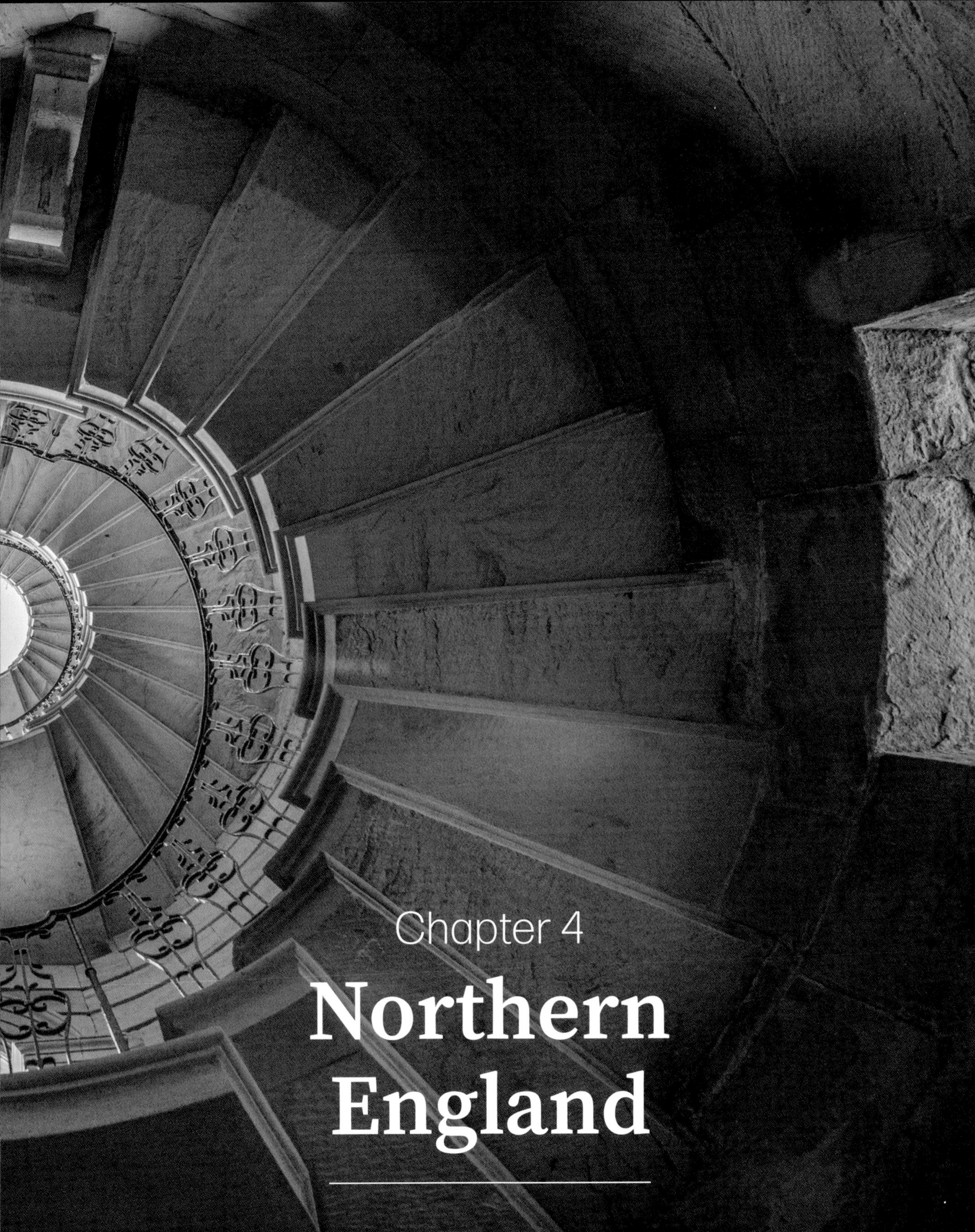

Chapter 4

Northern England

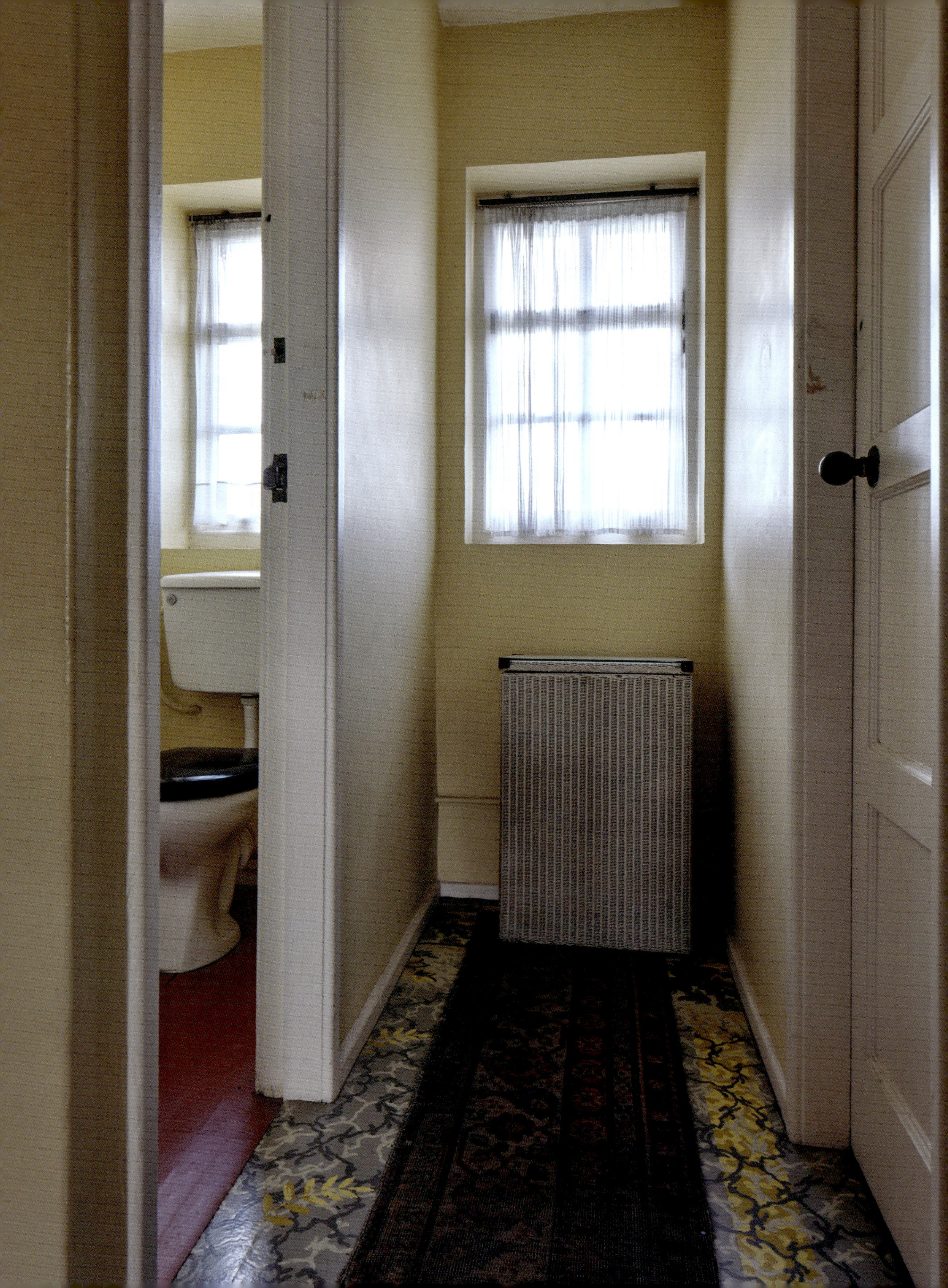

If Walls Could Sing

Lost Beatles Graffiti

20 Forthlin Road, Merseyside

This modest, mid-terrace house in the Allerton area of Liverpool was the rehearsal space of arguably the most influential band of the rock and roll era. What these walls bore witness to, and what is known to be sketched onto them, constitute the beginnings of The Beatles. Here, the world's best-known songwriting partnership began.

Paul McCartney met John Lennon in the summer of 1957, when Paul was just 15 and John 16, two years after Paul had moved to 20 Forthlin Road with his parents, Jim and Mary, and younger brother Mike. John invited Paul to join his band at the time, The Quarrymen, and soon the two boys were writing songs together. In Paul's words: 'When John and I decided to start to try and write songs, the most convenient location to do this was my home in Forthlin Road. My father went out to work and this left the house empty all day, so I would take off school, "sagging off" we called it, and John would take off from art college.'

A few years later, on 5 October 1962, 'Love Me Do' was released, propelling The Beatles into the musical stratosphere, from which they've never returned; 'Now and Then' was released in November 2023 and topped the charts on both sides of the Atlantic. But The Beatles' impact on popular music has less to do with single sales, or downloads, and more to do with the incalculable influence their songs and lyrics have had and continue to have on artists of every genre.

When the National Trust took the opportunity to buy 20 Forthlin Road in 1995, the decision surprised a few, it being so very different

< The smallest room in the house that was home to one of the biggest names in rock and roll.

from the sorts of properties the Trust is known for, but, as ordinary as the house might appear, it occupies an extraordinary place in the record of our country's social and cultural history – one which had a global impact.

In keeping with its ordinariness, the house is not shown as a Beatles museum, but instead appears as a record of life in 1950s Britain. Paul's mother, Mary, was very taken with her new home and took care with its decoration, notably the Sanderson wallpaper that she hung in the parlour. This was a designer that she much admired, but a whole room decorated in Sanderson paper was more than the family could afford, so she used inexpensive roll-ends, which meant that all walls were hung with her favourite paper but in three different designs.

Mary did not have long to enjoy her home. She died from breast cancer in October 1956, a loss felt so keenly by her sons that it was all the more important that the house should be presented with respect and, as far as possible, as it would have been when Mary lived here.

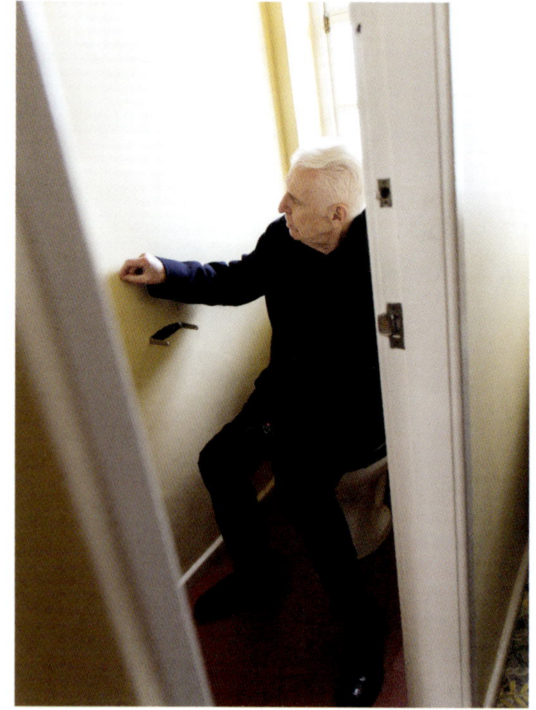

^ Mike McCartney helped the National Trust to identify the likeliest location of the young boys' graffiti.

Exceptions were made, however, as a time capsule would not have reflected Paul's development as a musician and Mike's as a photographer. So the boys' bedrooms tell of the time that their father introduced them to rock and roll, feeding Radio Luxembourg into their rooms from the radiogram downstairs, so that they could listen to the music of Elvis Presley and others. Displayed throughout the property are black and white photographs of the family taken by Mike, including pictures of Paul playing guitar, John and Paul jamming together and other scenes that capture the early days of their creative partnership. It is because

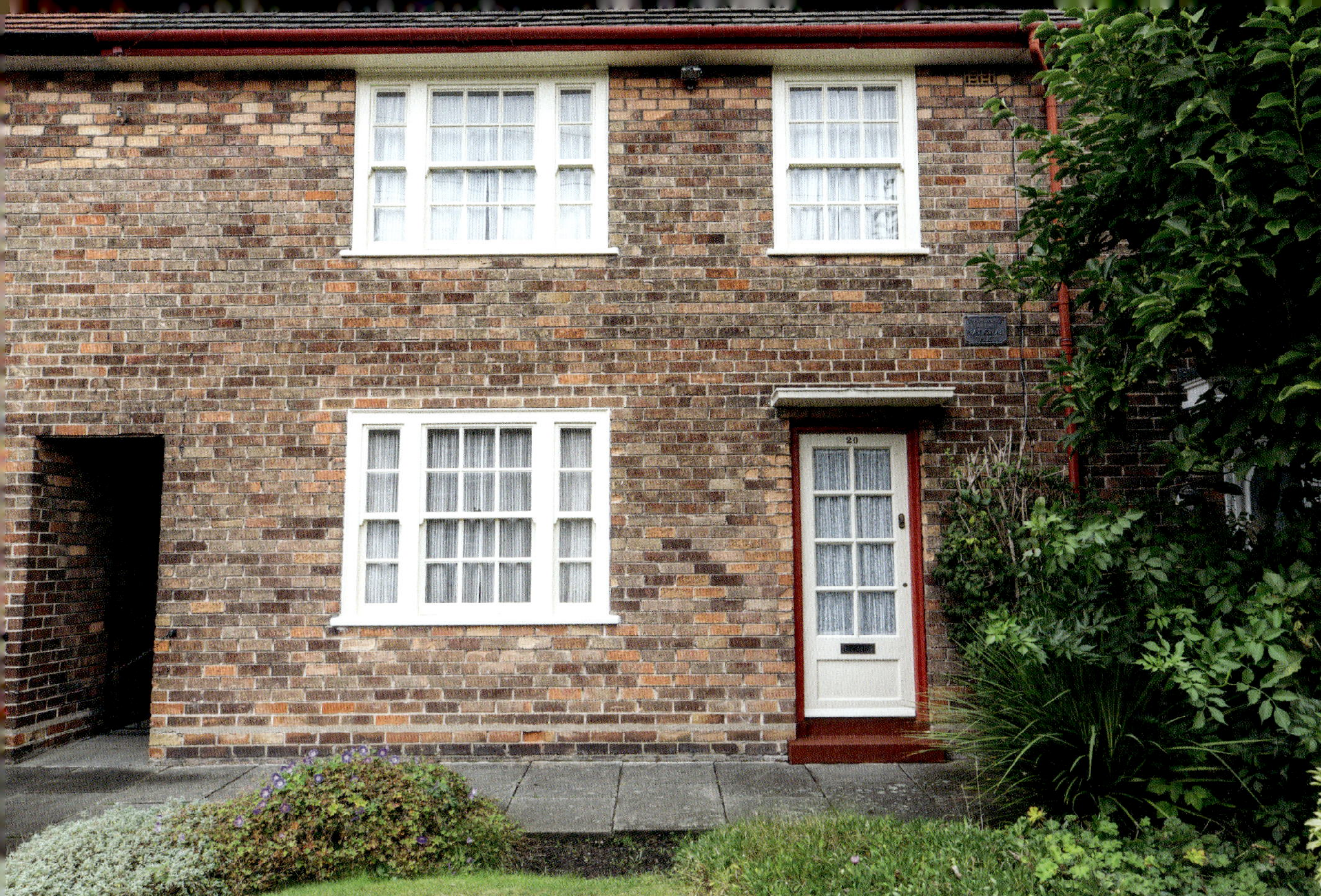

of these photographs that the National Trust was able to re-create the house as the McCartneys' home.

The smallest room in the house, in other words the lavatory, has also been subject to the same careful study and consideration over how to present it in the most meaningful way. The house at 20 Forthlin Road might appear outwardly unremarkable, but it is a record of a significant change in housing built in the post-War period, prior to which indoor toilets were luxuries not affordable by ordinary people.

The man responsible for the design of 20 Forthlin Road and many like it – around 6,000 council houses in Liverpool – was Sir Lancelot Keay, City Architect and Director of Housing. He believed in building houses that offered simplicity in layout but quality in construction. The house is a prime example of his work and the fact that this mid-century,

^ This mid-century, mid-terrace house offers a fascinating insight into the lives of many ordinary people and a few very famous ones.

mid-terrace property has an indoor toilet, let alone an upstairs convenience, is something of interest to students of architecture – but there is yet another aspect of this room that makes it of interest to many more besides.

Paul and John may have gone on to become musicians of mythic consequence, but when they were boys, mates messing around and making music, they behaved like boys. This included – no doubt to the consternation of Paul's father – scratching words and drawings into the toilet wall. As Mike recalled: 'I remember us – I don't know who started it … I'm going to say my elder brother! – just doodling on the wall. So I wouldn't be surprised if we had cartoons on there.'

'I remember us – I don't know who started it … I'm going to say my elder brother! – just doodling on the wall.'

Such hugely valuable recollections meant that the young Beatles' doodles were known to exist even though they had long since been obscured by periodic redecorating down the decades. The property's resident Beatles expert and tour guide, Peter Grant, tells the story of how, when the McCartneys moved out – partly because Paul's wealth meant that they were able to and partly because the intense interest in the house

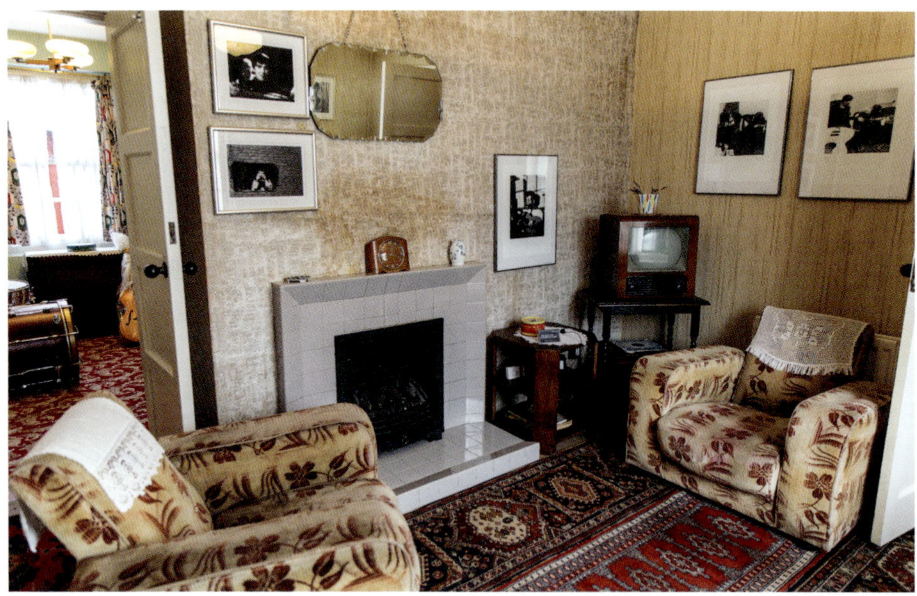

from fans made living there intolerable – their aunties and uncles came to help and painted over all the walls.

No detail is spared by National Trust curators, so when the story of the Beatles' doodles came to light, wall painting conservator Tobit Curteis was called in to investigate. Trained at The Courtauld Institute of Art, and with a host of prestigious international clients, Tobit was presented with the unusual challenge of restoring this cloakroom graffiti.

The first clue as to where Tobit should begin his investigations was that the doodlers in question used to make their marks while seated. This significantly narrowed down the search radius to the areas at arm's length from this position.

While the scenario was novel, the process was familiar, and Tobit began by carrying out tests to ascertain how many layers of paint were on the wall and which layer was the most likely to contain the graffiti. As Mike recalled that they would use pencil and felt-tip pens, not the most durable media, hopes of finding anything of significance were low. In Tobit's words: 'One of the things about graffiti is that it is not intended to last; it's just something that is there temporarily, so from a conservation point of view, it's a real challenge.'

A total of four layers of paint were found and the base layer was deduced to be the one bearing the historic markings. Tobit succeeded in locating three areas containing tell-tale traces of ink, proving the existence of the Beatles' doodles, but these were beneath a layer of well-applied paint – a credit to the aunties' and uncles' decorating skills, but to the detriment of efforts to further expose the graffiti.

However, with the location of the doodles established, their continued conservation is guaranteed. It is exciting to think that there are secrets in store on the loo wall, but until such time as conservation techniques, which are always improving, are available to more fully reveal them, the Trust has decided to let it be.

< 20 Forthlin Road is not presented as a Beatles museum, but rather as a record of life in 1950s Britain.

Skills and Techniques
The Writing on the Wall

Graffiti found a new form and established a whole culture in the movement that began in New York in the 1960s, but it has existed for as long as humans have had systems of writing and tools to make marks. Many examples have been found dating back to the classical civilisations of Greece and Rome. These empires built temples and monuments, and Roman emperors were sure to have their names carefully carved into architraves so that everyone would know who was responsible for these architectural wonders. But of equal historical interest are the marks of ordinary people, be they miners, masons or builders, recuperating soldiers or tourists passing through. After all, those with power and wealth generally have their stories carefully documented, ordinary folk less so. Historical graffiti can offer a glimpse of the everyday past and help to tell an alternative social history. 'If walls could speak ...', are words often offered up in historic buildings such as those looked after by the National Trust, but sometimes they can. Here are just a few examples.

At Sissinghurst Castle in Kent, graffiti was found scratched into the wall of the tower. Outlines of ships as well as names and dates were found etched into the soft stone during conservation work in 2018. The markings have been dated back to the Seven Years War (1756–63), a conflict between France and nations across Europe and the Americas. It's thought that up to 3,000 French prisoners were incarcerated at Sissinghurst. Overcrowding and the brutality of the guards meant that Sissinghurst was considered one of the worst military prisons in the country. Prisoners were at least permitted to send letters to their families, in some of which the inmates refer to their prison as 'Chateau de Sissinghurst', one reason the house is known today as Sissinghurst Castle.

In the gardens of Anglesey Abbey in Cambridgeshire are a recumbent lion and lioness thought to have been cast in the eighteenth century. The statues were acquired by Lord Fairhaven after he bought the property, together with his brother in 1926, with the aim of creating an elegant country house with the

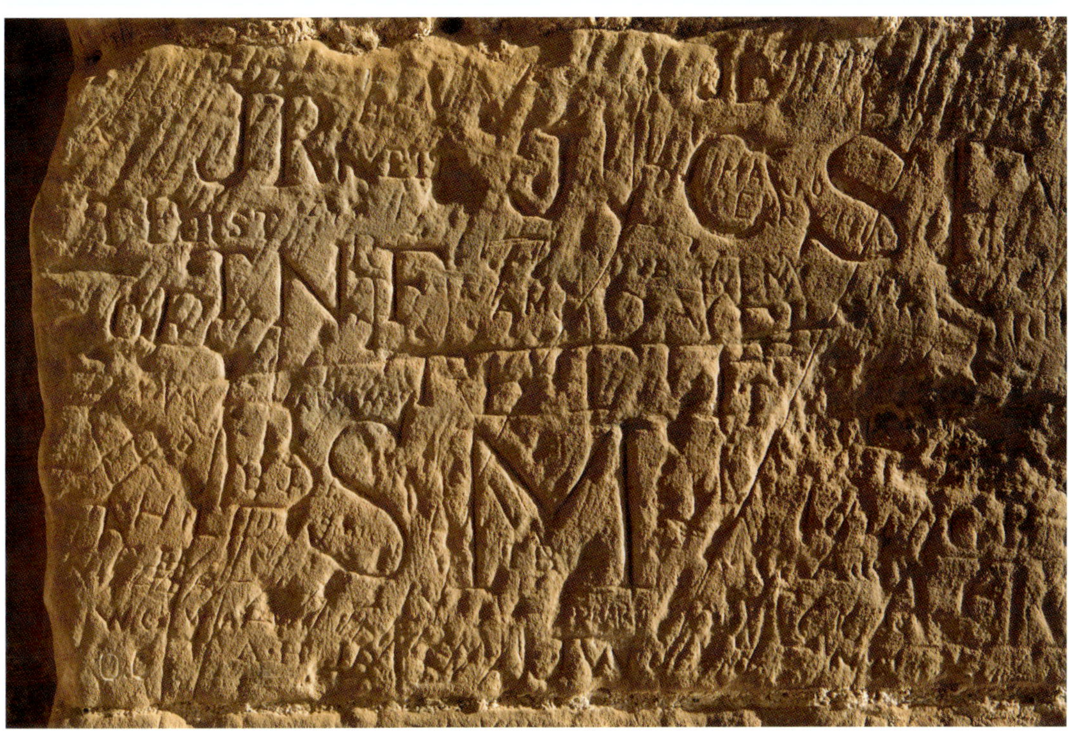

air of something much older. A profusion of initials, names and dates, such as 'C. E. Fox 1883', predate Lord Fairhaven's acquisition, and suggest that the lions were once mounted in a public place or institution.

At Bodiam Castle, built in the fourteenth century, masons' marks can be seen on the walls. Each mason had their own symbol, in effect their own 'tag', to mark the stones that they had worked on. These marks helped the master mason to identify exactly who had done what and how much they were to be paid – a useful visual guide for him, but also an invaluable source of information to archaeologists about how the castle was constructed. Also in the stonework of Bodiam Castle are many initials etched by visitors and tourists dating from the seventeenth century, and spanning hundreds of years. Destructive graffiti is naturally not encouraged in the present day, but these historic marks are of tremendous value for the extra perspective they give on the past.

^ Ancient graffiti carved into the stonework at Bodiam Castle, East Sussex.

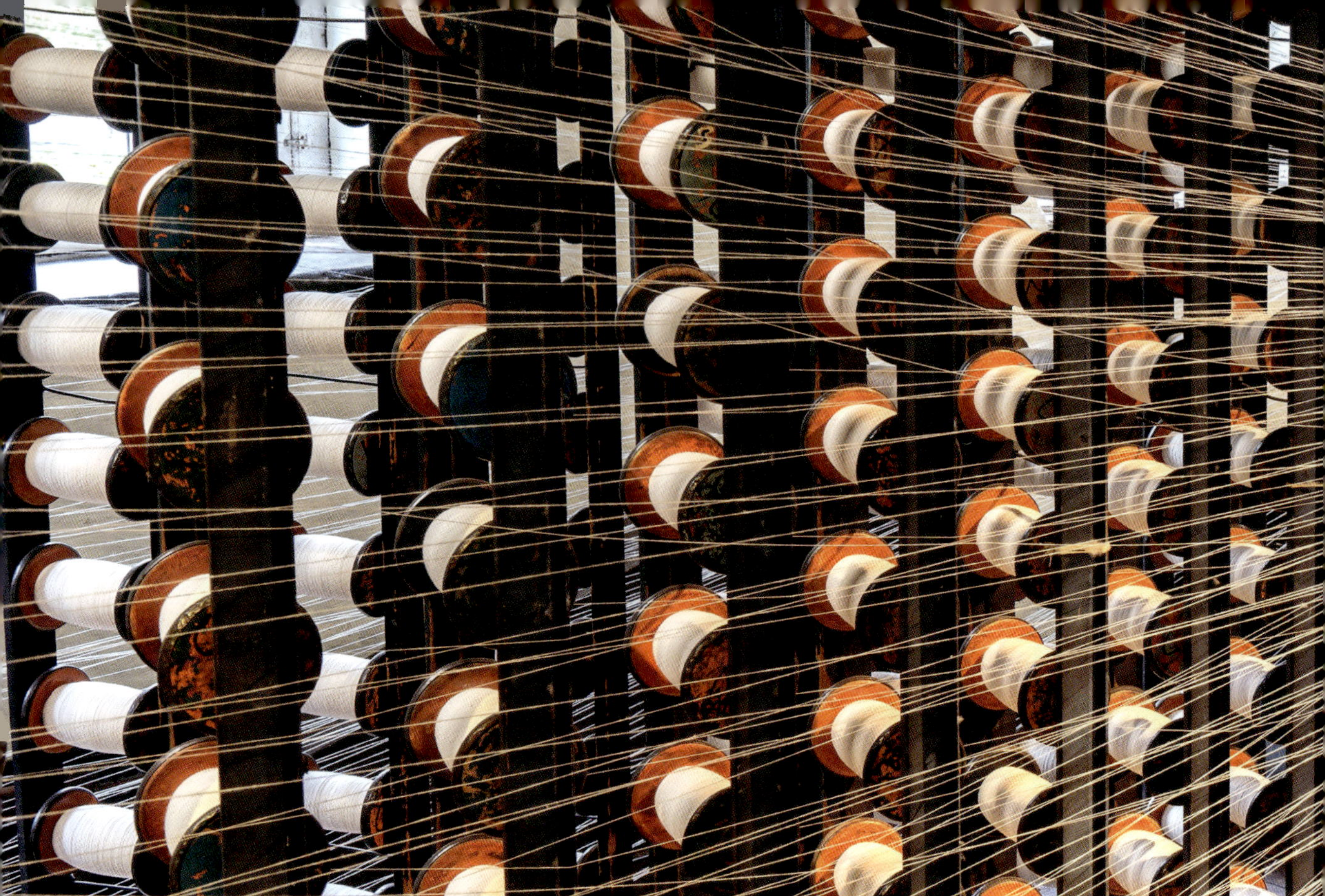

Spinning Yarns into Real Stories

Textile Factory

Quarry Bank Mill, Cheshire

Welcome to 'Cottonopolis', the centre of an industry that at one time produced half the world's cotton cloth. In 1853, the number of cotton mills in the UK peaked at 108. Quarry Bank Mill was one of many, but it proved more successful than the rest, and was productive for nearly 200 years. It is now cared for by the National Trust as a museum of the

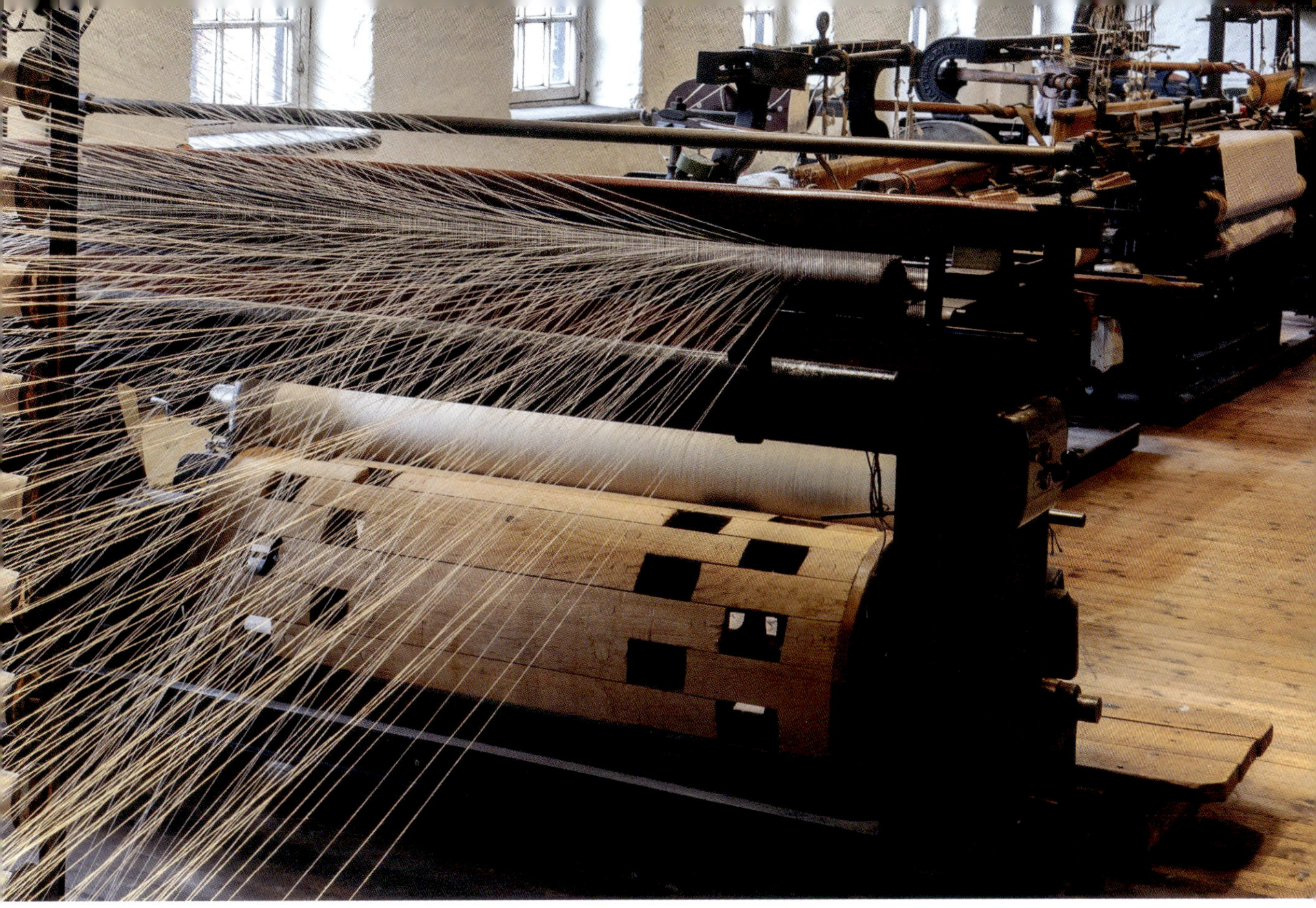

cotton industry and one of the best-preserved textile mills of the Industrial Revolution. What's more, the recent Quarry Bank Project, lasting five years and costing £9.4 million, has made more accessible than ever the material details of people's lives and brought to life their stories from the archives.

Quarry Bank was one of the first mills to be built, in the 1780s. Other early entrants took advantage of the development of steam power, but Quarry Bank's founder, Samuel Greg, chanced upon an especially good site for his mill. On the banks of the River Bollin and close to a road link to the Bridgewater Canal, it was fed by the natural power of the river and a constant supply of raw cotton from the port of Liverpool. However, it was more than just finding a propitious plot that led Quarry Bank Mill to become the largest and most successful cotton

^ Working machinery loaded with cotton at the recently restored Quarry Bank Mill.

mill in the UK. Samuel Greg not only founded a cotton mill here, but a whole community.

The complex began as a four-storey block of red brick, with a stone-coped pediment and a cupola, housing a bell, on its roof. It also bears an inscription, 'Quarry Bank Mill built by Samuel Greg Esquire of Belfast Ireland Anno Domini 1784'. The cotton-spinning machinery it contained was initially powered by a single water wheel. By 1796, the building had doubled in length, and a fifth storey and second water wheel were added. When Samuel handed the business over to his son, Robert, the mill began weaving cloth in addition to spinning yarn. The mill developed a reputation over and above their competitors for innovations in machinery, but also in how it managed its workforce.

The word often used to describe Samuel Greg's approach to labour relations is 'paternalistic', which is to say, outwardly benevolent but ultimately controlling. Where this attitude is seen most starkly is in the indenture of child apprentices, where a child was legally bound to their employer for a certain number of years, a practice that was not unusual at the time. While the water wheels powered the beams, spindles and looms, children were an excellent and plentiful source of labour, fetching, carrying and feeding materials into the machines. At the start of the mill's operation, it's thought that over half of Samuel Greg's workforce were poor and orphaned children, mostly girls. It may be that they were better off at Quarry Bank Mill than living with their families in poverty, or being placed in workhouses, but their days were long – 12 hours a day, six days a week – and their work could be dangerous – small fingers were often caught in or severed by machines. However, Samuel Greg provided food and accommodation, medical care and basic education.

In 1790, Samuel Greg built the Apprentice House to accommodate all the child workers, as many as 90, sleeping two to a bed. As a part of the Quarry Bank Project, the Apprentice House has been re-interpreted using material from the archives and the knowledge of historical advisers, such as Professor Hannah Barker of The University of Manchester.

> The mill was at the centre of a complex that included workers' accommodation, a school, a chapel and also areas in which to grow food.

What was once a rather bare space has been filled with objects to convey something of the material culture of the apprentices. As Hannah explained at the time: 'We will be introducing apprentices' boxes to tell the individual children's stories. These boxes would have been common amongst servants and other mobile employees in the eighteenth century, and would have been used to both transport one's possessions and to keep them safe. From surviving records in the Quarry Bank archive, we do know that it was likely that each apprentice had at least two sets of clothes, and that they sometimes worked extra hours to buy other items, such as a new gown, shoes, a sliding rule, a flute and even a watch. Recreating some of these possessions, and the boxes in which they were kept, alongside providing details of the lives of their owners, will give us a much stronger sense of these children's experiences working and living at Quarry Bank. I hope it will help visitors to feel a closer connection with these child workers and to develop a clearer sense of what being an apprentice at the mill would have been like.'

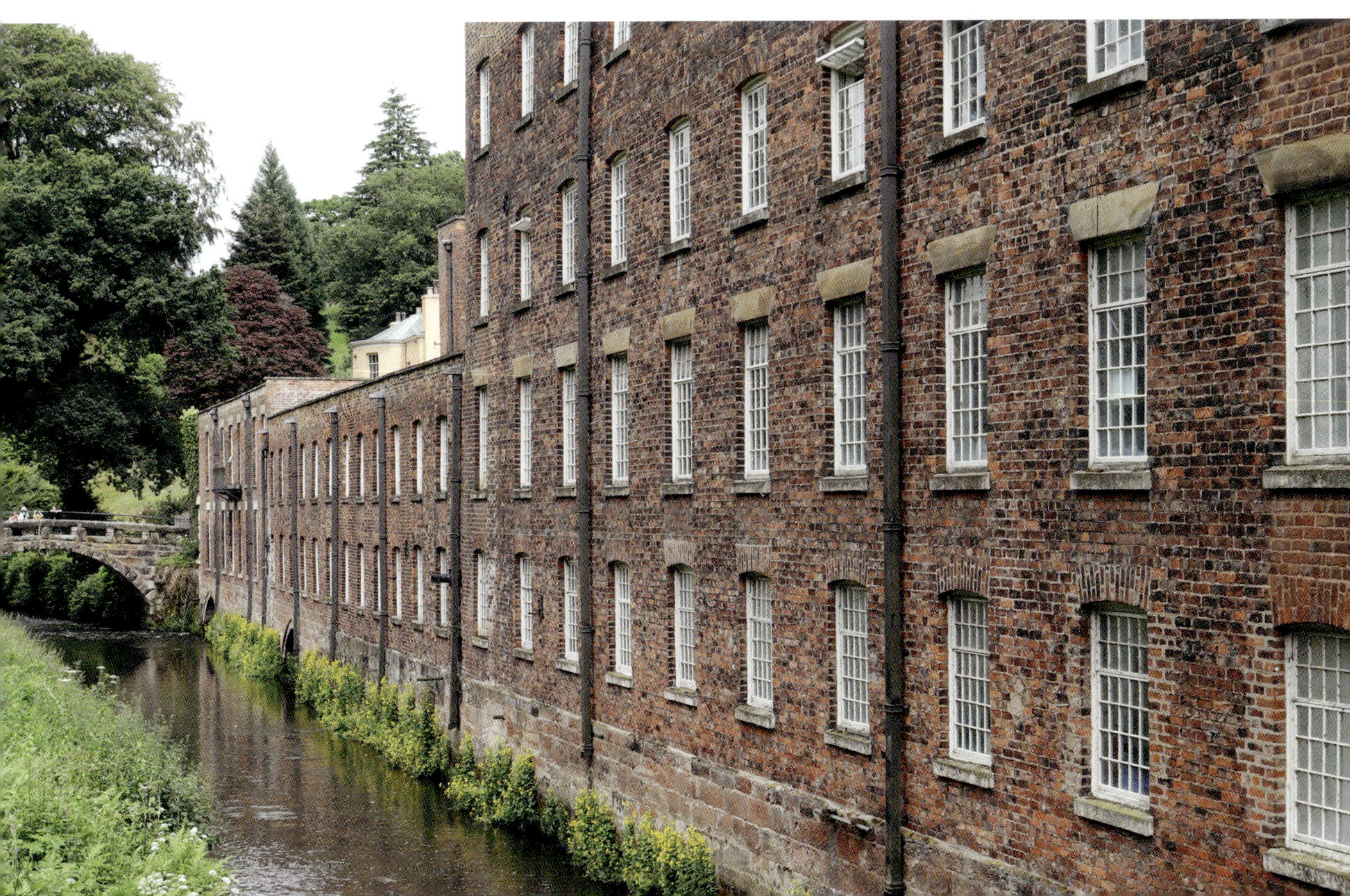

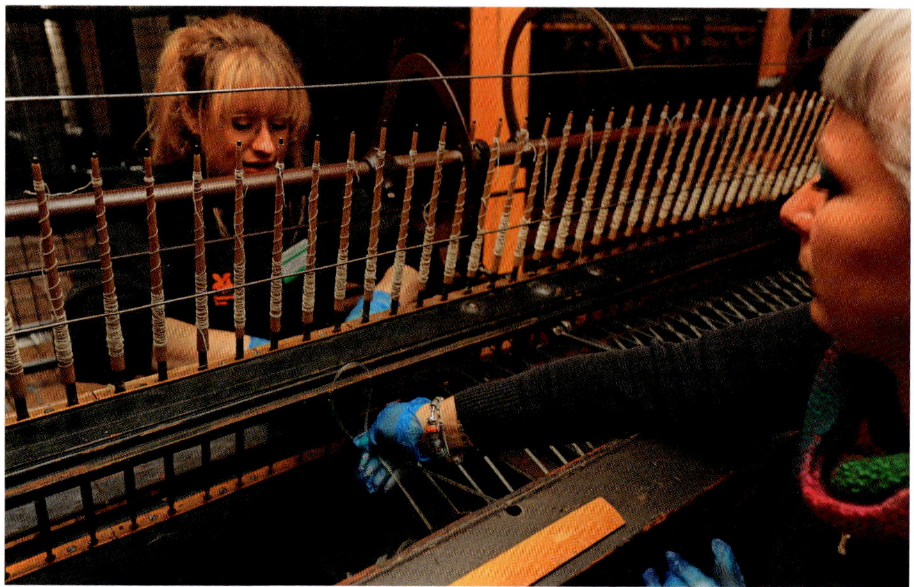

The Gregs built housing to accommodate other workers, initially by converting barns, and later added more workers' homes, as the mill increased in size. In the 1820s a new terrace of cottages, called Oak Cottages, was built. These were two-up, two-downs – two bedrooms upstairs, a parlour and a scullery downstairs, and a cellar – and would have housed large families and mixed households made up of lodgers and sub-tenants, living in all four rooms as well as the cellar. Each cottage benefitted from a back yard with its own privy, which was a decided advantage over houses in the towns, which often had one privy shared by an entire street. As a part of the Quarry Bank Project, one of these dwellings, 13 Oak Cottages, has been opened to the public. Locally known as Pickled Cottage as it is so little changed, it avoided modernisation in the 1960s and so it has been possible to present this space in a way that powerfully conveys what it would have been like to live here. Professor Hannah Barker was also involved in the re-interpretation of 13 Oak Cottages, and had to find ways of making the interiors readily understandable from a time when there were none of the

^ Demonstrations of the machinery give visitors a sense of how the mill sounded as well as looked.

formal distinctions of space that we're used to today. As she explained: 'It seems quite possible that inhabitants would sleep and sit and socialise and cook and eat in the room we might think of as the front room on the ground floor, while the back room might have been a form of kitchen (though without running water). It is also likely that unrelated individuals would have shared bedrooms, and probably beds.'

The cottages also came with some allotments for the tenants' use, while the Gregs had their own walled garden complete with extensive glasshouse; these have also been recently restored. Again, the archives were consulted, helping the garden team to recreate the space and grow the variety of seasonal vegetables that would have been nineteenth-century staples. The 1830s glasshouse, however, is more likely to have supplied the Gregs' dinner table with exotics and tender fruits, as the proprietors made their home on site, at Quarry Bank House, also recently restored and reopened to the public. Here the Gregs naturally afforded themselves luxuries and decorations not seen elsewhere, which have all been carefully conserved, not least the large stone floor tiles, every one of which was lifted, labelled, cleaned and reinstalled.

But it is the workers' stories that stand out the most. Following the Quarry Bank Project, all five floors of the mill are now accessible and visitors are guided by an audio-visual experience accompanied by the clattering of machines throughout. A brand-new lift shaft has been built using 8,000 bespoke and weathered bricks, making the whole site accessible.

The five-storey mill, the Apprentice House, 13 Oak Cottages, the walled garden and the Gregs' comfortable Georgian house all add up to a large and important piece of our industrial history, but there are yet more pieces to be discovered to complete the picture. Researchers will, in time, fully investigate, digitise and publicise the archives. Everyone who has worked on the project can be rightly proud of what Quarry Bank Mill communicates to its visitors, but the work is continuing. In the words of Eleanor Underhill, general manager at the time the project was conceived and delivered: 'Quarry Bank is a unique and very magical place but [there is] so much more to do to complete the jigsaw and enable everyone to experience the history of the whole estate.'

Modelled on the Past

The Dying Gaul

Fountains Abbey and Studley Royal Water Garden, North Yorkshire

This ruined abbey and water garden are part of a World Heritage Site, such are their singularity and importance. Beyond their obvious aesthetic appeal lie layers and layers of human history and the ways subsequent generations sought to shape the landscape around them. One of the remarkable things John Aislabie, followed by his son William, was able to achieve here at Fountains Abbey and Studley Royal, was the accumulation of a series of landscaping styles, whereas in so many other cases older designed landscapes and fashions were swept away by new. John Aislabie created his own version of a French-influenced water garden, and later William was able to buy the Gothic ruins of the abbey, and around it created a more naturalistic, romantic landscape that linked to his father's creation.

A politician turned landscape designer, John Aislabie switched between parties but managed to attain wealth and high office before becoming embroiled in a scandal that cost him his career. In 1721, he was expelled from his position as Chancellor of the Exchequer. His crime was to accept money to promote the South Sea Island Company, a public-private partnership, that was granted a monopoly to supply enslaved people from Africa to islands in the 'South Seas' and South America. Given Britain's involvement in the War of the Spanish Succession, it was highly unlikely the company would have been able to make a profit, but trading in its shares reached a frenzy before the stock price collapsed, leaving thousands of investors ruined.

> *The Dying Gaul* reflected in John Aislabie's water garden.

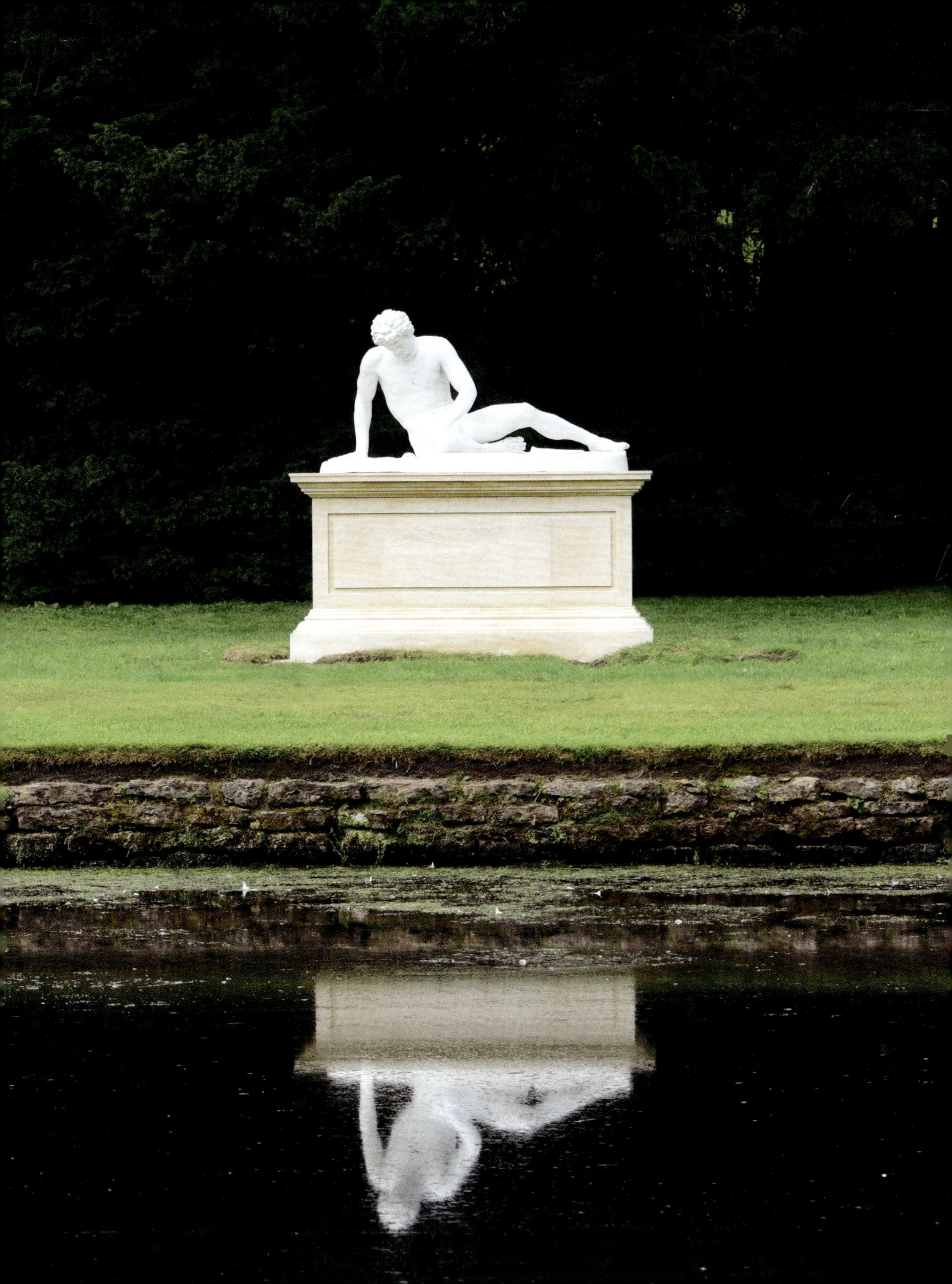

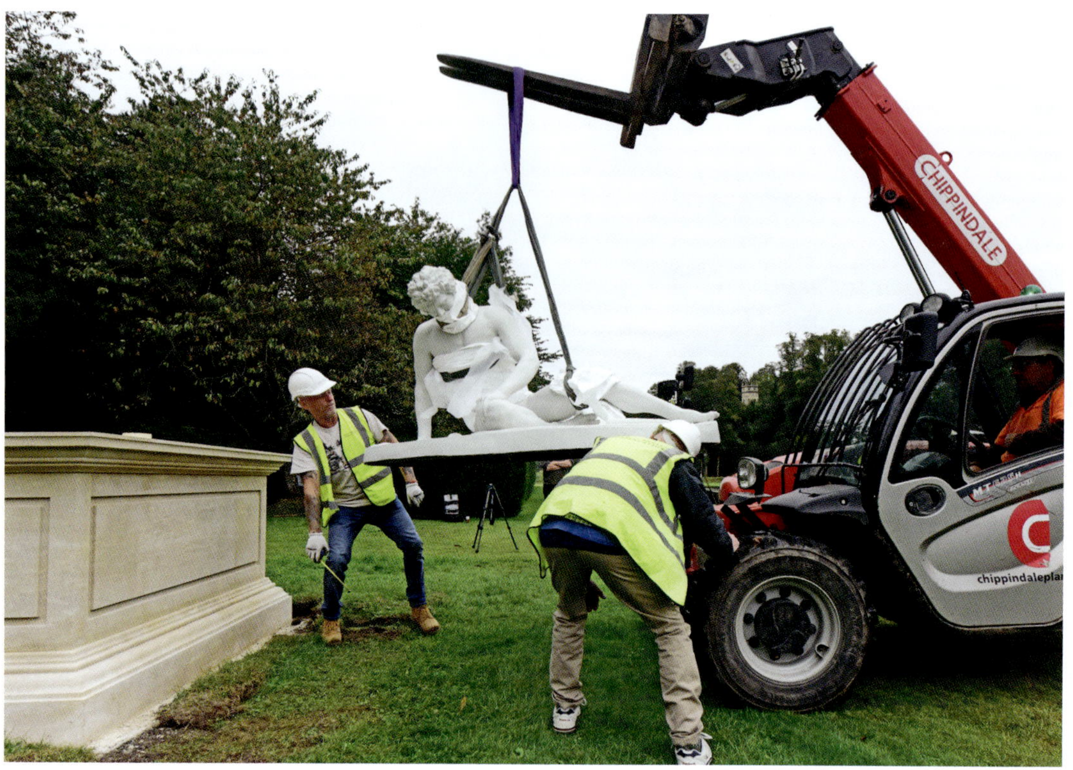

^ The new replica of *The Dying Gaul* is moved to his final resting place.

After a spell in the Tower of London and payment of a fine of £45,000, Aislabie spent his retirement creating the finest water garden the country had ever seen. In a landscape of sublime beauty were buildings and statues that would have been familiar to classically educated Georgians, who would have recognised their forms and been pleased by the references. *The Dying Gaul* was one of the most celebrated works to have survived from antiquity – a Roman copy in marble of a now lost Greek statue in bronze – and facsimiles in the form of engravings and statues were much sought after by the educated classes in the seventeenth and eighteenth centuries. For that reason, John Aislabie was bound to use it to adorn his water garden. But as a once-great man humbled, did he perhaps choose the image of a fallen hero as a reference to himself?

This statue is of a naked man, pierced in his side with his head bowed as he slumps to the floor. Since the excavation of the original in around

1620 from the site of the ancient Gardens of Sallust in Rome, *The Dying Gaul* was commonly known as *The Dying Gladiator*. After restoration – it was missing its right arm, left knee, toes, left thumb, nose, penis and portions of the base, including the sword – it went on display at the Capitoline Museums. The statue's remarkable realism and expressive pathos captivated seventeenth- and eighteenth-century audiences and became a must-see on the Grand Tour. Lord Byron saw it during his journeys around the Mediterranean, and commemorated it in *Childe Harold's Pilgrimage*:

> 'I see before me the Gladiator lie:
> He leans upon his hand – his manly brow
> Consents to death, but conquers agony,
> And his drooped head sinks gradually low –
> And through his side the last drops, ebbing slow
> From the red gash, fall heavy, one by one,
> Like the first of a thunder-shower; and now
> The arena swims around him – he is gone.'

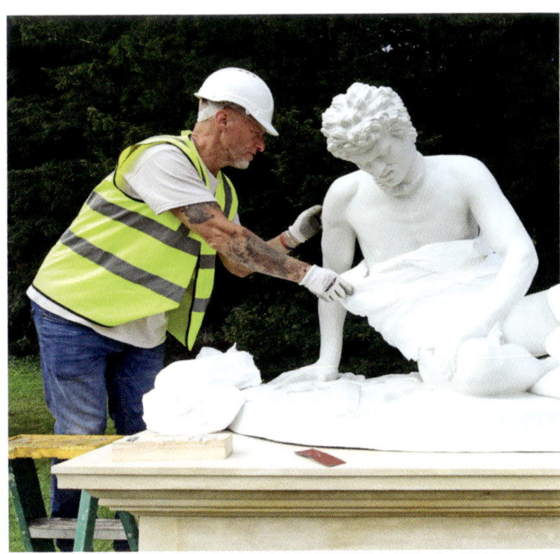

^ Missing since the nineteenth century, *The Dying Gaul* returns to Studley Royal.

There are no records of John Aislabie's Grand Tour, but we do know his son William completed his in 1720. At this time John was still Chancellor, but he had begun work on his water garden a number of years before he found himself with extra time on his hands.

He had begun to lay out the water gardens at Studley Royal in 1718, and had been a subscriber to John James's *Theory and Practice of Gardening*, a translation of a French work by Antoine-Joseph Dezallier d'Argenville. The geometric design

John chose for his water garden did indeed follow the French fashion and was clearly influenced by the kind of formality seen at the Château de Chantilly and the Palace of Versailles.

Part of John's original design are the Moon and Crescent Ponds beside a canalised section of the River Skell that flows through the estate and wraps around the ruins of Fountains Abbey. To achieve the stillness and tranquillity of the ponds' mirrored surfaces required an extraordinary amount of earthmoving and manpower. By 1726, approximately 100 men were working to create water features, which included canals, cascades and ponds.

By the 1730s John was able to add the finishing touches to his newly created landscape and he introduced five classical statues that were cast in lead and painted off-white to better reflect in the surfaces of the ponds. The subjects of these statues included: Neptune, Roman god of the sea, in an appropriately aquatic setting; Bacchus, the god of wine and revelry, as these were pleasure gardens after all; the Wrestlers, which was the subject of much scholarly attention at the time and demonstrated John's culture and learning; and a beautiful young man, thought to be Endymion, a shepherd loved by the moon goddess Selene.

The fifth statue is *The Dying Gladiator*, as the statue was then titled. By the time Fountains Abbey and Studley Royal came into the ownership of the National Trust in 1983, the statue had long-since vanished, it is thought in the late nineteenth century. By this time, it had been re-identified as a 'barbarian' and a 'Gaul', owing to the tell-tale facial hair (young men in classical Greek and Roman statuary are invariably clean-shaven), the torc around his neck and the wind instrument lying between his legs, which is known as a carnyx and was used by the Celts.

Whether a Roman gladiator or a Celtic barbarian, without it John Aislabie's water garden could not be considered complete. After conservation work had been carried out on the existing four statues, thoughts turned to the missing figure. As Sarah France, World Heritage Co-ordinator at the site, explained: 'In 2016 we reinstated the white finish to the existing lead statues, and inspired by that work we started to think about returning the "missing" statue. We have no idea why *The Dying Gladiator* statue disappeared in the late nineteenth century, but

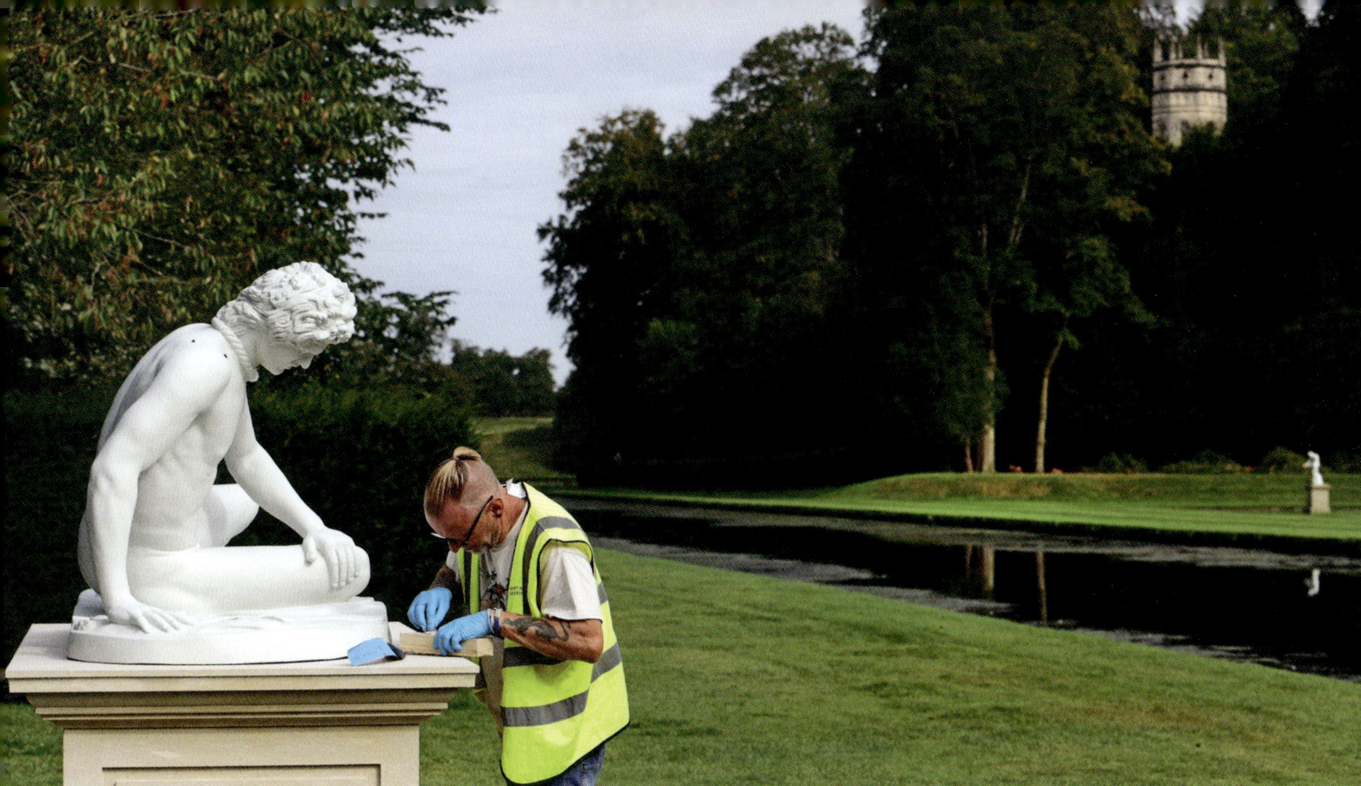

^ John Aislabie commissioned *The Dying Gaul* as one of a set of five classical statues for his water garden.

after detailed research and working closely with experts in lead statuary, we were sure we could make a replica of the missing statue that would enhance the exceptional beauty of the gardens.'

Its form was of course well known, having been replicated in gardens all around the world, and archaeological surveys had revealed its original position beside the Moon Pond. When funds were found, thanks to the generous support of visitors and the local community and the proceeds of a floodlit fun run around the estate, a brand-new statue was cast by expert statue conservators, Rupert Harris Conservation. In addition to the statue, a plinth measuring over 6½ feet (2 metres) in length and 3¼ feet (1 metre) in width and height was manufactured at Cadeby Stone's Doncaster works.

Happily, beside the Moon Pond and completing the scene at Studley Royal, there is now a fine reproduction of a Georgian copy of a Roman replica of the Greek original. Sadly, for *The Dying Gaul*, his final moments of agony will play out for many years to come.

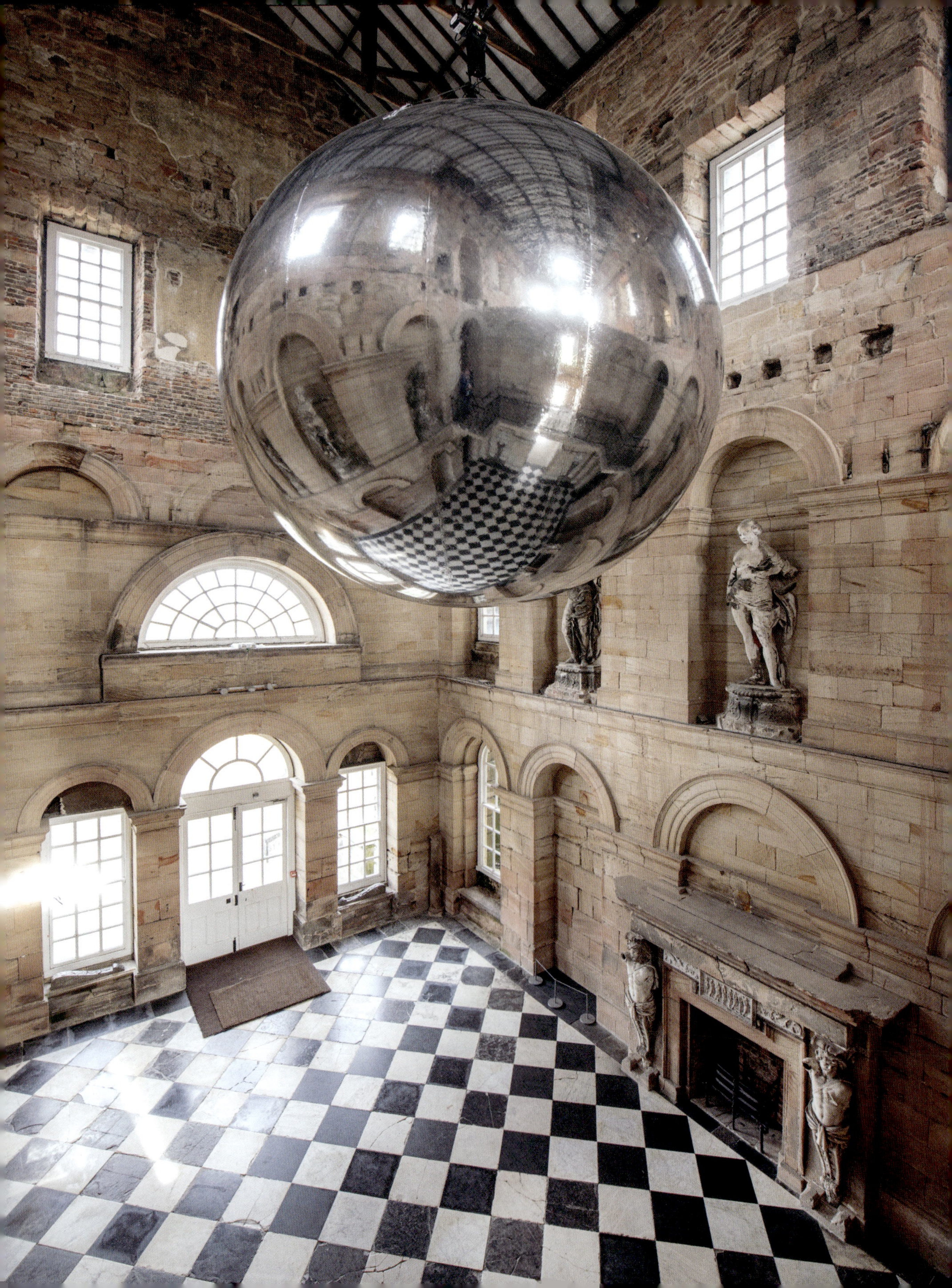

A Theatrical Reveal

'The Curtain Rises'

Seaton Delaval Hall, Northumberland

When Seaton Delaval Hall came into the care of the National Trust in 2009, the quality of the property's architecture, even in its ravaged state, was clear. Its once magnificent interiors had suffered from decades of abandonment after partial destruction in a ruinous fire of 1822. Despite twentieth-century rejuvenation, it can fairly be said that Seaton Delaval Hall has a history as chequered as the floor in its iconic Entrance Hall. Indeed, standing inside that space today, you get a very clear sense that this is a place that has seen its share of times both good and bad. Presenting such layers of history while a major conservation project takes place requires inventiveness and imagination. Fortunately, Seaton Delaval Hall is just the place to inspire those things.

In 1718, Admiral George Delaval commissioned the country's leading architect, Sir John Vanbrugh, to design a magnificent new house. Sadly, neither client nor architect lived to see their vision realised: Admiral George died in 1723 and Vanbrugh three years later. It fell to the Admiral's nephew, Captain Francis, and his wife Rhoda Apreece to continue the work.

The couple completed construction of the mansion and executed it brilliantly. Seaton Delaval Hall is considered by some to be one of the finest examples of Vanbrugh's work. Its relatively unaltered state is partly due to the length of time it was occupied – around a century only.

< The mirrored sphere in the Entrance Hall of Seaton Delaval Hall suggests a novel way of reflecting on history.

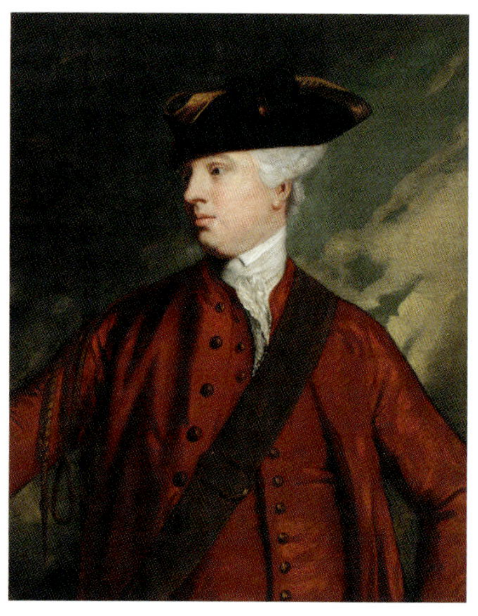

^ Sir Francis Blake Delaval by Sir Joshua Reynolds.

However, though the Delavals lived here for a relatively short period of time, they lived *large*.

Captain Francis and Rhoda had 12 children – eight sons and four daughters – so you can imagine a clamorous family home. But Seaton Delaval Hall became much more than that. By the time the eldest of the boys, Sir Francis Blake Delaval, came into his inheritance, it played host to such scenes that it became the talk not just of the town but of the entire country. The exploits of the Gay Delavals, as the Georgian press dubbed them, became legendary. William Howitt, not a tabloidist but a historian and chronicler of his own times, wrote of Francis's gatherings: '... the vast and almost perpetual crowds of company entertained; the fêtes given, when this beautiful house and gardens became in truth a perfect fairyland of light, and beauty, and music; with floating throngs of gay and lovely creatures, that were ready to rush into the most extraordinary frolics and scenes of mischief imaginable.'

The Delavals' hosting was certainly generous but sometimes their guests were the source of the entertainment. Francis and his siblings were partial to a practical joke and it's said that one of their japes included putting drunken guests to bed in a dark room in which they'd wake to find themselves apparently lying on the ceiling. Legend does not preserve how this prank was executed, but one can imagine inverted pictures on the walls, and chairs and tables suspended from the ceiling.

Francis's personal favourite form of entertainment appears to have been the theatre. Many of his friends were actors and he spent large sums of money staging theatrical performances in London, in which he cast his brothers, sisters and friends.

Fortunately there were other Delavals more minded to make money than spend it. Francis's brother John assumed management of the estate, under whose stewardship the family's fortunes soared to even greater heights. It was John and his brother Thomas who, in the 1760s, oversaw improvements to the harbour at Seaton Sluice and the creation of a deep-water dock that allowed for the export of far greater quantities of goods.

This situation was not to last. By the following century, local industries were in decline and the last of the eight brothers had died without a male heir, meaning Seaton Delaval Hall passed to Sir Jacob Henry Astley, the son of the eldest sister, Rhoda. His primary home was elsewhere, so the family was not present when that disastrous fire of 1822 broke out. House staff and estate workers were unable to contain the fire and it burned for five hours before the flames could be brought under control. It is said to have burned with such intensity that it was mistaken for a sunset of unusual brilliance by sailors in nearby Whitley Bay.

Such are the varied fortunes and dramas of Seaton Delaval Hall, like scenes in a play. Previous acts included the family reroofing the Central Hall in the 1860s and extensive conservation work in the twentieth century. The latest act, a major programme of restoration and conservation, was played out in full view of visitors, taking inspiration from the fun and the theatrics Seaton Delaval Hall played host to, with Vanbrugh's building providing a dramatic backdrop.

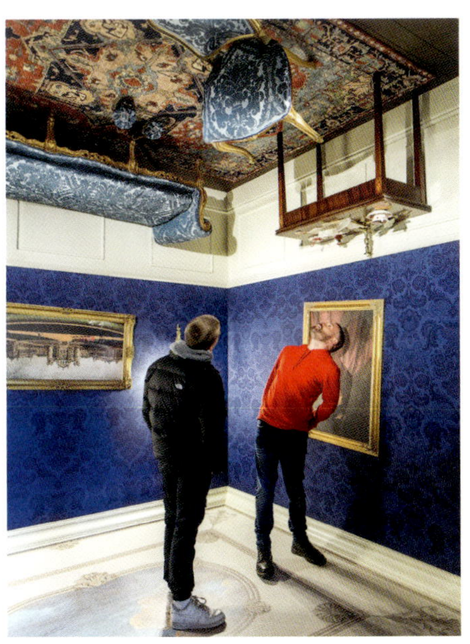

^ Taking practical jokes to new heights in the Upside Down Room.

In 2018, with support from the National Lottery Heritage Fund and other donors, the National Trust embarked on a major, four-year-long project of conservation and restoration under the title 'The Curtain Rises'. This included the urgent work of stabilising and re-roofing the surviving West Wing. In the central block, extensive conservation was carried out on the iconic and exquisitely created spiral staircases, which had become worn and structurally unsound over time. Another area of focus for the project was to address water ingress in the Basement, with new flooring and the addition of a damp-proof membrane beneath the South Portico steps. All of this, and more, consolidated many of Seaton Delaval Hall's most important features – which is all well and good, but you might be wondering where the Delaval-inspired sense of fun comes into it.

Inside the hall, the theatricality of the Delavals is presented in a variety of surprising ways. Step into the Central Hall, cast your eyes to the rafters and you might see a large, mirrored sphere that reflects back new and playful views of Vanbrugh's impressive double-height interior. In the re-roofed West Wing, you'll find the Upside Down Room, evoking the elaborate and mischievous pranks the Delavals played on their guests. In the West Wing's former kitchen there's a travelling Baroque theatre, where visitors can act out their own entertainments, as the Delavals would have done. In the Basement, there is a full-size anchor, which both references the Delavals' maritime interests but also the idea of anchoring the story of this family's fortunes in the space occupied by its workers, this workforce being invisible but essential to any great estate.

'The Curtain Rises' has set the stage at Seaton Delaval Hall, but there is much conservation work still to do and stories to share. The show will most certainly go on.

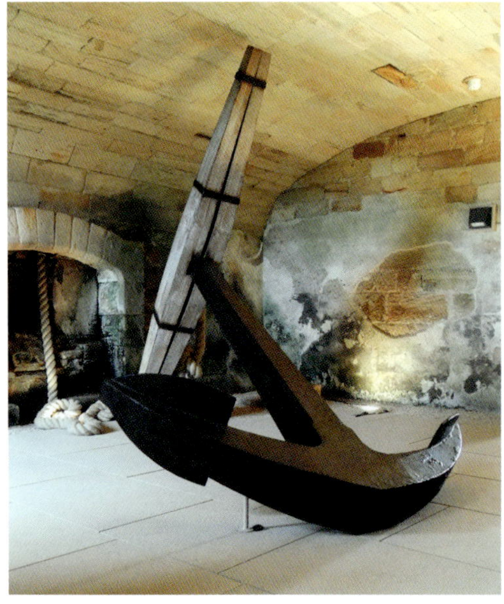

< A full-size anchor in a domestic space is one of many curiosities at Seaton Delaval Hall.

> Seaton Delaval Hall's iconic spiral staircases were the subject of extensive conservation.

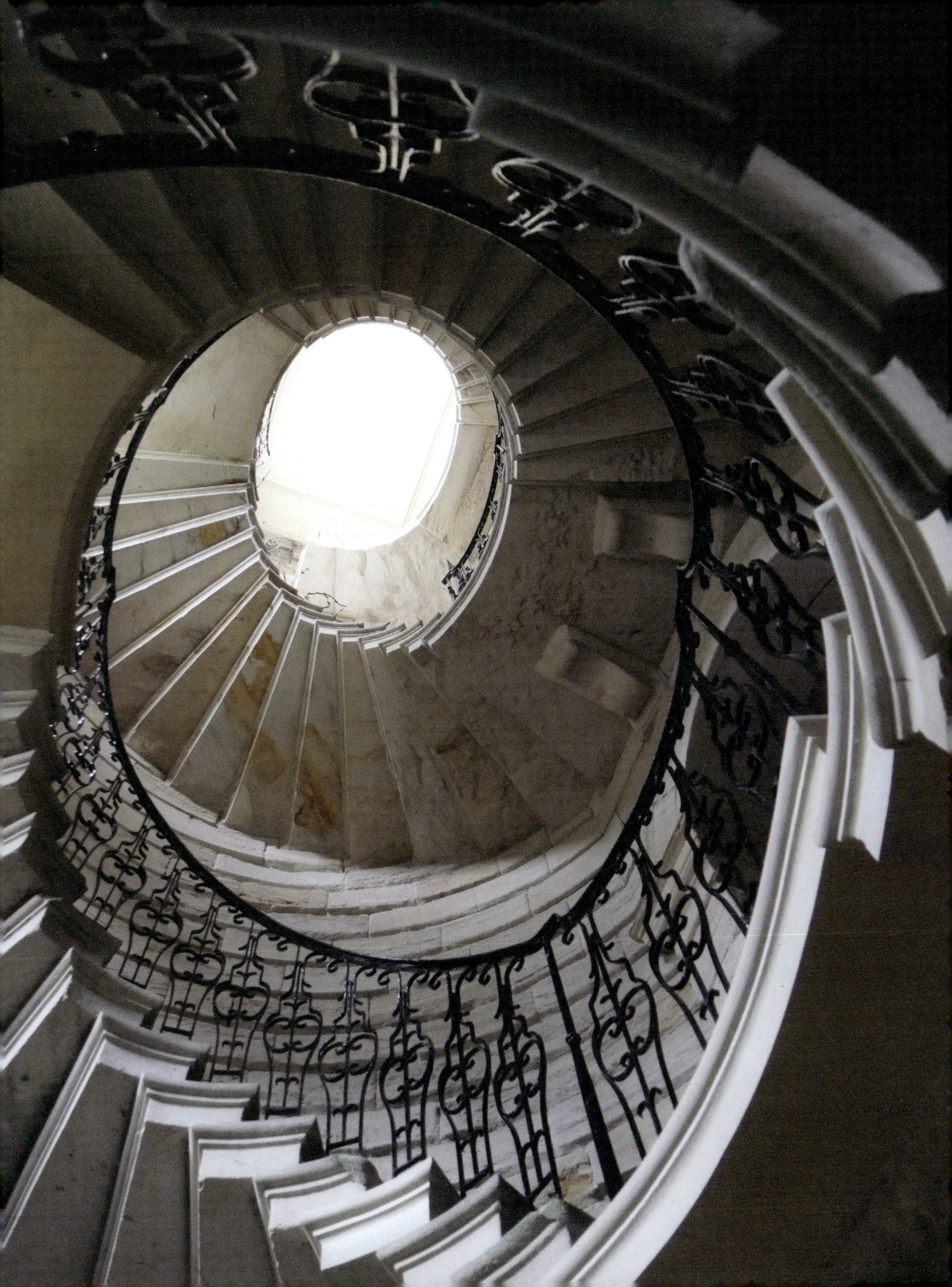

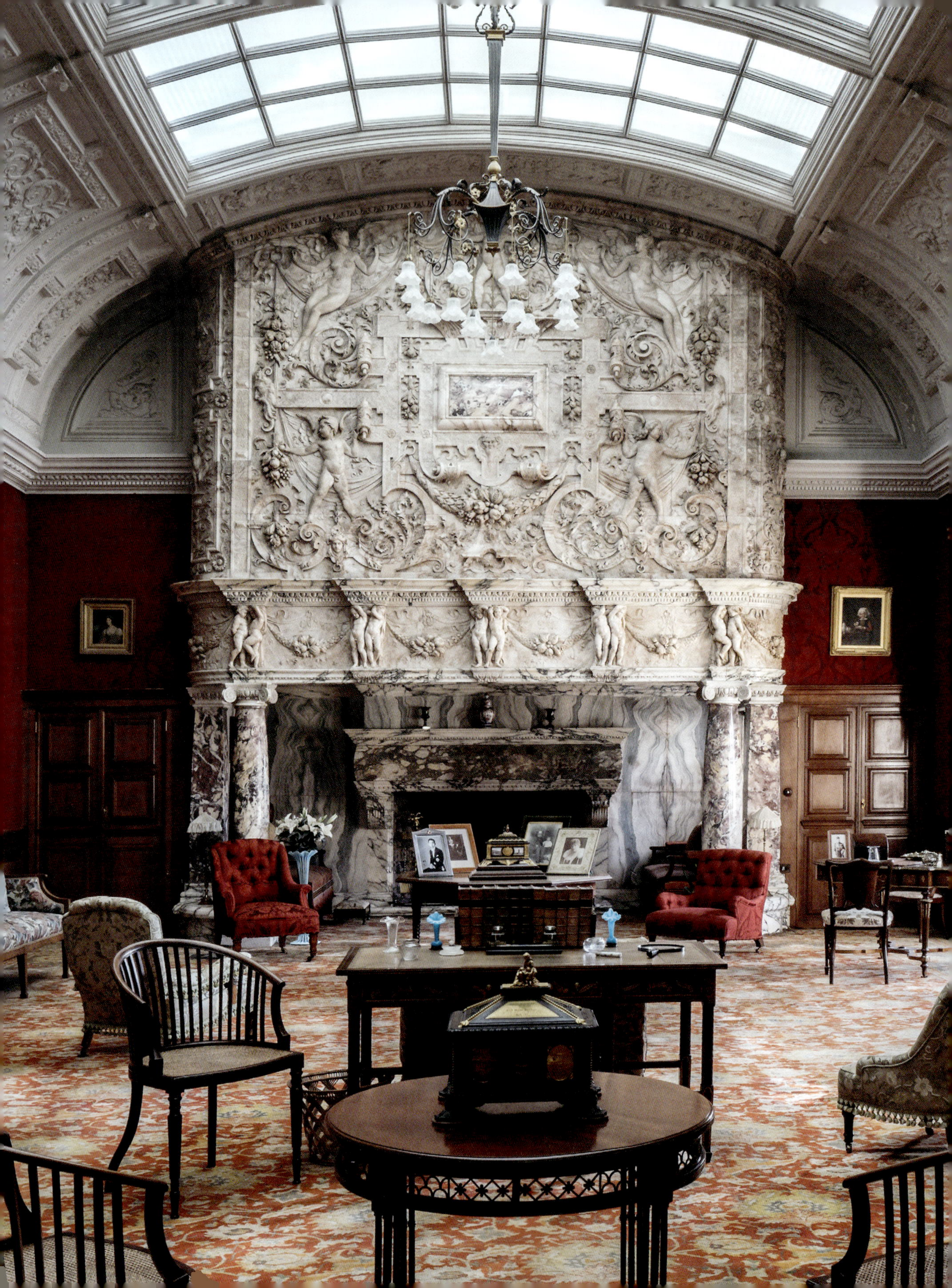

When Water Is Stronger Than Stone

Marble and Alabaster Fireplace

Cragside, Northumberland

That Cragside was the first house in the world to be lit by hydroelectric power is a known and celebrated fact (for more on hydropower at Cragside, see page 246). So it is something of an irony that water should threaten to blight two of the stand-out features in Lord Armstrong's magnificent Drawing Room.

In 2021, a year-long project began to conserve the marble fireplace that dominates that room and also the remarkable, vast chenille carpet underfoot.

Lord Armstrong deliberately made his Drawing Room a showpiece, a place in which to entertain royalty and impress the clients of his armaments business. The 20-foot (6-metre) floor-to-ceiling chimney piece, carved from a mixture of Italian marble and alabaster, was commissioned by Lord Armstrong from his architect Richard Norman Shaw, and designed by Shaw's assistant, William Lethaby. It was completed in time for a visit from the Prince and Princess of Wales, who would go on to become King Edward VII and Queen Alexandra; the latter is depicted with her daughters and Margaret, Lady Armstrong, in a painting by H. H. Emmerson of the Drawing Room at Cragside in front of the enormous fireplace.

Whether the royal couple were impressed is not recorded, but responses to the fireplace have certainly been mixed. In 1904, German

< Lord Armstrong's spectacular floor-to-ceiling chimney piece was carved from Italian marble and alabaster.

architect and author Hermann Muthesius described the fireplace as a 'splendid example … with finely composed relief decoration'. On the other hand, author Reginald Turnor writing in 1950 expressed his distaste for the room's 'flamboyant and rather sickening detail'.

It continues to divide opinion in visitors today and Cragside's property curator Clara Woolford conceded: 'It is ridiculously extravagant and is in stark contrast to the rest of the house, which was intentional … It is definitely visibly spectacular and all our visitors are wowed by it. It gets talked about and is one of the centrepieces of a visit to Cragside, but yes, it is not to everybody's taste.'

The floor-to-ceiling chimney piece was completed in time for a visit from the Prince and Princess of Wales, who would go on to become King Edward VII and Queen Alexandra.

The fireplace's immensity, however, does not make it immune from environmental factors and this colossal edifice, reputed to weigh 10 tonnes, is as susceptible to the damaging effects of water as anything else. When salts were observed on the surface of the fireplace, a phenomenon known as salt efflorescence, alarm bells began to ring. As Clara explained: 'It is caused by moisture moving through the stone and then evaporating. When the salt builds up in the pores of the material it ultimately breaks apart. Almost like a disease, it starts in a small area and spreads through the weak sections of stone – in this case the veins of the marble. If untreated, the fireplace could crumble quickly.'

Specialist stone conservators were brought in to carry out repairs. Having brushed away the salts, they filled losses in the veining and surface of the marble with specialised mortars, carefully mixed with aggregates to match the colours of the stone. Once this delicate work was completed, the next phase, altogether more industrial in scale, could begin. Behind the fireplace are two ferrous steel beams, a material as vulnerable to the effects of water ingress as the stone. Every inch of those beams needed to be coated with marine paint to protect them from rusting further.

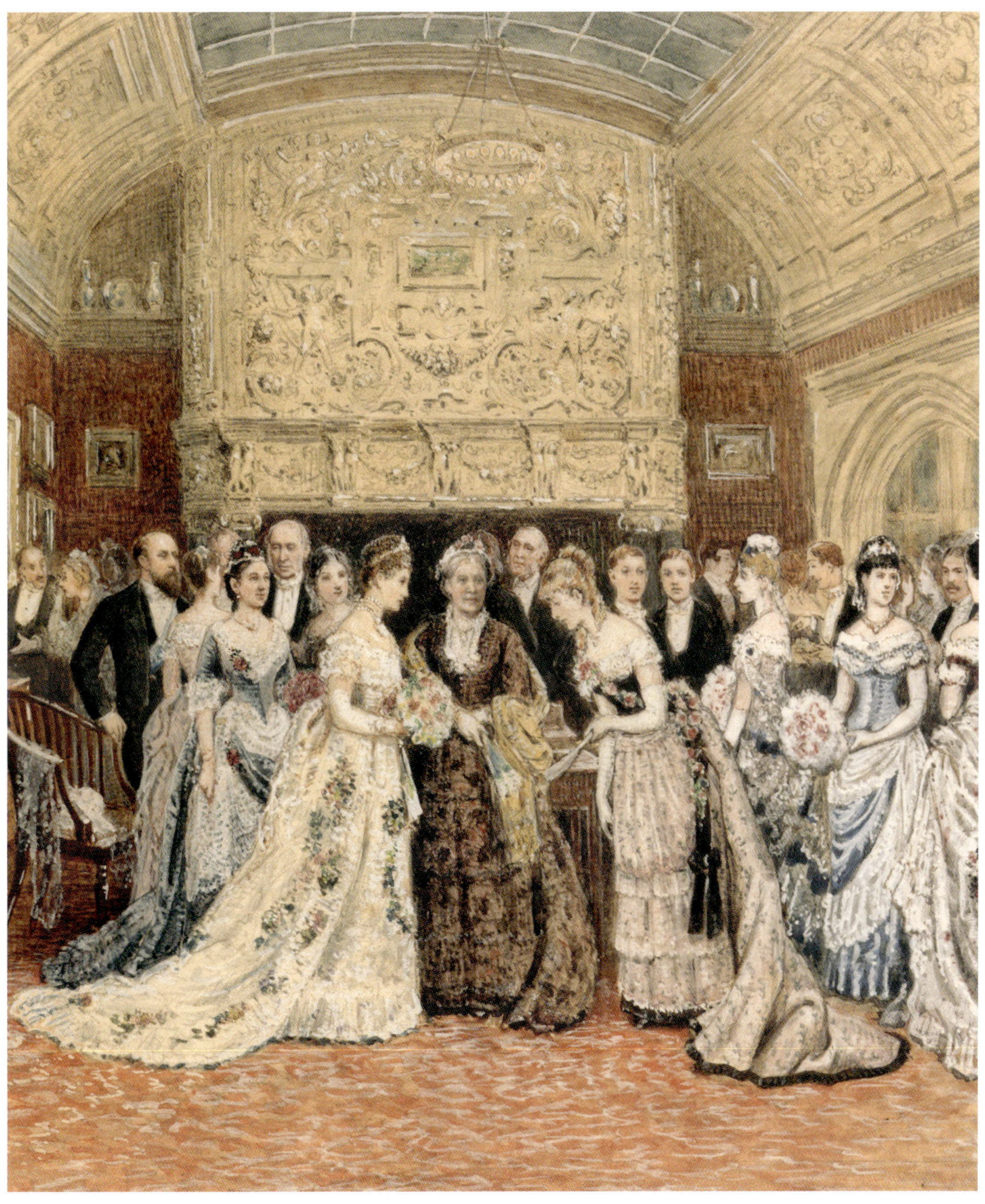

^ *Princess Alexandra with Lady Armstrong in Drawing Room*, from an album entitled *Royal Visit to Cragside August 1884*, illustrated by H. H. Emmerson.

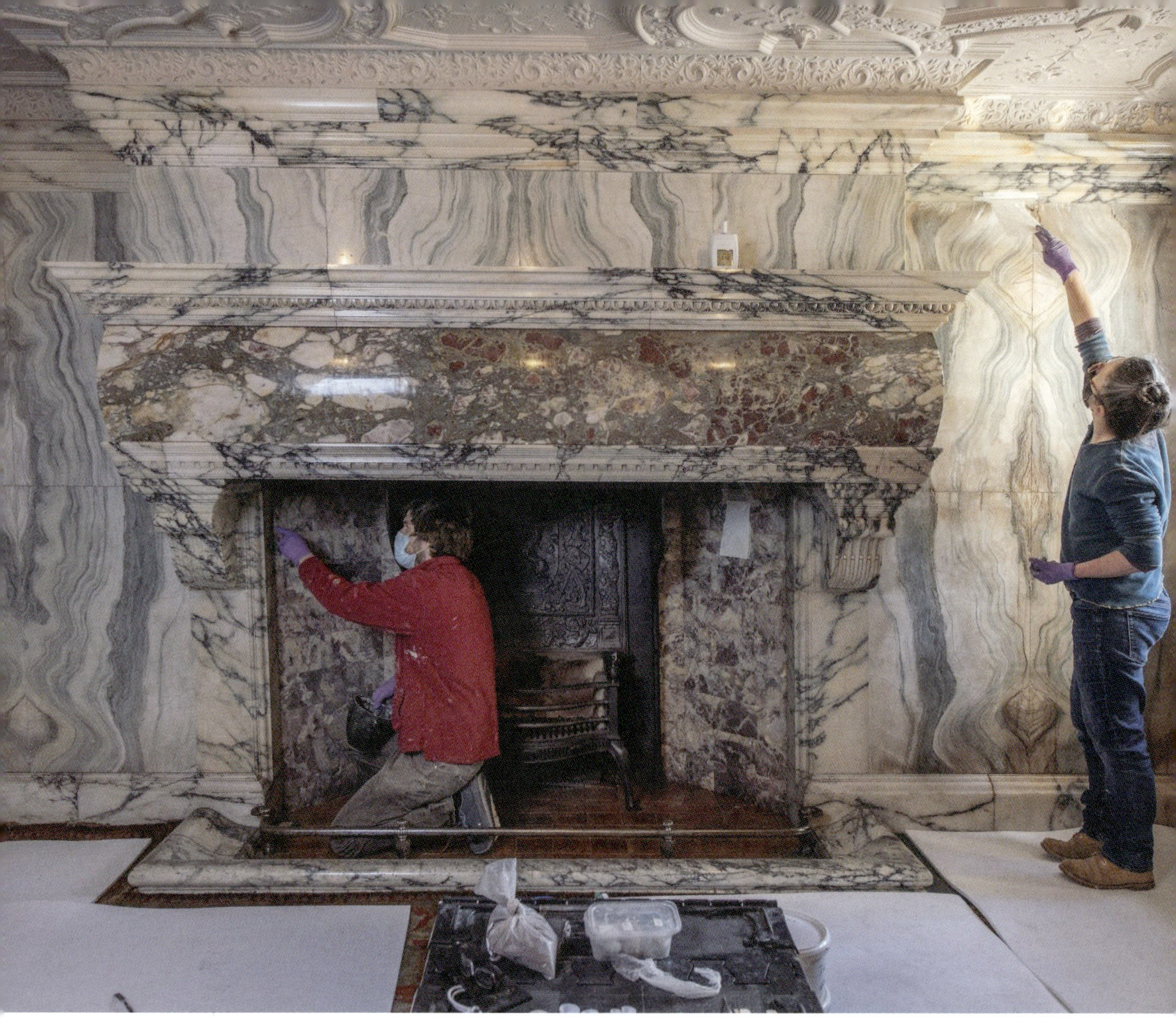

^ Conservators Alex Rickett and Chloe Stewart carrying out repairs to the marble in the inglenook of the fireplace.

Moving from the interior to the exterior, surveyors were brought in to take detailed photography of Cragside's masonry with the use of a drone. When overlaid with the results of a thermal imaging survey, cracks and voids in the walls that would be otherwise impossible to detect were identified. This provided information for another specialist team, who then had to repair these gaps in the masonry using lime mortar and rake out any cement-based mortar used in historic repairs before repointing.

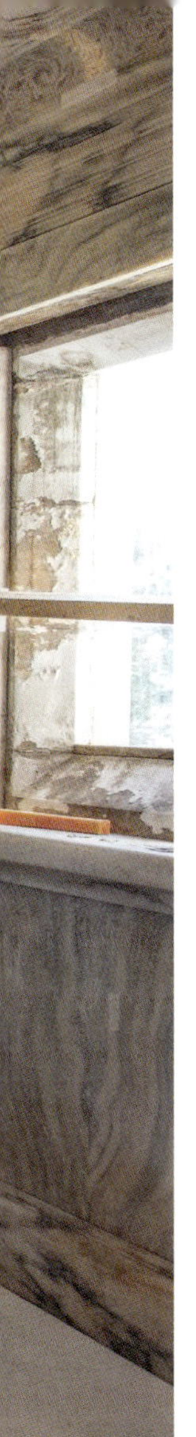

Past damage fixed, Cragside then needed to be made more resilient to future water ingress. Ever since Cragside was built in the second half of the nineteenth century, our weather patterns have changed markedly. As Clara put it: 'The Victorian drainage system doesn't support twenty-first-century weather conditions. Winters at Cragside are wetter and much longer, due to climate change. We are more prone to significant bursts of rain and stormy weather.' The complex system of guttering and downpipes on this side of the building was assessed, repaired and modified, making the building more able to cope with extremely wet weather.

While Cragside was being made more weatherproof, yet more specialist conservators were at work on the Drawing Room's huge chenille carpet. The National Trust has no more than a dozen chenille carpets in its collection, and this one is a rare and very significant example due to its astonishing size and it being original to Cragside. It is also exceptional for being one of the first carpets in the world to be woven using engineering techniques invented during the Industrial Revolution. You would expect nothing less from Lord Armstrong, a titan of industry and engineering.

The condition of the carpet had suffered in areas where it is thought three large planters had once been placed, causing the wool pile and underlying woven structure to deteriorate. Just as the damage to the fireplace would have spread if left unchecked, the gaps in the pattern of the carpet where the weft was broken would have only increased in size. In the summer of 2021, conservators worked on site to stabilise the woven structure and to patch the gaps in the pile with specially made inserts, embroidered in the conservator's studio to match the design and colour of the missing areas.

The Drawing Room conservation project entailed the skills and expertise of many specialist teams, hardly surprising given the scale that Lord Armstrong liked to work at. Water is being brought once more under close control at Cragside, befitting the house that did so much to advocate for its potential.

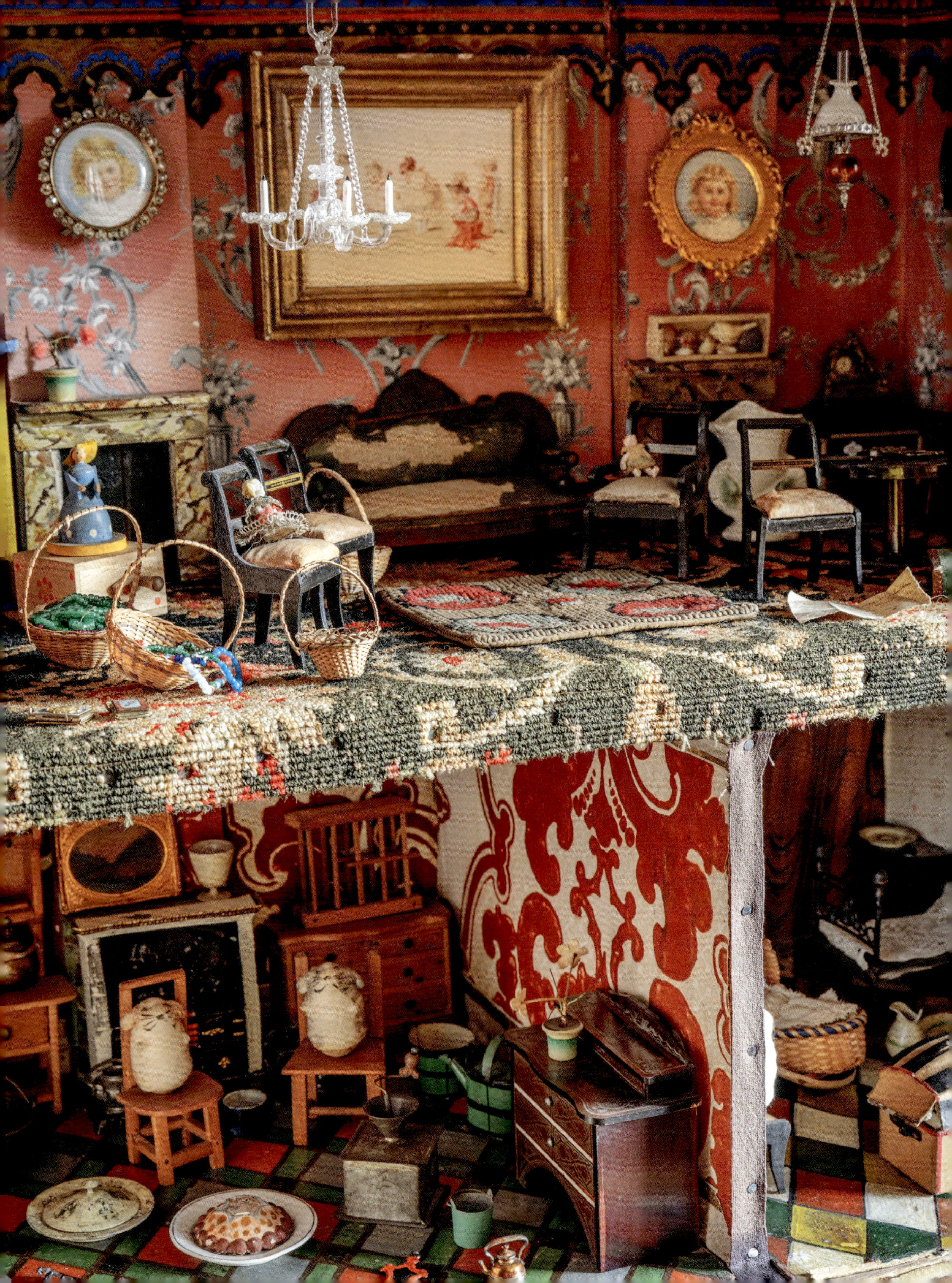

Gifts From a Lost Love

Doll's House Accessories

Hill Top, Cumbria

By the time Beatrix Potter bought Hill Top in 1905, she had won acclaim as a children's author, but also lost the man she loved. In this farmhouse, the world-famous writer-turned-sheep-farmer aspired to a simpler life, one lived closer to nature. Hill Top was a far cry from the opulence of her childhood home but she retained a few valued pieces and added to them treasured items that sparked her imagination or memories. One of her greatest treasures is a doll's house containing items that featured in one of her famous tales, but that also tells another story. As that doll's house has recently been the object of careful attention and conservation treatment, it's time for this tale of lost love to be told.

Beatrix Potter published her first children's book in 1902. That book was *The Tale of Peter Rabbit*, of which 40 million copies have been sold worldwide. Over the next three decades she published a total of 23 children's books, all of which became classics of the genre, beloved by children then and ever since. Her tales of rabbits and squirrels, cats and mice, ducks and foxes, frogs and hedgehogs, and more besides, delighted readers and those to whom they were read. Just as captivating, however, were her illustrations for the stories.

A story featuring particularly meticulous drawings was *The Tale of Two Bad Mice*, published in 1904, about two rodents that go on a rampage through a little girl's doll's house. You might reasonably expect

< These tiny toy treasures, kept by Beatrix Potter long after she had retired from writing children's stories, were clearly of great sentimental value to her.

this to be a work of fantasy, so it may surprise you to learn that Beatrix's illustrations of mice making a nuisance of themselves in the miniaturised world of a doll's house were drawn from life.

The dedication on the frontispiece of *The Tale of Two Bad Mice* reads: 'FOR W. M. L. W. THE LITTLE GIRL WHO HAD THE DOLL'S HOUSE'. That little girl was Winifred Warne, niece of Norman Warne, son of the publisher Frederick Warne, and a partner in the firm following his father's retirement in 1894. Norman was also Beatrix's editor and, very briefly, fiancé.

After the success of *The Tale of Peter Rabbit*, Beatrix was a regular visitor to the offices of Frederick Warne & Co. The working relationship between author and editor blossomed into a friendship and, during the development of *The Tale of Two Bad Mice*, they grew closer still. It was Norman who made Winifred's doll's house and, at the end of 1903, he built and sent Beatrix a glass-fronted house for her two pet mice, Tom Thumb and Hunca Munca, with a ladder to an upstairs nesting loft so she could observe and draw them. Norman also went to Hamley's, the famous toy shop in London, and bought a variety of doll's house props, again for Beatrix to sketch and incorporate into her illustrations for the book.

In Beatrix's illustrations, the story's protagonists, also called Tom Thumb and Hunca Munca, peep out from their mousehole, cautiously enter the doll's house, attempt to eat the fake food and, when they discover the ham is made of plaster and the fish is stuck to the plate, go on a wrecking spree. Then the pragmatic mice realise some non-edible items might be useful –

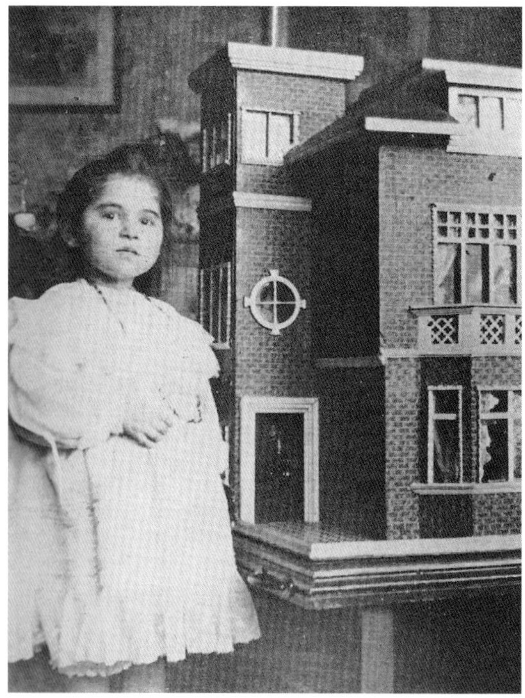

^ Winifred Warne, niece of Beatrix's editor Norman Warne.

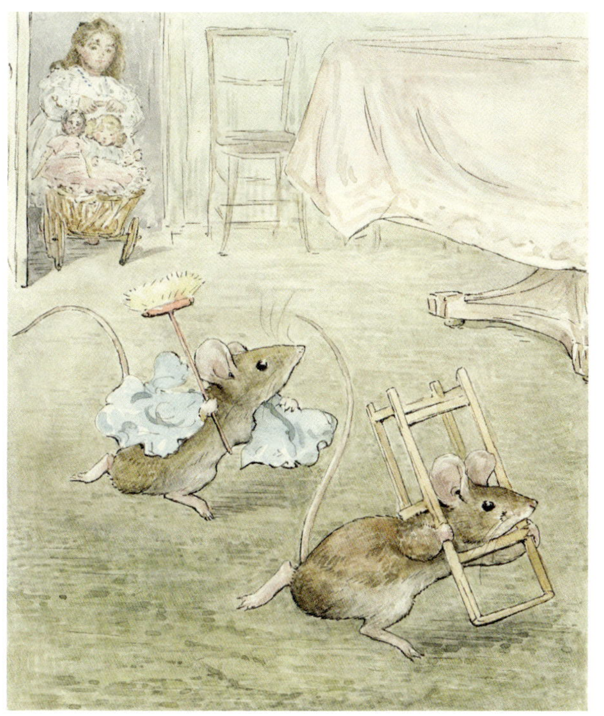

^ Hunca Munca and Tom Thumb making off with items from the little girl's doll's house.

'a chair, a book-case, a bird-cage, and several small odds and ends' – and they attempt to make off with them. So, for the illustration of the two mice on the stairs with a feather bolster between them, thanks to Norman's gift, Beatrix was able to sketch her pet mice on the loft ladder in believable postures, which she then translated into her drawings.

Beatrix had to draw Winifred's doll's house from photographs, however. Norman had invited Beatrix to his brother's house so that she could sketch it, but her parents, disapproving of the growing intimacy between the pair, refused her use of the family carriage.

Still, Beatrix was able to carry on working with Norman, and the two clearly delighted in her developing tale of two mice – and she in the props Norman was sending her – of which she remarked: 'the things will do beautifully; the ham's appearance is enough to cause indigestion. I am getting almost more treasures than I can squeeze into one small book.'

Beatrix kept these 'treasures' when she bought Hill Top Farm in 1905, the same year that she and Norman got engaged, but sadly also the same year in which Norman died, just a month after his proposal. He was 37 years old. Hill Top became Beatrix's sanctuary, a place where she could heal and a place where she could fully pursue her love of landscape and nature. She continued to write, but she also used the proceeds from her writing to buy land, around 4,000 acres (1,600 hectares) of it, and learned the techniques of fell farming and rearing livestock, including pigs, cows, chickens and sheep.

When Beatrix died, aged 77, she left Hill Top and its contents, along with all her Lakeland property, to the National Trust, a gift that comprises much of what exists today and forever more as the Lake District National Park.

The tiny toy treasures that Norman sent her are now contained in a doll's house at Hill Top, one that she acquired long after the publication of *The Tale of Two Bad Mice*, when she was around 73 and had been married to William Heelis for over 20 years. Beatrix had been asked by Winifred's father to look after the doll's house immortalised in her illustrations, but she had suggested it be lent to a children's hospital. After the children's hospital it's thought that the doll's house found a new home, but one that was destroyed in the Blitz.

∨ Winifred's father offered the doll's house to Beatrix but she thought it better given to a children's hospital instead.

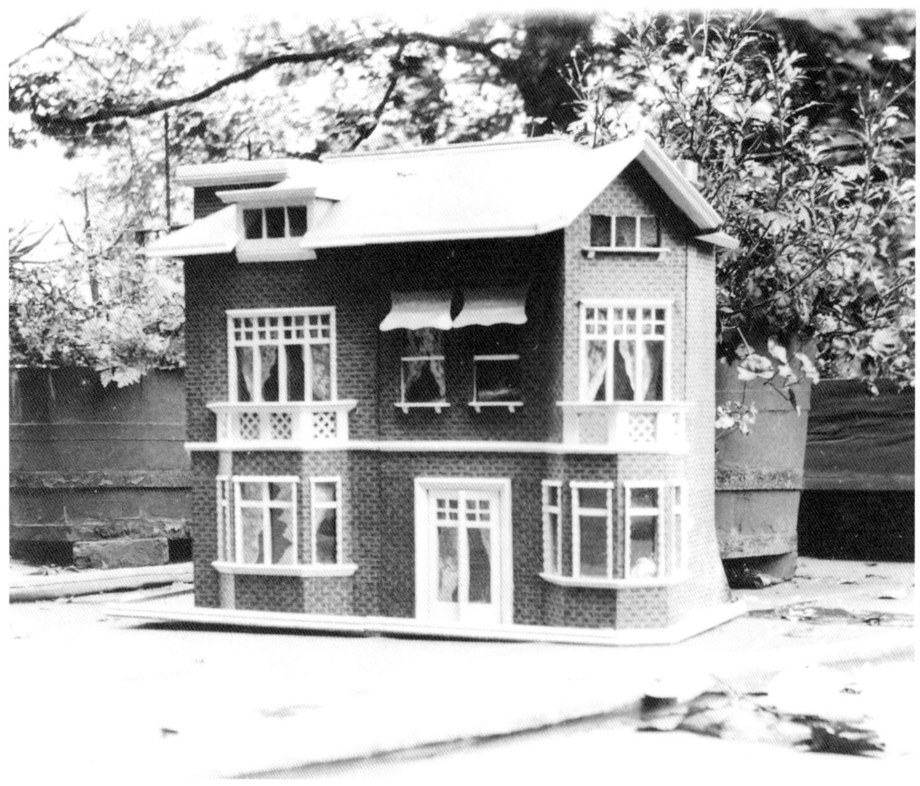

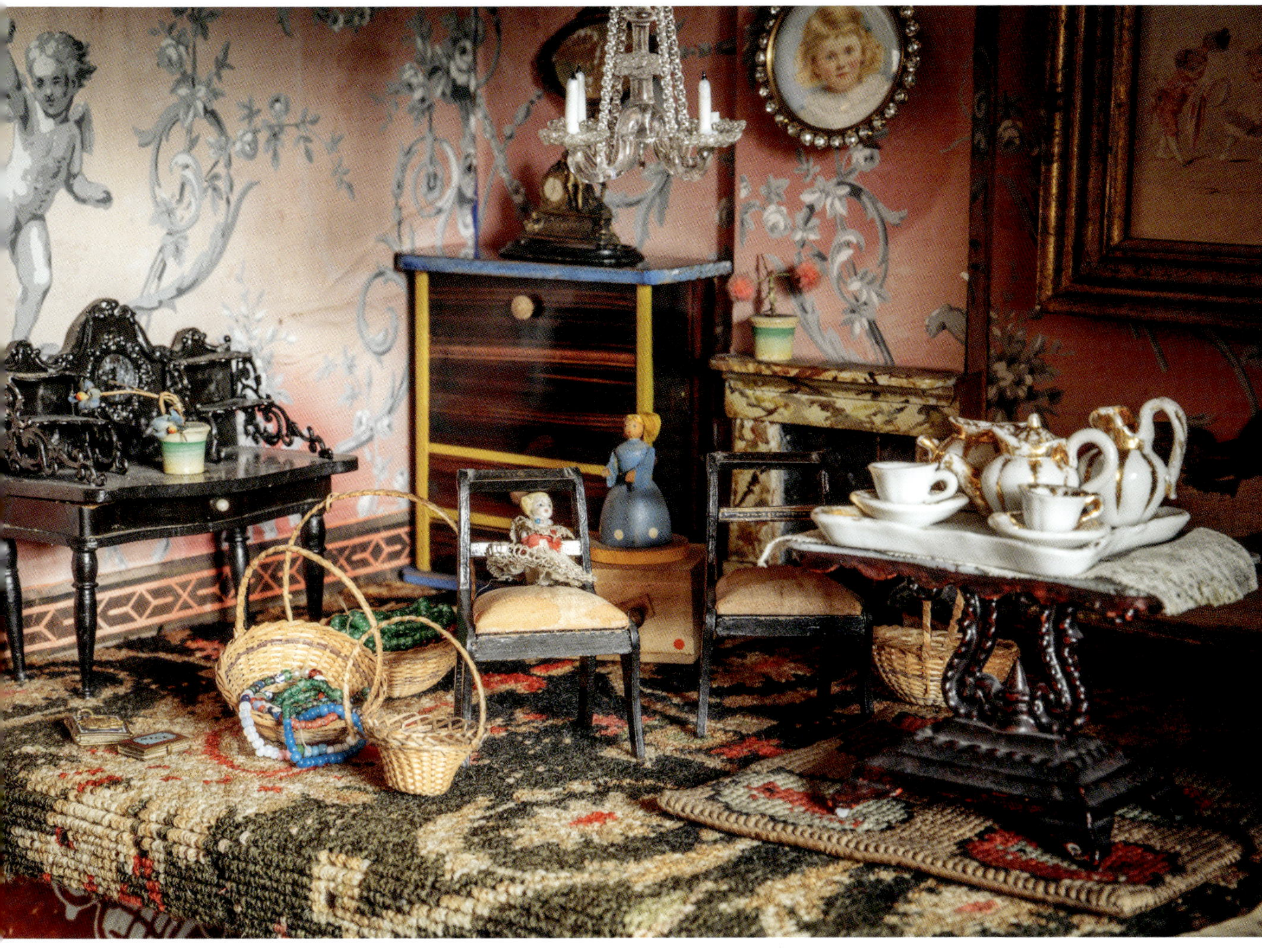

Whether Beatrix chose to keep and display a number of 35-year-old doll's house accessories out of sentimentality towards her story, or out of respect for her first love, we can never know. However, they provide us with tantalising clues about the private life of this world-famous author, an extraordinary woman, who left not only a legacy of cherished children's stories but also a gift that has preserved in perpetuity one of the country's most beautiful landscapes.

^ As an old woman, Beatrix bought this doll's house in which to keep some of the tiny treasures sent to her by her first love.

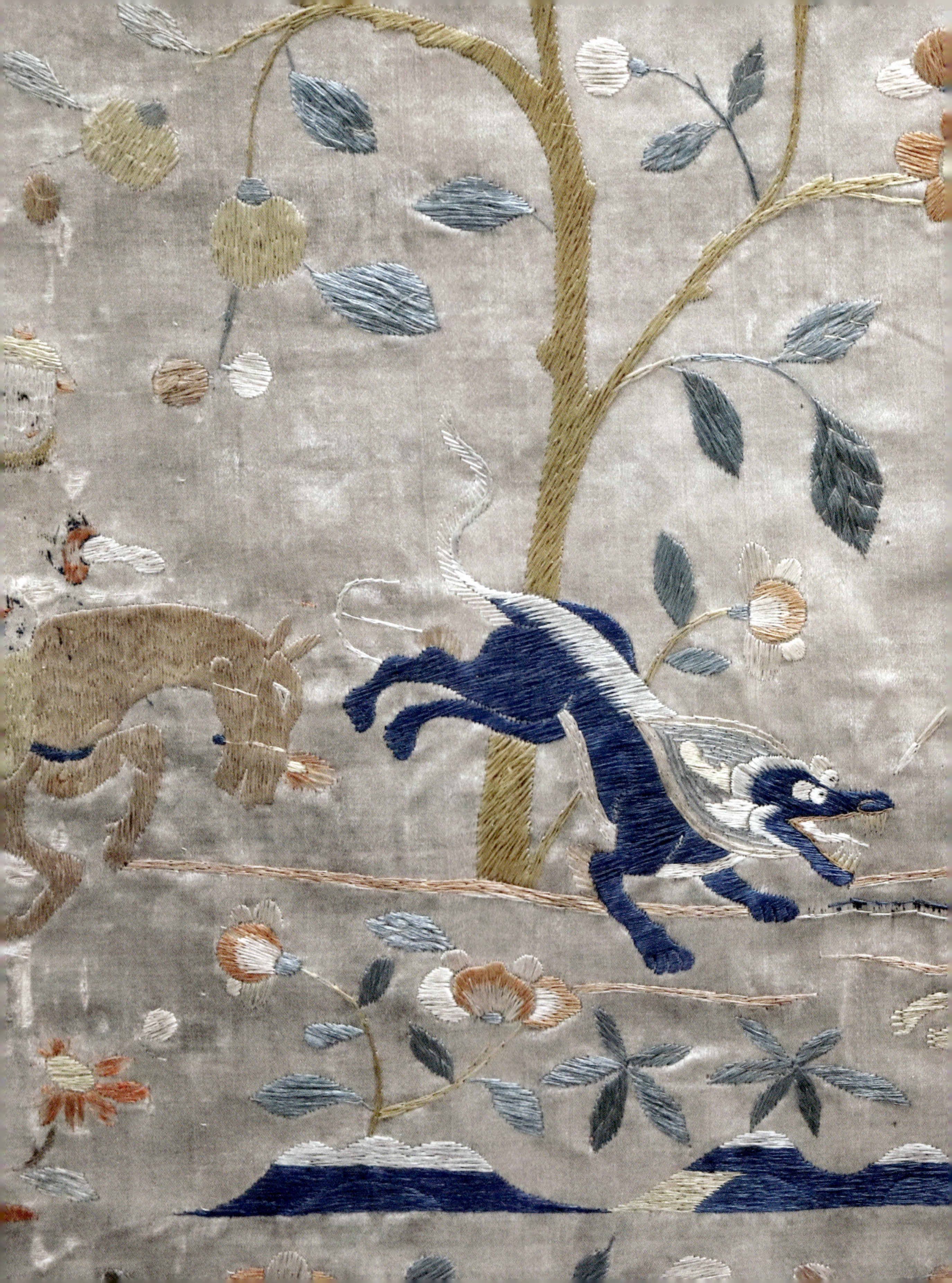

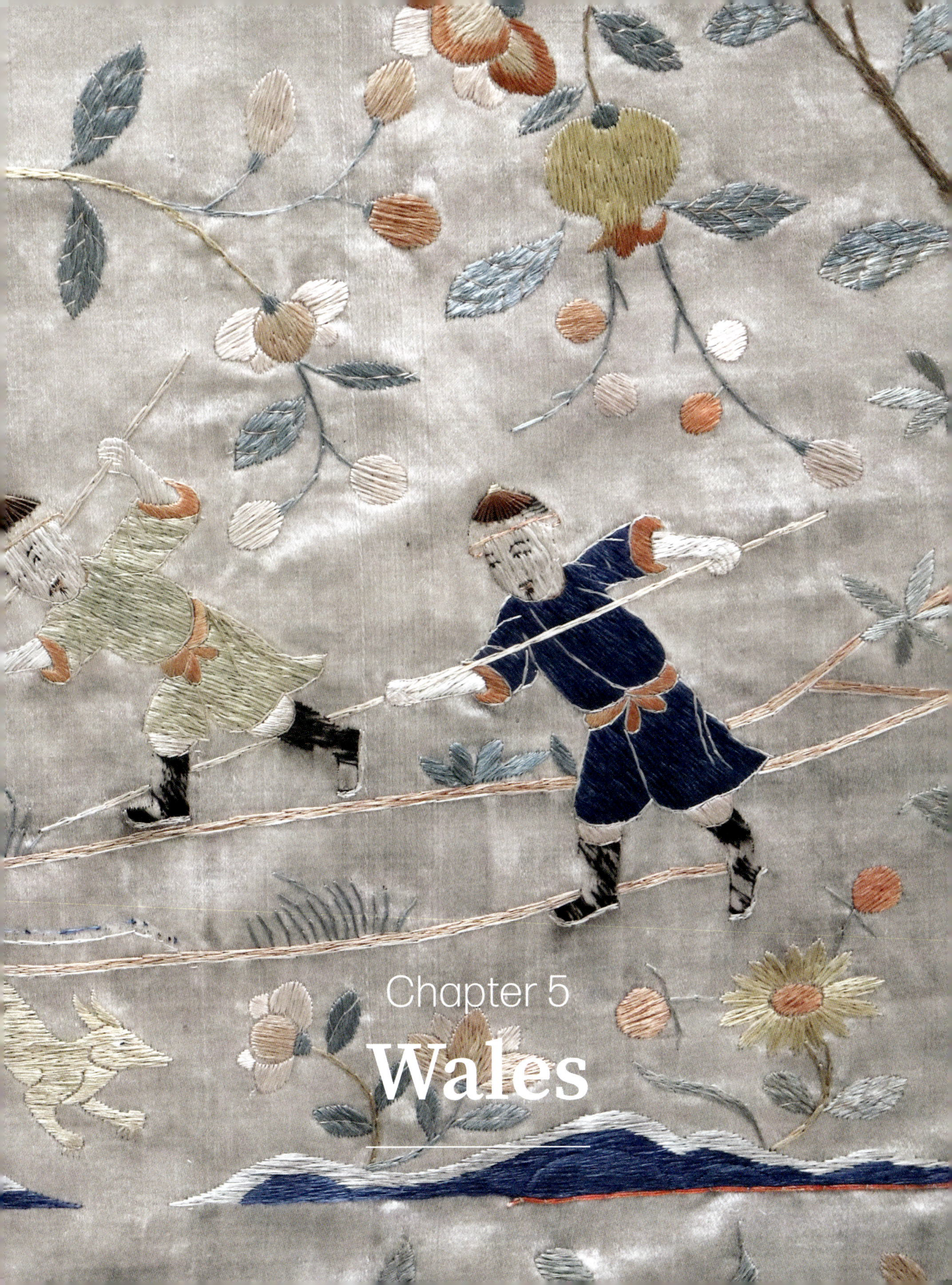

Chapter 5

Wales

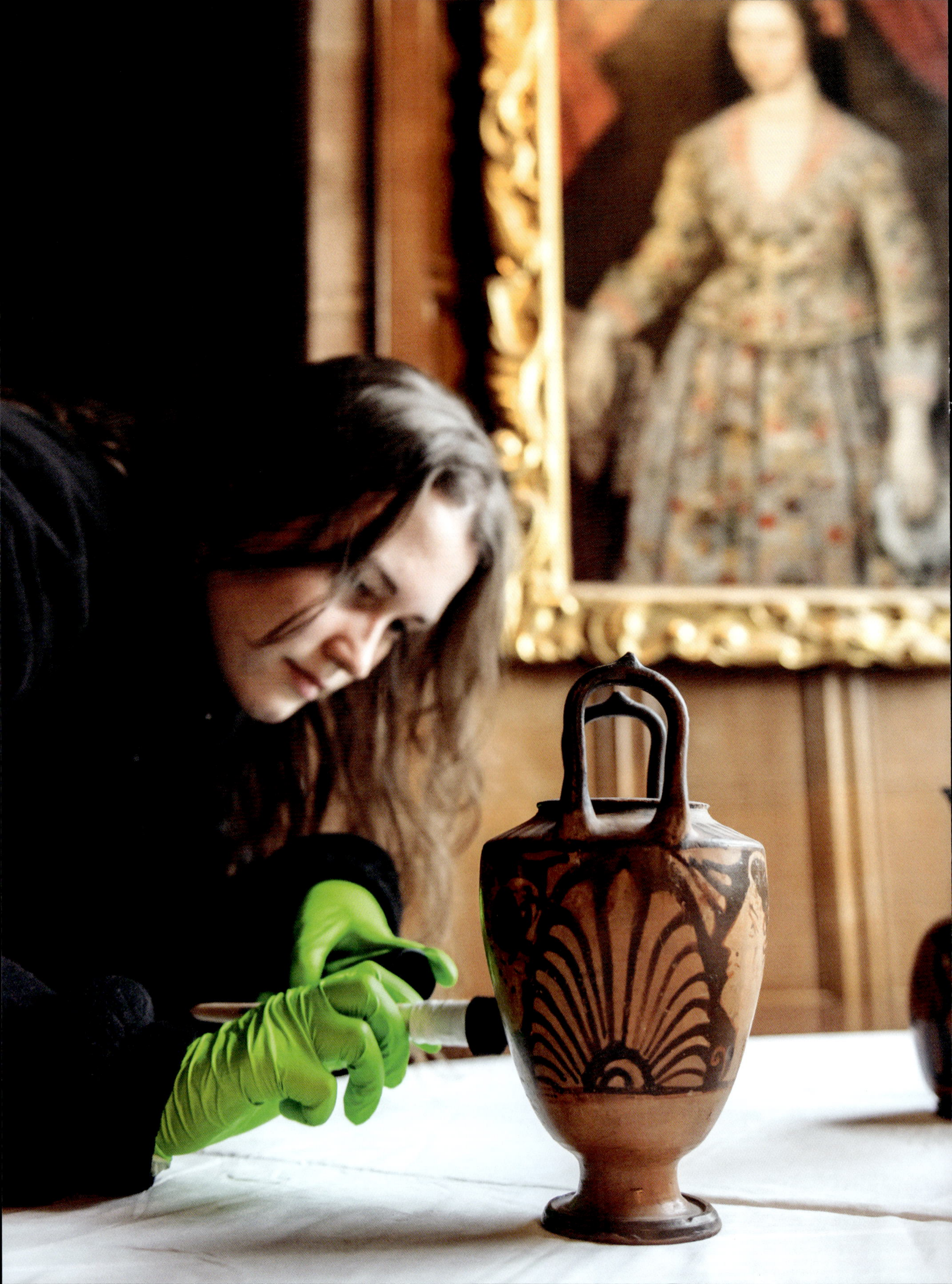

A Once in a Decade Deep-Clean

Etruscan Vases

Powis Castle, Welshpool

The study of Classics, that is the literature of the ancient Greek and Roman civilisations, was once a key component of any elite education. The Grand Tour of Europe was the 'finishing school' for these students and an opportunity for young men (and some young women) to furnish the country homes they were destined to inherit with souvenirs that showcased their education.

At Powis Castle, generations of family members completed their Grand Tours and their ancestral home contains a wonderful array of ancient artefacts. In fact, Powis Castle can lay claim to having one of the world's greatest collections of art and historical objects, with over 13,500 items in its care. Such a rich repository poses challenges as well as opportunities.

When you consider that from the seventeenth to the early nineteenth century, most upper-class young men completed Grand Tours, the country houses now cared for by the National Trust contain an almost unimaginable number of objects collected from many countries and many centuries. This raises the question of how to display such a collection while simultaneously conserving and studying it.

Greek vases are a relatively unexplored area of the Trust's collection, so there is much to be discovered about these objects. That collection

< Collections Assistant, Megan Alexander, cleaning a *lebes gamikos*, a form of ancient Greek pottery used in marriage ceremonies.

numbers over one million items, so it's safe to say that not everything in it is fully known and understood. When an object receives its conservation clean – and, incredibly, everything does, in a strict rotation – the National Trust increasingly uses this as an opportunity to conserve and study the item in full view of visitors.

Take the six Etruscan vases displayed in the Library at Powis Castle – an obvious place to showcase the owner's classical education. These 2,000-year-old pieces usually live high up on an inaccessible shelf – sensible for items of such antiquity – but once a decade they are taken down for cleaning. For the most recent clean, a 16-foot (5-metre) scaffold was built to get the vases safely down, after which they were removed to the castle's Gateway Room, where visitors had the chance to observe conservators cleaning them. It took around five hours for each vase to be assessed and cleaned, allowing them to be closely studied and photographed.

These pieces date from around 350 BC, towards the end of the ancient Greek civilisation, marked by the death of Alexander the Great in 323 BC, and long before the founding of the Roman Empire in 27 BC. The style of the vases harks back to the Greek tradition, but they were made in a region of central Italy known as Etruria. The Etruscan people were strongly influenced by the Greeks, and they particularly prized Greek vases, which they collected in great numbers. The vases they produced and painted themselves were accordingly evocative of Greek forms and styles and depicted scenes from Greek mythology.

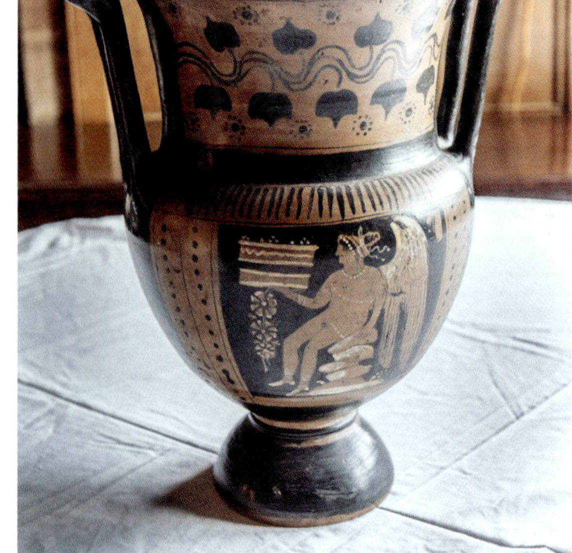

> *Krater* vases such as this were used for mixing wine and water.

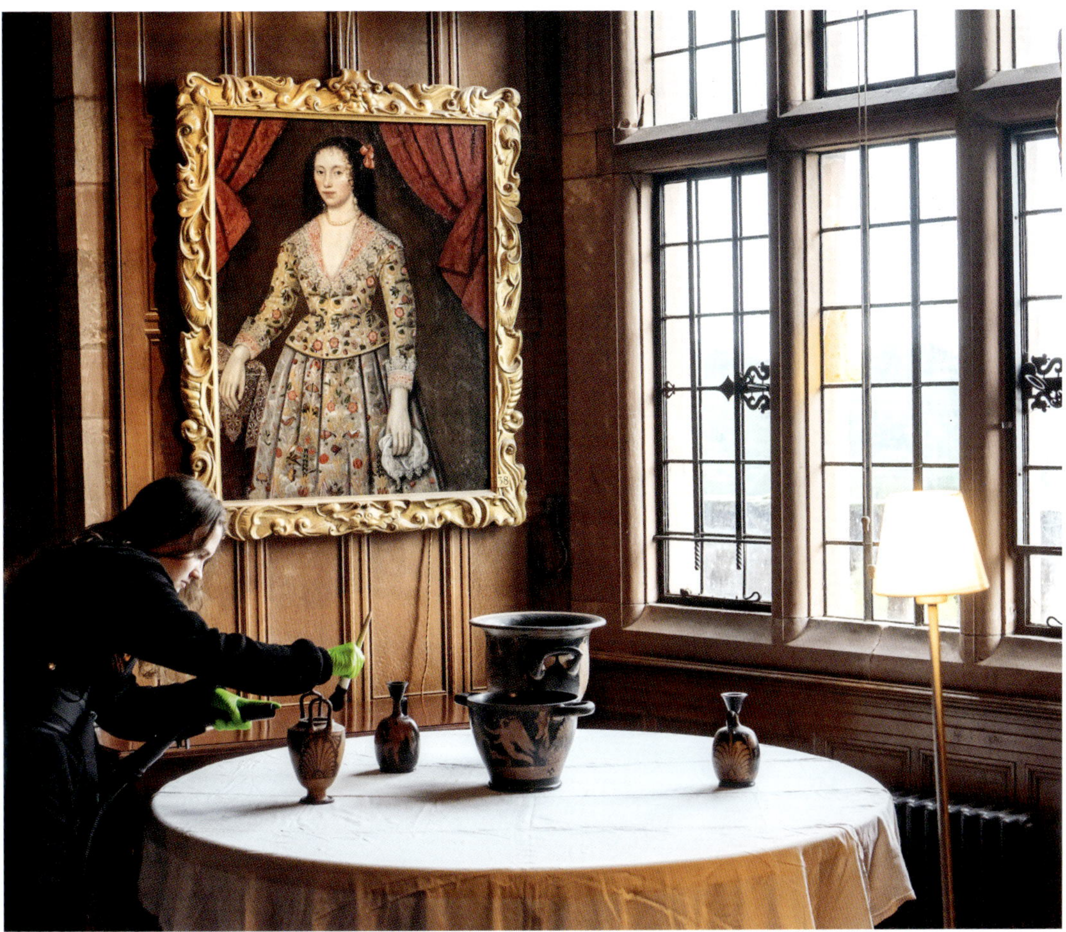

The six vases at Powis Castle are thought to have been acquired by a family member in the late 1700s, perhaps George Herbert, 2nd Earl of Powis, or his sister, Henrietta, and her husband, Edward Clive, 2nd Lord Clive, or possibly Edward's father, Robert Clive, 1st Lord Clive, known as 'Clive of India'. They may have been brought back from the same Grand Tour or gathered from multiple trips. They vary in size and shape, representing their different original functions. There are two vases known as *krater* that have a large round body and a wide mouth, and they were used for mixing wine and water. The two narrow-bodied vessels with a

∧ These 2,000-year-old pieces require an extremely careful and delicate hand when being cleaned.

single handle attached to the neck are called *lekythoi*, and would have been used either to hold scented oil (perfume), or oil for household purposes such as cooking. The large two-handled cup is a *skyphos*, a large drinking vessel. Finally, the collection includes a *lebes gamikos*, a two-handled, round-bottomed vase. This was a form of pottery used in connection with marriage ceremonies, possibly to hold water for the ritual bath taken before the wedding by the bride – and, perhaps, also by the groom – or it may have been a container for the couple's food.

Assisting with the cleaning of these exceptionally ancient objects was Lynne Edge, specialist ceramics conservator. Her work is of course careful and meticulous but also a source of fascination. As she put it: 'We use specialist brushes with bristles made of soft pony and sable hair, along with natural rubber smoke sponges to ensure an effective

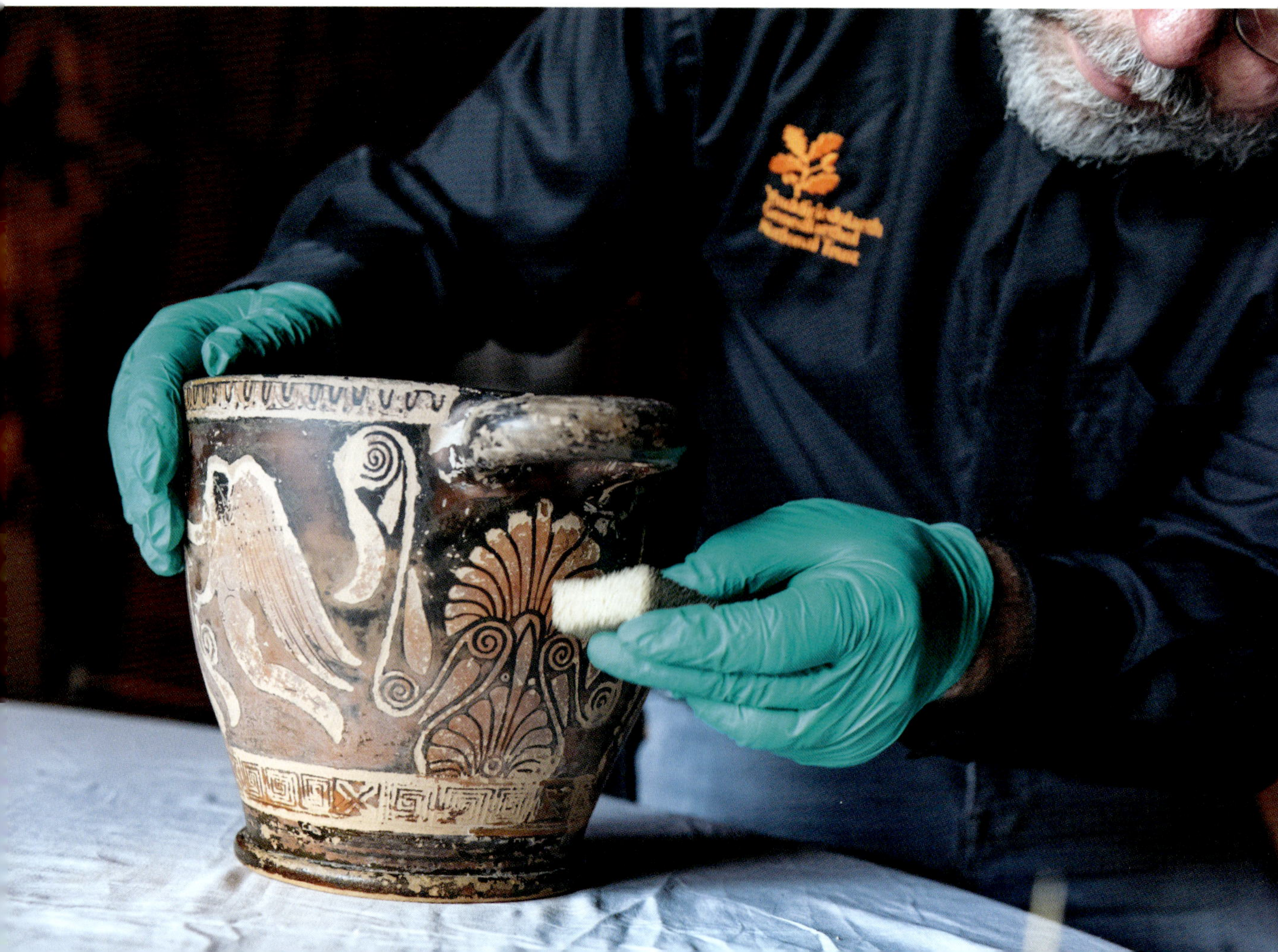

clean while being careful of the delicate decoration. It's a privilege and honour to handle such beautiful ancient objects. Often impressions of the fingerprints of the original maker can be found, connecting me to the object's past as I work to conserve it for the future.'

Alex Turrell is the Senior Collections and House Officer at Powis Castle, and oversaw this conservation clean, carried out in full view of visitors: 'We are delighted to be able to give visitors a once-in-ten-year chance to have a closer look at the delicate Etruscan vases and watch conservation in action at Powis. Dusting and cleaning are continual jobs in caring for the collections here, but fragile objects such as the vases are cleaned less often. It's amazing to think that these vases have been successfully preserved for two millennia, and we're so pleased to be able to share this exciting occasion with visitors.'

While the vases were being cleaned, lighting was added to the position they occupy in the Library. Now returned to their safe perches, they can be seen and appreciated far more clearly.

As for the other Greek vases scattered across the country houses of the National Trust, they have been the subject of a National Trust Partnership, an award-winning research collaboration with Oxford University. Curator Abigail Allan has located, catalogued and researched the Trust's collections of ancient Greek vases, before curating new displays in key properties. The teams at Nostell, Charlecote Park and Sudbury Hall have staged temporary exhibitions, each focusing on a different aspect of Greek vases. At Nostell, the collection was considered in terms of what it said about their collectors, and what these objects meant to them. At Charlecote, it was more object-focused, looking in detail at the artistry and iconography employed on these vases, thought to be the finest in the National Trust. Finally, at the Children's Country House at Sudbury, the theme was travel, adventure, myths and monsters.

So just as the task of cleaning the objects in the collections of the National Trust has no end, the opportunities to learn from them and consider them in new ways are limitless.

< This *skyphos* was used as a drinking vessel.

Skills and Techniques
Miniature Portrait of Lord Herbert

Smaller than a piece of A4 paper, this miniature portrait of Sir Edward Herbert is exceptionally rare. It was acquired in 2016 for the collection at Powis Castle, the seat of the Herbert family. Before being put on display, it was sent away to the Hamilton Kerr Institute, the painting conservation department at the Fitzwilliam Museum in Cambridge. There it was put under the microscope, but also examined using electromagnetic and X-ray technology. While these processes revealed more about its condition, the pigments used and their application, and any reworkings or corrections by the artist, research by curators revealed yet more layers of information.

To begin with, it is worth mentioning that the word 'miniature' is not derived from the Latin *minimum*, as is often and understandably assumed, but comes from *minium*, the Latin word for the bright orange-red pigment that was widely used in the Middle Ages for the decoration of manuscripts. Portrait miniatures grew out of the tradition of manuscript illumination rather than being a sub-genre of portrait painting.

But as to the specifics of *this* miniature, it was painted in 1613–14 by Isaac Oliver, the official miniature painter of James I's queen, Anne of Denmark. Its subject, Sir Edward Herbert, 1st Lord Herbert of Cherbury, was by then noted both for his courtly accomplishments and his courage in battle. He was a poet, philosopher and musician, acquiring admirers such as the poet John Donne, who applauded him for his 'obscurenesse'. Another admirer was Lady Ayres, a lady-in-waiting to the queen, who secretly commissioned a miniature copy of a painting of Sir Edward from Oliver. So enraged was Lord Ayres on finding this item hung 'about her neck soe lowe that she yet hid it under her brestes' that he ambushed his supposed rival with a gang of men near Whitehall Palace in London and stabbed him in his side with a dagger.

Despite being seriously injured, Sir Edward survived the attack, and continued to distinguish himself for his gallantry, as denoted by his

> A miniature of Sir Edward Herbert, later 1st Lord Herbert of Cherbury, painted by Isaac Oliver in 1613–14.

handsomely liveried horse and squire waiting in the background of this painting. Sir Edward's lance leaning against a tree suggests he's resting after a royal jousting tournament. However, the contemporary viewer would recognise his attitude as that of a melancholic young man, rather than one who is simply tired. Renaissance thinkers regarded melancholy as a disorder of the mind, but one that conferred benefits, being considered conducive to creativity and deep philosophical meditation. Sir Edward would certainly have been keen to be portrayed as a deep thinker.

The motto and image chosen to adorn Sir Edward's shield are of course more symbolic than decorative, and intended to convey some personal quality or belief of the bearer. Sir Edward's choice of a heart engulfed in flames proclaims him as a man who loves ardently, be that romantic love or sworn allegiance to his king. Or it could convey both simultaneously, while also fitting the mood, as 'lovesickness' was thought to induce melancholia.

Isaac Oliver gives us a gallant knight, a deep thinker and a lovesick hero all in one, rendered in a quality rarely matched, making this a marvel in miniature.

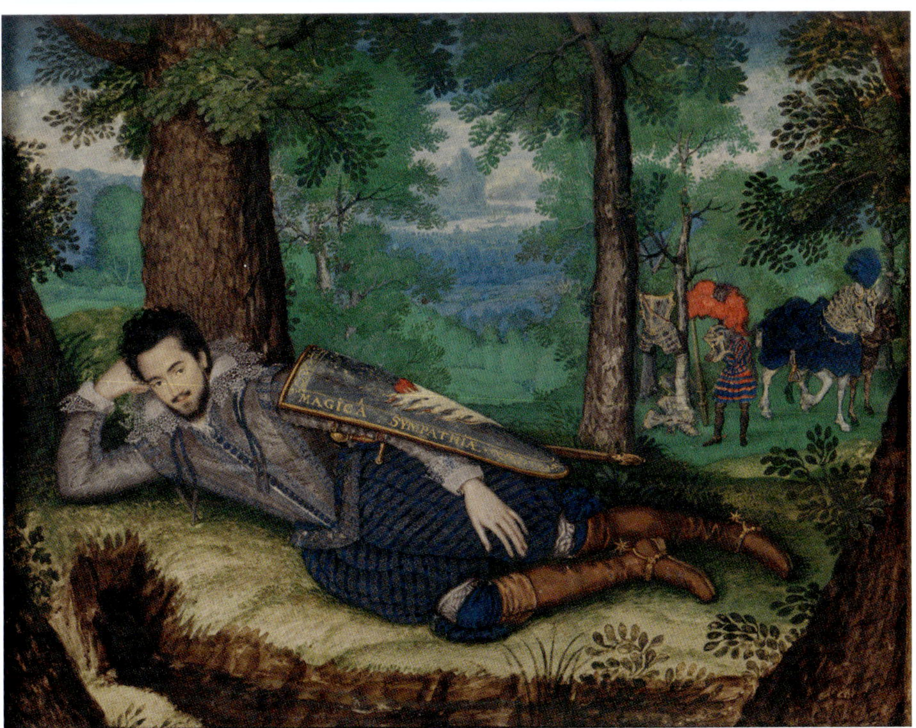

How the Other Half Sleep

The State Bed

Erddig, Wrexham

Erddig's collection, numbering in the region of 30,000 items, is one of the largest in the National Trust. Consequently, its size and variety call for an array of different conservation techniques.

Erddig was home to the Yorke family from 1733, until it was given to the National Trust by Philip Yorke III in 1973. During that time, it would seem the Yorkes had a tendency to accumulate material things – from the extravagant to the everyday – and threw little away.

The collection at Erddig is so varied that it provides a particularly rich and detailed account of life both above and below stairs. The Yorkes were somewhat unusual in commemorating their servants and household staff in portraits, poems and photographs. Attesting to how life was lived above stairs, at the other end of the social scale, Erddig boasts its very own State Bedroom. This room was filled with rare and delicate furnishings, although this didn't prevent it from being regularly used by visiting guests.

The room is hung with beautiful, hand-painted Chinese wallpaper and contains a rare surviving example of a *lit à la duchesse* canopy bed dating from 1720. Because the Yorkes would never consider replacing or renewing it, the bed retains its original hangings of silk satin embroidered with Chinese designs. This makes it, perhaps, Erddig's greatest treasure but one that, due to its fragility, is displayed behind a glass screen.

> Erddig's State Bed in a state of undress during conservation work.

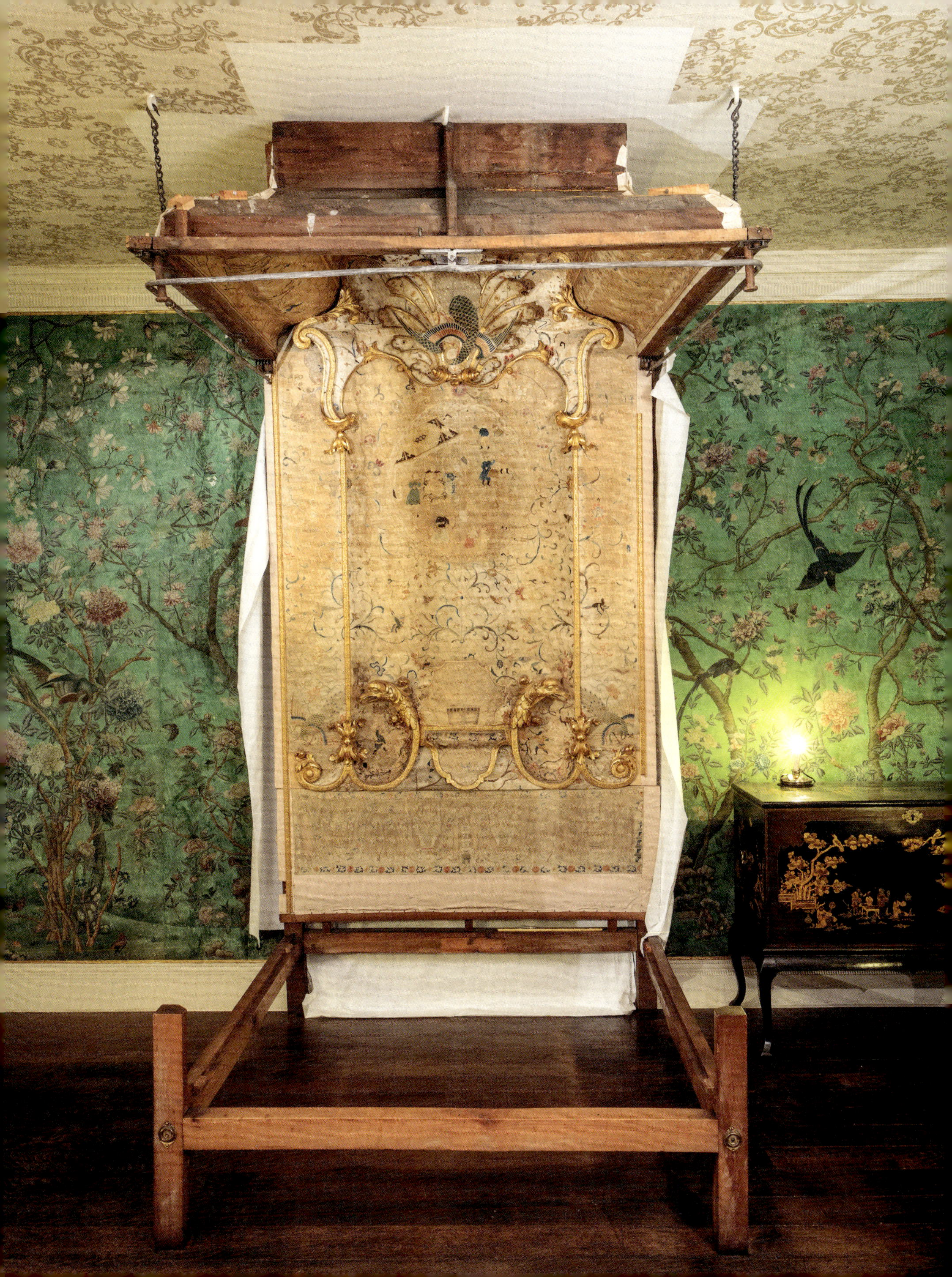

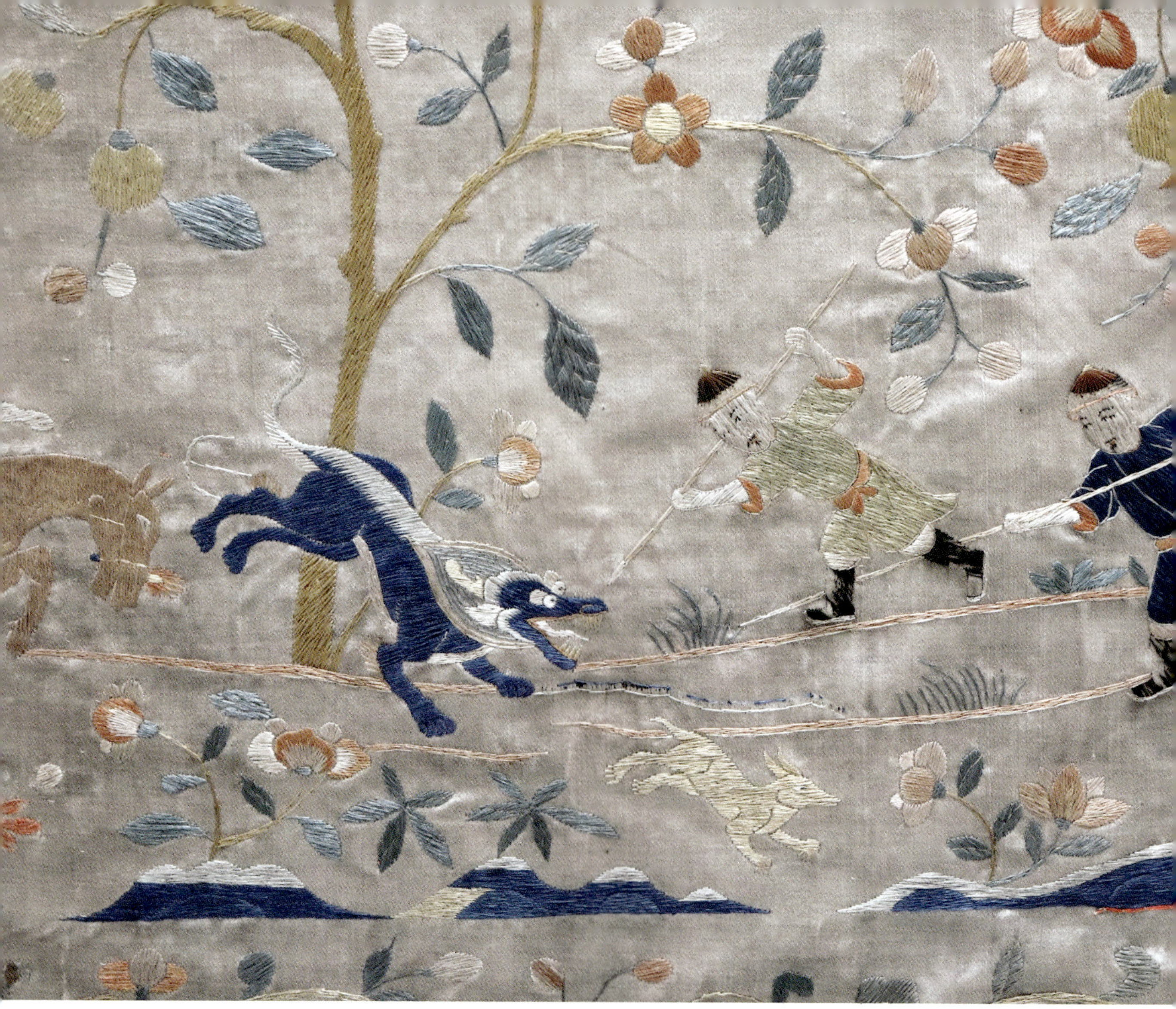

Susanne Gronnow, Erddig's property curator, recalled: 'I first saw the bed over 20 years ago, but because it's so fragile it's the one object in Erddig Hall that has always been looked after by external specialists.'

Erddig certainly boasts a wealth of material items but there hasn't always been the money available to keep them in the best condition. In the 1920s, Europe was still reeling in the aftermath of the First World War. A social change was taking place that would see country houses like Erddig struggle to continue as before, and the estate began to decline.

^ A detail of a hunting scene embroidered onto silk satin.

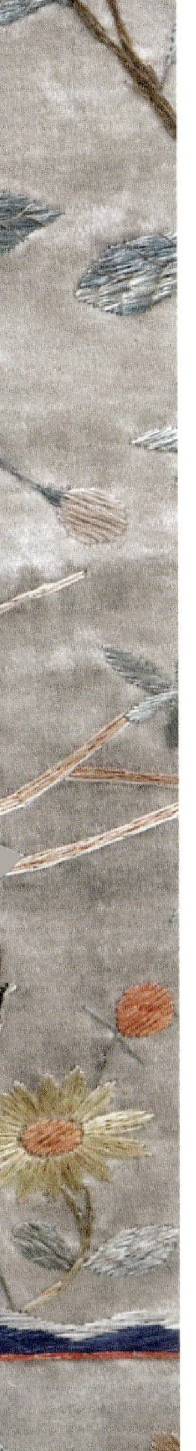

Simon Yorke IV, who inherited Erddig in 1922 at the age of 19, was something of a recluse, eschewing modern comforts such as electricity, mains water, gas or telephone. This general lack of intervention on his part saw the property fall into a state of disrepair, but it also meant that Erddig remained remarkably unaltered at a time when other historic houses were being demolished. It was partly thanks to Simon's determination that Erddig didn't go the same way as so many others. When the time came for his brother, Philip Yorke III, to hand the estate over to the National Trust, he said: 'My only interest for many years has been that this unique establishment for which my family have foregone many luxuries and comforts over seven generations should now be dedicated to the enjoyment of all those who may come here and see a part of our national heritage preserved for all foreseeable time.'

That was in 1973, when Erddig was literally and metaphorically on the brink. A few years earlier there had been a collapse of a shaft that ran from a nearby coal mine under the house. This came after years of subsidence, which had already caused much damage, fracturing the building and allowing water to penetrate in many places. But now the situation was far more critical and without urgent remedial work the house might have fallen into ruin. Using compensation of £120,000 paid by the National Coal Board, who also agreed to stop mining underneath the house, the National Trust was able to carry out the necessary work. This ensured Erddig's immediate survival, but it was not enough. With Philip Yorke III's agreement, the decision was made to sell off part of the estate to pay for repairs arising from decades of neglect and subsidence.

None of this was wilful neglect; it was simply the result of having too much to do with too little. The most valuable and highly treasured items, such as the hangings on the State Bed, did receive specialist attention when they were sent away to London's Victoria & Albert Museum in 1968.

Unsurprisingly, after more than 50 years those repairs had started to fail and the embroidery had started to split and fray. So in 2019 the National Trust team began a six-year conservation project to restore the bed, generously funded by the Wolfson Foundation, the Royal Oak Foundation and a legacy gift. Various elements – cornices, curtains and valances – had to be dismantled with the utmost care and dispatched to the National Trust Textile Conservation Studio at Blickling in Norfolk (see page 152), with the headboard conserved *in situ*.

Out of the whole project's estimated 5,000 hours, the bed curtains alone underwent 1,200 hours of restoration. Once returned to Erddig, they were hung, not on the State Bed, but in a custom display. Property curator Susanne said of the display: 'Even I had never seen the detail close enough to appreciate its beauty. The new display enabled visitors to get much closer to the curtains than before, to take their time and notice the details, such as the embroidered birds and butterflies flying through the flower-laden tree branches.'

The conservation of the State Bed's hangings was a lengthy and complex exercise, given their fragility and long history of repairs, some more successful than others but all part of the story. When attention was turned to the bed cover, conservators were presented with a new set of challenges. For, testifying to the Yorkes' make-do-and-mend approach, it was found that the bed cover was more of a composite than had previously been appreciated, with 300-year-old Chinese silk peacocks cut out and applied to the corners of a nineteenth-century Welsh quilt. Furthermore, underneath Chinese embroidered silk added during the conservation work done by the Victoria & Albert Museum, conservators discovered panels of eighteenth-century British embroidery attached around the edge of the bed cover. This mixture of materials was remarkably well executed, but it is not known for certain by whom. Louisa Yorke's memoir from 1919 records the repair of the bed cover, but not in sufficient detail to answer all the conservators' questions.

These discoveries have now been presented, along with the conserved bed cover, in their own custom display at Erddig, allowing visitors to marvel at the intricacy of the bed cover's various components and unravel the story of its repair.

> Detail of the wood-mounted, embroidered peacock from the canopy of the State Bed.

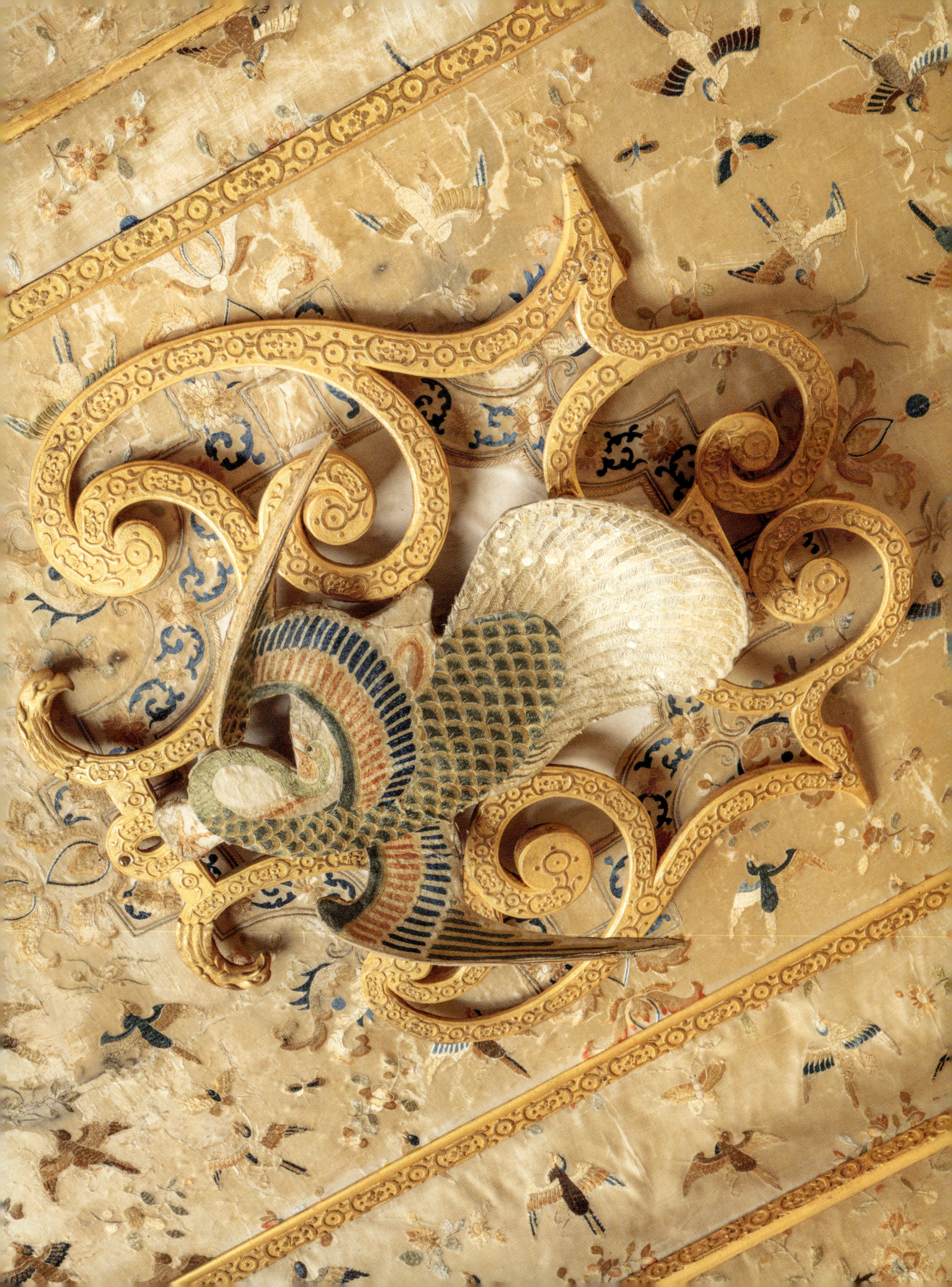

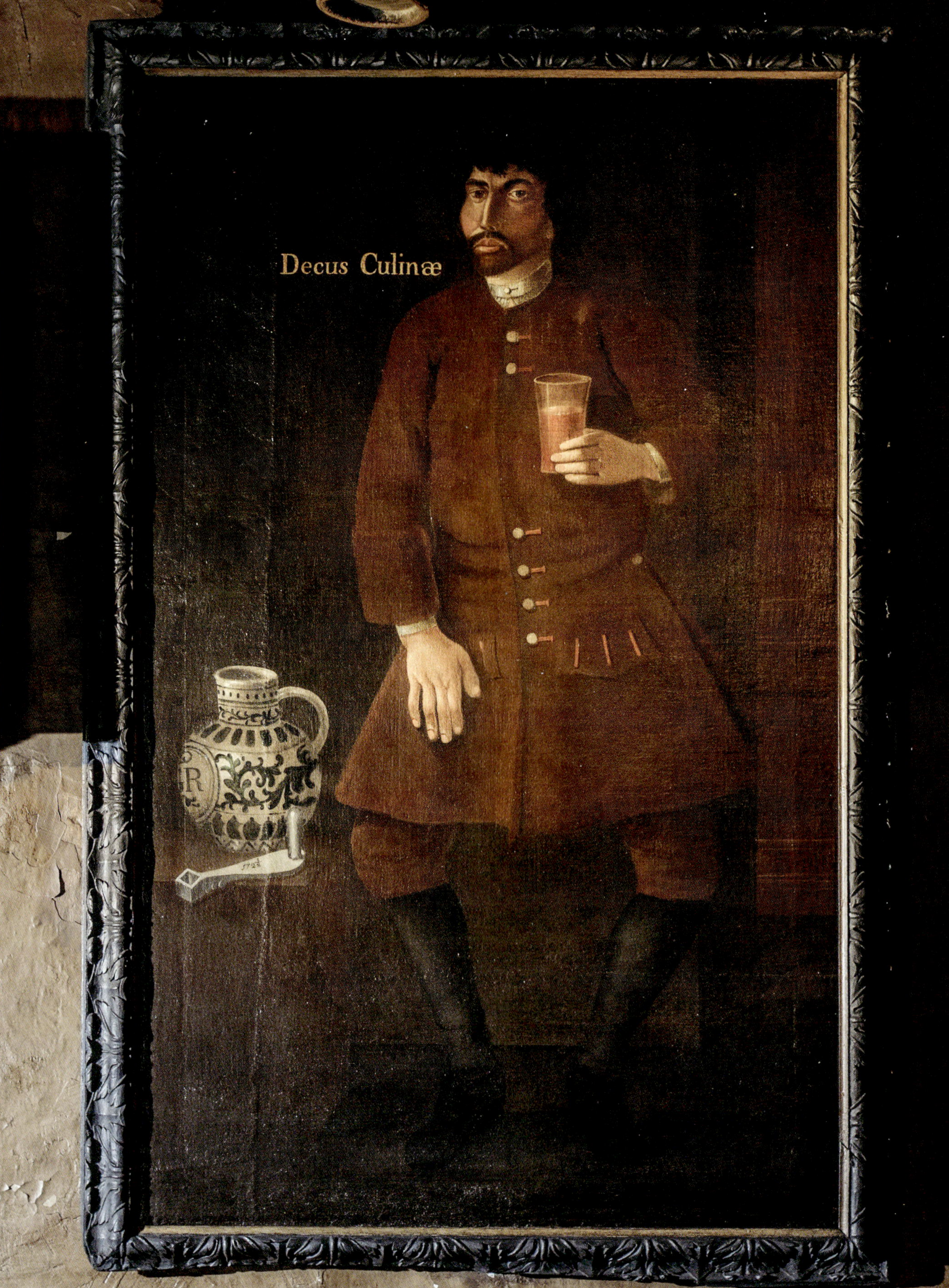
Decus Culinæ

An Unusual 'Below Stairs' Painting

John Wilton's Portrait

Chirk Castle, Wrexham

For the last 300 years, a full-length portrait has hung in the kitchen, and later the Servants' Hall, at Chirk Castle. Already this may strike you as strange, for a life-size oil painting to be hanging 'below stairs' and, more unusual still, for that imposing picture to be a portrait of a member of the household staff.

The servant's name was John Wilton and the Latin motto in gold – prior to conservation one of the more prominent details still visible under the soot and layers of darkened varnish – proclaims him *Decus culinae*, 'glory of the kitchen'. We also know the name of the artist, Mr Whitmore, although this is not a name likely to be familiar even to those expert in the field of portraiture.

Records from the eighteenth century tell us that John Wilton was described as 'a deformed Cripple taken into the Family by Sir Richard Myddelton [3rd Baronet (1655–1716)], and kept for Charity from his Youth to his Death which happen'd in October 1751 – near sixty years old.' The date of the painting, 1728/9, puts the sitter in his thirties, when he was clearly a much-valued member of the castle's staff, and suggests that the portrait may have been painted over an extended period.

It shows Wilton with his head inclined slightly to the left, confidently holding the spectator's gaze. His hair is short, his beard neatly trimmed,

< John Wilton's portrait after conservation reveals a variety of fascinating details previously obscured by layers of soot and discoloured varnish.

and in his left hand he holds a tumbler of liquid, possibly ale. There is a glimpse of a white shirt and a jacket with shiny buttons, which suggests he may have been dressed in his best clothes. In front of the jug on the table to his right there is some kind of handled tool. But before conservation, a combination of dirt and aged varnish had obscured large parts of the portrait, such that Wilton's legs were barely visible and it wasn't possible to tell whether he was sitting or standing.

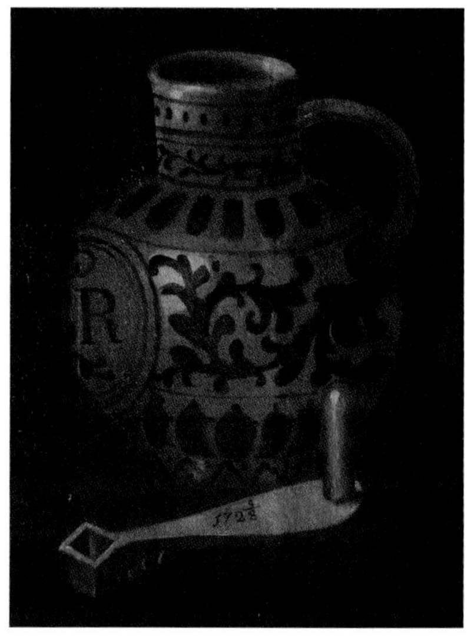

^ This tool could have been a removable handle used to turn a roasting jack, or a winding key for the turret clock.

Already there was much intrigue surrounding this painting, its surface blackened by dirt, so when the time came to send the painting away to be conserved, anticipation of what would be revealed was high. The job of removing centuries of soot and grime fell to paintings conservator Annabelle Monaghan.

As Annabelle removed the layers of sooty surface dirt and old discoloured varnish, Wilton began to come out of the shadows to reveal himself – his strong, aquiline nose, his pale, hazel-coloured eyes and his cheeks reddened, perhaps by the heat of the kitchen. Most revealing of all was the way in which the artist had painted Wilton's legs and feet; his legs are shown quite bowed and one shoe appears to have a stacked heel. It seems likely that this depiction shows the disability that Wilton is described as having in the estate records.

While Annabelle was bringing Wilton back into the light, John Chu, Senior National Curator for Pictures and Sculpture, and Karen George, Collections and House Manager at Chirk Castle, were delving into the archives to find out more about John Wilton. What they found was surprising and moving in equal measure.

In an accounts book dated 20 October 1723, Karen found details of a payment of £2 2s that was made to a Mr Whitmore for a number of jobs around the castle: painting and gilding in the summerhouse, some repairs to glazing and Wilton's portrait. While specialist portrait painters did exist at this time, it was quite common for a painter-decorator to work across many different trades – including portraiture. Yet the rarity of a painting such as this can't be overstated. As John explained: 'What this commission resulted in is a full-length, highly sensitive depiction of one working man painted by another working man, and in that respect this is unbelievably rare, if not unique.'

Other entries in the household accounts relating to John Wilton include a payment to his mother for cloth enough to make him two shirts, and a payment to a shoemaker for new shoes, as well as repairs to his old ones. The latter is especially interesting, given that he was described in the historical record as having a disability – of which there may be evidence in his portrait – but evidently not one that kept him off his feet, as his shoes were so worn down they needed to be repaired. The final entry in the castle's ledgers that mentions Wilton is perhaps the most poignant: a payment in October 1751 for the ale provided at his funeral.

Meanwhile, Annabelle was making discoveries of her own: 'It seems clear that the intention was for this painting to be full-length and life-size. John Wilton in the painting measures approximately 165 centimetres [5 feet 5 inches], which is about the average height for a man at that time. The artist started off with a fairly large piece of canvas that was ready primed, and he could easily have painted the portrait on this single piece of canvas. Wilton would have been reduced in size, but it still would have been a good-size portrait for a commission like this. Instead, Whitmore went to the trouble of stitching on four additional pieces of canvas to give himself enough space to paint Wilton life-size and include the jug and crank handle. It feels like a real statement on the part of the artist or the person who commissioned it.'

Conservation is about so much more than improving the appearance of something. As John Chu said: 'Conservation has made this an even more important painting for us, partly because we can see John Wilton so much more clearly, but also because it spurred us to go back to those records and find out much more about him than we ever previously knew.'

A Quarryman Painter's View

View in Penrhyn Quarry by John Thomas Parry

Penrhyn Castle, Gwynedd

Wales is renowned for its castles; it has over 600, more castles per square mile than any other country in Europe. The people of this land have been fortifying for centuries: there is evidence that the Romans built some of their strongholds on old Iron Age settlements; the Normans erected hundreds of castles as the noblemen sought to defend their newly acquired lands in the eleventh century; other castles were built both before and after the Norman invasion; and then there are castles such as Penrhyn.

It may surprise you that this enormous edifice, that manages to dominate its surroundings even against the jaw-slackening backdrop of the Menai Strait and Eryri (Snowdonia), is only 200 years old. Penrhyn was originally built for Richard Pennant in the style of a castellated Gothic fortress, but the castle we see today was made for George Hay Dawkins-Pennant in a neo-Norman style. It has the outward appearance of an impregnable castle, but was intended as a comfortable mansion – the kind of design that led architect Augustus Pugin to quip: 'Who would hammer against nailed portals, when he could kick his way through the greenhouse?' But then defence was never Penrhyn's purpose. It was built to impress and express its owner's vast wealth, which had come originally from the family's sugar plantations in Jamaica, worked by enslaved people.

So already Penrhyn has a challenging past. The Pennants' overseas

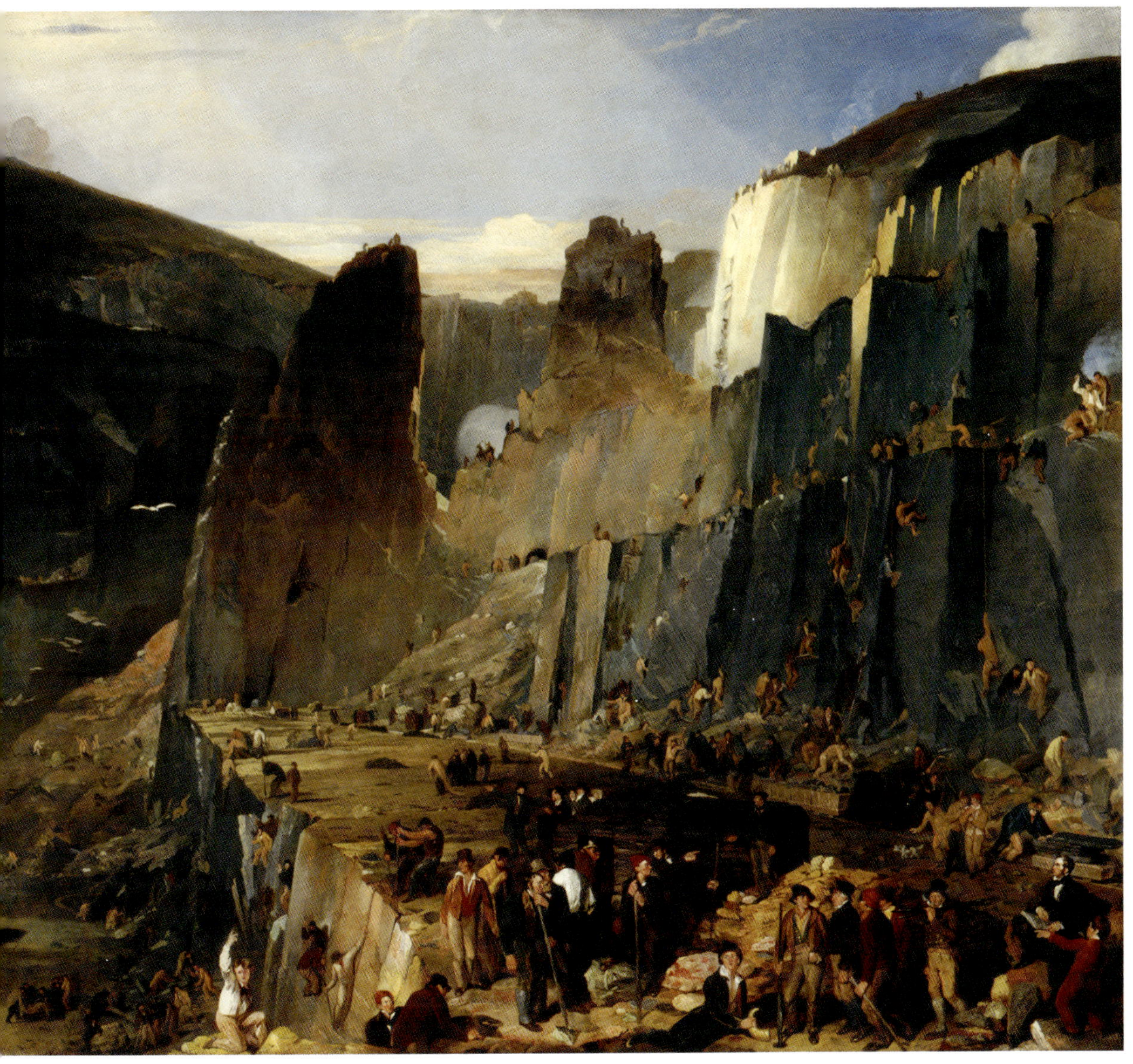

^ *The Penrhyn Slate Quarry*, painted by Henry Hawkins in 1832.

business operations entailed the enslavement of people trafficked from Africa, and made the family very rich. This revenue was invested into the family estates and allowed the development of the quarry, the building of Port Penrhyn and the railway between those two sites. Profits from the quarry were then spent on the building of the current Penrhyn Castle. We can't deny the Pennants' business acumen; we might, however, take issue with how they sourced and treated their workers. At the quarry, too, the actions of the family during the Great Strike would be the cause of great suffering, destroying a community that up until then relied almost entirely on the estate for employment, and inflicting wounds to the people of Bethesda that to this day have not fully healed.

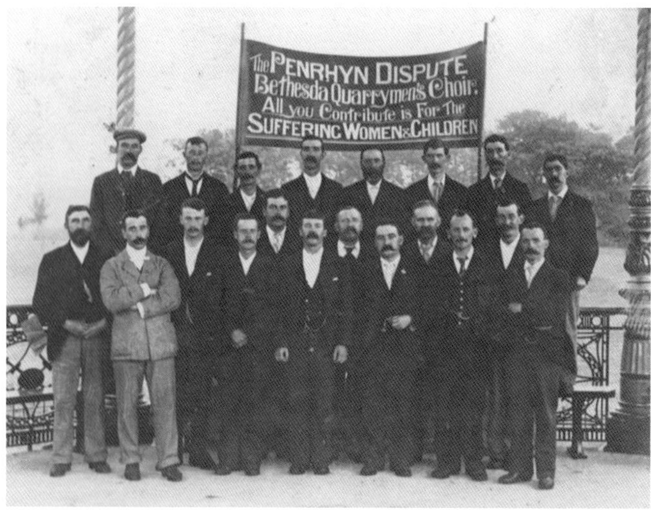

^ The Bethesda Quarrymen's Choir sought to raise funds for the families of striking miners.

> A pen and watercolour drawing of Penrhyn Quarry by quarryman John Thomas Parry, signed and dated Oct. 3rd 1891.

It was during the time of George Sholto Douglas-Pennant, 2nd Baron Penrhyn, that long-simmering tensions and dissatisfaction over working conditions boiled over into industrial action. There had been walkouts prior to this, but the Great Strike lasted three years beginning in 1900, and in that time reduced hundreds of local families to poverty. In 1901, faced with starvation, 400 quarrymen returned to work; a decision for which they were branded traitors. It was an impossible situation – stand with your fellow workers or feed your family. By 1902, over 1,200 men had left the area. Bethesda was being slowly torn apart.

After three years and seven months, those that remained had no choice but to return to work, but on Lord Penrhyn's terms. The community's suffering had been equal to its defiance, and the legacy of the losses – the divisions between neighbours, the men forced from their homes in search of work – are felt to this day, with many descendants of quarrymen refusing to go near the castle.

Very aware of these feelings still present in the local community, National Trust staff at Penrhyn have for some time been trying to engage with the residents of Bethesda, inviting them to come to the castle and share their families' stories about the Great Strike. For one such event, collections assistant Miriam Parry was tasked with going through the archives to find objects that might be of interest to those who could overcome their objections and attend.

Whether it was the shared name or just the very real poignancy of the piece, she chose a watercolour painted by quarryman John Thomas Parry. He also painted in oils, on pieces of slate he had himself quarried, which he would then sell on for a few shillings. His watercolour of a view inside Penrhyn Quarry, painted in October 1891, shows real artistry in conveying depth and delicacy in the detail.

In the run-up to the event, as a National Trust employee but also as a child of Bethesda, Miriam admitted to mixed feelings: 'I'm quite nervous to see what the reaction to the event is going to be. I've always felt like a bit of a traitor myself. I'm working in the castle and now I'm working here, taking care of Lord Penrhyn's collection.'

People came, not in their droves, but into double figures, and they brought both their own memories and those handed down through families, as well as photographs and objects, bringing new life to this story of old strife. Barri, whose great-great-grandfather was one of the striking quarrymen, said: 'There was a strong sense of connection and that is a good thing. We all had different stories to share. Let's hope we can keep doing this again in the future.'

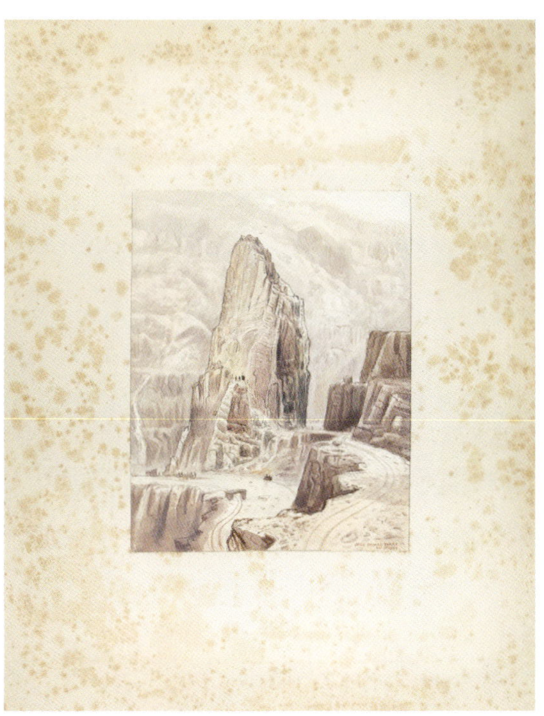

Speaking not as a National Trust employee but as someone conscious of her own family links stretching back to the strike and beyond, Miriam summed up the event: 'It is about reclaiming our history. This is our castle now.'

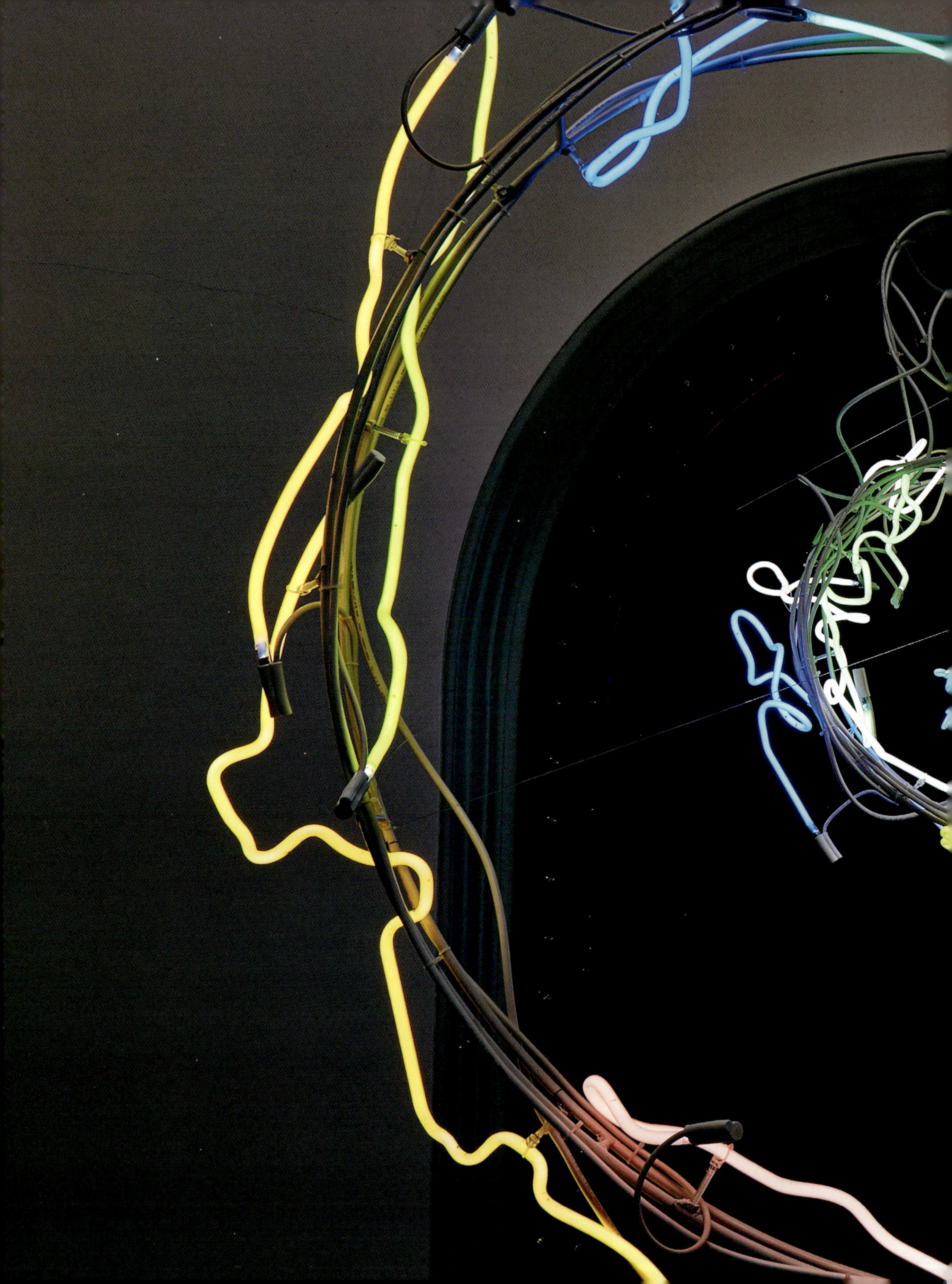

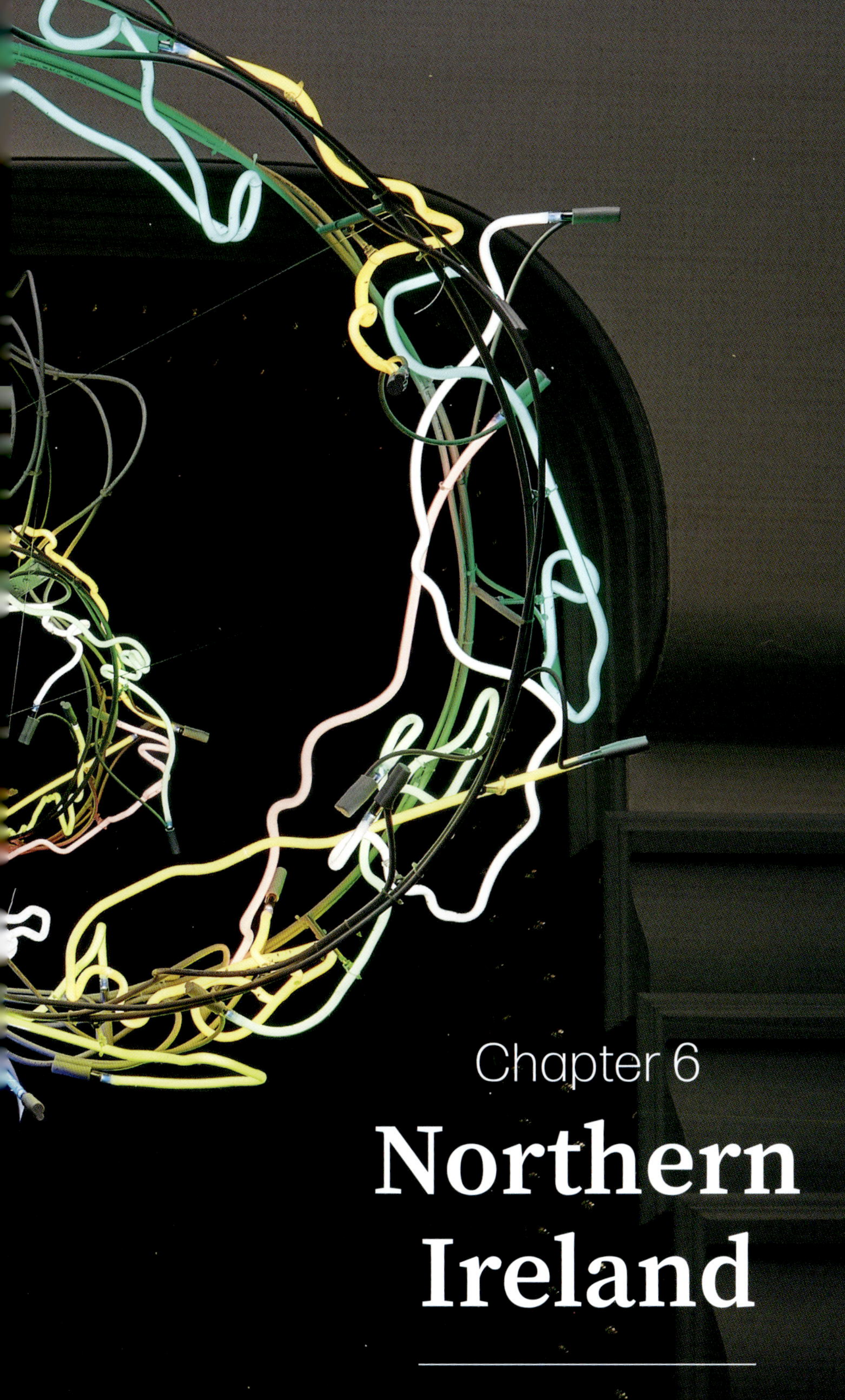

Chapter 6

Northern Ireland

Staging a Comeback

Red Squirrels

Castle Ward, County Down

As a conservation charity, the National Trust is responsible for the upkeep of hundreds of properties and the amassed collections they contain. But the built environment makes up just a proportion of the places cared for by the National Trust, which includes over 600,000 acres (250,000 hectares) of farmland, around 780 miles (1,250 kilometres) of coastline and in excess of 500 historic properties, gardens and nature reserves. As one of the UK's largest landowners, the National Trust plays a vital role in helping to stem the decline in our biodiversity. The loss of our wildlife leaves us all poorer – and the species most at risk need their habitats to be conserved if we are to keep these living treasures.

Arguably the most recognised species that has seen its numbers plummet in the last hundred years is the red squirrel. It is widely known that the grey squirrel was introduced to England from North America, and subsequently outcompeted the smaller reds, so that they now only survive in a few places, such as remote pine forests in Northumberland or islands cut off from the mainland. What is less well known is that the grey squirrels were introduced as an ornamental species to populate the grounds of stately homes. The first recorded introduction was in 1876 and, in a rather ironic twist, the person perhaps most responsible for their spread was the 11th Duke of Bedford, Herbrand Russell. He was greatly concerned with animal conservation, and was president of the Zoological Society of London from 1899 to 1936, but he also released

> From an estimated UK population of 3.5 million in the 1870s when the grey squirrel was introduced, reds now number between 120,000 and 160,000 individuals.

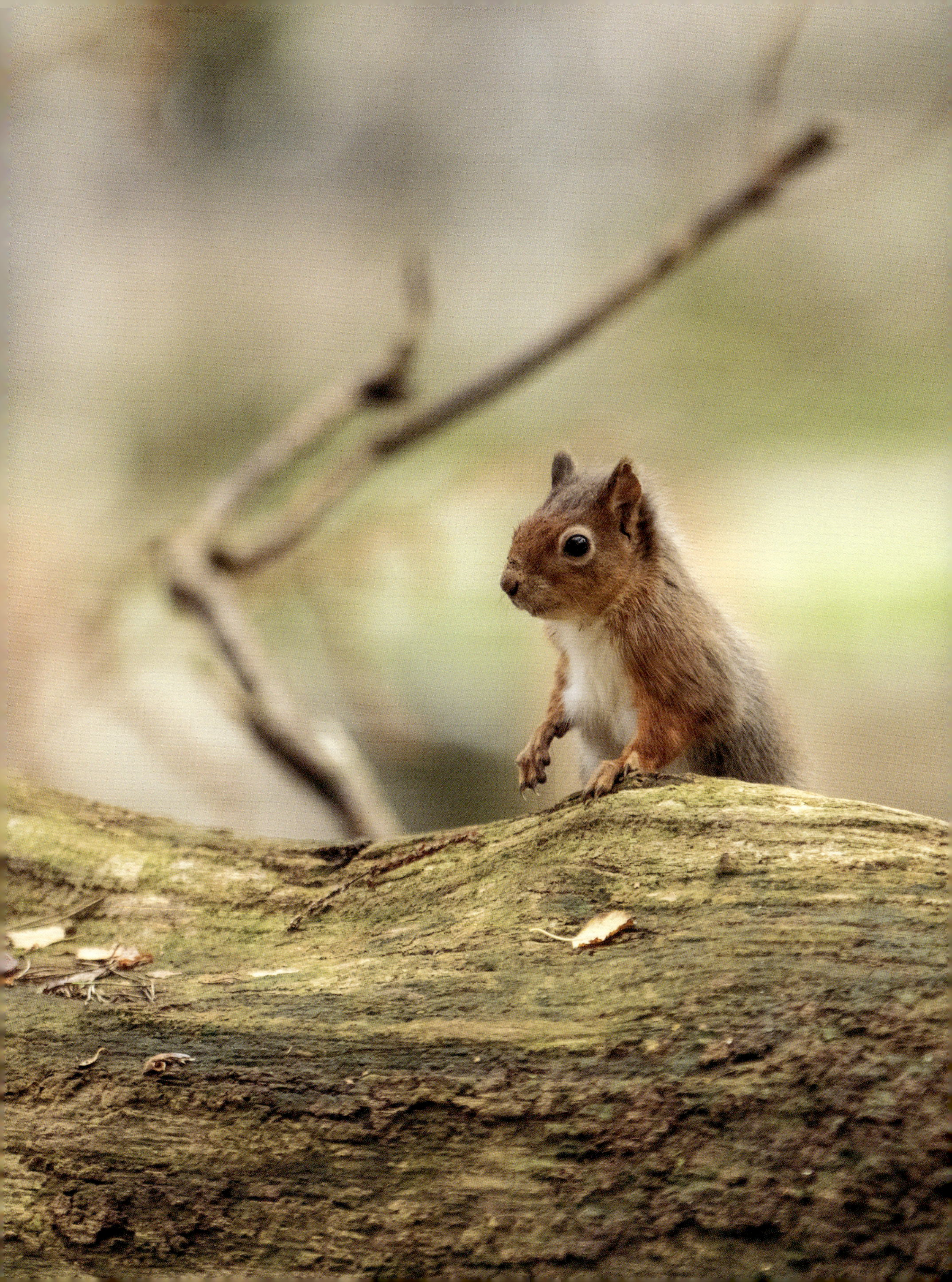

and made gifts of many grey squirrels from his home on the Woburn Estate in Bedfordshire.

When grey squirrels were introduced in the 1870s, the UK's population of reds was estimated to be around 3.5 million. Today that figure has dropped to between 120,000 and 160,000 individuals. To save the red squirrel population from further decimation and to reverse that decline, several Wildlife Trusts have been pursuing conservation projects in England, Wales and Scotland. Meanwhile in Northern Ireland, a National Trust property has been at the forefront of initiatives to reintroduce red squirrels.

Castle Ward, situated on the shores of Strangford Lough, is an unusual eighteenth-century mansion comprising two distinct architectural styles. The house that Bernard Ward and his wife Lady Ann Bligh built in the 1760s was a very sophisticated architectural project, which combined the traditional classical style of the entrance front – a formality appropriate to the 'public' façade as visitors approach – with

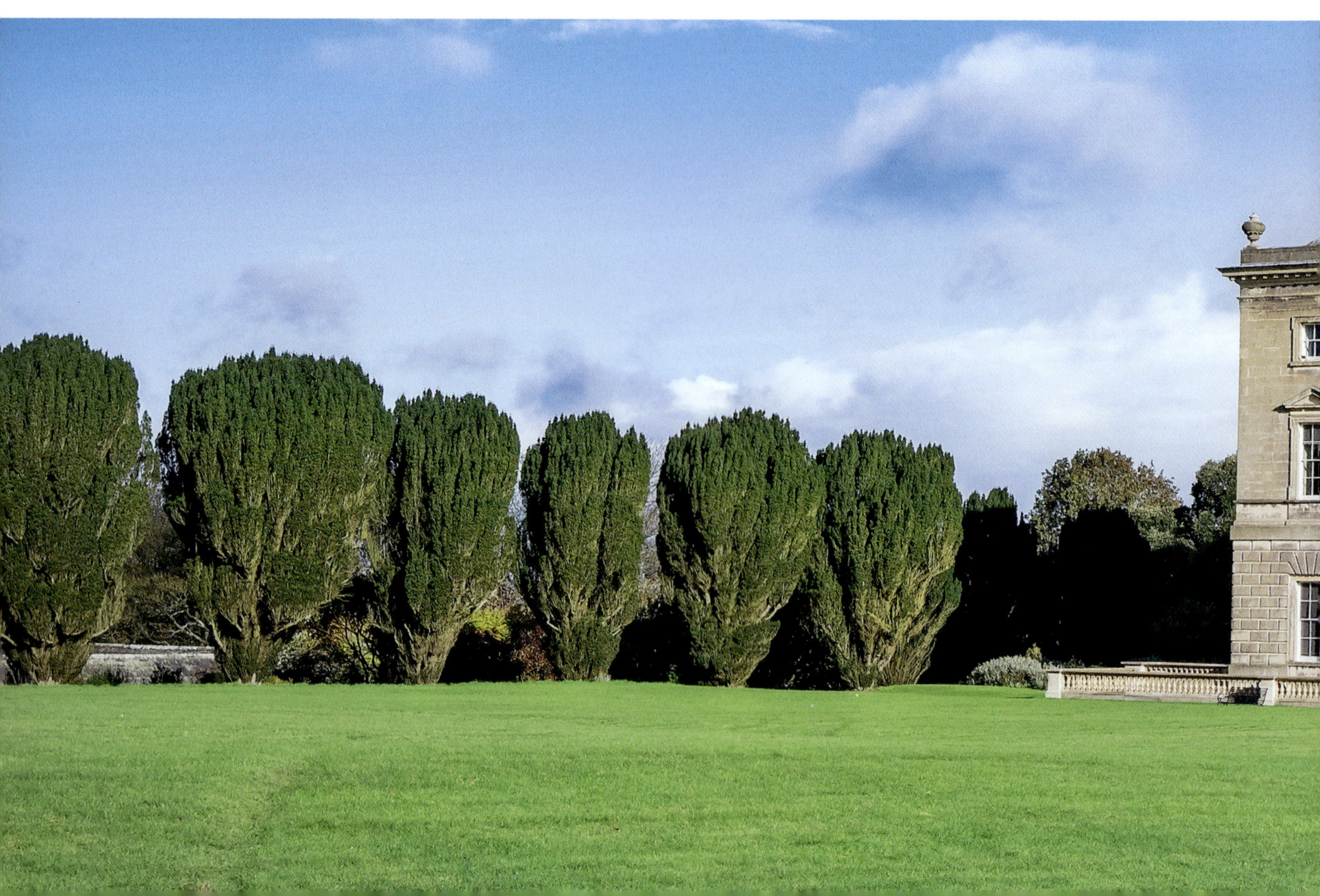

the modern, much more informal, Romantic style of the neo-Gothic 'garden front', with its splendid view of Strangford Lough. The two styles are also in evidence in the interiors, with a clear divide down the centre.

Another curiosity contained in Castle Ward is a set of five cases in which stuffed red squirrels are posed as if participating in a boxing match. One wears a red sash and the other a blue sash, and the fight plays out through five scenes until the victorious, red-sashed squirrel stands over the fallen blue squirrel.

Taxidermy may not be to our taste today, but this display serves as an interesting counterpoint to the fightback that is going on outside the walls of Castle Ward and within its woodland. Castle Ward was chosen as a release site by Belfast Zoo, as it has ample woodland habitat but, more

∨ The grand and formal entrance front of Castle Ward is in contrast to the rather more romantic neo-Gothic elevation that looks out over Strangford Lough.

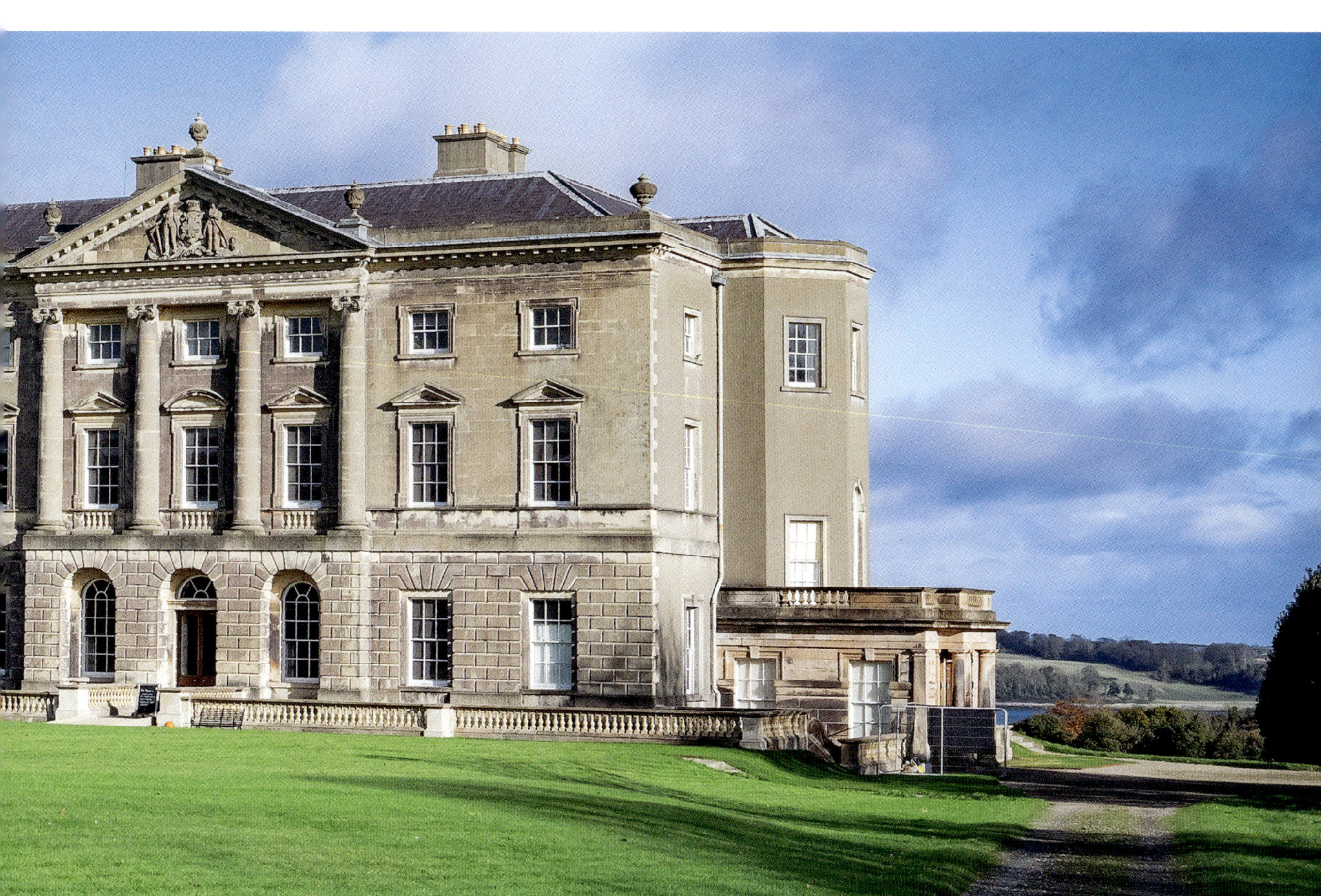

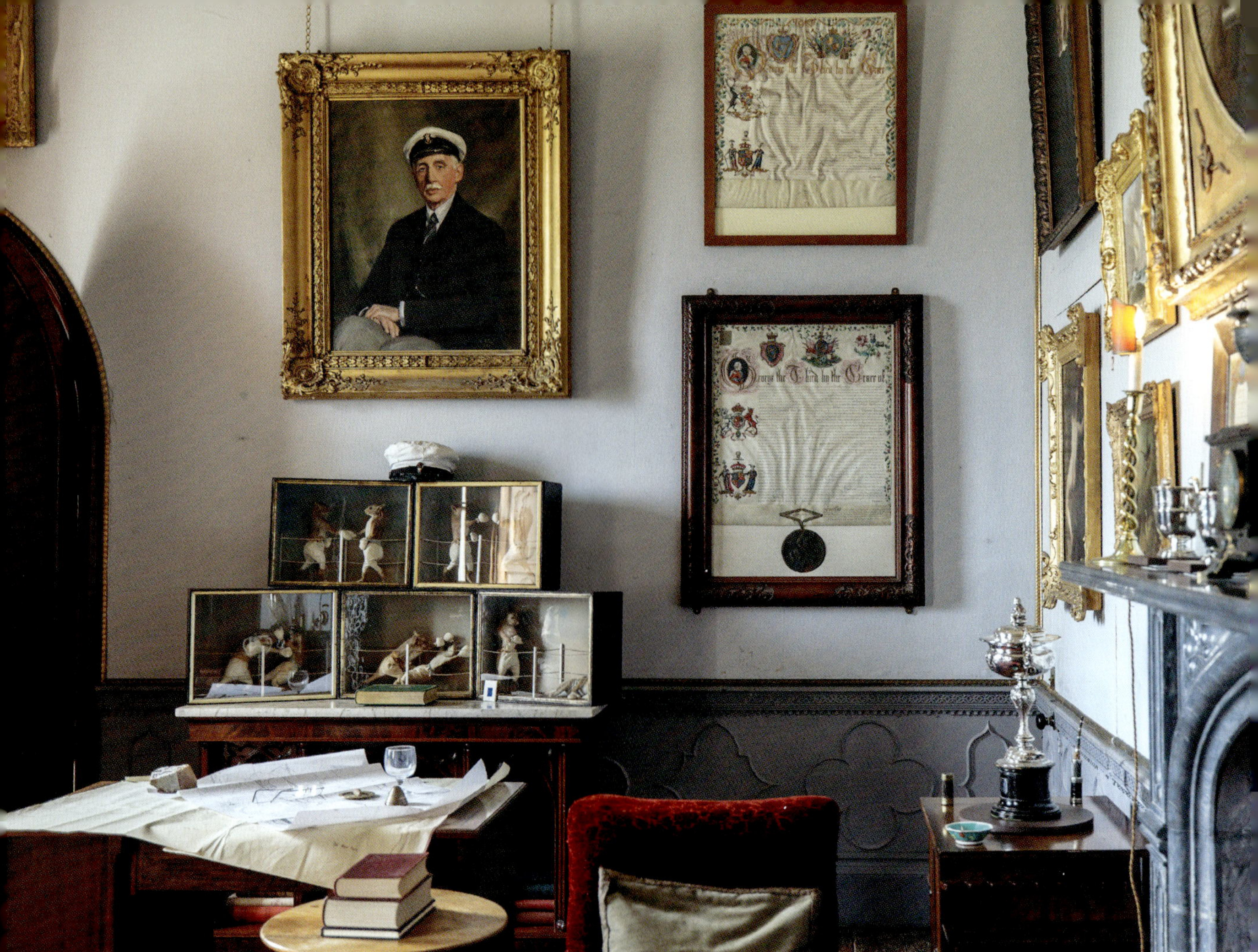

crucially, those woods do not contain grey squirrels. It also contains a healthy population of pine martens, the natural predator of grey squirrels, whereas pine martens and reds, two indigenous species, have learned to successfully co-exist over the millennia.

Castle Ward is the seventh site used by Belfast Zoo into which squirrels bred in captivity have been released. In this initiative, which saw Belfast Zoo working together with the National Trust, Ulster Wildlife, Northern Ireland Environment Agency and the Heart of Down Red Squirrel Group, four squirrels travelled to their new home in hay-lined

^ Preserved by Victorian taxidermist Edward Hart in 1834, the red squirrels in these five cases make up a tableau called 'The Prize Fight'; today the National Trust's approach to animal conservation is very different.

nest boxes, before being released into a temporary enclosure in the woodland, to allow them to acclimatise to their new surroundings.

Katy Bell, Senior Conservation Officer at Ulster Wildlife, said: 'This much-needed project to introduce red squirrels to Castle Ward has been in planning with partners for a number of years and we are delighted to see it finally come to fruition with the red squirrels now settled into their new home. Partnership working is vital in helping to ensure the long-term future of red squirrels in Northern Ireland and we hope to see this new population flourish, breed and spread out into other areas in County Down and beyond, with continued collaboration between organisations, landowners and volunteers.'

Since the release of the red squirrels at the end of 2022, and another in April 2023, estate staff and volunteers regularly top up feeders and monitor the health of the squirrels using specialised cameras. Danielle Shortall, National Trust Nature Recovery Project Officer, said: 'Our ranger team really enjoy keeping the feeders topped up and keeping an eye out for the wee furry folk in our wooded areas, but we couldn't do it without the help of a great group of volunteers and the Heart of Down Red Squirrel Group. Positive community involvement – from monitoring the squirrels and carrying out supplementary feeding to local people reporting sightings – is at the heart of this exciting project and we are grateful for everyone's support.'

Feelings of positivity appear to be well placed, as these new inhabitants have been seen on camera in various locations around the estate, so they are fully exploring their new home, and volunteers and staff have enjoyed seeing them at play. Their energetic nature is perhaps demonstrated most clearly during the mating season, when they take part in chases where they race round and round a tree trunk, up and down, before suddenly leaping from one tree to another and continuing their spiralling game of tag.

Hopefully Castle Ward's woodlands will be the scene of many more of these chases as its little population goes from strength to strength. Certainly, it's expected that the living specimens on the estate should soon far outnumber the Victorian squirrels in their display cases.

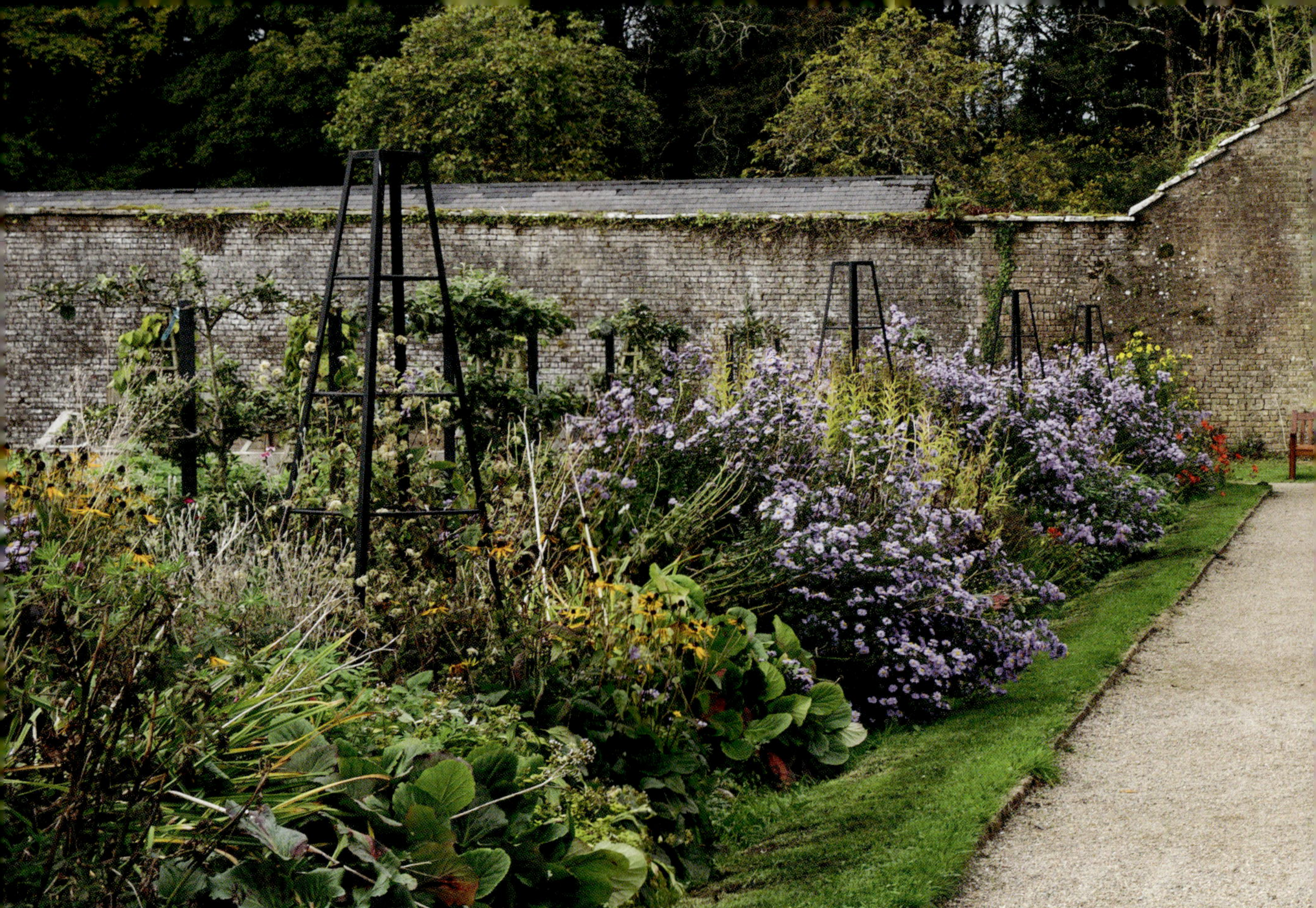

A Growing Community

Kitchen Garden

Florence Court, County Fermanagh

For decades, the walled garden at Florence Court was hidden from sight, visible only in surveys, photographs and archaeological records. As any gardener knows, when these spaces are left to their own devices, they rapidly lose their form. The project to return the walled garden to its former productive glory spanned years, and drew on contributions from staff, volunteers, funders and supporters.

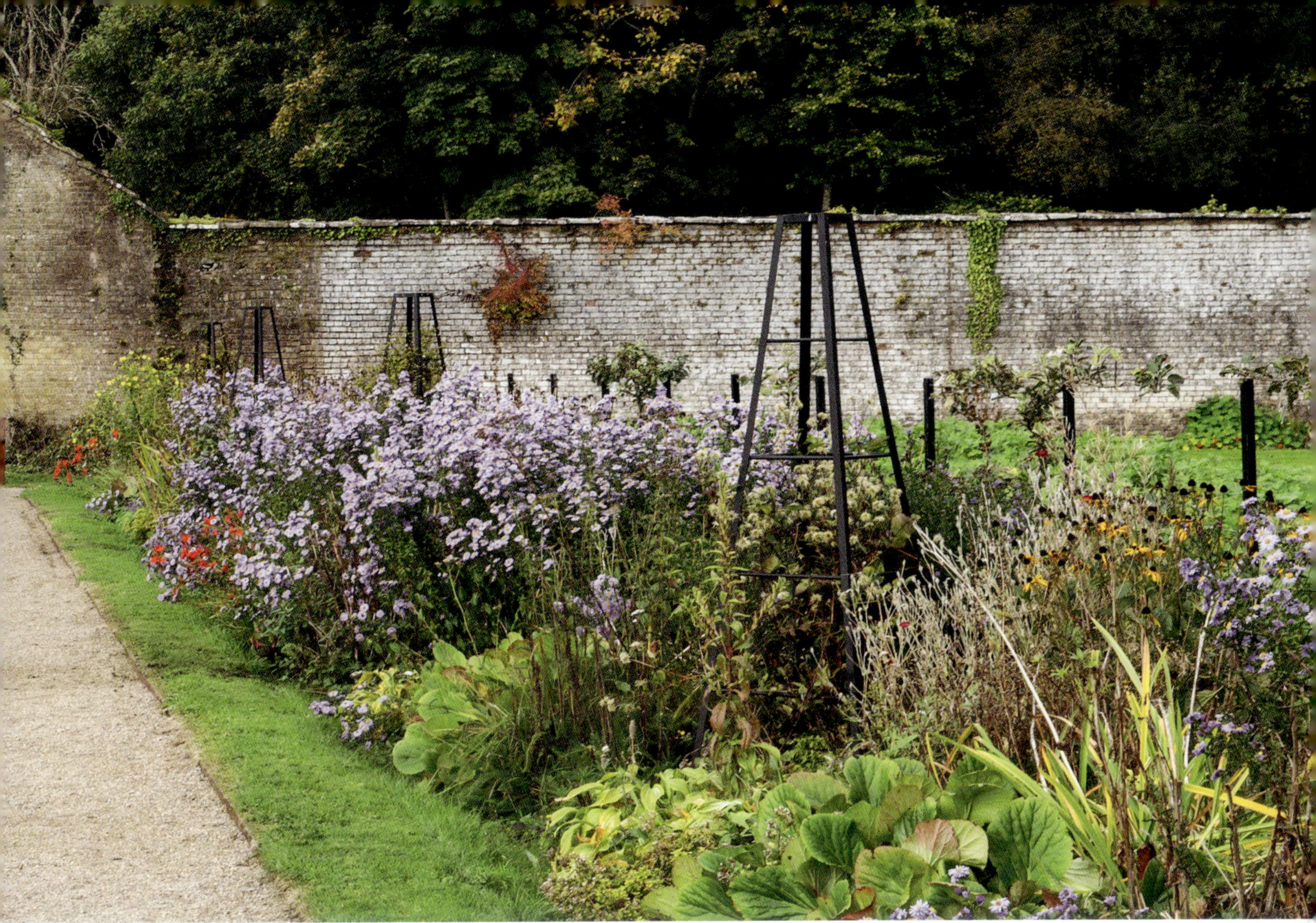

^ The walled garden at Florence Court is bearing fruit, flowers and vegetables once more.

Florence Court was once the seat of the Cole family, the earls of Enniskillen. The Georgian mansion at its heart is known for its exquisite Rococo decoration and fine Irish furniture, but it is equally celebrated for its views. Located in the west of the county, in the foothills of Cuilcagh Mountain and surrounded by expansive parkland and thick woodland, it boasts the most majestic countryside setting.

The Cole family lived here for over 250 years, during which time their fortunes naturally waxed and waned. By the time the family decided to give Florence Court to the National Trust in 1953, the estate had suffered from the combined effects of the Second World War, falling agricultural prices and rising wage costs. Still, what they presented to the National Trust was one of the finest examples of an historic Irish demesne.

In addition to grazing for livestock and horses, a large deer park and arable land for crops, the estate included a pottery works that made drainage pipes, bricks and tiles, and a sawmill that produced everything from fence posts and gates to railway sleepers and coffins.

Supplying the house was the walled garden, built in the late eighteenth century, which was greatly developed by Charlotte Cole, 4th Countess of Enniskillen. Covering an area of 4 acres (1.6 hectares), it contained both ornamentals and edibles, and was laid out in a pleasing formality intended to provide a feast for the eyes, as well as flowers for the house and food for the table. Charlotte had her head gardener, James Sutherland, lay out a rose garden and build a pergola to support climbing roses and clematis. They planted an orchard of native Irish apples, and Viscount Cole commissioned glasshouses that ran the length of the garden's north wall, enabling the cultivation of grapes and apricots.

In the 1920s there were at least 12 gardeners at Florence Court; by the 1930s there were six, plus the head gardener. However, when the last head gardener, James Sheppard, left in 1947, the garden fell into disuse and its buildings into disrepair. The glasshouses, along with a mushroom house and potting shed, were in such a poor state that they were demolished in 1974. It took an archaeological survey in 2014 to discover the original footprint of the glasshouses, but several more years

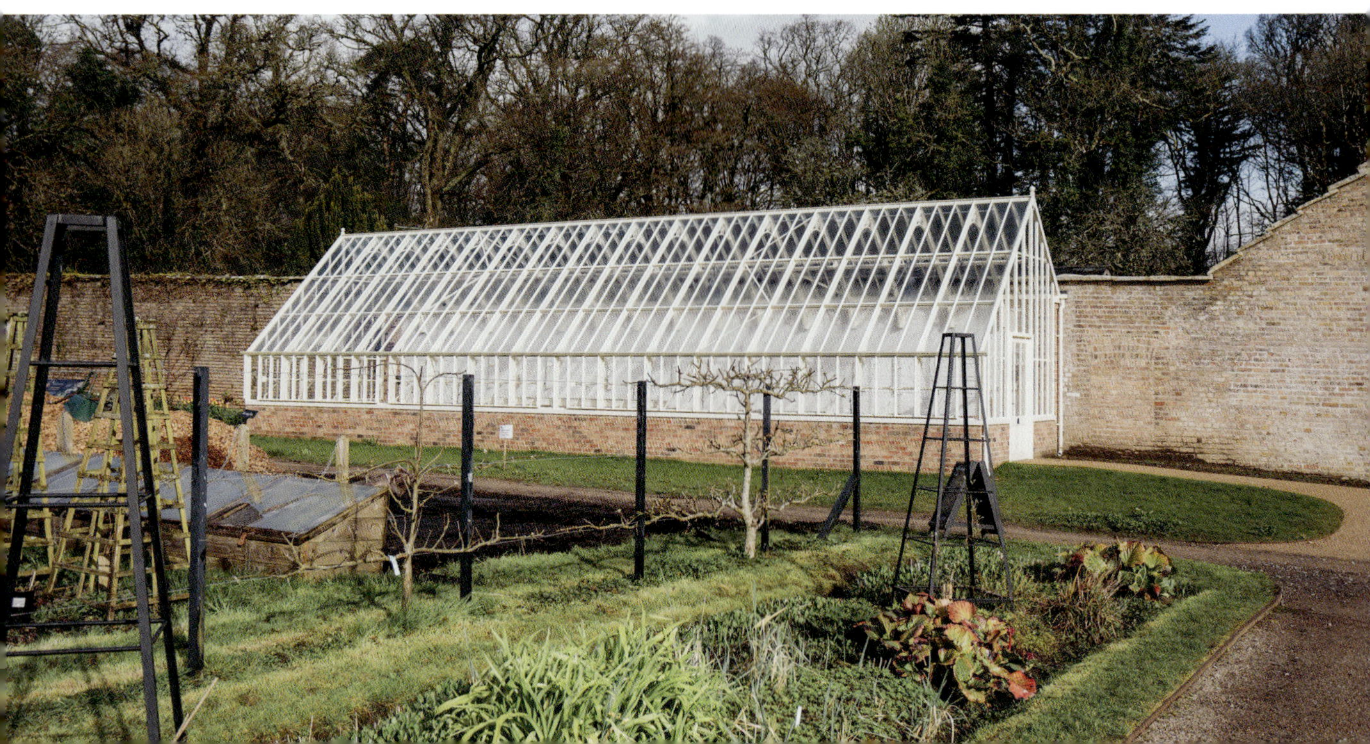

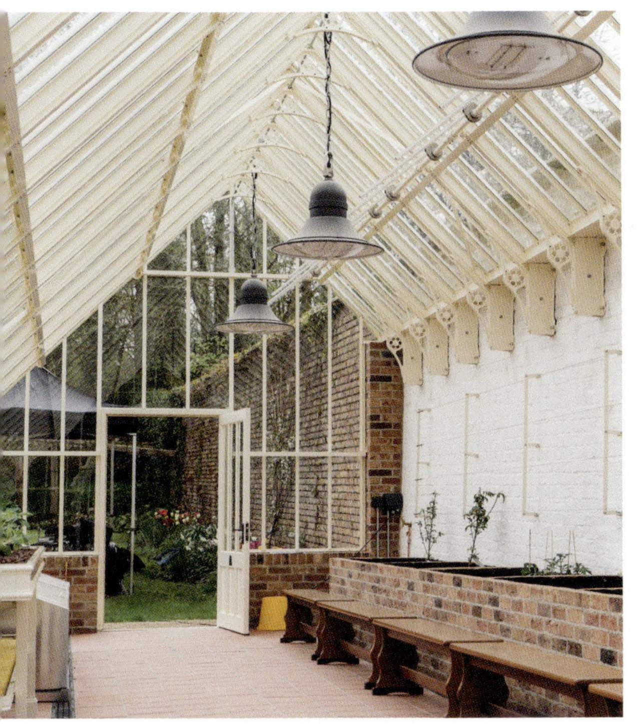

of research and fundraising were needed before work could begin on the restoration of the walled garden.

Over many years the vision to restore the walled garden was developed and led by former head gardener, the late David Corscadden. The structure and planting of today's garden are largely due to David's expert leadership, and he also oversaw a significant expansion of Florence Court's Irish Apple Tree collection. In 2022 it fell to the next head gardener, Ian Marshall, to see the project through to its final stages, which culminated in the summer of that year with the delivery and installation of the new glasshouses.

Throughout, Ian was assisted by a team of passionate volunteers. When describing the project, Ian said it was 'about building a community as much as a garden'. Around 30 volunteers came to work in the garden for a day or two each week, which they did for years. Visitors to Florence Court can now see the restored walled garden, which also hosts regular community groups, as it did throughout the project, as, after all, it wouldn't have been possible without community involvement. Speaking about his team of volunteers, Ian said: 'They are a hard-working and dedicated bunch, and without them the garden wouldn't exist,' and of the walled garden: 'I think we have the peace, the tranquillity, but also the craic in here. That's what I think people are here for, they come to learn new skills but they also come to meet new people and have a bit of fun.'

^ The design of the new glasshouses was inspired by the original buildings, modified for modern uses.

< Construction and installation of the two glasshouses took 40 weeks to complete.

Skills and Techniques
Conservation of Energy

When we talk of kitchen gardens, most likely the image conjured up is a Victorian walled acre or two, of the type seen at Florence Court, but the Victorians did not invent them. So, too, with hydropower; you might imagine only large twentieth-century dams constructed of concrete to hold vast quantities of water and harness its power. But again, hydropower in the UK has been utilised for a lot longer than you may think. Of course, it's the Greeks who can claim the earliest use of hydropower, with Archimedes' invention of the water screw, but on these islands, it was those ingenious and industrious Victorians who introduced the concept, even if they didn't manage to make it affordable and more widely available.

William George Armstrong, 1st Baron Armstrong, was the first engineer to be raised to the peerage. Alongside his wife, Margaret, he created Cragside in Northumberland, during the second half of the nineteenth century. A visionary inventor and engineer, he built Newcastle's Swing Bridge and the hydraulic mechanism that operates London's Tower Bridge. He powered Cragside by harnessing water from artificial lakes to drive hydraulic machinery and to generate electricity, making Cragside the first known place in the world to be powered by hydroelectricity. His first scheme was installed in 1878, using relatively crude and dangerous arc lamps. In 1880, he made improvements, installing a series of Joseph Swan's newly invented incandescent light bulbs. At its peak, Lord Armstrong's hydroelectric system saw water channelled 340 feet (103 metres) vertically, descending from lakes high above the house down to the turbine and Crompton dynamo in the Power House below.

To a modern audience, when energy production from a natural and renewable source is a real and urgent necessity, this would read like very welcome news, but although Armstrong's work generated waves of interest, it didn't challenge the nation's reliance on coal. Now that Cragside is in the care of the National Trust, the use of hydropower continues to be developed, and in 2014 a new hydro-generator was installed to light the house. This time the generator is a 56-foot (17-metre) long Archimedes' Screw – a modern

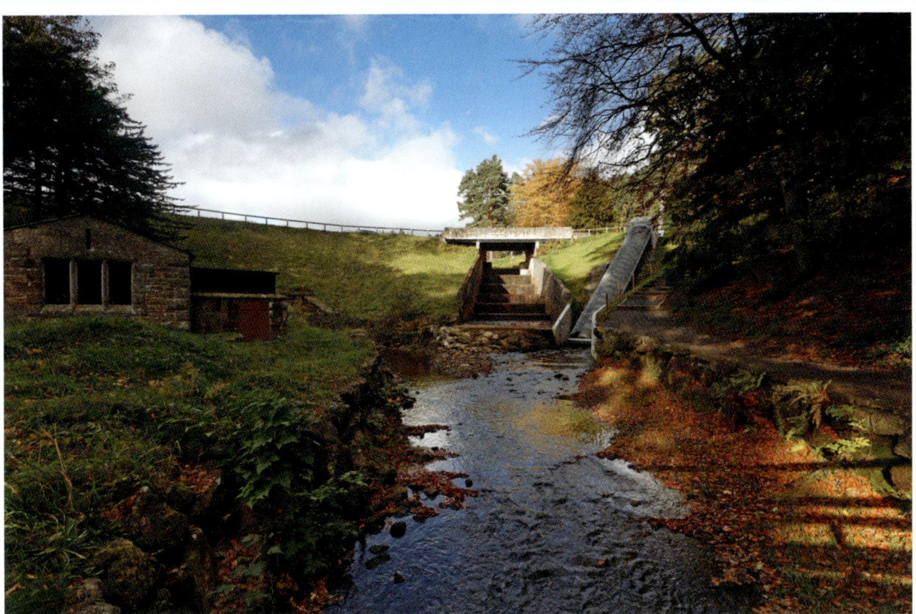

application of the much older technology – that is turned by water falling from the wonderfully named Tumbleton Lake, one of the series of artificial lakes created by Lord Armstrong. While not a direct continuation of his work, this certainly captures its spirit.

The National Trust has also introduced a hydroelectricity scheme at Hafod y Llan farm in Eryri (Snowdonia). Harnessing nature without affecting its beauty, it has been sensitively installed, and now generates enough energy a year to power over 610 homes.

In another beauty spot popular with walkers, the Stickle Ghyll hydro was installed in 2015, and uses fast-flowing water in the Langdale Valley, Cumbria, to power the Sticklebarn pub. A pint of beer after a long walk is usually a guilt-free experience, but at this pub even more so.

Gibson Mill in West Yorkshire was one of the first cotton mills of the Industrial Revolution, but today it is powered by hydroelectricity and roof-mounted solar panels. It has been off grid for 10 years and is the National Trust's flagship sustainable building.

^ The Archimedes' Screw hydro-electric turbine at Cragside uses water from Tumbleton Lake to create power for the house.

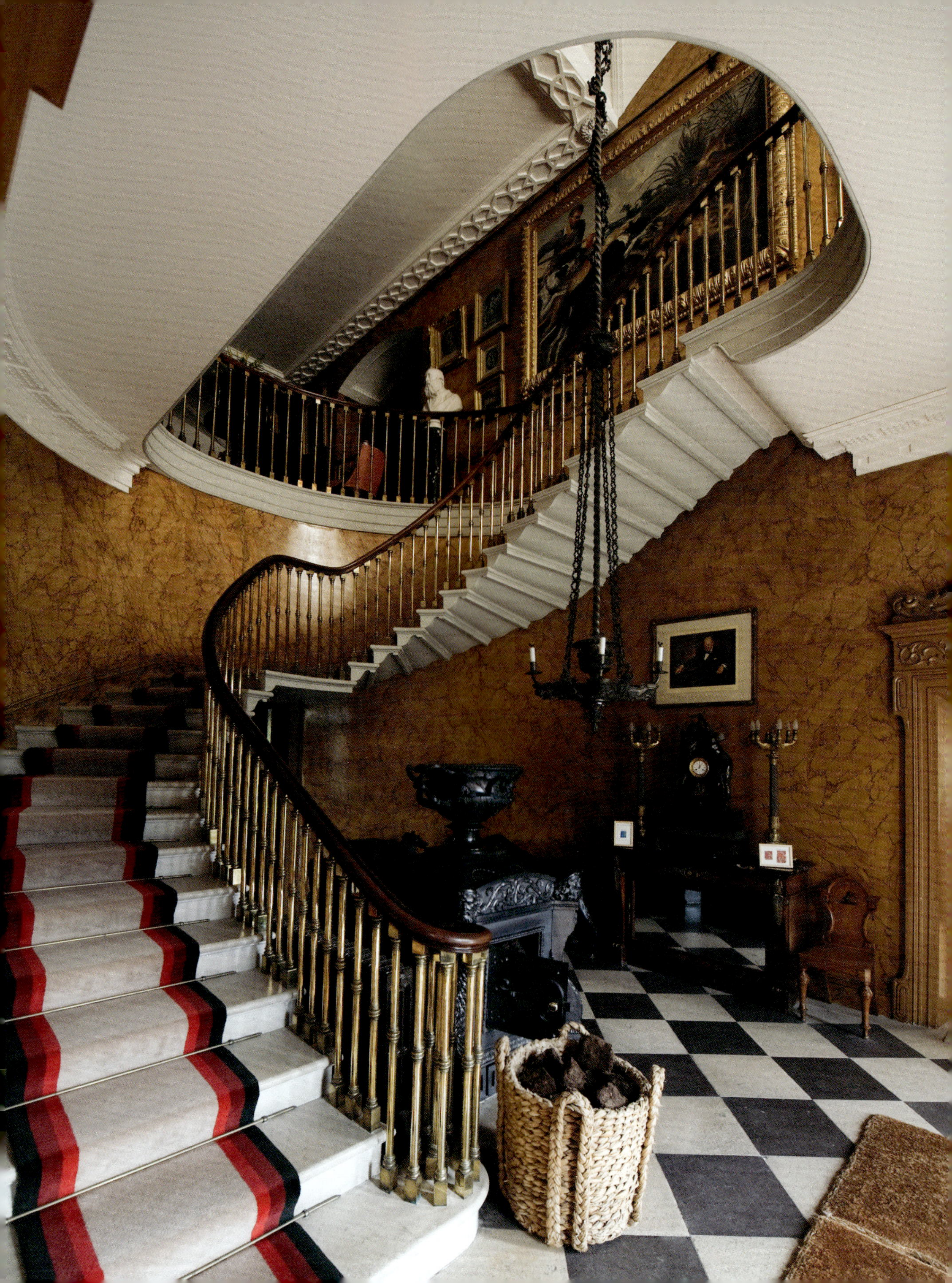

An Illuminating Story

Acetylene Gas Lighting

The Argory, County Armagh

The Argory was built in the 1820s, following something of a quirk in a will, and is itself full of quirks. Its story begins in 1817 when a man named Joshua MacGeough died, leaving two sons and three daughters. He all but left his first son out of his will, bequeathing the family home at Derrycaw to his second son, Walter. However, the terms of the will stipulated that Walter couldn't bring a wife to live with him, as long as his sisters remained unmarried. That they did, so, seeking independence, Walter decided to build his own house, The Argory.

Walter was a wealthy barrister and his tastes when furnishing his new home tended towards opulence. The West Hall makes that clear; it has a remarkable cantilevered stone staircase on three sides with gleaming brass balusters supporting a mahogany handrail. Suspended above it is a large, double-height brass light fitting. The Argory also has two impressive Argand lamp chandeliers, which ran on oil, and were named after their Swiss inventor. However, they were converted to run on gas (becoming gasoliers), when Walter's son, Captain Ralph MacGeough Bond Shelton, inherited The Argory.

When Captain Shelton installed an acetylene gas plant in 1906, he was joining a growing number of country-house owners doing likewise. Acetylene gas was a popular source of heating, lighting and power during the late nineteenth and early twentieth centuries. It is indeed the hottest and most efficient of all the fuel gases – it is also widely used in welding

< Originally an entrance hall designed to make a big impression, the West Hall contains a remarkable wraparound cantilevered staircase and double-height light fitting.

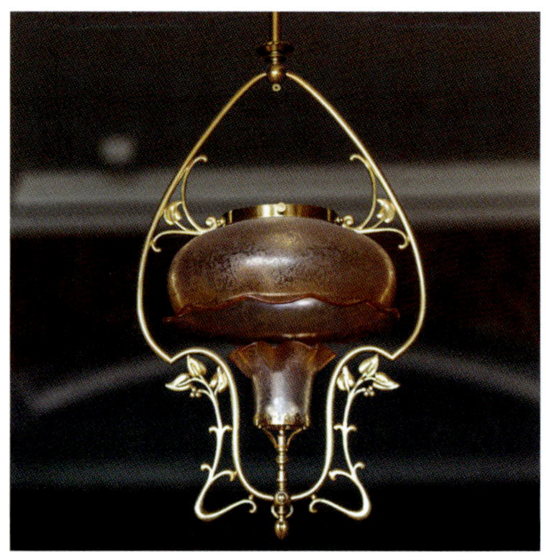

^ The Argory's acetylene gas lighting system is a remarkable survivor.

– but it is rather unstable in air and highly flammable. Consequently, most acetylene gas fittings were later converted to electricity (if the house they had been lighting hadn't been incinerated by then). Captain Shelton and subsequent owners – his nephew Sir Walter MacGeough Bond, who inherited in 1916, Sir Walter's son Nevill and the National Trust, to whom Nevill donated The Argory in 1979 – decided to leave all the light fittings untouched. In fact, The Argory continued to run on acetylene until as recently as the 1980s and the gas was lit for the last time in July 1981, the day the house opened to the public.

This decision to retain The Argory's acetylene lighting system and fittings, in their original state, and resist the temptation to convert to electricity, as happened in so many other country houses, makes this an exceptionally rare survivor.

Incidentally, Captain Shelton was himself a survivor, having been on board HMS *Birkenhead* when it sank off the coast of South Africa in shark-infested waters – a story he apparently never tired of telling. Having inherited the family home where he grew up with his six siblings, Captain Shelton made The Argory a party house, where he entertained lavishly. He was a generous and attentive host and insisted that his guests were wined and dined until they could wine and dine no more. Testament to this is the weighing chair and record book he set up in the hall to check that his guests left heavier than when they arrived.

However, this is just another of The Argory's quirky asides, and the National Trust has the serious task of keeping the home of Mr Bond (as Nevill MacGeough Bond was known) just as he wished. Though the light fittings haven't been in use since the 1980s, they require regular cleaning and occasional full-scale conservation. A project to conserve all of the light fittings began in 2013, beginning with the shades in the

Drawing Room. Being over 100 years old and made of delicate pink silk, they required specialist attention and so were sent away to the National Trust's Textile Conservation Studio at Blickling in Norfolk (see page 152). Then there were the fittings themselves, all of which had to be removed from the walls and sent away to a specialist metalwork studio to have any necessary repairs made, and to be cleaned, polished and lacquered. This included the double gasolier in the West Hall, which required scaffolding to bring it safely down. It took three years to remove, conserve and reinstate all of the light fittings.

Though the West Hall gasolier was not operational, it naturally left something of a gap while it was being worked on in the metalwork studio. The National Trust took the bold decision to use the space left by the gasolier to display something rather different.

Kevin Killen is a member of the Royal Society of Sculptors and a visual artist who sculpts with neon light. His work aims to explore unseen boundaries and capture evanescent moments. Kevin visited The Argory and met with house steward Matthew Morrison, who gave him a tour of the house as he talked about The Argory's history and its people, pointing out interesting features as he went. Matthew did all of this in near darkness with a bulb affixed to his right index finger.

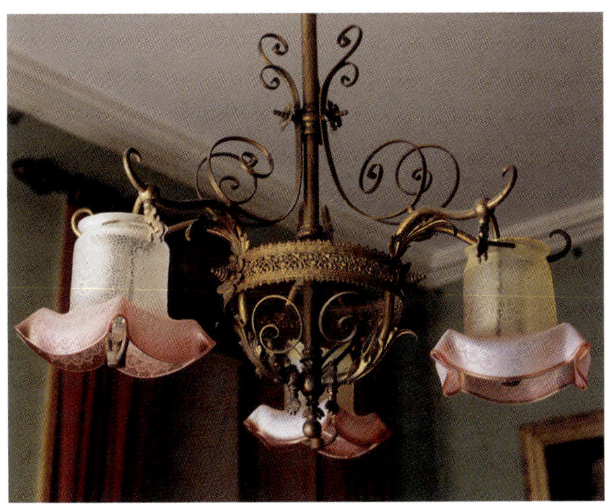

^ The ornate three-arm gasolier with pink-flushed glass shades that hangs in the Study.

While this must have struck Matthew as something of a departure from the house tours he was used to giving, Kevin described his approach: 'My work uses neon light to map peoples' stories, histories and lives. While we do it in very different ways, the National Trust also preserves these things, so working with them has been an interesting experience. Using the tour of the house as a starting point, I photodocumented a staff member traversing the tour route and translated that into a neon map. The piece embodies the owners, staff and visitors throughout the house's history, while the spiral shape is inspired by the spiral patterns found in the house's décor.'

The piece, entitled *Artificial Sunshine*, was temporarily suspended over the West Hall, spiralling down into that space, measuring four and a half metres in length and over a metre at its widest point. The neon light wasn't static; rather, it pulsed and changed colour. It certainly made an impression on visitors. As Matthew said: 'The blue of the china, pink of the lampshades, the green of the grass and so on, it's very modern and although some people don't like it, the majority find it fascinating and in keeping with the last owner's collection of modern art.'

As Mr Bond, who gave The Argory to the National Trust, was an avid collector and patron of modern and contemporary art, the idea was to celebrate the fascinating history of lighting within the house, while at the same time referencing Mr Bond's interest in artistic innovation and experimentation, and his encouragement of young artists from Northern Ireland. It told that story in a novel and highly creative way, and it undoubtedly got people talking. Matthew was certainly convinced: 'I spend most of my time living in the past telling stories and showing off the collections but we're always delving into history to come up with something new and this interpretation is something special.'

The original Argand gasolier from the West Hall has since been reinstated, as have all the other conserved light fittings around the house. The original neon artwork was taken apart, and the pieces re-used by Kevin Killen to create a second artwork commissioned by the Trust. Called *Artificial Sunshine II*, this is another spiral artwork, which is mounted on a wall in the back stair, alongside a number of Mr Bond's works of modern art – the few that remain in the house of a collection that once contained some 400 artworks. Hopefully Mr Bond would approve.

> *Artificial Sunshine* by Kevin Killen referenced both The Argory's fascinating history of lighting and the house's former owner's commitment to contemporary art.

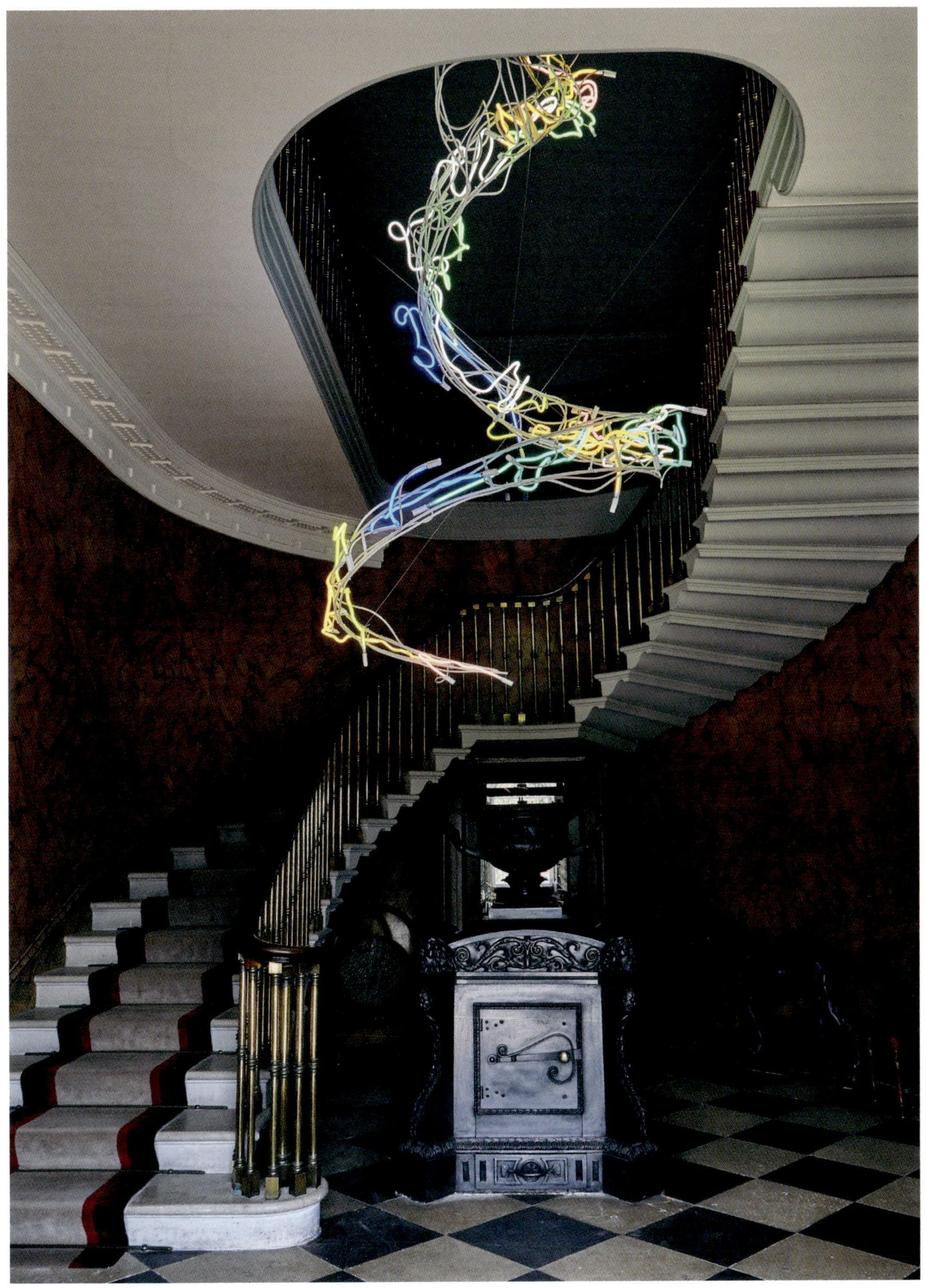

Extinction Resurrection

Concrete Dodo and Stegosaurus

Mount Stewart, County Down

Returning to Strangford Lough, but this time to its northern shores, we come to our final conservation project and we meet again the stonework conservator who worked on the Philae Obelisk at Kingston Lacy (see page 33).

Douglas Carpenter, this time aided by Sam Peacock, was called in to rescue two cast-concrete sculptures of animals that have already suffered one extinction. Mount Stewart enjoys a benign microclimate thanks to two things: its position close to sea level, which means frosts and extremely cold temperatures are kept at bay; and a nearby woodland that was planted in the early nineteenth century and has grown into a dense shelter belt. However, this is not enough to protect Mount Stewart and its gardens from destructive winds, which is the fate that befell these stone sculptures of a dodo and a stegosaurus. The dodo had suffered less damage out of the two, with the loss of a toe and a broken plinth, but the stegosaurus looked like it had been struck by a meteorite – a broken tail, a broken leg, some of its spine plates chipped with others completely missing, and extensive cracking on its back legs.

The gardens at Mount Stewart benefitted not only from the topographical features mentioned above, but also from having an exceptional gardener, a woman who was as enthusiastic as she was knowledgeable. Edith Vane-Tempest-Stewart, Marchioness of

> The dodo restored to its plinth once more.

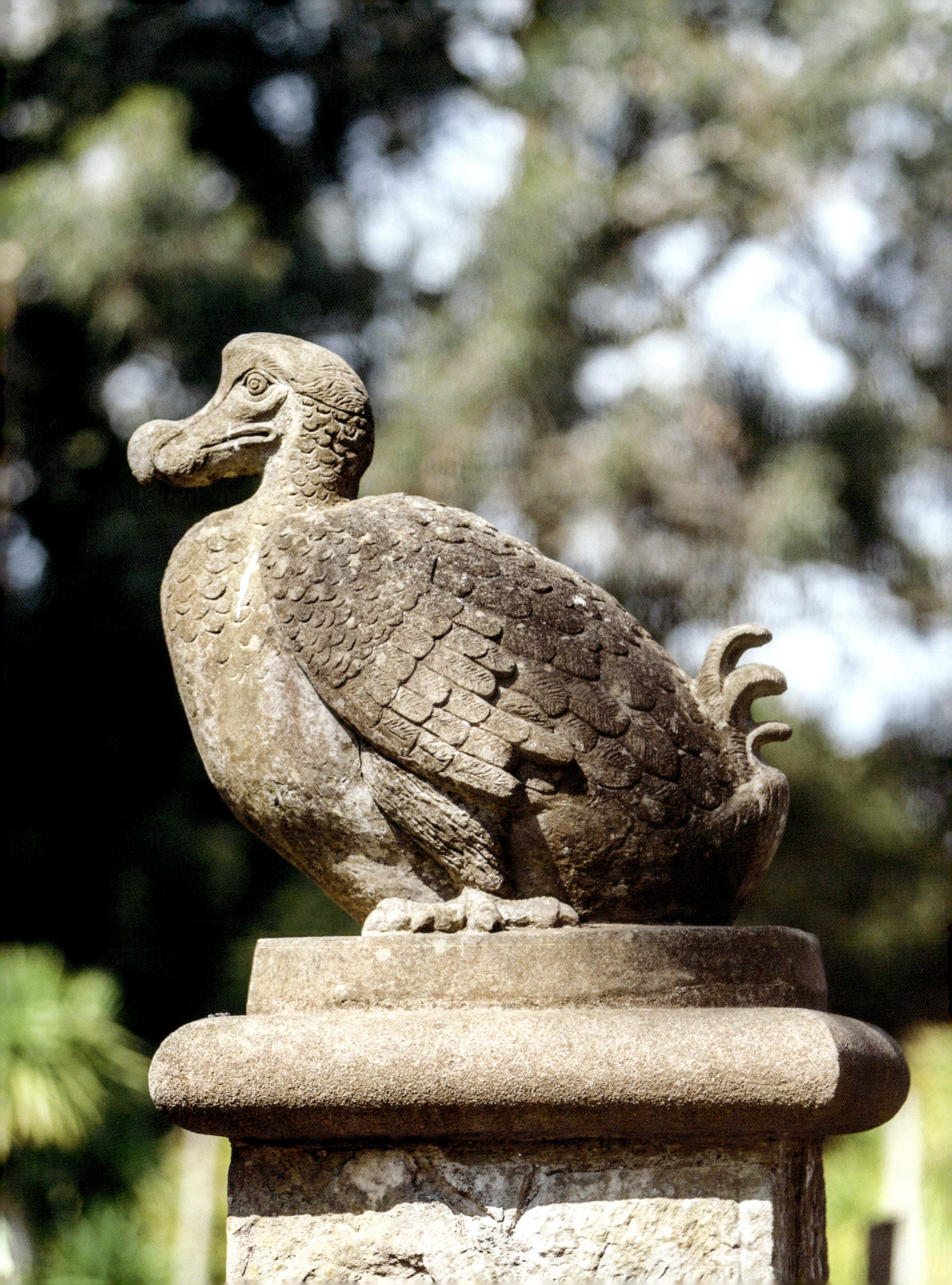

Londonderry, came to Mount Stewart with her husband Charles in 1919, and over the next four decades she created a garden that remains one of the finest in the world. Aided by the famous plant hunter Frank Kingdon-Ward and the area's clement climate, she was able to push the boundaries with her planting, using tender species from exotic climes that might have perished elsewhere. She also had the assistance of head gardener Tomas Bolas, who had trained at Chatsworth, and whom she directed in the creation of the South Terrace and Italian Garden.

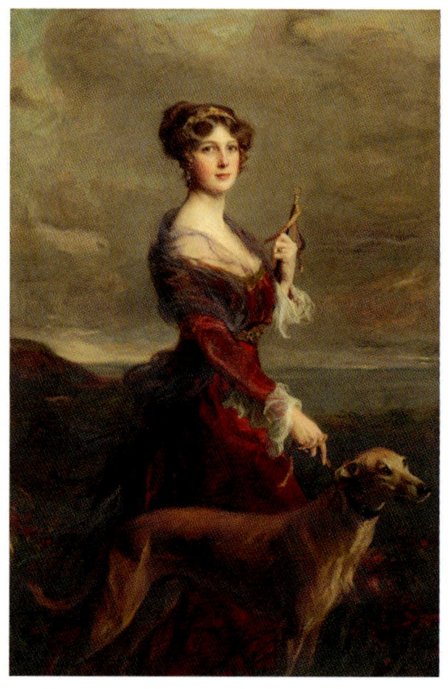

^ Edith, Marchioness of Londonderry, with her favourite greyhound Fly.

That's not to say Edith was not every bit a hands-on gardener. She would give some orders but she would also take up tools herself and expect her guests to help out. It's said that she would send visitors away with a wheelbarrow and instruct them to 'weed the lily walk by lunchtime'. She would pore over planting plans and seed catalogues in her study, and if she needed to be in her garden in a hurry – and her energetic character meant she always was – she would clamber out of her window, pursued by her very many dogs. Edith was irrepressible and inspired, and at every turn in the gardens at Mount Stewart you can see her creativity and horticultural expertise – and there is no shortage of her humour and theatricality either.

This is especially demonstrated by the Dodo Terrace beside the Italian Garden. It is the height of whimsy, but reflects on a very dark period of history, closely and personally experienced by Edith and Charles. He saw active service for much of the First World War, witnessing first-hand the mass slaughter of the Battle of the Somme. During those years the couple called their London home the 'Ark', opening it up as a retreat for friends involved in the war effort. When the war was over and work on the gardens could begin, Edith incorporated this into her designs, and had local sculptor Thomas Beattie cast a series of concrete sculptures to reflect on that period.

A variety of animals, extant and extinct, are arranged around a concrete sculpture of Noah's Ark, the design inspired by an illumination in a medieval manuscript. Four dodos preside over the scene, with a cast of characters that includes a cheetah, frog, fox, hedgehog, rabbit, stegosaurus and more. If this seems an odd menagerie, and of course it is, the selection might make more sense when you learn that Edith had given each of their human visitors to the Ark a nickname. Her husband Charles was 'Charley the Cheetah', while Edith's father was the dodo due to his old-school manner. Charles had a number of marital affairs (Edith's resilience in dealing with this personal challenge was reflective

∨ Local sculptor Thomas Beattie was responsible for the Ark and its accompanying menagerie on the Dodo Terrace.

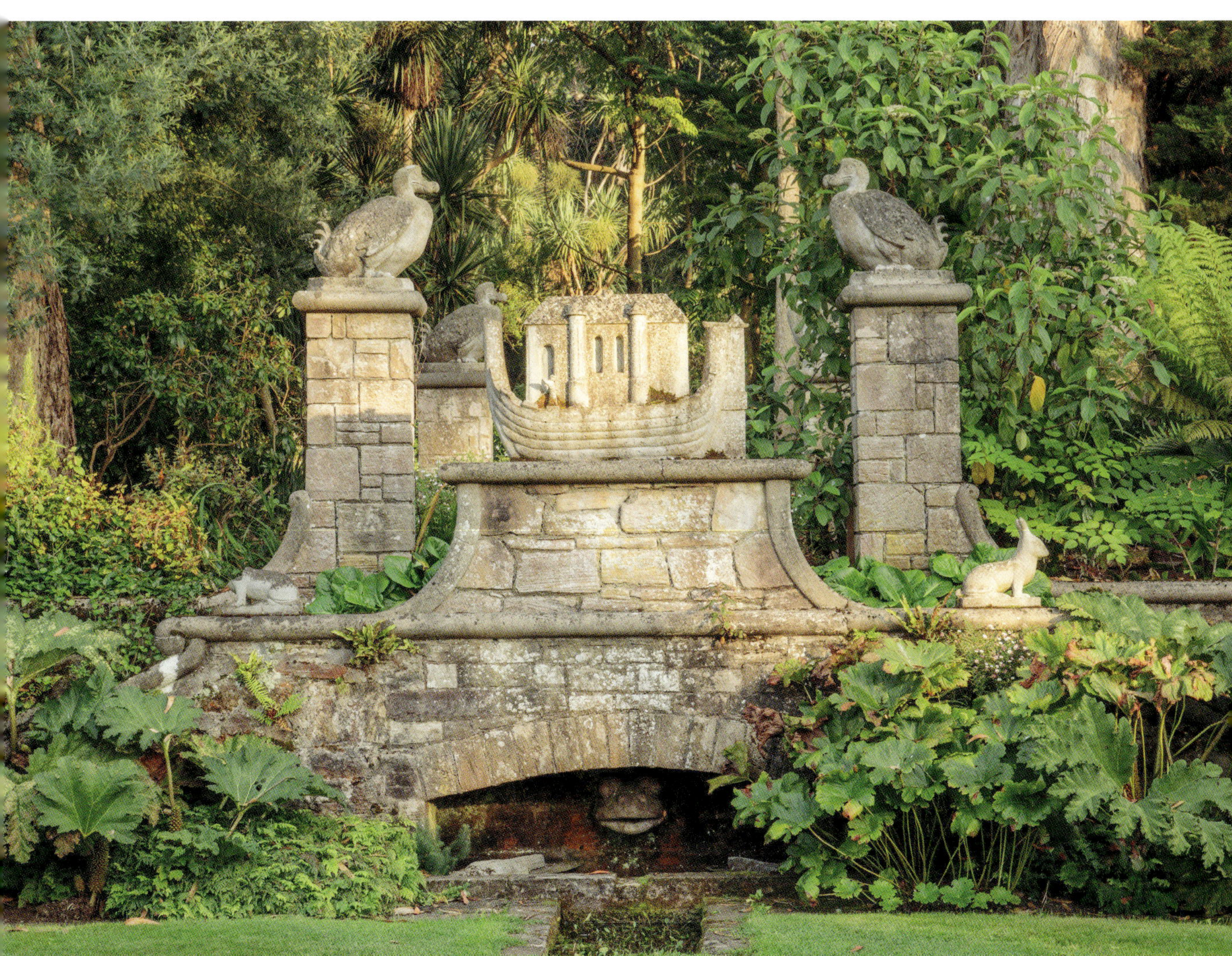

of her character), while 'Daddy the Dodo', Edith once remarked, was 'representative of an elder England' and of a type of landed gentry soon to become obsolete, just like the bird.

It goes without saying that these sculptures are unique and unlike anything the stonework conservators would have worked on before, but as you may recall from their visit to Kingston Lacy, encountering the unusual is a fairly common occurrence in the gardens of the National Trust. The dodo with the broken toe was a relatively straightforward procedure, as concrete is not an especially difficult medium to patch and match. Unfortunately the original toe was not found in the undergrowth, but a cast was taken from the toe of another dodo, which allowed for a near-perfect prosthetic, especially after Douglas's retouching.

The stegosaurus was a good deal trickier, as Beattie's sculptures also contain an iron sub-frame that is prone to rust and expansion when exposed to the elements, which can then shatter the surrounding concrete. The stegosaurus's inner structure was especially visible and its treatment was going to require a major operation.

As Sam began to work on the stegosaurus, its fragility became more and more apparent, so the removal of the protruding ironwork from its base required the delicate handling of an angle grinder. That done, the stegosaurus could be reseated on its plinth and be pieced back together or built back up where pieces were missing. Sam needed to be as creative with her 'mix' as with her shaping of the new

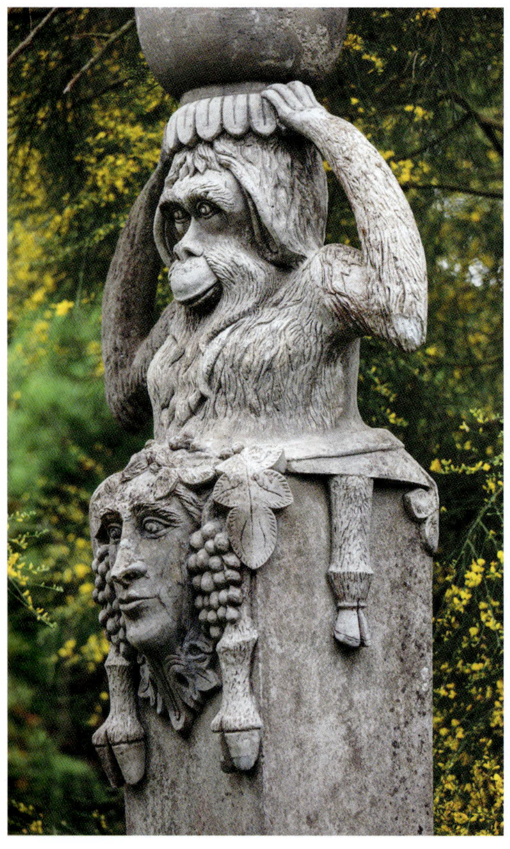

^ There is a sense of playfulness throughout the garden Edith created, but on the Dodo Terrace especially so.

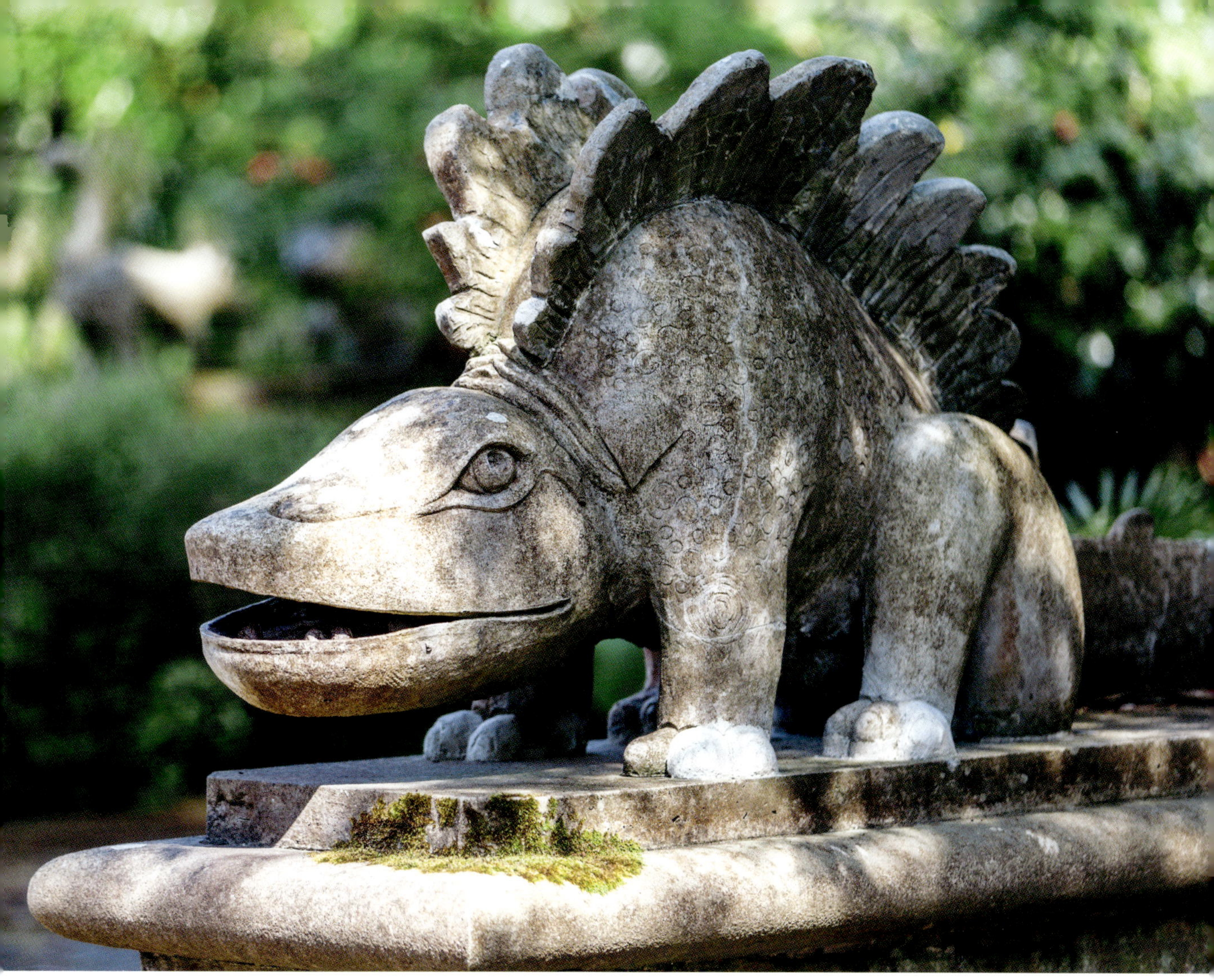

plates on the stegosaurus's back. Using a recipe of her own making that combined grit, various sands, quarry dust and cement, she applied her mix to resin-coated stainless-steel armatures and shaped the new material to match the style and size of the neighbouring plates. It was a complex repair but the greater the challenge, the greater the satisfaction. As Sam said: 'Some repairs are very hands-off; some like the stegosaurus you have to intervene a bit more. But you just need to respect whatever it is you're repairing. You want the object to sing,' adding: 'Definitely one of my favourite jobs.'

^ The stegosaurus restored and gracing the Dodo Terrace once more.

Index

Note: page numbers in **bold** refer to pictures.

Picture Credits

2: ©National Trust Images/James Dobson; 4–5: ©National Trust Images/Colin Davison; 7: ©National Trust Images/Andreas von Einsiedel; 9: ©National Trust Images/James Dobson; 11: ©National Trust Images/Arnhel de Serra; 12–13, 14: ©National Trust Images/Paul Harris; 16: ©National Trust Images/Angelo Hornak; 17, 19: ©National Trust Images/Paul Harris; 20–21: ©National Trust Images/Nick Meers; 22: ©Wiltshire Museum, Devizes; 25: ©Martin Papworth; 27: ©Royal Cornwall Museum; 28: ©National Trust Images/James Dobson; 29: ©National Trust Images/David Noton; 30: ©National Trust Images /Lynda Aiano; 31: ©Royal Cornwall Museum; 32: ©National Trust Images/Jay Williams; 35: ©National Trust Images/Derrick E. Witty; 37: ©Brick House Conservation Ltd; 38: ©National Trust Images; 40–41: ©National Trust Images/Jaron James ; 42: ©National Trust/Sophia Farley & Denis Madge; 43, 44: ©National Trust Images/Steve Haywood; 46: ©National Trust Images/David Levenson; 48: ©National Trust Images/William Shaw; 51, 52–53: ©National Trust Images/James Dobson; 54: ©National Trust Images/John Miller; 56: ©Historic England Archive; 57, 59: ©National Trust Images/Chris Lacey; 60–61, 62, 65, 67: ©National Trust Images/James Dobson; 69: ©National Trust/Jaron James; 70: ©Tate; 71: ©National Trust Images/John Hammond; 73: ©National Trust Images/Andreas von Einsiedel; 74, 76, 77: ©National Trust Images/James Dobson; 78: ©Blast Films & All3Media International; 79: ©National Trust Images/James Dobson; 80: ©National Trust Images/Charles Thomas; 82: ©National Trust Images/John Hammond; 83: ©National Trust Images; 84: ©Blast Films & All3Media International; 85: ©National Trust Images/Jonathan Buckley; 87: ©National Trust Images/James Dobson; 88: ©National Trust Images; 89: ©National Trust Images/Andrew Butler; 90: ©National Trust Images/James Dobson; 92 top: ©National Trust/Charles Thomas; 92 bottom: ©National Trust Images/James Dobson; 94: ©National Trust Images/Neil Campbell-Sharp; 96: ©National Trust Images/Derrick E. Witty; 97: ©National Trust Images/Stephen Robson; 98–99: ©National Trust Images/Megan Taylor; 101: ©National Trust Images/Andreas von Einsiedel; 102: ©National Trust Images/James Dobson; 103 top: ©National Trust Images/Andrew Fetherston; 103 bottom: ©National Trust Images/David Brunetti; 104: ©National Trust Images/James Dobson; 105: ©National Trust Images/James Beck; 106: ©National Trust Images/Katy Dunn; 108: ©National Trust Images/Matthew Hollow; 109, 110: ©National Trust Images/Vicki Marsland; 111: ©National Trust Images; 112: ©National Trust Images/Hugh Mothersole; 113: ©National Trust Images/John Hammond; 114, 115: ©National Trust Images/Hugh Mothersole; 116: ©Blast Films & All3Media International; 118: ©National Trust Images/John Millar; 120–121: ©National Trust Images/Gavin Repton; 123: ©National Trust Images/James Dobson; 124: ©National Trust Images/Matthew Hollow; 125, 127: ©National Trust Images/James Dobson; 128: ©National Trust Images/Andreas von Einsiedel; 131, 132, 133: ©National Trust Images/James Dobson; 134: ©National Trust Images/Gavin Repton; 136: ©National Trust Images/Andrew Patterson; 137, 139: ©National Trust Images/Gavin Repton; 141: ©National Trust Images/James Dobson; 142: ©The Royal Society; 143, 144: ©National Trust Images/James Dobson; 146: ©National Trust Images/Nick Guttridge; 148: ©National Trust Images/John Bethell; 149: ©Blast Films & All3Media International; 150: ©National Trust Images/John Hammond; 152: ©Blast Films & All3Media International; 154: ©Instinctive Photography; 157: ©Blast Films & All3Media International; 159: ©Mike Hodgson; 160: ©Alamy; 162: ©Mike Hodgson; 163: ©Blast Films & All3Media International; 164, 166, 167, 168, 169: ©National Trust Images/Arnhel de Serra; 170–171: ©National Trust Images/Colin Davison; 172: ©National Trust Images/Dennis Gilbert; 174, 175, 176: ©National Trust Images/Annapurna Mellor; 179: ©National Trust Images/John Miller; 180–181: ©National Trust Images/Paul Harris; 183: ©National Trust Images/Jemma Finch; 184: ©National Trust Images/David Watson; 187, 188, 189, 191: ©Anthony Chappel-Ross; 192: ©National Trust Images/Colin Davison; 194: ©National Trust Images/John Hammond; 195: ©National Trust Images/Annapurna Mellor; 196, 197: ©National Trust Images/Jo Hatchert; 198: ©National Trust Images/Andreas von Einsiedel; 201: ©National Trust Images/John Hammond; 202: ©Colin Davison Photography; 204: ©National Trust Images/James Dobson; 206: ©Alamy; 207: ©National Trust Images/Colin Liddie; 208: ©National Trust Images/Robert Thrift; 209: ©National Trust Images/James Dobson; 210–211: ©National Trust/Pete Huggins; 212, 214, 215, 216: ©National Trust Images/Paul Harris; 219: ©National Trust Images/Todd-White Art Photography; 221: ©National Trust Images/James Dobson; 222: ©National Trust/Pete Huggins; 225: ©National Trust Images/James Dobson; 226: ©National Trust Images/James Beck; 228: ©National Trust Images/Annabelle Monaghan; 231: ©National Trust Images/John Hammond; 233: © National Trust Images/Simon Harris; 234–235: ©National Trust Images/Simon Mills; 237: ©National Trust Images/James Dobson; 238–239: ©National Trust Images/Brian Morrison; 240, 242–243: ©National Trust Images/Annapurna Mellor; 244, 245: ©National Trust Images/Ronan McGrade; 247: ©National Trust Images/Chris Lacey; 248: ©National Trust Images/John Millar; 250: ©National Trust Images/Annapurna Mellor; 251: ©National Trust Images/W. Anderson-Porter; 253: ©National Trust Images/Simon Mills; 255: ©National Trust Images/Annapurna Mellor; 256: ©National Trust Images; 257: ©National Trust Images/James Dobson; 258: ©National Trust Images/Andrew Butler; 259: ©National Trust Images/Annapurna Mellor.

Front cover: The Green Closet, Ham House (©National Trust Images/Chris Davies). Back cover, top: Mezzotint by Christoph Le Blon, Oxburgh (©Mike Hodgson); middle: John Nash staircase, Attingham Park (©National Trust Images/James Dobson); bottom: Pagoda Clock, Anglesey Abbey (©National Trust Images/Arnhel de Serra). Page 2: Mount Stewart, County Down (©National Trust Images/James Dobson). Pages 4–5: Seaton Delaval Hall, Northumberland (©National Trust Images/Colin Davison). Chapter openers: pages 12–13: The Shell Gallery, A La Ronde, Devon (©National Trust Images/Paul Harris); pages 60–61: Chinese Wallpaper, Ightham Mote, Kent (©National Trust Images/James Dobson); pages 120–121: Mary Curzon's Peacock Dress, Kedleston Hall, Derbyshire (©National Trust Images/Gavin Repton); pages 170–171: Cantilevered spiral staircase, Seaton Delaval Hall, Northumberland (©National Trust Images/Colin Davison); pages 210–211: The State Bed, Erddig, Wrexham (©National Trust/Pete Huggins); pages 234–235: *Artificial Sunshine* by Kevin Killen, The Argory, County Armagh (©National Trust Images/Simon Mills).

Acknowledgements

Blast Films, the BBC and the National Trust would like to thank all those who have contributed to this publication and to the projects featured in it, including:

Gerry Alabone, Megan Alexander, Abigail Allan, Ben Alsop, Helen Antrobus, Lucy Armstrong-Blair, Richard Ashbourne, Axminster Carpets Limited, Abigail Bainbridge, Richard Ball, Rob Bandy, Hannah Barker, Siobhan Barratt, Emrhys Barrell, Claire Beale, Sir Henry Bedingfeld, Katy Bell, Eleanor Black, Niall Black, Felicity Bolton, Anita Bools, Dianne Britton, Emile de Bruijn, Nicholas Burnett, Tim Cambourne, Katy Canales, Douglas Carpenter, Katherine Carter, Tracey Chaplin, Matthew Charlton, Jim Chestnutt, Laura Christie, John Chu, Classic Masonry, Cliveden Conservation, Imogen Cloët, Eleanor Codman, Nathalie Cohen, Rachel Conroy, Constantine, Tarnya Cooper, Simon Cottle, Tobit Curteis, Daedalus Conservation, Alison Dalby, Kevin Dale, Danial Demaine, Amanda-Jane Doran, Ilana van Dort, Katrina Dowman, Jacob Downey, Louise Drover, David Duckham, Jane Eade, Lynne Edge, Rebecca Ellison, Scarlet Faro, Morgan Feely, James Finlay, Tom Flemons, Sarah France, Shannon Fraser, Rachael Freemantle, Miranda Garrett, Karen George, Rebecca Glover, Julia Glynn, Claire Golbourn, Rupert Goulding, Peter Grant, Liz Green, Southern Green, Elena Greer, David Gregory, Paul Grist, Susanne Gronnow, Becci Haigh, Fiona Hall, John Hall, The Hamilton Kerr Institute, Yoko Hanegreefs, Studio Hardie, Rupert Harris, John Hartley, Cath Lloyd Haslam, Rebecca Hellen, Drew Hill, Historic Property Ltd, Audrey Hoare, Hog and Fitch, Charlotte Holmes, Holywell Glass, Jock Hopson, Berenice Humphreys, Philippa 'Pip' Hunt, James Hunter, IMC, Inskip Gee Architects, Integrated Design Partnership, John Austin & Partners, April Johnson, Shona Johnston, Saraid Jones, Hannah Kay, Heather Kay, Sarah Kay, Christo Kefalas, Kevin Killen, Allan King, Barbara Kleiser, Paul Knibb, Naomi Kulasingham, Christopher Lane, Nigel Larkin, Rachel Lawson, Michelle Leake, Ana Logriera, Emily MacCormack, Sarah Maisey, Loredana Mannina, Graham Marley, Emma Marshall, Ian Marshall, Vicki Marsland, Tim Martin, Tony Martin, Claire Masset, Freddie Matthews, Hannah Mawdsley, Sarah Mayfield, Mike McCartney, Roisin McKenna, Rona McKnight, Julieanne McMahon, Emma Mee, Mildred, Howells & Co, Hannah Miles, John Mills, Momentum, Annabelle Monaghan, Jo Moody, Matthew Morrison, Newton's Ladder, Emma Nobes, Norman & Underwood, North Exhibition Services, Northumbria University students, Sharon Oldale, Elaine Owers, Stuart Page, Martin Papworth, Jim Parry, Miriam Parry, Sam Peacock, Alastair Peebles, Richard Pennington, Emma Philip, PLYable, Steve Priest, Lewis Proudfoot, Chris Purvis, Alexandra Radford, Roisin Rampley, Matthew Read, Alex Rickett, Melvyn Rodda, Royal Manufacturers De Wit, Royal Oak Foundation Conservation Studio, Helen Royall, Jackie Rumsey, Brian Russell, Alice Rylance-Watson, Sally Strachey Historic Conservation Ltd, David Salmo, Polly Saltmarsh, Maria Sanchez, Mark Sandiford, Emma Schmuecker, Helen Sharp, Katherine Sharp, Zoë Shearman, Danielle Shortall, Kristie Short-Traxler, Caroline Sigley, Sine, Emma Slocombe, Jane Smith, Troy Smith, Nur Sobers-Khan, Matt Spinks, Karen Stafford, Chloe Stewart, Ian Stimpson, Graeme Storey, Clare Stoughton-Harris, Alice Strickland, John Sutcliffe, Richard Swinscoe, Anna Tallon, Katie Taylor, Peter Taylor, Textile Conservation Studio, TigerGeo Limited, Christopher Tinker, Hugh Torrens, Philip Treece, Alex Turrell, Ruby Tyler, Eleanor Underhill, Seb vanden Bogaerde, Angus Wainwright, Christian Walker, Nicola Walker, Jonathan Wallis, Paul Walton, Catriona Ward, Liz Waring, David Watson, Rosamund Weatherall, Megan Wheeler, Dom Wierzbowski, Rowena Willard-Wright, Mann Williams, Nadine Wilson, Barbara Wood, Clara Woolford, Ian Wright, Kris Zykubek.